T0210988

Communications in Computer and Information Science 1868

Editorial Board Members

Joaquim Filipe⬤, *Polytechnic Institute of Setúbal, Setúbal, Portugal*
Ashish Ghosh⬤, *Indian Statistical Institute, Kolkata, India*
Raquel Oliveira Prates⬤, *Federal University of Minas Gerais (UFMG),*
Belo Horizonte, Brazil
Lizhu Zhou, *Tsinghua University, Beijing, China*

Rationale

The CCIS series is devoted to the publication of proceedings of computer science conferences. Its aim is to efficiently disseminate original research results in informatics in printed and electronic form. While the focus is on publication of peer-reviewed full papers presenting mature work, inclusion of reviewed short papers reporting on work in progress is welcome, too. Besides globally relevant meetings with internationally representative program committees guaranteeing a strict peer-reviewing and paper selection process, conferences run by societies or of high regional or national relevance are also considered for publication.

Topics

The topical scope of CCIS spans the entire spectrum of informatics ranging from foundational topics in the theory of computing to information and communications science and technology and a broad variety of interdisciplinary application fields.

Information for Volume Editors and Authors

Publication in CCIS is free of charge. No royalties are paid, however, we offer registered conference participants temporary free access to the online version of the conference proceedings on SpringerLink (http://link.springer.com) by means of an http referrer from the conference website and/or a number of complimentary printed copies, as specified in the official acceptance email of the event.

CCIS proceedings can be published in time for distribution at conferences or as post-proceedings, and delivered in the form of printed books and/or electronically as USBs and/or e-content licenses for accessing proceedings at SpringerLink. Furthermore, CCIS proceedings are included in the CCIS electronic book series hosted in the SpringerLink digital library at http://link.springer.com/bookseries/7899. Conferences publishing in CCIS are allowed to use Online Conference Service (OCS) for managing the whole proceedings lifecycle (from submission and reviewing to preparing for publication) free of charge.

Publication process

The language of publication is exclusively English. Authors publishing in CCIS have to sign the Springer CCIS copyright transfer form, however, they are free to use their material published in CCIS for substantially changed, more elaborate subsequent publications elsewhere. For the preparation of the camera-ready papers/files, authors have to strictly adhere to the Springer CCIS Authors' Instructions and are strongly encouraged to use the CCIS LaTeX style files or templates.

Abstracting/Indexing

CCIS is abstracted/indexed in DBLP, Google Scholar, EI-Compendex, Mathematical Reviews, SCImago, Scopus. CCIS volumes are also submitted for the inclusion in ISI Proceedings.

How to start

To start the evaluation of your proposal for inclusion in the CCIS series, please send an e-mail to ccis@springer.com.

Leonid Sokolinsky · Mikhail Zymbler
Editors

Parallel Computational Technologies

17th International Conference, PCT 2023
Saint Petersburg, Russia, March 28–30, 2023
Revised Selected Papers

Editors
Leonid Sokolinsky (iD)
South Ural State University
Chelyabinsk, Russia

Mikhail Zymbler (iD)
South Ural State University
Chelyabinsk, Russia

ISSN 1865-0929   ISSN 1865-0937 (electronic)
Communications in Computer and Information Science
ISBN 978-3-031-38863-7   ISBN 978-3-031-38864-4 (eBook)
https://doi.org/10.1007/978-3-031-38864-4

© The Editor(s) (if applicable) and The Author(s), under exclusive license
to Springer Nature Switzerland AG 2023

This work is subject to copyright. All rights are reserved by the Publisher, whether the whole or part of
the material is concerned, specifically the rights of translation, reprinting, reuse of illustrations, recitation,
broadcasting, reproduction on microfilms or in any other physical way, and transmission or information
storage and retrieval, electronic adaptation, computer software, or by similar or dissimilar methodology now
known or hereafter developed.
The use of general descriptive names, registered names, trademarks, service marks, etc. in this publication
does not imply, even in the absence of a specific statement, that such names are exempt from the relevant
protective laws and regulations and therefore free for general use.
The publisher, the authors, and the editors are safe to assume that the advice and information in this book
are believed to be true and accurate at the date of publication. Neither the publisher nor the authors or the
editors give a warranty, expressed or implied, with respect to the material contained herein or for any errors
or omissions that may have been made. The publisher remains neutral with regard to jurisdictional claims in
published maps and institutional affiliations.

This Springer imprint is published by the registered company Springer Nature Switzerland AG
The registered company address is: Gewerbestrasse 11, 6330 Cham, Switzerland

Preface

This volume contains a selection of the papers presented at the 17th International Scientific Conference on Parallel Computational Technologies, PCT 2023. The PCT 2023 conference was held in St. Petersburg, Russia, during March 28–30, 2023.

The PCT series of conferences aims at providing an opportunity to report and discuss the results achieved by leading research groups in solving practical issues using supercomputer and neural network technologies. The scope of the PCT series of conferences includes all aspects of the application of cloud, supercomputer, and neural network technologies in science and technology such as applications, hardware and software, specialized languages, and packages.

The PCT series is organized by the Supercomputing Consortium of Russian Universities and the Ministry of Science and Higher Education of the Russian Federation. Originating in 2007 at the South Ural State University (Chelyabinsk, Russia), the PCT series of conferences has now become one of the most prestigious Russian scientific meetings on parallel programming, high-performance computing, and machine learning. PCT 2023 in St. Petersburg continued the series after Chelyabinsk (2007), St. Petersburg (2008), Nizhny Novgorod (2009), Ufa (2010), Moscow (2011), Novosibirsk (2012), Chelyabinsk (2013), Rostov-on-Don (2014), Ekaterinburg (2015), Arkhangelsk (2016), Kazan (2017), Rostov-on-Don (2018), Kaliningrad (2019), Perm (2020), Volgograd (2021), and Dubna (2022).

Each paper submitted to the conference was scrupulously evaluated in a single-blind manner by three reviewers based on relevance to the conference topics, scientific and practical contribution, experimental evaluation of the results, and presentation quality. The Program Committee of PCT selected the 25 best papers from a total of 71 to be included in this CCIS proceedings volume.

We would like to thank the respected PCT 2023 platinum sponsor, RSC Group, golden sponsor NORSI-TRANS, and track sponsor, Karma Group, for their continued financial support of the PCT series of conferences.

We would like to express our gratitude to every individual who contributed to the success of PCT 2023. Special thanks to the Program Committee members and the external reviewers for evaluating papers submitted to the conference. Thanks also to the Organizing Committee members and all the colleagues involved in the conference organization from ITMO University, South Ural State University (national research university), and Moscow State University. We thank the participants of PCT 2023 for sharing their research and presenting their achievements as well.

Finally, we thank Springer for publishing the proceedings of PCT 2023 in the Communications in Computer and Information Science series.

June 2023

Leonid Sokolinsky
Mikhail Zymbler

Organization

Steering Committee

Berdyshev, V. I.	Krasovskii Institute of Mathematics and Mechanics, UrB RAS, Russia
Ershov, Yu. L.	United Scientific Council on Mathematics and Informatics, Russia
Minkin, V. I.	South Federal University, Russia
Moiseev, E. I.	Moscow State University, Russia
Savin, G. I.	Joint Supercomputer Center, RAS, Russia
Sadovnichiy, V. A.	Moscow State University, Russia
Chetverushkin, B. N.	Keldysh Institute of Applied Mathematics, RAS, Russia
Shokin, Yu. I.	Institute of Computational Technologies, RAS, Russia

Program Committee

Dongarra, J. (Co-chair)	University of Tennessee, USA
Sokolinsky, L. B. (Co-chair)	South Ural State University, Russia
Voevodin, Vl. V. (Co-chair)	Moscow State University, Russia
Zymbler, M. L. (Academic Secretary)	South Ural State University, Russia
Ablameyko, S. V.	Belarusian State University, Belarus
Afanasiev, A. P.	Institute for Systems Analysis, RAS, Russia
Akimova, E. N.	Krasovskii Institute of Mathematics and Mechanics, UrB RAS, Russia
Andrzejak, A.	Heidelberg University, Germany
Balaji, P.	Argonne National Laboratory, USA
Boldyrev, Yu. Ya.	St. Petersburg Polytechnic University, Russia
Carretero, J.	Carlos III University of Madrid, Spain
Gazizov, R. K.	Ufa State Aviation Technical University, Russia
Glinsky, B. M.	Institute of Computational Mathematics and Mathematical Geophysics, SB RAS, Russia
Goryachev, V. D.	Tver State Technical University, Russia
Il'in, V. P.	Institute of Computational Mathematics and Mathematical Geophysics, SB RAS, Russia
Kobayashi, H.	Tohoku University, Japan

Kunkel, J.	University of Hamburg, Germany
Kumar, S.	South Ural State University, Russia
Labarta, J.	Barcelona Supercomputing Center, Spain
Lastovetsky, A.	University College Dublin, Ireland
Likhoded, N. A.	Belarusian State University, Belarus
Ludwig, T.	German Climate Computing Center, Germany
Mallmann, D.	Jülich Supercomputing Centre, Germany
Malyshkin, V. E.	Institute of Computational Mathematics and Mathematical Geophysics, SB RAS, Russia
Michalewicz, M.	A*STAR Computational Resource Centre, Singapore
Modorsky, V. Ya.	Perm Polytechnic University, Russia
Pan, C. S.	Cloudflare, UK
Prodan, R.	Alpen-Adria-Universität Klagenfurt, Austria
Radchenko, G. I.	Silicon Austria Labs, Austria
Shamakina, A. V.	HLRS High Performance Computing Center Stuttgart, Germany
Shumyatsky, P.	University of Brasilia, Brazil
Sithole, H.	Centre for High Performance Computing, South Africa
Starchenko, A. V.	Tomsk State University, Russia
Sterling, T.	Indiana University, USA
Sukhinov, A. I.	Don State Technical University, Russia
Taufer, M.	University of Delaware, USA
Tchernykh, A.	CICESE Research Center, Mexico
Turlapov, V. E.	Lobachevsky State University of Nizhny Novgorod, Russia
Wyrzykowski, R.	Czestochowa University of Technology, Poland
Yakobovskiy, M. V.	Keldysh Institute of Applied Mathematics, RAS, Russia
Yamazaki, Y.	Federal University of Pelotas, Brazil

Organizing Committee

Bukhanovsky, A. V. (Chair)	ITMO University, Russia
Klimova, A. S. (Deputy Chair)	ITMO University, Russia
Khramova, A. V. (Secretary)	ITMO University, Russia
Antonov, A. S.	Moscow State University, Russia
Antonova, A. P.	Moscow State University, Russia
Goglachev, A. I.	South Ural State University, Russia
Kraeva, Ya. A.	South Ural State University, Russia

Mamieva, D. G.	ITMO University, Russia
Nikitenko, D. A.	Moscow State University, Russia
Nizomutdinov, B. A.	ITMO University, Russia
Polyanichko, A. V.	ITMO University, Russia
Sidorov, I. Yu.	Moscow State University, Russia
Sobolev, S. I.	Moscow State University, Russia
Voevodin, Vad. V.	Moscow State University, Russia
Yurtin, A. A.	South Ural State University, Russia
Zymbler, M. L.	South Ural State University, Russia

Contents

Supercomputer Simulation

High Performance Architectures, Tools and Technologies

Evaluating the Impact of MPI Network Sharing on HPC Applications

Anna Khudoleeva$^{(\boxtimes)}$, Konstantin Stefanov , and Vadim Voevodin

Lomonosov Moscow State University, Moscow, Russian Federation
khudoleeva.anna98@gmail.com, {cstef,vadim}@parallel.ru

Abstract. In any modern supercomputer system, a so-called noise inevitably occurs. It can be defined as an external influence of the software and hardware environment leading to a change in the execution time or other properties of applications running on a supercomputer. Although the noise can noticeably affect the performance of HPC applications in some cases, neither the nature of its occurrence nor the degree of its influence have been investigated in detail. In this paper, we study how much a certain type of noise, caused by sharing of MPI network resources, can impact the performance of parallel programs. To do this, we conducted a series of experiments using synthetic noise on the Lomonosov-2 supercomputer to determine to what extent such noise can slow down the execution of widely used benchmarks and computing cores.

Keywords: Supercomputer · Noise · Noise influence · MPI · Performance analysis

1 Introduction

A supercomputer is an extremely complex system in which a huge number of different software and hardware components work and interact simultaneously. The supercomputer environment is not static but changes over time, which leads to changes in execution time, performance, and other properties of identical launches of user applications. "Noise" is often the cause of such changes. There is no unambiguous definition of the concept of noise; we define it as the influence of the software and hardware environment that leads to a change (most often slowdown) in the execution time or other properties of applications running on a supercomputer.

At the moment, the influence of noise on HPC applications is rather poorly studied. It has been shown, though, that this influence can be very significant in some cases [8,10,15]. For this reason, it is exceptionally important to study how significant the impact of noise on different applications can be.

In this work, which is part of the ExtraNoise project [14], aimed at disclosing and tackling key questions of system-noise influence on HPC applications, we focus on a particular type of noise associated with sharing a communication network. We consider situations when some external program (another user

© The Author(s), under exclusive license to Springer Nature Switzerland AG 2023
L. Sokolinsky and M. Zymbler (Eds.): PCT 2023, CCIS 1868, pp. 3–18, 2023.
https://doi.org/10.1007/978-3-031-38864-4_1

application or some system process) interferes with the workflow of a user parallel application since it occupies a shared resource: the communication network for transferring MPI messages. We have studied two different situations: 1) noise is present on the same computing node where the parallel application is running, and 2) noise is present on other computing nodes. Our task was to find out how much that noise can slow down the execution of various widely used applications and benchmarks. For this purpose, we manually added synthetic noise to interfere with the analyzed programs.

The main contribution of this paper is the study and description of the impact of MPI-related noise on the execution time of different parallel applications. The research showed which applications are more or less affected by this noise and how significant such an influence can generally be. The experiments were carried out on the Lomonosov-2 supercomputer [20], but the conclusions regarding the influence on applications are valid for other systems.

The paper is structured as follows. Section 2 outlines existing studies related to the supercomputer noise topic. We provide a thorough description of the analyzed tests and noise generators in Sect. 3. Section 4 is devoted to the description and analysis of the conducted experiments. Section 5 summarizes the results obtained.

2   Related Work

Several studies have dealt with the influence of noise on the behavior of supercomputer applications. However, we cannot say that the topic has received enough consideration. Even more, there are only a few studies investigating what the source of the noise is. Those papers pay the most attention to the OS noise. For example, papers [3,5–7,11,18] are devoted to the study of specific OS noise sources and methods to exclude them. Other sources of noise have been studied to a much lesser extent. We can single out the papers [16,17], in which the mutual influence of applications simultaneously running on different nodes of a supercomputer is considered. This influence is caused by the parallel use of any shared resource as the file system or communication network. These papers describe an approach that allows assessing the impact of applications on each other via dividing them into segments, which are then analyzed and clustered based on system monitoring data.

Several studies do not focus on the source of noise. These include, for example, the paper [15], considered one of the first works devoted to this topic. The authors of that work investigate the causes of performance loss on a particular supercomputer and looked for ways to reduce the detected noise. The paper [13] explores the possibility of noise reduction using SMT technology. The effect of noise on the execution of collective MPI operations is also studied (see, for instance, [2,9]). The so-called "idle waves" are considered in the paper [2]. These waves arise because different processes in a parallel program are idle while waiting for slower processes (slowed down by the influence of noise), and with each next collective operation, this effect can accumulate or decrease. The changes in the behavior of applications caused by the noise from the monitoring system as a result of collecting data from performance monitoring counters in multiplexing mode are considered in [21].

One of the most extensive studies on noise is described in [10]. The authors researched in detail the impact of noise on application performance, considered many works on this topic, and proposed a model and its implementation to simulate the noise impact, thereby helping to evaluate the behavior and scalability of applications in a noisy environment.

3 Description of Noise Generators and Tests

The source of MPI-related noise can be another parallel application or system process executed simultaneously and using the same communication resources as the analyzed user application. We will hereinafter refer to a parallel program that simulates noise as a *noise generator* and to a parallel program that is analyzed under noise influence as a *test*. We assume that such noise (simulated by noise generators in our case) can have a significant impact, so we want to study it in detail.

3.1 Tests

We chose the following widely used benchmarks and typical computing cores to study noise effect:

- MPI implementation of NPB benchmarks [4] (npb-bt, npb-cg, npb-ft, npb-is, npb-lu, npb-mg, npb-sp).
- OSU benchmarks osu_alltoall and osu_multi_lat. These tests operate with long messages.
- Tests based on MPI_Barrier and MPI_Allreduce (barrier, allreduce). These simple tests, developed at MSU Research Computing Center, are used as the most noise-sensitive benchmarks. Their principal part is a loop with many corresponding collective operations. The allreduce test operates with short messages.

The NPB tests were chosen to evaluate the noise impact on real-life applications. With the OSU tests, we intended to assess the effect on widely used MPI benchmarks. In our opinion, barrier and allreduce are the most susceptible to the influence of the studied noise.

3.2 Test and Noise Layout

Figure 1 depicts the noise generator and test layout cases on a supercomputer. Some of the parameters of noise generators, such as the number of nodes or the number of processes per node, are specific to each platform. The research was carried out on the computing nodes of the Lomonosov-2 supercomputer. Each is equipped with one Intel Xeon E5-2697 processor, featuring 14 physical cores (plus hyper-threading, for a total of 28 logical cores). Eight computing nodes are connected through nonblocking FDR InfiniBand switches, linked in a flattened butterfly topology [12]. Although the layout is specific to our target HPC architecture, we present a generalized description of noise options that can be extended to other platforms.

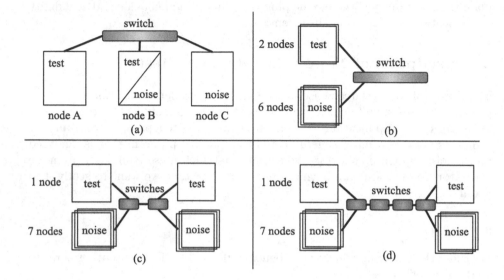

Fig. 1. Different test and noise generator layouts on a supercomputer

The following four cases of the noise generator and test mapping on computing nodes are studied.

Case 1: the test and the noise generator use the same supercomputer node. This case corresponds to the real-life situation of the nonexclusive launch of user applications on one node (allowed at some supercomputers) or system services actively using the communication network (an abnormal situation that needs to be detected). In this case, we launch the noise generator and the test application on two nodes, one of which is shared between the two programs (Fig. 1a). Both programs send MPI data to the shared node or receive MPI data from it. Shared MPI-related resources in this case are the network card on the node B and one communication link between this node and a network switch.

Cases 2–4: the test and the noise generator run on separate nodes. Applications on different computing nodes can have a noticeable effect on each other due to competition for a shared resource: the communication network. In this case, we take into account the network topology since different mappings of applications can affect the impact of noise. We study three variations of noise when separate nodes are used:

- The nodes are connected to one switch (Fig. 1(b)). We consider the situation when the test involves two nodes and the generator runs on the remaining nodes connected to the same switch, i.e., on six nodes in the case of the Lomonosov-2 supercomputer. Noise generator processes do not communicate within nodes, so messages are sent between nodes only. This allows us to study whether there is a way to load a switch with enough data transfer to affect the performance during the test.
- The nodes are divided into two equal groups. The nodes in one group are connected to one switch. Adjacent switches are used (Fig. 1(c)). The test runs on two nodes; each node is connected to its own switch. The noise generator uses 14 nodes; seven of them are connected to its own switch. The generator sends messages from nodes of the first switch to nodes of the second switch only. Here we study the effect of the high load on the communication link between adjacent switches.
- Same as in the previous case, but switches are not adjacent (Fig. 1(d)). This option is introduced to study whether noise influence and load on shared resources change when applications run on more distant nodes.

3.3   Selection of Noise Generators

We intend to measure the performance of test applications in the presence of the heaviest possible load on the communication network. Therefore we want to choose a noise generator that creates the most interference in it for each case of noise layout. Usually, two main characteristics are used to describe communication networks: throughput and latency. Throughput is important when sending large amounts of data. Latency, on the other hand, plays a role in the transmission of small messages. Thus we select two generators: one uses the maximum bandwidth (further referred to as BW); the other one produces the maximum number of MPI packets per second (MR). We conducted a series of experiments to choose generators that meet the requirements for each case of noise placement and stress the communication network the most. Below we point out the generators chosen in each case. Noise generators are implemented via MPI OSU benchmarks [1].

Test and Noise Share One Node. As said before, we want two types of noise generators: one with maximum BW and one with maximum MR. Moreover, since the direction of data transfer in the noise generator can be essential, we consider the following variants: the generator sends messages from node B to node C, from node C to node B, or in both directions (as shown in Fig. 1a). Thus we need six generators in total. The MPI OSU benchmarks listed below were heuristically chosen as the most suitable.

- Noise with maximum BW:
    - The osu_bw benchmark is used for unidirectional data transfer. Further, we refer to it as bw_send when sending data from the shared node and bw_receive when sending data to the shared node. This benchmark shows

a bandwidth of 6.5 GB/s, a very heavy load, amounting to 95% of the theoretical peak throughput of 6.8 GB/s.
- The osu_put_bibw benchmark is used for bidirectional data transfer (further, bw_bidir).

All BW benchmarks are used with long messages of 4 MB.
- Noise with maximum MR:
  - The osu_mbw_mr benchmark is used for unidirectional data transfer. Further, we refer to it as mr_send when sending data from node B to C and mr_receive when sending data from node C to B.
  - The osu_put_bibw benchmark is used for bidirectional data transfer (further, mr_bidir).

All MR benchmarks are used with short messages of 1 byte.

One-directional noise generators are based on OSU benchmarks that call standard point-to-point operations MPI_Send/MPI_Recv. Bidirectional generators use one-sided operations MPI_Put/MPI_Get. Although there is a minor difference, we can make a qualitative comparison of these two types of noise. We consider noise generators with different numbers of processes per node, from 1 to 14.

Test and Noise Run on Separate Nodes. In this case, the same OSU benchmarks were used to generate maximum BW and MR. The direction of data transfer also plays a role; however, this depends on whether one or more switches are involved. This point is clarified further on.

The nodes are connected to one switch (see Fig. 1b). Lomonosov-2 computing nodes are connected to nonblocking FDR InfiniBand switches. One switch unites eight nodes. As it was mentioned before, we want to study the test performance in the presence of maximum noise, which means the load on the switch should have the biggest impact. Thus we place noise on the maximum available number of nodes, which is six since at least two nodes are needed for the test. Generating load on six separate nodes is a nontrivial task since there are many ways to do it. We decided to use the following noise generators in this case:

- All-to-all noise generator. Fourteen copies of the OSU benchmark osu_alltoall run on all six nodes allocated for noise, no communication happens within a node. We assume that the maximum load is created by using the maximum number of processes per node, so 14 copies of the benchmark are used.
- Noise generator via point-to-point operations. Each node sends messages to the remaining five nodes and receives messages from them. We implement two options for this generator using two different OSU benchmarks.
- Six noise nodes are divided into three pairs. The messages are sent only within each pair of nodes. Fourteen copies of the osu_bw benchmark are used on each pair of nodes.

It should be noted that the noise direction does not matter in this case. Thus a total of eight different generators were used.

The nodes are connected to two switches (see Figs. 1(c) and 1(d)). We consider the same noise generators when nodes are connected to adjacent or nonadjacent switches. The direction of noise data transfer between nodes matters in this case since it affects the operation of the communication links between switches. Therefore, three noise generators were considered: 1) noise data is transmitted in the same direction as the test; 2) noise is transmitted in the opposite direction; 3) both directions are used for noise. The first two variants were implemented using osu_bw, and the last one using osu_put_bibw. The evaluation showed that the bidirectional noise generator has the maximum impact; the influence of the same-direction generator is slightly less, and the test slowdown is insignificant when the generator sends packets in the opposite direction. Thus, only the bidirectional noise generator was further considered.

4   Experimental Results

As mentioned above, all the experiments were conducted on the Lomonosov-2 supercomputer. All jobs were submitted using the Slurm resource manager in the test partition. We used the same computing nodes in each set of experiments. We also set affinity to cores for both test and generator processes. All the experiments in all four cases of communication network noise were conducted in a similar vein. The same set of tests described in Sect. 3.1 was used for studying each type of noise.

We adhered to the following experiment plan. First, we measured the time of "clean" test runs (without noise) and then compared the value obtained to the time of test runs affected by noise. Each experiment was repeated at least ten times. Data outliers showing abnormal execution times were manually excluded from the dataset. We resorted to 95% confidence intervals (CI) to determine whether noise influence is statistically significant: if 1) the mean time for noisy runs is greater than the mean time for clean runs, and 2) CI for runs with noise does not overlap with CI for runs without noise, then the noise is considered statistically significant.

To interpret the results more thoroughly, we need to understand how these tests use the communicating network. This is quite easy for OSU benchmarks and also for barrier and allreduce but not for NPB benchmarks. Thus we performed the profiling of MPI usage in NPB employing the mpiP tool [19]. According to mpiP, npb-ft uses primarily MPI_Alltoall, and npb-is also uses MPI_Allreduce. The other tests mainly use point-to-point operations. All tests operate with long messages only.

4.1   Case 1: One Shared Node

The results of the experiments in Case 1 of noise mapping (described in Sect. 3.2) are illustrated in Tables 1 and 2. If the noise is statistically significant, we report the normalized mean difference (*mean diff, %*) between noisy and clean execution times. Otherwise, if the noise is negligible, we omit the mean difference and insert a dash in the corresponding table cells. Table 1 contains the results of `barrier`, `allreduce`, and OSU tests. Table 2 presents the results of NPB tests. We launched the tests and generators on equal numbers of processes per node (pr./node): 1, 4, 7, and 14 for `barrier`, `allreduce`, and OSU tests; 1, 2, 4, and 8 for NPB tests (as most of them operate only on a number of processes equal to a power of 2). Different physical cores were used for test and noise in all cases, except for 8 and 14 pr./node since there are not enough physical cores in these cases, and it is necessary to use the logical cores available under hyper-threading.

Table 1. Case 1: noise on the shared node. Results of `barrier`, `allreduce`, and OSU tests

test	procs. per node	time, s no noise	normalized mean diff, %					
			noise types					
			bw_send	bw_receive	bw_bidir	mr_send	mr_receive	mr_bidir
barrier	1	1.53	216.46	197.70	377.83	–	144.21	1.90
	4	2.65	141.01	97.42	236.93	1.90	3442.47	3.85
	7	2.68	170.52	107.48	285.80	16.98	5933.66	64.52
	14	2.49	445.59	115.69	403.42	411.25	6142.20	154.12
allreduce	1	2.01	138.98	136.52	285.31	–	204.02	1.75
	4	3.18	114.80	94.31	185.54	1.72	3811.73	3.57
	7	3.20	134.83	95.90	190.42	12.21	5737.78	51.58
	14	2.72	208.03	100.06	271.42	367.96	5863.35	123.78
osu alltoall	1	21.44	64.45	68.00	87.73	–	103.20	2.32
	4	19.20	137.33	78.23	145.49	1.39	1555.78	13.24
	7	23.39	146.40	76.54	130.70	5.90	2402.32	23.92
	14	27.61	161.60	85.49	142.31	8.88	982.85	59.30
osu multi_lat	1	27.44	53.75	54.24	106.63	0.43	44.55	6.67
	4	20.69	52.65	51.66	102.34	0.83	1035.47	31.64
	7	26.25	56.52	51.87	101.95	2.14	1390.14	47.00
	14	27.93	55.55	49.90	93.28	7.75	1253.10	60.66

Noise influence on `barrier`, `allreduce`, *and OSU tests. Table 1.* We can see that `mr_receive` has a considerable influence on all the tests, resulting in a slowdown by a factor of up to 60 (!). It is strange since this noise is generated using the same program as in `mr_send` but with a different mapping of MPI ranks to nodes, so that messages flow in the opposite direction. The reason is presumably as follows. The MPI `eager` protocol is used when transferring small messages (1 byte is sent in each MPI message in the case of `mr_receive`), and the overheads of the `eager` protocol are significantly different when sending and when receiving messages. The MPI message is sent only on the sender side, but its processing can be postponed on the receiver side if there are too many messages, so the message has to be saved to the buffer, which should be allocated in advance. The results show that MPI overheads can be vastly different in these two seemingly alike cases. We tested several OpenMPI parameters and managed to reduce the `mr_receive` noise to the level of `mr_send` by changing various parameters (for instance, by enabling RDMA and increasing the buffer size). However, everywhere below, we give the results without parameter optimization to demonstrate the impact of this effect.

The following interesting points can also be highlighted in connection with the results in Table 1:

– MR noise (except the abnormal case of mr_receive) has a lesser impact than BW noise. It means that applications that occupy the entire bandwidth are noisier than programs sending packets at the maximum rate.
– MR influence grows as the number of processes per node increases. The impact of mr_send on barrier and allreduce exceptionally grows when hyper-threading is on (case of 14 pr./node) and even exceeds the mr_bidir noise.
– BW noise, unlike MR noise, does not scale with the number of processes per node. Probably, BW generators put a load heavy enough on the bottleneck even when running on 1 pr./node.
– We can only provide a qualitative comparison of unidirectional and bidirectional noises since OSU noise generators are based on different MPI operations (see 3.3). As expected, the experiments proved that bidirectional noise has a higher impact than unidirectional message passing.
– osu_alltoall produces a less pronounced slowdown than tests with other collective operations, presumably due to the use of long messages in this test.

We also showed that barrier and allreduce are more exposed to all types of noise than other tests as they use the communication network more intensively. Interestingly, even though barrier does not send any user MPI data, it is more exposed to noise influence than allreduce.

Noise influence on NPB tests. Table 2. As expected, the impact of noise on NPB tests is less significant than in the previously shown tests. The following three results are the same as for the previously discussed test group:

– MR noise is less than BW noise. Moreover, MR noise is often negligible in this case.
– Bidirectional noise is stronger than the unidirectional load (except for npb-is and the abnormal case of mr_receive explained earlier).
– MR noise increases when hyper-threading is used (also true for BW noise in this case). We can see that the noise impact grows significantly if hyper-threading is on, even though only two hyper-threading logical cores are used (the test and noise occupy 16 cores, although the processor has 14 physical cores). However, this impact can partially be caused by the computational part of NPB tests, which is also somewhat slowed down under hyper-threading.

Table 2. Case 1: noise on the shared node. Results of NPB tests

test	procs. per node	time, s no noise	normalized mean diff, % noise types					
			bw_send	bw_receive	bw_bidir	mr_send	mr_receive	mr_bidir
MG	1	19.16	–	–	–	–	–	–
	2	10.50	–		4.94	–	5.60	–
	4	5.19	8.25	8.49	13.56	1.47	16.89	2.28
	8	3.91	17.90	21.38	33.64	19.41	53.46	19.71
CG	1	142.03	1.95	–	5.59	–	–	–
	2	74.00	2.50	3.15	5.96	–	2.11	–
	4	31.52	–	–	–	–	11.80	–
	8	18.12	22.09	15.95	23.53	16.31	62.63	30.97
FT	1	96.67	–	–	–	–	–	–
	2	50.32	3.52	–	4.77	–	10.58	–
	4	26.55	11.48	9.03	13.29	2.05	117.58	2.87
	8	16.13	19.70	18.40	26.38	13.53	299.28	23.88
IS	1	3.49	18.52	15.12	11.04	–	–	–
	2	47.77	12.59	9.78	12.99	–	26.60	–
	4	29.11	10.67	8.64	8.81	–	102.65	–
	8	18.09	29.69	14.80	25.00	–	602.83	6.33
LU	1	254.23	–	–	–	–	–	–
	2	129.45	4.36	4.70	4.89	3.63	3.79	4.31
	4	74.38	2.93	3.79	5.63	2.03	4.28	2.36
	8	43.48	27.06	28.10	33.97	29.15	34.51	31.26
BT	2	207.46	4.07	4.27	4.92	3.67	–	–
	8	65.58	40.07	41.58	49.44	46.06	57.87	45.91
SP	2	161.60	3.77	4.51	7.66	2.23	4.11	2.10
	8	65.27	12.14	18.83	28.16	12.07	22.79	14.06

Note that the abnormal slowdown caused by mr_receive is most significant for npb-is and npb-ft, that is, the only NPB tests using MPI collective operations. We can also observe that the slowdown of tests does not directly correlate with the percent of the time the tests perform MPI operations. For instance, according to the mpiP profiling, npb-bt spends 11% of runtime in MPI on 8 pr./node, while npb-mg 32%, but the slowdown of the first is noticeably more pronounced. This indicates that, apart from other reasons, the impact of noise depends on peculiarities in the interaction with the communication network of each particular application, e.g., on the frequency of MPI calls.

4.2   Case 2: One Shared Switch

Here we consider Case 2, when the test and noise generators are launched on nodes connected to one InfiniBand switch (see 3.2). As we already stated, the switch is nonblocking. It should manage any load without slowing down, but we wanted to find out whether this is true in practice. We conducted the experiments using the two tests most sensible to the noise, namely, barrier and osu_bw with long messages. We used 14 pr./node and tried out eight noise generators (see Sect. 3.3).

The noise from all eight generators, both BW and MR, proved insignificant in all cases. We concluded that parallel applications do not affect each other when running on nodes connected to one switch since the switch handles all the load and cannot be a bottleneck when using a shared MPI communication network.

4.3   Case 3: Two Adjacent Switches

Tables 3 and 4 contain the results of the experiments in Case 3.2. We studied six noise-generator configurations: both BW and MR noise on 1, 4, and 7 nodes per switch.

Noise influence on barrier, allreduce, *and OSU tests. Table* 3. In this case, the tests were launched on two nodes, one node per switch. The results of the experiments show that noise on separate nodes can slow down the execution by a factor of as much as 21. Here, unlike the case of a shared node, MR noise has a more significant impact than BW noise. The reason is supposedly that processing a large number of packets, in case of congestion in the link between InfiniBand switches, has a more significant impact on the switches than link bandwidth exhaustion. We noticed that the slowdown in the tests is proportional to the number of nodes with noise, which points to a linear growth of overheads. Tests with collective operations suffer from additional load more than the osu_multi_lat test, which is based on MPI point-to-point operations, although the slowdown of the last is still significant. As in the case of a shared node (see Table 1), barrier performance deteriorates the most. At the same time, osu_alltoall is less influenced by noise than other collective operations. A possible explanation is that the ratio of communications between nodes connected to one switch is higher for MPI_Alltoall than for other collective operations, as a result of the difference in difficulty of the implemented MPI algorithms.

Table 3. Case 3: noise on nodes connected with adjacent switches. Results of barrier, allreduce, and OSU tests

test 1 node per switch	time, s	mean diff, %					
	no noise	noise type					
		BW			MR		
		noise nodes per switch			noise nodes per switch		
		7	4	1	7	4	1
barrier	2.65	1573.81	1098.00	194.55	2146.96	1097.99	173.71
allreduce	2.65	1428.79	824.11	177.21	1966.45	1011.73	144.41
osu_alltoall, short msgs	10.90	778.67	443.06	93.51	1076.29	571.03	90.21
osu_multi_lat	35.65	747.35	433.15	106.67	944.84	519.24	121.71

Noise influence on NPB tests. Table 4. NPB tests were launched on the following configurations:

- With different numbers of processes and nodes: 2 nodes (1 per switch), 16 processes in total; or 8 nodes (4 per switch), 64 processes in total.
- Using two options for the distribution of processes per node: balanced (bl) or nonbalanced (nb). In the balanced configuration, 8 pr./node are always used; in the nonbalanced, the maximum number of processes (14) is launched on the nodes of one switch, and the rest (2) are launched on the nodes of the other switch.

Table 4. Case 3: noise on nodes connected with adjacent switches. Results of NPB tests with a balanced distribution of processes

number of nodes with test	test	time, s	mean diff, %					
		no noise	noise type					
			BW			MR		
			noise nodes per switch			noise nodes per switch		
			7	4	1	7	4	1
2 nodes, 1 per switch 16 processes	MG	3.91	10.14	5.50	1.04	13.98	6.42	1.50
	CG	17.28	14.16	7.33	1.71	19.46	8.75	2.24
	FT	16.09	73.12	41.58	10.34	102.07	47.54	11.40
	IS	17.18	135.67	76.63	21.17	186.64	87.72	20.16
	LU	43.56	1.27	–	–	2.24	0.72	–
	BT	65.59	2.64	0.87	–	3.73	1.34	–
	SP	65.53	4.47	2.46	0.42	5.94	2.72	0.51
8 nodes, 4 per switch 64 processes	MG	1.05		6.43	–		7.60	–
	CG	3.14		29.92	8.08		33.38	8.32
	FT	5.41		55.48	13.46		66.91	15.24
	IS	9.41		62.33	15.49		78.78	17.62
	LU	11.94		–	–		–	–
	BT	16.07		–	–		4.43	–
	SP	13.29		11.89	2.05		15.99	2.40

In Table 4, we see the results of bl runs. The NPB slowdown is again significantly less than that of tests shown in Table 3. NPB is more sensitive to noise when more nodes are used since more transfers flow through the shared link between the switches. Noise on more nodes is more noticeable for the same reason. The measurements of npb-is and npb-ft tests are outstanding; these tests show the greatest slowdown since they are the only NPB tests using MPI collective operations. It can also be noted that the performance of npb-is with MPI_Allreduce deteriorates more than that of npb-ft with MPI_Alltoall. Such relation corresponds to the results shown in Table 3: `allreduce` slowdown is greater than `alltoall` slowdown. Other NPB tests are less sensitive to noise, with `npb-lu` and `npb-bt` not changing at all.

We found out that the influence of noise on `nb` runs is less than on `bl` runs. The noise is not detected for almost all `nb` tests with point-to-point MPI operations on two nodes. We detected the mean difference for `npb-is` and `npb-ft` (tests with collective operations), but it was smaller by a factor of three to four. It is generally the same for runs on eight nodes. We explain this result by the fact that more communication happens within processes on one node in `nb` runs, which means that fewer data are transferred between switches. However, we should mention that the "clean" time of `bl` NPB runs is less than that of `nb` runs. Thus, on the one hand, launching applications with a balanced distribution of processes is optimal compared to the nonbalanced mapping of processes. On the other hand, the noise impact on the performance of tests is less if done the second way. For example, in the presence of noise, nonbalanced variants of `npb-is` and `npb-ft` run faster than their balanced counterparts, while it is the opposite when no noise is introduced.

4.4   Case 4: Two Nonadjacent Switches

All experiments in Case 3.2 were conducted in the same manner as in Case 3 but on different sets of nodes. Half of the nodes remained the same; the other nodes were from a different rack of the Lomonosov-2 supercomputer. It was estimated that the route between switches runs through two additional switches, meaning that an MPI message has to traverse through five network links and four switches in total.

The experiment measurements showed that Case 4 is very similar to Case 3. Therefore all Case 3 results are also valid when several switches are used. The only difference is the slowdown of `barrier`, `allreduce`, and OSU tests, which is noticeably less in this case. This is apparently caused by the following reasons: 1) the work with MPI is organized less efficiently since sending the messages takes longer because of the greater distance between nodes, which increases the baseline time of "clean" runs; 2) in Case 4 (unlike the case of adjacent switches), the additional load caused by the noise can be balanced across several switches. These two reasons lead to a lesser noise impact.

According to the obtained results, NPB tests showed exactly the same performance as in Case 3. Thus it does not matter whether NPB tests are launched on close or distant nodes.

5   Conclusions

In this paper, we presented the results of extensive testing of noise influence on HPC applications. We focused on MPI-related noise, which can happen if some external program (another user application or some system process) interferes with the workflow of a user parallel application since it occupies a shared resource: the communication network for transferring MPI messages. We studied the maximum possible noise in terms of bandwidth and MPI message rate and measured the slowdown for a set of well-known tests and benchmarks. All experiments were conducted on the Lomonosov-2 supercomputer, but the conclusions regarding the influence on applications are valid for other systems.

We found out that competition for the MPI communication network within a computing node can significantly affect the execution time of user applications. For example, we showed that performance can be severely degraded if a lot of short messages are received on a node. Also, we showed that high-bandwidth noise has a greater impact than high-message-rate noise, and it has more influence on MPI collective operations (especially on MPI_Barrier) than on point-to-point operations. NPB tests were less affected by the noise, but their slowdown can also be significant and noticeable, especially when using collective operations.

We confirmed the assumption that parallel programs do not interfere with each other when running on nodes connected to one switch, i.e., the tested InfiniBand switch can handle such a load. However, if the parallel program uses computing nodes connected to two adjacent switches instead, then the link between them can become a bottleneck, leading to a noticeable deterioration of the application performance in some situations. In this case, unlike the case of one shared node, high-message-rate noise has a more significant impact than high-bandwidth noise. We can conclude that congestion in the link between switches caused by a large number of messages affects the performance more than link bandwidth exhaustion. Moreover, MPI collective operations prove more susceptible to this type of noise than point-to-point operations. Thus, among NPB tests, the IS and FT benchmarks, which use collective MPI operations, slow down the most in the presence of noise. For other tests, the slowdown is minor or even negligible in this case. The overall picture remains basically the same when an MPI program uses the connections between nonadjacent switches.

Acknowledgments. The reported study was funded by the Russian Foundation for Basic Research (project № 21-57-12011). The research was carried out on shared HPC resources at Lomonosov Moscow State University.

References

1. OSU Micro-benchmarks. https://mvapich.cse.ohio-state.edu/benchmarks/
2. Afzal, A., Hager, G., Wellein, G.: Propagation and decay of injected one-off delays on clusters: a case study. In: 2019 IEEE International Conference on Cluster Computing (CLUSTER), pp. 1–10. IEEE (2019). https://doi.org/10.1109/CLUSTER.2019.8890995
3. Akkan, H., Lang, M., Liebrock, L.: Understanding and isolating the noise in the Linux kernel. Int. J. High Perform. Comput. Appl. **27**(2), 136–146 (2013). https://doi.org/10.1177/1094342013477892
4. Bailey, D., Harris, T., Saphir, W., Van Der Wijngaart, R., Woo, A., Yarrow, M.: The NAS parallel benchmarks 2.0. Technical report, Technical Report NAS-95-020, NASA Ames Research Center (1995)

5. Beckman, P., Iskra, K., Yoshii, K., Coghlan, S.: The influence of operating systems on the performance of collective operations at extreme scale. In: 2006 IEEE International Conference on Cluster Computing, pp. 1–12. IEEE (2006). https://doi.org/10.1109/CLUSTR.2006.311846

6. De, P., Kothari, R., Mann, V.: Identifying sources of operating system jitter through fine-grained kernel instrumentation. In: Proceedings - IEEE International Conference on Cluster Computing, ICCC, pp. 331–340 (2007). https://doi.org/10.1109/CLUSTR.2007.4629247

7. De, P., Mann, V., Mittal, U.: Handling OS jitter on multicore multithreaded systems. In: Proceedings of the 2009 IEEE International Parallel and Distributed Processing Symposium, IPDPS 2009, pp. 1–12. IEEE Computer Society (2009). https://doi.org/10.1109/IPDPS.2009.5161046

8. Ferreira, K.B., Bridges, P., Brightwell, R.: Characterizing application sensitivity to OS interference using kernel-level noise injection. In: 2008 SC - International Conference for High Performance Computing, Networking, Storage and Analysis, SC 2008 (2008). https://doi.org/10.1109/SC.2008.5219920

9. Garg, R., De, P.: Impact of noise on scaling of collectives: an empirical evaluation. In: Robert, Y., Parashar, M., Badrinath, R., Prasanna, V.K. (eds.) HiPC 2006. LNCS, vol. 4297, pp. 460–471. Springer, Heidelberg (2006). https://doi.org/10.1007/11945918_45

10. Hoefler, T., Schneider, T., Lumsdaine, A.: Characterizing the influence of system noise on large-scale applications by simulation. In: Proceedings of the 2010 ACM/IEEE International Conference for High Performance Computing, Networking, Storage and Analysis, SC 2010, pp. 1–11. IEEE (2010). https://doi.org/10.1109/SC.2010.12

11. Jones, T.: Linux kernel co-scheduling for bulk synchronous parallel applications. In: Proceedings of the 1st International Workshop on Runtime and Operating Systems for Supercomputers, pp. 57–64 (2011). https://doi.org/10.1145/1988796.1988805

12. Kim, J., Dally, W.J., Abts, D.: Flattened butterfly: a cost-efficient topology for high-radix networks. In: Proceedings - International Symposium on Computer Architecture, pp. 126–137 (2007). https://doi.org/10.1145/1250662.1250679

13. León, E.A., Karlin, I., Moody, A.T.: System noise revisited: enabling application scalability and reproducibility with SMT. In: 2016 IEEE International Parallel and Distributed Processing Symposium (IPDPS), pp. 596–607. IEEE (2016). https://doi.org/10.1109/IPDPS.2016.48

14. Nikitenko, D.A., et al.: Influence of noisy environments on behavior of HPC applications. Lobachevskii J. Math. **42**(7), 1560–1570 (2021). https://doi.org/10.1134/S1995080221070192

15. Petrini, F., Kerbyson, D.J., Pakin, S.: The case of the missing supercomputer performance: achieving optimal performance on the 8,192 processors of ASCI Q. In: Proceedings of the 2003 ACM/IEEE Conference on Supercomputing, SC 2003, p. 55. IEEE (2003). https://doi.org/10.1145/1048935.1050204

16. Shah, A., Müller, M., Wolf, F.: Estimating the impact of external interference on application performance. In: Aldinucci, M., Padovani, L., Torquati, M. (eds.) Euro-Par 2018. LNCS, vol. 11014, pp. 46–58. Springer, Cham (2018). https://doi.org/10.1007/978-3-319-96983-1_4

17. Shah, A., Wolf, F., Zhumatiy, S., Voevodin, V.: Capturing inter-application interference on clusters. In: Proceedings - IEEE International Conference on Cluster Computing, ICCC (2013). https://doi.org/10.1109/CLUSTER.2013.6702665

18. Tsafrir, D., Etsion, Y., Feitelson, D.G., Kirkpatrick, S.: System noise, OS clock ticks, and fine-grained parallel applications. In: Proceedings of the 19th Annual International Conference on Supercomputing, pp. 303–312 (2005). https://doi.org/10.1145/1088149.1088190

19. Vetter, J., Chambreau, C.: mpiP: lightweight, scalable MPI profiling (2005). http://gec.di.uminho.pt/Discip/MInf/cpd1415/PCP/MPI/mpiP_LightweightScalableMPIProfiling.pdf

20. Voevodin, V., et al.: Supercomputer Lomonosov-2: large scale, deep monitoring and fine analytics for the user community. Supercomput. Front. Innov. **6**(2) (2019). https://doi.org/10.14529/js190201

21. Voevodin, V., Stefanov, K., Zhumatiy, S.: Overhead analysis for performance monitoring counters multiplexing. In: Voevodin, V., Sobolev, S., Yakobovskiy, M., Shagaliev, R. (eds.) RuSCDays 2022. LNCS, vol. 13708, pp. 461–474. Springer, Cham (2022). https://doi.org/10.1007/978-3-031-22941-1_34

Parallel Data Preprocessing Library for Neural Network Training

Dmitry Buryak[1], Vadim Vakhrushev[1(✉)], Mikhail Shubin[1], Nina Popova[1], Kamil Khamitov[1], and Oleg Ivanov[2]

[1] Lomonosov Moscow State University, Moscow, Russian Federation
pristmanabern@yandex.ru, popova@cs.msu.ru
[2] Federal Register of Experts in the Scientific and Technical Sphere, Moscow, Russian Federation

Abstract. Data preprocessing is a commonly used method to improve the efficiency of neural network training algorithms. In this paper, we suggest an approach for organizing parallel computations that makes it possible to preprocess data against the background of neural network training. We assume that data preprocessing is performed on the processor using multiprocessing calculations, whereas training involves graphic processors. The proposed algorithms differ in the way of organizing parallelism and interprocess communication. The methods are implemented in Python and C++ and presented as a software library. We describe the results of comparing the efficiency of the methods with the implementation of parallel preprocessing within the PyTorch framework on various test problems. Also, we give some recommendations on the method choice depending on the dataset and the batch preprocessing algorithm.

Keywords: Data preprocessing · Neural network training · HPC · Multiprocessing · Python

1 Introduction

At present, neural networks are widely used in solving applied problems. The amount of data required to train modern deep-learning models increases every year. In this regard, there is a problem with the scalability of data preprocessing algorithms for training neural networks. During the training stage, there may arise situations when the time required for preprocessing the input data is comparable to the time spent directly on training the neural network or even exceeds it. Such an effect may occur for various reasons, for example, because of a relatively small number of neural network parameters or when the training stage includes GPU computing which significantly speeds up the learning process. In such cases, training data can be preprocessed more slowly than the neural network will process them. Therefore one must be able to prepare data batches in parallel and asynchronously with the learning algorithm. There is

© The Author(s), under exclusive license to Springer Nature Switzerland AG 2023
L. Sokolinsky and M. Zymbler (Eds.): PCT 2023, CCIS 1868, pp. 19–32, 2023.
https://doi.org/10.1007/978-3-031-38864-4_2

also the question of whether it is possible to single out classes of datasets featuring characteristics that allow solving the problem of parallel data preprocessing more efficiently.

The paper proposes an approach supporting data preprocessing on many-core hardware platforms. The approach has been implemented as a library providing the user with several parameters for setting the preprocessing according to the particular task. This implementation offers a solution to the CPU Load Balancing issue which often arises in multicore systems.

2   Related Work

Parallel and asynchronous preprocessing of data batches is critical for efficient neural network training. For this reason, the most popular modern deep learning frameworks, such as PyTorch, Keras, and TensorFlow, provide extensive support for this kind of data preparation.

In TensorFlow and Keras, the preprocessing process is considered an ETL (Extract, Transform, and Load) pipeline in which individual stages can be parallelized [1]. The module that implements parallel data preprocessing is written in C++, which allows for the use of multithreading instead of multiprocessing, thereby avoiding the *global interpreter lock*, which is specific to the Python language.

In [1], a preprocessing library for TensorFlow is considered. The tf.data API provides operators that can be parameterized with user-defined computation, composed, and reused across different machine learning domains. These abstractions enable users to focus on the logic features of applying data processing, while tf.data's runtime ensures that pipelines run efficiently.

The Nvidia Data Loading Library (DALI) [2] is an approach alternative to the proposed. DALI can accelerate data preprocessing operations using GPU-accelerated data preprocessing operations. DALI also prefetches and pipelines the data fetch and preprocessing with the GPU compute, similar to the default dataloader in PyTorch. Though DALI shows high efficiency, the CPU Load Balancing issue remains in the system. The CoorDL library is presented in [3]; this library uses DALI and can be used as a drop-in replacement for the default PyTorch dataloader.

Let us now consider the implementation of parallel data preprocessing in the PyTorch framework (Fig. 1). Each worker process has its own input queue, in which the master process writes the indices of the objects that need to be preprocessed and combined into a batch. Also, the main process writes the serial number of this batch. Then, each worker process prepares the corresponding batch and puts it along with its serial number in a single output queue, shared among all worker processes. The master process keeps the serial number of the next required batch to pass to the neural network. When extracting another batch from the queue, the master process compares the serial number of this batch and the number of the required batch and, if they do not match, caches the batch to return it immediately when the corresponding batch number matches

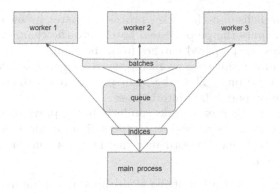

Fig. 1. Data preprocessing scheme in the PyTorch framework

the required number. Such algorithms guarantee that the batches are fed to the input of the neural network in a deterministic order.

3   Overview of the Proposed Methods

Before proceeding to the analysis of the implemented methods, we should highlight several general points that are taken into account in our implementation. All developed algorithms support two modes of operation: blocking and nonblocking. In blocking mode, the main process waits for the next batch, consisting of completely new data, to be prepared. In nonblocking mode, the main process does not wait for the next batch to be prepared but samples the required number of objects from the buffer of previously preprocessed batches. The advantage of this approach is that there are no delays in waiting for the preparation of the next batch. However, in this case, the neural network will receive duplicate input objects during one epoch, which can lead to overfitting. This negative effect can be reduced by increasing the size of the buffer of preprocessed batches. As the buffer size increases, each object will be sampled fewer times during the current training epoch.

Also, note that deep learning tasks in many cases require reproducibility of results. Therefore, the developed algorithms support ordered and unordered data preparation modes. In ordered mode, it is guaranteed that the results of the preprocessing algorithm will be the same in different runs with the same input parameters. In unordered mode, reproducibility is not guaranteed, but the learning process may be accelerated. The reasons for this effect will be explained below, with a detailed analysis of the implemented algorithms.

It is important to point out that the developed library does not depend on any third-party libraries or frameworks and uses only Python 3 multiprocessing library.

Let us describe the implemented methods:

- Batch-level parallelism: each worker process prepares its own data batch at a time. Then it puts the preprocessed batch into the channel, and the main process retrieves the prepared batches from the channel.
- Object-level parallelism: each worker process prepares several objects and puts them into the pipe. Then the main process reads them from the pipe and groups the prepared data into batches.
- Shared memory buffer use: it works similarly to the previous method, except that the shared memory is used as a process interaction method instead of pipes. It leads to higher performance but imposes some restrictions upon preprocessed data.

Before a detailed description of the algorithms, it will be useful to describe the method used for distributing objects among worker processes. Each process prepares one data chunk at a time. The definition of the chunk changes depending on the method. For batch-level parallelism, K is equal to the batch size. For object-level parallelism and the shared memory buffer algorithm, K may be an arbitrary positive integer number.

Consider the situation when there are N objects in a dataset, and K is a chunk size. In this case, the number of data chunks is

$$S = \left\lceil \frac{N}{K} \right\rceil. \tag{1}$$

Then the maximum chunk index is equal to $R = S - 1$.

Assume the case of three worker processes. Under these assumptions, chunk indices are distributed among the processes in the following way:

$$0: \ 0, 3, \ldots, R - (R \mod 3),$$
$$1: \ 1, 4, \ldots, R - ((R-1) \mod 3),$$
$$2: \ 2, 5, \ldots, R - ((R-2) \mod 3).$$

3.1   Batch-Level Parallelism

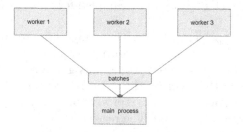

Fig. 2. Batch-level parallelism preprocessing scheme in the case of ordered data preparation

In this method, worker processes use channels to communicate with the master process. In the case of the ordered batch preparation method, each process has its own channel, which makes it possible to obtain batches in a strictly defined order and avoid the memory cost of caching on the side of the main process. In unordered mode, all processes have one shared channel, so the main process reads the fastest prepared batch, which can lead to a gain in time (Fig. 2).

It is important to note that this approach does not take into account the internal structure of the batch, which makes it universal: different batches, in general, can have different sizes, for example, when training recurrent neural networks [4]. Also, if some union operation must be performed on individual objects to form the batch, it will be done asynchronously with the learning algorithm, in the worker process; this may lead to a significant gain in time if the union operation is heavy.

The disadvantages of this approach include the fact that during the training of a neural network at the beginning of each epoch, the preparation time of the first batch coincides with that of the sequential implementation. In practice, this delay is negligible since the number of batches is usually much larger than one.

Advantages of the method:
1. No assumptions about the internal structure of the batch.
2. Grouping objects into a batch can be done asynchronously in the worker process.
3. Relative ease of implementation and lack of complex synchronization models.

Disadvantages of the method:
1. The preparation time of the first batch is the same as in the serial implementation.
2. Pipes may not be the fastest means of inter-process communication; it takes additional time to serialize, transfer, and deserialize a batch.

3.2 Object-Level Parallelism

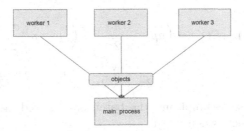

Fig. 3. Preprocessing scheme with object-level parallelism in the case of ordered data preparation

This method, in contrast to the previous one, works at the level of objects instead of batches (Fig. 3).

Since the preparation of one batch, in general, is carried out by several processes, the procedure for grouping objects into a batch has to be performed in the main process synchronously with the training of the neural network. Also, note that if the process prepares fewer objects than the batch size, the master process will have to read data from the channel several times to form a data batch.

Let us now compare the efficiency of batch preparation in the cases of batch-level and object-level parallelism when the object preparation time is not constant. For simplicity, consider an example when there are two processes, each prepares a batch for batch-level and an object for object-level parallelism, and the batch size is n. Also, assume that the object preparation time is a normally distributed random variable with parameters (μ, σ). Then, if all objects are prepared independently, the time required to prepare one batch in batch-level parallelism is $X = \min(X_1, X_2)$, $X_1 \sim N(n\mu, n\sigma^2)$, $X_2 \sim N(n\mu, n\sigma^2)$, where $N(a, b)$ is a normally distributed random variable with parameters (a, b); in object-level parallelism, this time is $Y = n \cdot \min(Y_1, Y_2)$, $Y_1 \sim N(\mu, \sigma)$, $Y_2 \sim N(\mu, \sigma)$ since in this case we always take the first object that is ready. We neglect the time required to transfer data from worker processes to the main process.

Let us calculate the expected value of these random variables [5]:

$$E(X) = n\mu \cdot \Phi\left(\frac{n\mu - n\mu}{\sqrt{n\sigma^2}}\right) + n\mu \cdot \Phi\left(\frac{n\mu - n\mu}{\sqrt{n\sigma^2}}\right) - \sqrt{n}\sigma \cdot \phi\left(\frac{n\mu - n\mu}{\sqrt{n\sigma^2}}\right)$$

$$= n\mu - \frac{\sqrt{n}\sigma}{\sqrt{2\pi}}, \tag{2}$$

$$E(Y) = n\left(\mu \cdot \Phi\left(\frac{\mu - \mu}{\sqrt{\sigma}}\right) + \mu \cdot \Phi\left(\frac{\mu - \mu}{\sqrt{\sigma}}\right) - \sigma \cdot \phi\left(\frac{\mu - \mu}{\sqrt{\sigma}}\right)\right)$$

$$= n\mu - n\frac{\sigma}{\sqrt{2\pi}}, \tag{3}$$

where $\Phi(x)$ and $\phi(x)$ are, respectively, the cumulative distribution function and the probability density function of the normal distribution.

Thus,

$$E(X) - E(Y) = \left(n\mu - \frac{\sqrt{n}\sigma}{\sqrt{2\pi}}\right) - \left(n\mu - n\frac{\sigma}{\sqrt{2\pi}}\right)$$

$$= n\frac{\sigma}{\sqrt{2\pi}} - \frac{\sqrt{n}\sigma}{\sqrt{2\pi}} = (n - \sqrt{n})\frac{\sigma}{\sqrt{2\pi}}. \tag{4}$$

Thus, under these assumptions, the batch is prepared faster in the case of parallelism over objects when $n > 1$.

The advantages and disadvantages of this method are the following:

Advantages of the method:
1. Flexibility of the algorithm depending on the choice of the value K.
Disadvantages of the method:
1. Grouping objects into a batch is performed synchronously in the main process, which increases the time cost of the algorithm.

2. The main process can perform several reads of objects from the channel
   to form a batch.

3.3   Shared Memory Buffer Use

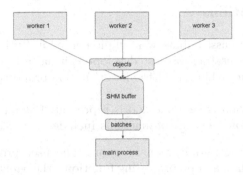

Fig. 4. Scheme of preprocessing using a buffer in the shared memory, in the case of ordered data preparation

The difference between this approach and the previous one is the use of shared memory instead of channels. Shared memory is usually the fastest of interprocess communication tools, but it imposes some restrictions upon input data (Fig. 4).

As in the previous method, the master process waits for each worker process to preprocess its part of the batch. In this method, instead of putting the objects into the pipe, they are placed in the shared memory immediately after processing, without serialization, so as to improve performance. Accordingly, after reading data from memory, deserialization is not required. This leads to a restriction upon the object size after preprocessing: the objects must have the same shape since the shared memory buffer, which is a multidimensional array, has a certain size when created, and in general, it is impossible to predict what the size should be to accommodate batch objects. If all objects after preprocessing have the same shape object_shape, the number of objects in the batch is K, and L batches are placed in the buffer, then the shared memory buffer will have the shape $(L, K, \texttt{object\_shape})$. Note that a significant part of deep learning problems, in particular, computer vision, satisfies the object homogeneity constraints after preprocessing.

This method significantly reduces the time required to transfer an object from the worker process to the main process. Thus, this method is an extension of the idea of using object-level parallelism instead of batch-level parallelism and corrects the disadvantages of the previous method, while introducing some restrictions on input data.

Advantages of the method:
   1. It significantly reduces the cost of transferring a batch between worker
      processes and the main process by using shared memory instead of pipes.
Disadvantages of the method:
   1. Occurrence of restrictions on the preprocessed objects.

4   Implementations

All three methods discussed above were implemented in Python3. For the third
idea, a C++ implementation was also developed (it has a Python3 user's interface, provided by the pybind11 [6] framework). The proposed library is called
Parloader.

The implementation of each method is represented as a single module providing several functions. The set of functions includes:

- `init_dataprep`: the initialization function. The user provides the *dataset
  object* (contains data and preprocessing function), the *batch size* (used during
  the training process), the *number of processes* (the number of workers that
  will preprocess data), a *flag of blocking/nonblocking mode*, as well as other
  technical parameters.
- `start_dataprep`: a procedure that starts preprocessing;
- `stop_dataprep`: a procedure that stops preprocessing;
- `rqst_batch`: a function that returns batches with preprocessed objects.

Other parameters for `init_dataprep` include the *size of the buffer* (for the
shared-memory version; it is used for storing processed objects), the *union function* (a function that groups objects into a batch), and the *initialization function*
(it will be called in every worker process before preprocessing).

The core of the library is the use of parallel processes (rather than threads).
The reason for this solution is that threads are not useful when Python-code
parallelism is required because of the presence of the *global interpreter lock* in
Python. The C++ implementation (of the same library interface) also presents
this problem because the preprocessing function remains "Python-side", so the
thread mechanism is also worthless in this case.

The Python 3 implementation employs the `multiprocessing` module for
this, while the C++ implementation uses the `fork` mechanism.

5   Experiment Results

We conducted experiments for various tasks, such as image processing, video
processing, and time series processing. We built three plots for each task: one that
reflects the dependence of execution time (including preprocessing and training)
on the number of processes when learning with blocking mode, a similar plot
for nonblocking mode, and a plot of the fraction of unique objects processed
by the neural network during the epoch. The results were averaged over five

epochs. The batch size in all experiments was 64, and the K parameter for both object-level parallelism and shared memory algorithms was set to 1.

The experiments were carried out on a node of the Lomonosov-2 supercomputer [7] equipped with an Intel Xeon Gold 6126 (2.60 GHz, 12 cores) CPU and an Nvidia Tesla P100 GPU.

5.1   Image Processing

In this experiment, we used Alexnet [8] as a neural network and the "bee-vs-wasp" [9] task as a dataset (a set of pictures of bees, bumblebees, and other insects). The machine learning task was to classify the objects into three classes. In this experiment, the same set of transformations was applied to each object during preprocessing.

The results (execution time for blocking and nonblocking modes) are shown in Fig. 5. We can see that the method that uses shared memory outperforms other methods from the point of view of execution time. It can be explained by the fact that the time spent reading data from the shared memory is significantly less than the time spent reading from a channel or queue, as in other methods.

The PyTorch implementation and the batch-level parallelism implementation perform approximately on the same level. This happens because PyTorch also uses batch parallelism. However, the proposed implementation offers more lightweight channels for interprocess communication, unlike the queue used by PyTorch.

Object-level parallelism performs worse than the above-mentioned methods. This happens, most likely, because the overheads of transferring data between processes in this method are the highest in comparison with others. Also, the function of grouping objects into a batch is called synchronously when a batch is requested, unlike the previous methods.

The worst performance is shown by the C++ implementation. It uses the `pickle` module for converting Python objects to byte arrays and back. The merging function also works synchronously in the main process. There are significant overheads, thus the speed of this implementation is lower than that of Python libraries. As for the nonblocking mode, the execution time increases with an increase in the number of processes and then reaches an asymptote. The reason for this is that the time spent preparing the batch decreases as the number of processes increases. This in turn leads to an increase in the running time of the batch since the function for obtaining a batch in nonblocking mode immediately returns the previously prepared data if the new batch is not ready yet. In the experiment, at a certain point, the processing time of the batch by the neural network is equal to or greater than the batch preprocessing time, therefore the execution time in the nonblocking mode is equal to the execution time in the blocking mode.

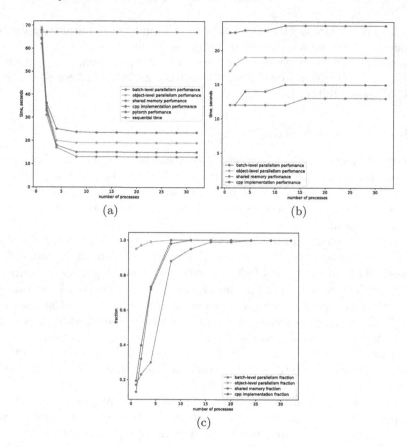

Fig. 5. Image processing, execution time: (a) blocking mode, (b) nonblocking mode, (c) nonblocking mode, fraction of unique objects

It should be noted that the greater the fraction of unique objects the neural network gets during the epoch, the longer the data is prepared in the nonblocking mode.

5.2 Time Series Processing

In this experiment, the task of time series prediction was solved using the double Stacked GRU neural network. The dataset was automatically generated using trigonometric functions with random noise added. In tasks of time sequence prediction, the shared memory approach is not, generally speaking, applicable since the input object for the neural network is a sequence with a length that can vary from object to object, and this does not satisfy the homogeneity restrictions for preprocessed data.

The results (execution time for the blocking and nonblocking modes) are shown in Fig. 6.

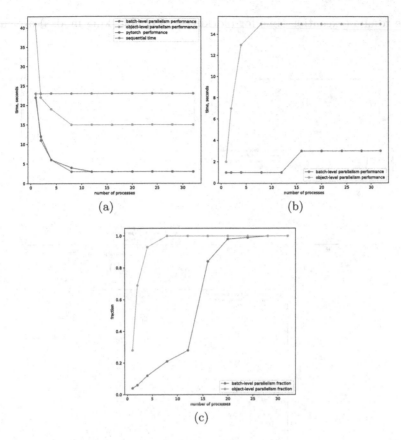

Fig. 6. Time series processing, execution time: (a) blocking mode, (b) nonblocking mode, (c) nonblocking mode, fraction of unique objects

In these experiments, as we can see, the object-parallel version is also inferior to the batch-parallel version and PyTorch implementations. In this case, the function of grouping objects into a batch is relatively heavier than in the previous task, which results in more lag compared to the previous experiment.

As for the nonblocking mode, the conclusions remain the same as in the previous paragraph.

5.3 Video Processing

The experiment consisted of the task of recognizing a number in a picture. The dataset was artificially generated by placing a number in a random place in the picture. The architecture used was that of a convolutional neural network [10]. During the generation and preprocessing of the object, a random number of augmentations was used, which significantly distinguishes this experiment from the first one and leads to a significant spread in the preparation time of one object.

The results (execution time for blocking and nonblocking modes) are shown in Fig. 7.

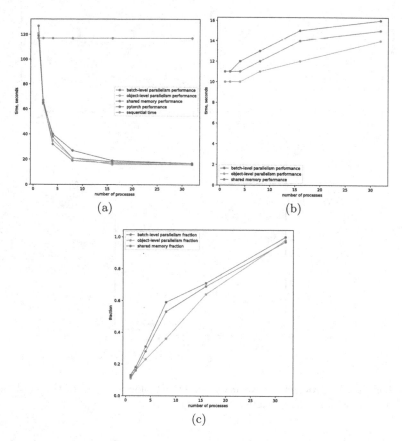

(a)

(b)

(c)

Fig. 7. Video processing, execution time: (a) blocking mode, (b) nonblocking mode, (c) nonblocking mode, fraction of unique objects

As we can see, the methods that can simultaneously prepare a small number of objects, such as object-level parallelism and shared memory, show slightly better results than PyTorch and batch-level parallelism. This supports the assumption that the methods that operate on objects rather than batches can be faster when the object preparation time shows a large spread.

6   Conclusions

The following general conclusions can be drawn based on the analysis of the experiments:

1. When all objects after preprocessing are homogeneous (i.e., they have the same shape), it is most likely that the shared memory method shows the highest performance.
2. If the function of grouping objects into a batch is not heavyweight and the object preparation time is not constant, then, most likely, it is best to use object-level parallelism.
3. Otherwise, batch-level parallelism is the most suitable.

In this paper, we presented an approach to applying multiprocessing for preliminary data preparation on multicore systems. The approach was implemented as a library called Parloader, which provides the user with parameters for setting the efficiency according to the particular task. Also, we performed an experimental study of the library in the case of the PyTorch framework. The experiments showed that the Parloader library outperforms PyTorch DataLoader in almost all cases. An important advantage of the Parloader library is that it can be used as an independent module not only in the PyTorch framework but also in other neural network applications and frameworks.

We plan further research on Parloader efficiency with other frameworks, such as its adaptation for the *hard mining* task, i.e., that of searching for the hardest samples for training.

Acknowledgments. The study was partly funded by the Russian Foundation for Basic Research (research project № 20-07-01053). The research was carried out on shared HPC equipment at Lomonosov Moscow State University research facilities [7].

References

1. Murray, D.G., Simsa, J., Klimovic, A., Indyk, I.: tf.data: a machine learning data processing framework (2021). arXiv:2101.12127
2. NVIDIA DALI Documentation. https://docs.nvidia.com/deeplearning/dali/. Accessed 29 Sept 2022
3. Mohan, J., Phanishayee, A., Raniwala, A., Chidambaram, V.: Analyzing and mitigating data stalls in DNN training. Proc. VLDB Endow. **14**(5), 771–784 (2021). https://doi.org/10.14778/3446095.3446100
4. Sherstinsky, A.: Fundamentals of Recurrent Neural Network (RNN) and Long Short-Term Memory (LSTM) Network (2018). Elsevier "Physica D: Nonlinear Phenomena" Journal **404** (2020). Special Issue on Machine Learning and Dynamical Systems. arXiv:1808.03314. https://doi.org/10.1016/j.physd.2019.132306
5. Nadarajah, S., Kotz, S.: Exact distribution of the max/min of two Gaussian random variables. IEEE Trans. Very Large Scale Integr. (VLSI) Syst. **16**(2), 210–212 (2008). https://doi.org/10.1109/TVLSI.2007.912191
6. pybind11—Seamless operability between C++11 and Python. https://github.com/pybind/pybind11. Accessed 16 May 2022

7. Voevodin, V.V., et al.: Supercomputer Lomonosov-2: large scale, deep monitoring and fine analytics for the user community. J. Supercomput. Front. Innov. **6**(2), 4–11 (2019). https://doi.org/10.14529/jsfi190201
8. Krizhevsky, A., Sutskever, I., Hinton, G.E.: ImageNet classification with deep convolutional neural networks. In: Advances in Neural Information Processing Systems, vol. 25 (2012)
9. https://www.kaggle.com/datasets/jerzydziewierz/bee-vs-wasp
10. O'Shea, K., Nash, R.: An introduction to convolutional neural networks (2015). arXiv:1511.08458

An Efficient LRnLA Algorithm and Data Structure for Manycore and Multicore Computers with Hierarchical Cache

Vadim Levchenko and Anastasia Perepelkina

Keldysh Institute of Applied Mathematics, Moscow, Russian Federation
lev@keldysh.ru, mogmi@narod.ru

Abstract. According to the Roofline model, low arithmetic intensity is the main performance bottleneck for multidimensional simulation with stencil data access. This bottleneck can be eliminated using LRnLA (locally recursive nonlocally asynchronous) algorithms, which take advantage of all levels of cache. We introduce the new algorithm FArShFold, a development of previously published Torre-type LRnLA algorithms by using data arrays aligned with a space-time wavefront. The novelty is in the distribution of data between threads and the decomposition in the time axis for parallelism. In this paper, we present the implementation of the algorithm for the solution of fluid dynamics problems with the LBM method and its scaling on AMD zen2/3 processor architectures. The obtained performance for single precision D3Q19 LBM is more than 1.4 GLUps on the AMD Ryzen R9 5950X processor.

Keywords: GPU · LRnLA · LBM · Stencil computing · Roofline

1 Introduction

Modern supercomputers can surpass the performance of 10^{18} double-precision floating-point operations (FLOP) per second (FLOPS). This is a qualitative breakthrough: the number of FLOP performed in parallel is now more than 10^9, which is, in turn, more than the number of serial FLOP that can be performed per second. As a matter of fact, parallelism is the primary source of performance.

Together with the growth in the number of transistors, the number of computing cores in new processors also increases. Multicore processors inherit the concepts of SMP and NUMA architectures, and even of many-node clusters. Physical integration enables better intercore connectivity, as well as the connectivity with other parts of the system. It is also important to note that shared resources, such as power consumption, data bus, last level cache (LLC), and memory controllers can be redistributed to benefit one or two cores in a multicore system thereby decreasing the latency in a critical path.

Scaling of multicore processors is achieved through the use of the intermediate core hierarchy level (Intel core clusters or AMD core complexes) with shared

© The Author(s), under exclusive license to Springer Nature Switzerland AG 2023
L. Sokolinsky and M. Zymbler (Eds.): PCT 2023, CCIS 1868, pp. 33–48, 2023.
https://doi.org/10.1007/978-3-031-38864-4_3

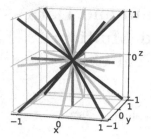

shell	points
0	1: $(0,0,0)$
1 ——	6: $(\pm 1,0,0),(0,\pm 1,0),(0,0,\pm 1)$
2 ——	12: $(\pm 1,\pm 1,0),(\pm 1,0,\pm 1),(0,\pm 1,\pm 1)$
3 ——	8: $(\pm 1,\pm 1,\pm 1)$

Fig. 1. LBM shells

cache. Further scaling requires more hardware resources. Manycore processors, made specifically for massively parallel tasks, are capable of a less prominent dynamic redistribution of resources and may not support the effective coherency of local caches. In this case, thread synchronization becomes expensive.

The consideration of modern trends in multicore processors leads us to the following conclusion. It is crucial to utilize all available parallelism since the processing power relies mainly on it, and the code architecture has to take advantage of all types of core interconnectivity, clustering, and local and shared resources. Our goal is to find the most efficient and convenient way to implement codes for the numerical simulation of physical phenomena. To this end, we use the method of LRnLA (locally recursive nonlocally asynchronous) algorithm construction [6].

2   Computational Aspects of LBM

Computational Fluid Dynamics (CFD) is an excellent test bed for algorithm development. CFD codes are relevant to many scientific and engineering purposes. The choice of the numerical schemes is flexible in terms of computational cost, data, and locality. A good example is the Lattice Boltzmann Method (LBM) and its many variations [4]. In the context of the current paper, it is an appropriate illustration of a scheme with variable data size and a stencil access pattern.

There are Q scalar values f_q (populations) associated with a node in a lattice. The lattice step and the time step are equal to 1 in nondimensional units. The local collision operation at node $\vec{x}_i$ at the discrete-time instant t^k can be written as

$$f_q(\vec{x}_i, t^k) = \Omega_q(f_1^*(\vec{x}_i, t^k), \ldots, f_Q^*(\vec{x}_i, t^k)), \quad q = 1, \ldots, Q, \tag{1}$$

where Ω_q is a collision operator. We use the basic BGK collision operator and a second-order expression for the equilibrium distribution [4].

The second step of LBM is the streaming step, which consists of Q separate transfers of f_q values in the $\vec{c}_q$ direction from each node to its neighbors:

$$f_q^*(\vec{x}_i + \vec{c}_q, t^k + 1) = f_q(\vec{x}_i, t^k), \quad q = 1, \ldots, Q. \tag{2}$$

In this paper, the vectors $\vec{c}_q$ are from the shells listed in Fig. 1, and all variants of LBM used here are given in Table 1. A 3D LBM with $Q = q$ is often

Table 1. Parameters of different configurations. FLOP: single-precision floating-point operation; FMA: fused multiply–add operation. Since processors operate in FMA operations, the FMA metric is more precise when there is an imbalance between two types of FLOP. LU: lattice site update. PU: population (f_q) update.

code	Q1	Q7	Q13	Q19	Q9	Q15	Q21	Q27
shells in Fig. 1	0	0,1	0,2	0,1,2	0,3	0,1,3	0,2,3	0,1,2,3
FLOP/LU	30	78	150	198	126	174	246	294
2FMA/LU, $\mathcal{O}$	30	114	246	330	206	290	422	506
FLOP/PU	30	11	12	10	14	12	12	11
2FMA/PU	30	16	19	17	23	19	20	19
$\mathcal{I}_{\mathrm{SW}}$, F32 FLOP/byte	3.8	1.4	1.4	1.3	1.8	1.5	1.5	1.4

denoted by D3Qq. Note that D3Q19 and D3Q27 (cube stencil) may be relevant to fluid dynamics, and D3Q7 (cross) is frequently used in the solution of advection-diffusion equations. Others are added here for the study of algorithmic tendencies.

As for the code, in the basic implementations, two data copies per node are stored to avoid read conflicts that can occur due to the interdependence of neighbor cells. Alternatively, we can use one of the streaming patterns possessing the in-place modification property, such as the AA-pattern [1], Esoteric Twist [3], or compact update [12].

In this paper, we use the compact update [12,23] and only one data copy. Thus the streaming is split into the 'compact' and the 'de-compact' steps. All exchanges in a $2 \times 2 \times 2$ group of lattice nodes are performed, followed by the exchanges in a group that is shifted by one node in each direction. Each of the two substeps requires access only to a cube of eight nodes (compact group) and overwrites data in place.

3   LRnLA Algorithms

Let us outline the basics of the method of LRnLA algorithm construction [6].

Express the simulation task with a dependency graph in space-time. Let us consider a discrete lattice with $2N$ nodes along each of d spatial axes and the task of update of all these nodes N_T times according to a numerical scheme with a local stencil. In the dependency graph constructed for this task, the node at (x, y, z, t) ($d = 3$) in space-time is an operation of scheme update at this point, and the nodes are connected with links that are data dependencies.

Fold the dependency graph. This step is not required for the method developed in this paper. Still, we decided to use it since it has proven to be an efficient method for localization of boundary processing, effortless use of AVX vectorization, and multinode parallelism [9,10]. When the dependency graph is folded once on the axis a, every node with index $N \leq i_a < 2N$ along this axis is put in the same

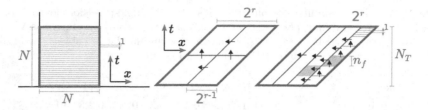

Fig. 2. Left: A simulation task ($d = 1$) decomposed into flat subtasks for stepwise execution. Center: The ConeFold LRnLA algorithm and its subdivision. Arrows show data dependencies. Right: Four ConeTorre. The rightmost one is decomposed into lower CTs. The orange areas are an example of two asynchronous subtasks. (Color figure online)

place as the node with index $N - 1 - (i_a - N)$, that is, in the position that is mirror-symmetric with respect to the center of the domain. Thus: (1) each node is assigned twice as many data and operations, (2) the first node is in the same place as the last one, (3) all vectors in the numerical scheme in the mirrored domain are reversed, and (4) the application of the periodic boundary condition is local [8,9]. We perform the folding operation on all axes and obtain a dependency graph with N nodes along each direction. Folding can be omitted in the algorithm construction. If that is the case, we consider a simulation domain with N nodes along each axis from the start.

Decompose the dependency graph and analyze the dependencies between subtasks. An LRnLA algorithm is defined through a shape in space-time that has dependency graph nodes inside it and a rule of subdivision of this shape. This reflects the subdivision of the task into subtasks. The whole dependency graph can be described by a box of size $N^d \times N_T$ that covers it. In the case of a traditional *stepwise* (SW) traversal, an external 'for' loop in time exists. This is described by a decomposition of the $N^d \times N_T$ box into $N^d \times 1$ layers with sequential dependencies (Fig. 2). In the same manner, the task of updating all nodes N_T times can be subdivided into N_T subtasks of updating all nodes once. LRnLA algorithms are described by the shapes that contain the nodes on several time layers.

The *ConeFold (CF) LRnLA algorithm* [6] (see Table 3 for all notations in the text) is described by a prism shape (Fig. 2). The lower base of a CF with a specified rank r is a cube with 2^r nodes along each edge on some time layer. Its upper base is a cube shifted by 2^r time steps in time, and if the stencil width is equal to 1, shifted by 2^r nodes in the positive direction of each spatial axis. It is a convenient shape both for the algorithm description and implementation. That is why here we discuss a task with $N = 2^{\mathrm{MaxRank}+1}$ nodes and $N_T = 2^{\mathrm{MaxRank}+1}$ layers in time. Tasks with other dimensions can be constructed with such building blocks. Each CF can be decomposed into 2^{d+1} CFs of lower rank. This decomposition can be done recursively down to an elementary update of a dependency graph node. Alternatively, CFs can be decomposed into ConeTorres.

The *ConeTorre (CT) LRnLA algorithm* [10] has the same shape as CF, but the N_T parameter is an arbitrary positive integer and is not fixed by the MaxRank parameter (Fig. 2, right). It contains $N^d N_T$ nodes and can be either

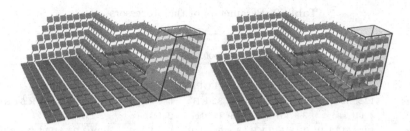

Fig. 3. FArSh Data for exchange in CT type algorithms ($d = 2$). FArSh stores the data on the CT slopes in the cell lines aligned with the direction of the CT execution. On each floor of a CT, a gnomon of lattice node data is read, and these data are overwritten with the output data on the other side of the CT. Here $d = 2$ and FArSh is a 2D array, namely, an array of lines of nodes, each line having N_T nodes. On the left and right, we see the states of FArSh, correspondingly before and after the execution of the pictured CT. (Color figure online)

decomposed into lower CTs (height n_f) or processed stepwise. In the latter case, CT can be implemented by a 'for' loop, in which, on each iteration, a cube of nodes is updated and the next cube is shifted by one cell in the positive direction of each axis.

To cover the whole dependency graph with CF shapes, we place some of the ConeFold shapes so that their upper or lower bases (or both) are outside the domain (Fig. 4). For the parts outside the domain, there are no operations. Thus CFs with MaxRank, as well as smaller CF/CTs on the boundary, have different numbers of operations inside them.

An example of possible parallelism is illustrated in Fig. 2. Even more asynchronous tasks can appear if $d > 1$.

3.1 Data Structures

Each CF/CT task has input and output data dependencies, which can be found as the dependency graph links coming in and out across the faces of the prism. Optimally, the data structure for storage of mesh node data has to be organized in the order that data are read in the algorithm. We use two types of data layouts. First, the data of the upper and lower bases of the prism are synchronized on the same time layer, i.e., $t = 0$ on the lower base and $t = N_T$ on the upper base (Fig. 3, blue). The base cube is a multidimensional array in d spatial dimensions. Since the CT size is flexible, the best practice is to organize the data according to the Morton Z-order curve.

Data of the second type are read on the inclined faces of the prism. The diagonal order of access in the Z-order array is inconvenient. It is not aligned for cache prefetching, and overhead integer operations are required to find the index of the required node. Thus we use the FArSh data structure introduced in [11] (Fig. 3, red). FArSh data have $d - 1$ spatial dimensions and one time dimension.

Table 2. Parameters of the processors

	AMD Ryzen			Intel Core-i	
	R9 3900	R9 5950X	R7 5800X3D	i7-7800X	i5-1240P
cores	12	16	8	6	4P+8E
peak F32	1.4 TFLOPS	2 TFLOPS	1 TFLOPS	0.7 TFLOPS	0.8 TFLOPS
L1 size	12×32 KB	16×32 KB	8×32 KB	6×32 KB	4×48 KB $+ 8 \times 64$ KB
L1 BW	3 TB/sec	3.8 TB/sec	1.9 TB/sec	2 TB/sec	2 TB/sec
L2 size	12×512 KB	16×512 KB	8×512 KB	6×1 MB	4×1.25 MB $+ 2 \times 2$ MB
L2 BW	1.5 TB/sec	2 TB/sec	1 TB/sec	750 GB/sec	1 TB/sec
L3 size	4×16 MB	2×32 MB	96 MB	8.25 MB	12 MB
L3 BW	1.3 TB/sec	1 TB/sec	500 GB/sec	500 GB/sec	350 GB/sec
RAM type	DDR4-3200			DDR4-2400	LPDDR5-4800
RAM size	64 GB	128 GB	64 GB	128 GB	16 GB
RAM BW	50 GB/sec	50 GB/sec	50 GB/sec	75 GB/sec	75 GB/sec
FLOP/byte	28	40	20	9	11

3.2   Algorithmic Issues

Arithmetic Intensity (AI) $\mathcal{I}$ is the number of operations per byte of data bandwidth. The Roofline model [21] uses AI to determine the peak performance of the code:

$$\Pi \le \min\left[\Pi_{\mathrm{CPU}}, \Theta\mathcal{I}\right], \tag{3}$$

where the CPU performance is denoted by Π_{CPU}, and Θ is the bandwidth of the data localization site. With this, the computing tasks are classified into two groups: compute-bound if $\mathcal{I} > \Pi_{\mathrm{CPU}}/\Theta$, and memory-bound if otherwise.

An SW simulation has a limit of optimization. Data are localized in RAM, and every population has to be loaded and saved at least once per time update. Realistically, the limit is hardly attainable since the populations in 3D simulations are also accessed when they are required by the neighbor cells.

The AI of such ideal SW codes ($\mathcal{I}_{\mathrm{SW}}$ in Table 1) is at least an order of magnitude less than the point of machine balance ($\Pi_{\mathrm{CPU}}/\Theta$) of modern processors (Table 2). Consequently, the memory bandwidth of the memory controllers is the key requirement for processors, and the achievements in the hardware parallelism development outlined in the introduction are irrelevant. A case in point is the fact that a 64-core AMD EPYC 7773X performs worse than an 8-core Intel Xeon Gold 6434 in the LBM speed test [16,17,19].

With LRnLA algorithms, the SW limit can be surpassed. In [9,10], a recursive CF subdivision was used for the LBM. CFs with a high rank r are localized in RAM, and the RAM bandwidth acts as a Roofline limit. However, if all data used in a CF of rank r' are localized on a higher level of the memory hierarchy (i.e., L3 cache), the performance of its subtasks, that is, CFs of lower rank ($r' - 1$), is limited by the L3 bandwidth [6]. Note that $\mathcal{I}_{\mathrm{CF},r}$ decreases with rank ($\forall r \; \mathcal{I}_{\mathrm{CF},r-1} < \mathcal{I}_{\mathrm{CF},r}$), but the bandwidth of the localization site increases with rank. Finally, we can estimate that the performance of a task can not be higher than the performance of any of its subtasks, therefore for the performance we have

$$\Pi \leq \min_{r}[\Pi_{CF,r}] \leq \min[\Pi_{CPU}, \Theta_{L3}\mathcal{I}_{CF,r'-1}, \Theta_{RAM}\mathcal{I}_{CF,r'}]. \tag{4}$$

This limit is found to be greater than the SW limit, and the SW performance is surpassed [9, 10].

The disadvantage of this approach is the limited asynchrony inside each CF. As a result, in the benchmarks on the 12-core AMD Zen2 [12], parallel scaling was close to linear only up to a factor of 4. The AMD Zen2 has 4 Core Complexes (CCX) with up to 4 active cores each. Within a CCX, the cores share the common 16MB of LLC cache space. The scaling is good as long as no more than one CF is localized per CCX. When more than one CF is launched in one CCX, less cache is available to each one. Although more threads are in use, the total efficiency is lower.

Our goal is to construct a new (optimal) algorithm with the following properties: (1) the computations are performed on data localized in L1, (2) LRnLA decomposition has enough degree of parallelism for manycore execution, and (3) the benefit of manycore execution is not lost due to the failure to localize data in the combined L2 and L3 cache.

3.3   Optimal Algorithm for Manycore CPUs

Let us define the criteria for the optimal algorithm that we aim to construct in this research. The AI of a CT with a base size equal to m groups of 2^d lattice nodes and height $2n_t \leq N_T$ can be expressed as

$$\mathcal{I}_{CT} \equiv \frac{\mathcal{O}_{CT}}{2\mathcal{S}_{CT}} = \frac{2n_t(2m)^d\mathcal{O}}{2\left((2m)^d + 2n_t\Gamma^{-}_{(2m)^d}\right)\mathcal{S}}, \tag{5}$$

where $\mathcal{O}_{CT}$ is the number of operations in the ConeTorre, and $\mathcal{S}_{CT}$ is the amount of data used in it. These data are loaded, updated, and saved. The factor 2 in the denominator accounts for the sum of load and save operations. No halo is added to $\mathcal{S}_{CT}$ because of the use of the compact update in LBM. Furthermore, $\mathcal{I}_{SW} = \mathcal{O}/2\mathcal{S}$ is the AI of the stepwise algorithm. On each time layer of a CT, a total of

$$\Gamma^{-}_{(2m)^d} \equiv (2m)^d - (2m-1)^d = d(2m)^{d-1} + \ldots + (-1)^d(2md-1)$$
$$= d(2m)^{d-1}(1 + O(1/2m)) \tag{6}$$

nodes (a cube gnomon) are loaded and saved. Thus, the first term in the denominator is the size of the CT base, and the second term is the size of FArSh.

We consider three cases. If $dn_t \ll m$, then CT is a low and wide layer; its AI can be approximated as $2n_t\mathcal{I}_{SW}$. In the second case, $m = n_t \equiv n \equiv 2^r$ for some integers n and r, and the CT is a ConeFold. In the CF, if the processed data are localized in a cache with fixed size $\mathcal{M}$, and $n \gg 1$, then the AI reaches its maximum value $\frac{2n}{d+1}\mathcal{I}_{SW}$. In the third case, we have $n_t \gg m$, so the CT

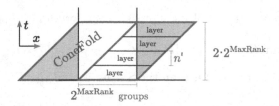

Fig. 4. Illustration of the construction of FArShFold for $d = 1$. A simulation domain with $2^{d \cdot \text{MaxRank}}$ groups is subdivided into 2^d ConeFolds. The pink areas contain no operations. Each CF is subdivided into layers. (Color figure online)

is narrow and long. The AI can be approximated as $\mathcal{I} \approx \mathcal{I}_{\text{SW}}(2m)^d / \Gamma^-_{(2m)^d}$. If $m \gg 1$, then it is proportional to m. If $m = 1$, then $\mathcal{I} = \frac{2^d}{2^d-1}\mathcal{I}_{\text{SW}} > \mathcal{I}_{\text{SW}}$.

Let us denote by n_{opt} the size n of the CF for which the processed data $\left((2n_{\text{opt}})^3 + 2n_{\text{opt}}\Gamma^-_{(2n_{\text{opt}})^3}\right)\mathcal{S}$ fit the combined L2 and L3 cache, $\mathcal{M}_{\text{L2+L3}} \approx 70$ MB. Consider a concrete example. For the single-precision LBM with $Q = 19$ and $Q = 27$ and taking into account the factor 8 from the dependency graph folding (Sect. 3), we have that $\mathcal{S} = Q \cdot 8 \cdot 4$ bytes and n_{opt} is in the range from 11 to 16. With this size, the ConeFold AI is $\frac{2n}{d+1} \approx 5$ to 8 times as high as the SW AI, and the performance peak is potentially higher by a factor of 5 to 8.

When several asynchronous tasks per CCX are executed, a lesser part of the L3 cache is available per task, and this estimate may not be reached. Therefore, we express the criteria of the optimal algorithm in the following way: the performance increase compared to the SW algorithm has to be no less than the theoretical estimate specified above.

4   FArShFold

Let us attempt to construct the optimal algorithm. Fold the domain (see Sect. 3) of $2^{d \cdot \text{MaxRank}}$ groups and decompose the dependency graph into CFs (Fig. 4). The data of such a CF base can only fit the CPU RAM. Decompose this CF into CTs with base size 2^{MaxRank} and height n' (an integer parameter of the algorithm). The resulting tasks are represented in the dependency graph space by flat layers ($dn' \ll 2 \cdot 2^{\text{MaxRank}}$) and are performed one after the other.

The layer is compute-bound. Indeed,

$$\Pi_{\text{layer}}(n_{\text{opt}}) \leq \min\left[\Pi_{\text{CPU}}, \Theta_{\text{RAM}}\mathcal{I}_{\text{layer}}\right] \approx \min\left[\Pi_{\text{CPU}}, \Theta_{\text{RAM}}2n_{\text{opt}}\mathcal{I}_{\text{SW}}\right] = \Pi_{\text{CPU}}.$$

Let us decompose the layer into CTs with height n' and only one lattice node group in the base ($m = 1$). When CT parallelism is used for GPU [13], the size of the CT base $n \ll N_T$ is chosen so that its data fit into the fastest memory level. In that case, this level is the register file and it is large enough to contain data for several node groups. On CPU, the fastest level is L1, which can contain no more than one group, that is why here we choose $m = 1$.

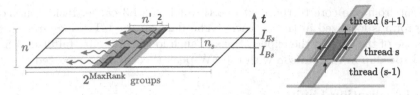

Fig. 5. Left: Illustration of the construction of FArShFold for $d = 1$. A layer is subdivided into CTs with a base size of 2^d lattice nodes. For parallelism, the layer is subdivided into slices; each slice is processed by a parallel thread. A thread processes CTs with height n_s, one by one in the reverse Z-order curve (for $d = 1$, in a line from right to left). If $n' = 2n_{\text{opt}}$, the grey CF can fit L3. Right: Data flow for the smallest CT. Here 2^d lattice nodes in the base (yellow) come from the other core through L3; n_s lattice nodes in the horizontal dependency (red, FArSh) are in the local cache of the same core. (Color figure online)

There are 2rd CTs in a layer. The order of execution is along the reverse Morton Z-curve since it provides the best memory reuse in the layer base.

The data for operation in a CT come from its base (vertical dependency) and from the neighboring CT (horizontal dependency). The data from the base fit the L1 cache and are localized there throughout the CT execution.

Our goal is to distribute the computation in the layer between cores and make each core localize the data it processes in its own cache (L2). We propose the following solution (Fig. 5). We decompose each CT into several slices, where each slice s is in the range $I_{Bs} \le i_t < I_{Es}$. The bases are still one group in size, but the amount of FArSh data per CT is less. Then we can localize FArSh in the local cache (L2) of each core.

Thus the complete flow of the recursive LRnLA decomposition is as follows (Fig. 4, 5). The ConeFold of rank MaxRank > 5 is decomposed into CTs with base MaxRank and height n' (layers). The layers are decomposed into N_C slices, where N_C is the number of cores. Each slice is processed by one processor core. Each slice is decomposed into CTs with one group in the base.

4.1 FArShFold Properties

As a result, multicore parallelism is implemented with the decomposition of the dependency graph in time. One core is to process updates for $I_{Bs} \le i_t < I_{Es}$; for the next core, $I_{B(s+1)} = I_{Es}$.

Note that the decomposition of the tasks into time slices is natural in the CT algorithm owing to the use of the FArSh data structure. The lines of FArSh nodes are cut into several smaller lines. Such a convenient implementation would not be possible if we used the main storage (Fig. 3, blue) for the exchange of data between CTs.

Each core processes CTs with one group in the base and a height equal to $n_s \equiv I_{Es} - I_{Bs} < n_{\text{opt}}$, one by one in the Z-order. These CTs are continued in their execution by the next core. In theory, the data of the group in the CT base are sent from one core to the next one through the L3 cache. Inside one core, this group is localized in the L1 cache. The data on the CT slopes stay in the L2 cache of the core. If the expectations of such localization are fulfilled, a 5- to 8-fold speedup in comparison with the SW peak (Sect. 3.3) is expected.

4.2 Localization Limits

The layer in Fig. 4 is compute-bound and fits RAM. It is decomposed into narrow CTs, and their AI is small. However, with the Z-order execution, we can expect the successive CTs to form a full task in the shape of a CF, and a CF is a task with the optimal AI for the chosen layer height n':

$$\Pi_{\mathrm{CF},n'} \leq \min\left[\Pi_{\mathrm{layer}}, \Theta_{\mathrm{RAM}}\frac{n'}{d+1}\mathcal{I}_{\mathrm{SW}}\right]. \tag{7}$$

Here, if $n' = 2n_{\mathrm{opt}}$, the CF data fit L3 (Sect. 3.3).

If we treat a CT as a subtask of a CF, and that CF fits L3, then its performance is limited by Θ_{L3} rather than by Θ_{RAM}:

$$\Pi_{\mathrm{FArShFold}} \leq \min\left[\Pi_{\mathrm{CF},n_{\mathrm{opt}}}, \Theta_{\mathrm{L3}}\frac{n_{\mathrm{opt}}}{d+N_C/2}\mathcal{I}_{\mathrm{SW}}\right],$$

where N_C in the denominator comes from the fact that there are N_C exchanges between cores through the L3 cache.

We also require FArSh to fit the L2 cache and the base (one group) to fit the L1 cache. Thus,

$$\Pi_{\mathrm{CT},1} \leq \min\left[\Pi_{\mathrm{FArShFold}}, \min\left(\Theta_{\mathrm{L3}}\frac{n_{L2}}{d}, \Theta_{\mathrm{L2}}\frac{n_{L1}}{d}, \Theta_{\mathrm{L1}}\frac{2^d}{2^d-1}\right)\mathcal{I}_{\mathrm{SW}}\right],$$

where n_{L1} and n_{L2} are the integers defined by the following condition: FArSh of a CT with base size n_{L1} (n_{L2}) and height n_s fits the L1 (L2) cache, i.e., $2n_s\Gamma_{n_{L2}} \leq \mathcal{M}_{\mathrm{L2}}/\mathcal{S}$.

4.3 Latency Limits

For a parallel algorithm, we have to take into account the possible latency. We have N_C cores. Let N_{CT} denote the maximal number of CTs that are executed at the same time. This parameter has to be adjusted to minimize the idle time of the threads. Since the parallelism is in the time axis, each narrow CT with height n' is processed by no more than one core at a time. Thus, to ensure there are enough asynchronous tasks for all cores, the condition $N_{\mathrm{CT}} \geq N_C$ must hold.

The total time to process a CT is $T_{\mathrm{pipe}} = n't_{\mathrm{calc}} + N_C t_{\mathrm{wait}}$, where t_{calc} is the time for the update of one group, that is, $\mathcal{O}_G = 2^{2d}\mathcal{O}$ operations, and data exchanges with FArSh; t_{wait} is the time for thread synchronization, which includes waiting for semaphores to open and the exchange of the group data $\mathcal{S}_G = 2^{2d}\mathcal{S}$ through the shared cache. According to Little's law, we have

$$\Pi_{\mathrm{CT},1} \leq \frac{N_{\mathrm{CT}}n'\mathcal{O}_G}{T_{\mathrm{pipe}}} = \frac{N_{\mathrm{CT}}n'\mathcal{O}_G}{N_C t_{\mathrm{wait}} + n't_{\mathrm{calc}}}. \tag{8}$$

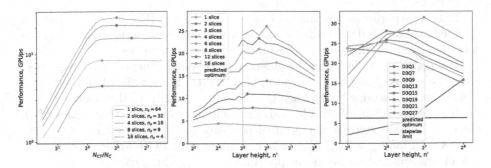

Fig. 6. Performance benchmarks for one full ConeFold update. The dots correspond to the maximal value on each graph.

5 Performance Tests

The algorithm was coded in C++20, gcc 11.3, and HWloc 2.5; the parallelism was implemented with standard library threads. The tests were performed on an AMD Ryzen R9 5950X processor if not stated otherwise. AVX vectorization was implemented through domain folding [9,10].

To perform the whole simulation, a 3D domain with $4 \cdot 2^{\mathrm{MaxRank}}$ LBM nodes along each axis is folded and subdivided into CFs. We set MaxRank $= 7$ and $Q = 19$ if not stated otherwise. All of the CFs of rank MaxRank are boundary CFs with many missing operations. Since the theory is constructed for a full CF task, we also perform several benchmarks for a full CF. In that case, the boundary condition is invalid, and such benchmarks are used only for parameter adjustments. Nevertheless, such full CFs can be valid if the initial task is first subdivided into CFs of rank equal to (MaxRank $-$ 1), and then FArShFold is applied to a CF which is entirely inside the domain.

To account for the memory-bound performance, we use the GPUps performance unit, i.e., billions of population updates per second, which is equal to the GLUps (billion of lattice node updates per second) metric multiplied by Q.

5.1 Parameter Adjustment

In theory, the construction goals in the implementation are achieved if $n' = 2n_{\mathrm{opt}}$. However, to account for the reality of the fixed local cache size of the cores, their bandwidth, and the possibility of suboptimal localization in the Z-order traversal, we decided that n' and N_{CT} should remain flexible parameters in the code.

We can use (8) and the performance dependence on N_{CT} and n_s (Fig. 6, left; $n' = 64$) to estimate $t_{\mathrm{wait}} \sim 30 \ \mu s$ and $t_{\mathrm{calc}} \sim 1.5 \ \mu s$ [15]. Thus, $t_{\mathrm{wait}} \gg t_{\mathrm{calc}}$ and synchronization overheads are high if n_s is low ($n'/N_C < t_{\mathrm{wait}}/t_{\mathrm{calc}}$).

This fact poses a problem. We have estimated the optimal height of the layer to be $n' = 2n_{\mathrm{opt}} = 32$, but if it is so, then n_s is low when the available parallelism of a 16-core processor is used.

Tests were performed for different values of n_s and n' (Fig. 6, center). Indeed, the predicted optimal value of n' does not lead to the best performance, and the deviation from the theoretical values increases as n_s decreases.

The t_{wait}/t_{calc} ratio varies for different Q. The dependence of the best performance versus Q and n' is shown in Fig. 6 (right). The predicted optimal value of $n' = 2n_{opt}$ is attained only when $Q = 27$ (cube stencil). In that case, t_{calc} has the highest value since both $\mathcal{O}_G$ and $\mathcal{S}_G$ are higher than for other values of Q. For $Q = 7$ (cross stencil), the optimal performance is found for $n' = 128$ and $n_s = 8$, and for $n_s = 2n_{opt}/N_C = 2$, it is more than twice lower. In this case, thread synchronization overheads prevail: $t_{wait} > t_{calc}2n_{opt}/N_C$.

5.2   Benchmark Results

Finally, we used the optimal values of N_{CT} and n' and measured the performance of our implementation (Fig. 7). Here, except for one case (one full CF), the simulation is for the whole domain: eight CFs tile the domain, some subtasks are empty, and the periodic boundary works correctly with the domain folding.

The performance result for the full CF is higher by a factor of about 5 than the SW limit when $Q = 7$ and by a factor of 4 when $Q = 27$. Thus, taking some possible overheads into account, the algorithm construction goals are satisfied.

The performance results for the full domain on the same graph are lower since the boundaries give rise to a worse load balance among parallel threads. When MaxRank is lower, the issue of synchronization overheads becomes prominent, and the performance decreases.

For MaxRank < 6, the condition $dn' < N_T$, which means that we can treat a layer as a flat CT (Sect. 3.2), is no longer satisfied. In that case, we can not estimate its AI as $n'\mathcal{I}_{SW}$, the premises of the FArShFold construction are not met, and the performance is further decreased. However, even in the worst case (MaxRank = 4), the performance remains higher than the limit for the SW codes.

For $Q = 19$, we studied the parallel scaling in the strong sense by increasing the number of cores with a fixed size of the domain (Fig. 7). The benchmark was run on different processors, listed in Table 2. In all the tests, the performance increases with N_C. The SW performance limit is surpassed with only two cores on any of the studied architectures. Up to $N_C = 4$, the scaling is close to linear, and the efficiency in relation to the performance peak is 20–40%. With more cores in use, the performance increases by at least a factor of 1.5. The probable reason for the slower increase here is the issue with synchronization overheads (Sect. 5.1).

Both for Intel and AMD processors, the change in the processor architecture gives a leap in performance, even when the core count is lower. In zen3, the increased shared cache gives a better performance, but this increase can not compensate for the twice lower number of cores and, thus, less local cache.

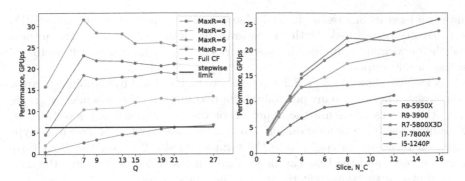

Fig. 7. Performance benchmarks

Table 3. Meaning of the notations used in the text

LBM	Lattice Boltzmann Method
d	number of spatial dimensions
group	lattice node group, a cube of 2^d lattice nodes
N	$2N$ is the number of mesh nodes of the simulation domain in each direction
N_T	number of time steps in the simulation task
$\mathcal{I}$, AI	Arithmetic Intensity
$\mathcal{O}$	operation count per lattice node update
$\mathcal{S}$	data size per lattice node, $\mathcal{S} = Q \cdot 4$ B
LRnLA	Locally Recursive non Locally Asynchronous (algorithms)
SW, CT, CF	Stepwise, ConeTorre, ConeFold
MaxRank	an integer parameter of the ConeFold algorithm, $N = N_T = 2 \cdot 2^{\text{MaxRank}}$
m	the CT base is a cube with m^d groups, i.e., $(2m)^d$ lattice nodes
n'	FArShFold parameter (see Figs. 4 and 5)
n_{opt}	the data of a CF of size $2n_{\text{opt}}$ fit the L3 cache

6   Related Work

LBM is a memory-bound scheme where high performance is relevant for many applications; for this reason, there are many studies devoted to improving its memory performance. Let us focus on several works targeting multicore CPUs. The majority of the implementations are stepwise and treat the stepwise performance as an ideal limit [22]. To get close to the peak, loop blocking [22] and spatial tiling [17] are used to take advantage of the multilevel cache. Here are some of the published results: 0.21 GLUps for single precision D3Q19 on Intel Xeon E5-2690v3 (12 cores, 68 GB/s memory bandwidth) [18]; 0.33 GLUps for double precision D3Q19 on AMD EPYC 7451 (24 cores, 130 GB/s) [22]; 0.27 GLUps for single precision D3Q19 on four Intel Xeon E5-4620 v4 processors (40 cores, 273 GB/s) [5]. The performance of the processors is different, but the memory bandwidths considered in these works are comparable to or higher than those we used in our research. This characteristic is more relevant since LBM is a memory-bound task. Both the performance limit estimated by the authors and the performance obtained in those works are lower than the results obtained in the current paper.

As we have shown in Sect. 3.2, the peak can be increased by combining several time layers. There are many possibilities for decomposing the dependency graph, and other works often use the approach of the one-dimensional wavefront [7, 20]. Our ConeTorre decomposition can also be described as a wavefront-type temporal blocking (in contrast to the temporal halo [2]). But the ConeTorre base is a cube, and the base can be localized in a smaller cache, while the data of a subtask in the wavefront tiling span the whole domain.

Finally, in comparison to other ConeTorre implementations [10, 14], the new algorithm introduced here shows better parallel scaling and, therefore, better efficiency on manycore CPUs.

7   Conclusions

In this work, we proposed FArShFold, a new algorithm of the LRnLA family. The algorithm allows the efficient use of manycore parallelism while taking advantage of the shared and local cache of the cores in a processor.

The algorithm is parallel in time, that is, time is divided into slices $I_{Bs} \leq i_t < I_{Es}$ and each slice is assigned only one core. This way, even the smallest cache levels (L1, L2) have their unique purpose in the algorithm.

This construction became possible with the use of the previous inventions associated with the LRnLA method: the recursive space-time subdivision and, most importantly, the use of the FArSh data structure for data exchange on the space-time slope.

Finally, note that the obtained performance result for single-precision D3Q19 LBM is more than 1.4 GLUps, and this value is at least 5–100 times as high as the recently published SW benchmarks [5], which include tests on many-node clusters with four Intel Xeon E5-4620 v4 processors. This fact proves the superiority not only of the FArShFold algorithm which is proposed here but also the optimality of the compact streaming pattern for LBM [23] and the nonlocal vectorization through domain folding [9, 10].

Acknowledgments. The research was supported by the Russian Science Foundation (grant № 18-71-10004).

References

1. Bailey, P., Myre, J., Walsh, S.D., Lilja, D.J., Saar, M.O.: Accelerating lattice Boltzmann fluid flow simulations using graphics processors. In: International Conference on Parallel Processing, ICPP 2009, pp. 550–557. IEEE (2009). https://doi.org/10.1109/ICPP.2009.38

2. Endo, T.: Applying recursive temporal blocking for stencil computations to deeper memory hierarchy. In: 2018 IEEE 7th Non-volatile Memory Systems and Applications Symposium (NVMSA), pp. 19–24. IEEE (2018)

3. Geier, M., Schönherr, M.: Esoteric twist: an efficient in-place streaming algorithms for the lattice Boltzmann method on massively parallel hardware. Computation **5**(2), 19 (2017). https://doi.org/10.3390/computation5020019

4. Krüger, T., Kusumaatmaja, H., Kuzmin, A., Shardt, O., Silva, G., Viggen, E.M.: The lattice Boltzmann method. Springer **10**(978-3), 4–15 (2017)

5. Lehmann, M., Krause, M.J., Amati, G., Sega, M., Harting, J., Gekle, S.: Accuracy and performance of the lattice Boltzmann method with 64-bit, 32-bit, and customized 16-bit number formats. Phys. Rev. E **106**(1), 015,308 (2022)

6. Levchenko, V., Perepelkina, A.: Locally recursive non-locally asynchronous algorithms for stencil computation. Lobachevskii J. Math. **39**(4), 552–561 (2018). https://doi.org/10.1134/S1995080218040108

7. Nguyen, A., Satish, N., Chhugani, J., Kim, C., Dubey, P.: 3.5-D blocking optimization for stencil computations on modern CPUs and GPUs. In: Proceedings of the 2010 ACM/IEEE International Conference for High Performance Computing, Networking, Storage and Analysis, SC 2010, pp. 1–13. IEEE (2010)

8. Osheim, N., Strout, M.M., Rostron, D., Rajopadhye, S.: Smashing: folding space to tile through time. In: Amaral, J.N. (ed.) LCPC 2008. LNCS, vol. 5335, pp. 80–93. Springer, Heidelberg (2008). https://doi.org/10.1007/978-3-540-89740-8_6

9. Perepelkina, A., Levchenko, V.: LRnLA algorithm ConeFold with non-local vectorization for LBM implementation. In: Voevodin, V., Sobolev, S. (eds.) RuSCDays 2018. CCIS, vol. 965, pp. 101–113. Springer, Cham (2019). https://doi.org/10.1007/978-3-030-05807-4_9

10. Perepelkina, A., Levchenko, V.: Synchronous and asynchronous parallelism in the LRnLA algorithms. In: Sokolinsky, L., Zymbler, M. (eds.) PCT 2020. CCIS, vol. 1263, pp. 146–161. Springer, Cham (2020). https://doi.org/10.1007/978-3-030-55326-5_11

11. Perepelkina, A., Levchenko, V.D.: Functionally arranged data for algorithms with space-time wavefront. In: Sokolinsky, L., Zymbler, M. (eds.) PCT 2021. CCIS, vol. 1437, pp. 134–148. Springer, Cham (2021). https://doi.org/10.1007/978-3-030-81691-9_10

12. Perepelkina, A., Levchenko, V., Zakirov, A.: New compact streaming in LBM with ConeFold LRnLA algorithms. In: Voevodin, V., Sobolev, S. (eds.) RuSCDays 2020. CCIS, vol. 1331, pp. 50–62. Springer, Cham (2020). https://doi.org/10.1007/978-3-030-64616-5_5

13. Perepelkina, A., Levchenko, V., Zakirov, A.: Extending the problem data size for GPU simulation beyond the GPU memory storage with LRnLA algorithms. In: Journal of Physics: Conference Series, vol. 1740, p. 012,054 (2021). https://doi.org/10.1088/1742-6596/1740/1/012054

14. Perepelkina, A., et al.: Heterogeneous LBM simulation code with LRnLA algorithms. Commun. Comput. Phys. **33**(1), 214–244 (2023). https://doi.org/10.4208/cicp.OA-2022-0055

15. Pershin, I., Levchenko, V., Perepelkina, A.: Qualitative and quantitative study of modern GPU synchronization approaches. In: Voevodin, V., Sobolev, S. (eds.) RuSCDays 2021. CCIS, vol. 1510, pp. 376–390. Springer, Cham (2021). https://doi.org/10.1007/978-3-030-92864-3_29

16. Pohl, T.: 619.lbm_s SPEC CPU®2017 benchmark description. https://www.spec.org/cpu2017/Docs/benchmarks/619.lbm_s.html

17. Pohl, T., Kowarschik, M., Wilke, J., Iglberger, K., Rüde, U.: Optimization and profiling of the cache performance of parallel lattice Boltzmann codes. Parallel Process. Lett. **13**(04), 549–560 (2003)
18. Riesinger, C., Bakhtiari, A., Schreiber, M., Neumann, P., Bungartz, H.J.: A holistic scalable implementation approach of the lattice Boltzmann method for CPU/GPU heterogeneous clusters. Computation **5**(4), 48 (2017)
19. SPEC: CPU®2017 benchmark results. http://spec.org/cpu2017/results/res2022 q1/cpu2017-20220228-31030.html. https://spec.org/cpu2017/results/res2023q1/c pu2017-20221205-33005.html
20. Wellein, G., Hager, G., Zeiser, T., Wittmann, M., Fehske, H.: Efficient temporal blocking for stencil computations by multicore-aware wavefront parallelization. In: 2009 33rd Annual IEEE International Computer Software and Applications Conference, vol. 1, pp. 579–586. IEEE (2009)
21. Williams, S., Waterman, A., Patterson, D.: Roofline: an insightful visual performance model for multicore architectures. Commun. ACM **52**(4), 65–76 (2009). https://doi.org/10.1145/1498765.1498785
22. Wittmann, M., Haag, V., Zeiser, T., Köstler, H., Wellein, G.: Lattice Boltzmann benchmark kernels as a testbed for performance analysis. Comput. Fluids **172**, 582–592 (2018)
23. Zakirov, A., Perepelkina, A., Levchenko, V., Khilkov, S.: Streaming techniques: revealing the natural concurrency of the lattice Boltzmann method. J. Supercomput. **77**(10), 11911–11929 (2021). https://doi.org/10.1007/s11227-021-03762-z

Parallel Numerical Algorithms

Implementation of a Fuzzy Inference Method with Nonsingleton Fuzzification Based on CUDA and GPGPU Technologies

Sergey Karatach[✉] and Vasiliy Sinuk

Belgorod State Technological University named after V. G. Shukhov, Belgorod, Russian Federation
karatach1998@yandex.ru

Abstract. This paper describes a fuzzy inference method using non-singleton fuzzification based on a fuzzy truth value. The described method offers an efficient convolution scheme based on the generalization principle, which reduces the computational complexity to the method to polynomial. For the described method, a parallel implementation using CUDA technology has been performed. The article describes the features of this implementation, as well as several possible improvements for it. The first improvement is to use the mechanisms of OpenGL technology when calculating fuzzy truth values. As a second improvement, we suggest an efficient algorithm for the convolution of fuzzy truth values is proposed for the case when a certain class of functions is used as some t-norms. The article presents the results of computational experiments for various modifications of the parallel implementation, including some of the proposed improvements. Based on the results obtained, we analysis is made on the feasibility of using one or another improvement at different degrees of sampling and with various numbers of inputs.

Keywords: Fuzzy inference · Non-singleton fuzzification · Parallel technologies

1 Introduction

Initially, the fuzzy systems described in [4] were a composition of a fuzzifier, a knowledge base, an inference module and a defuzzifier. Further development of the theory of fuzzy systems consisted in the modification of each of these components.

Thus, the fuzzification process, i.e., the expression of attribute values of input objects by means of fuzzy sets, in most ways of the practical application of fuzzy systems is formalized using singleton fuzzification. This type of fuzzification provides a speed of fuzzy inference acceptable for practical use. However, in some subject areas, with such a formalization of the attributes of input objects, the qualitative component of information about these objects is discarded.

© The Author(s), under exclusive license to Springer Nature Switzerland AG 2023
L. Sokolinsky and M. Zymbler (Eds.): PCT 2023, CCIS 1868, pp. 51–62, 2023.
https://doi.org/10.1007/978-3-031-38864-4_4

An alternative approach is fuzzification of the non-singleton type (NS) [3, 5, 8]. NS-fuzzification is used in fuzzy rule-based systems when the measurements that activate them are imperfect or uncertain (due to measurement noise, defects or deterioration of sensor's quality, etc.), or when their input data are natural language concepts. It models such measurements or concepts with fuzzy sets or more general linguistic variables. These objects of the theory of fuzzy sets and fuzzy systems to a greater extent reflect the original nature of numerical data or natural language concepts containing uncertainty or imperfection of measurement.

The main problem that arises when implementing inference in fuzzy MISO-structure systems using NS-fuzzification is an exponential increase in computational complexity. This article presents a fuzzy inference method using a fuzzy truth value (FTV), which reduces the computational complexity to polynomial. The proposed method makes it possible to implement the algorithm as a sequence of parallel calculations and reductions. The use of parallel computing technologies becomes especially justified, when implementing this algorithm in a generalized form, the discretization of membership functions is performed.

In the second section of the article, the problem of inference solved by a fuzzy is formulated. The third section describes the fuzzy inference method using fuzzy truth value and NS-fuzzification. The fourth section describes the features of the efficient implementation of this approach using CUDA and GPGPU technologies. Then, in the fifth section, a computational experiment was performed for the described implementation, according to the results of which conclusions were drawn about the justification of the proposed techniques for efficient implementation.

2   The Problem Statement

A linguistic model is a base of fuzzy rules R_k, $k = \overline{1, N}$, of the form

$$R_k \colon \text{if } x_1 \text{ is } A_{1k}, \ldots, \text{ if } x_n \text{ is } A_{nk}, \text{ then } y \text{ is } B_k, \tag{1}$$

where N is the number of fuzzy rules; $A_{ik} \subseteq X_i$, $i = \overline{1, n}$, and $B_k \subseteq Y$ are fuzzy sets that are characterized by membership functions $\mu_{A_{ik}}(x_i)$ and $\mu_{B_k}(y)$, respectively; $x_1, x_2, \ldots, x_n$ are input variables of the linguistic model, and

$$[x_1, x_2, \ldots, x_n]^T = \boldsymbol{x} \in X_1 \times X_2 \times \ldots \times X_n.$$

The symbols X_i, $i = \overline{1, n}$, and Y denote the spaces of input and output variables respectively. If you denote $\boldsymbol{X} = X_1 \times X_2 \times \ldots \times X_n$ and $\boldsymbol{A_k} = A_{1k} \times A_{2k} \times \ldots \times A_{nk}$, and

$$\mu_{\boldsymbol{A_k}}(\boldsymbol{x}) = \underset{i=\overline{1,n}}{T_1} \mu_{A_{ik}}(x_i),$$

where T_1 is an arbitrary t-norm, then rule (1) is represented as a fuzzy implication

$$R_k \colon \boldsymbol{A_k} \to B_k, \ k = \overline{1, N}.$$

The rule R_k can be formalized as a fuzzy relation defined on the set $\boldsymbol{X} \times Y$, i.e., $R_k \subseteq \boldsymbol{X} \times Y$ is a fuzzy set with membership function

$$\mu_{R_k}(\boldsymbol{x}, y) = \mu_{A_k \to B_k}(\boldsymbol{x}, y).$$

A logical-type model defines a function $\mu_{A_k \to B_k}(\boldsymbol{x}, y)$ based on known membership functions $\mu_{A_k}(\boldsymbol{x})$ and $\mu_{B_k}(y)$ using one of the implication functions proposed in [7, 10]:

$$\mu_{A_k \to B_k}(\boldsymbol{x}, y) = I(\mu_{A_k}(\boldsymbol{x}), \mu_{B_k}(y)),$$

where I is an implication function.

The task is to determine the fuzzy output $B'_k \subseteq Y$ for the system presented in the form (1) if the fuzzy sets are supplied at the inputs

$$\boldsymbol{A'} = A'_1 \times A'_2 \times \ldots \times A'_n \subseteq \boldsymbol{X} \text{ or } x_1 \text{ is } A'_1 \text{ and } x_2 \text{ is } A'_2 \text{ and } \ldots \text{ and } x_n \text{ is } A'_n,$$

with the corresponding membership function $\mu_{A'}(\boldsymbol{x})$ defined as

$$\mu_{A'}(\boldsymbol{X}) = \underset{i=\overline{1,n}}{T_3} \mu_{A'_i}(X_i). \tag{2}$$

A nonsingleton fuzzifier maps the measured $x_i = X'_i$, $i = \overline{1,n}$ to a fuzzy number, for which $\mu_{A'_i}(x'_i) = 1$ and $\mu_{A'_i}(x_i)$ are decreases from 1 to 0 as it moves away from the x'_i value.

Conceptually [6] NS fuzzification implies that a given input value x'_i is the value that will be the most possible of all nearby values; however, since the input is uncertain, neighboring values may also be possible, but to a lesser extent.

According to the generalized fuzzy rule *modus ponens* [10], a fuzzy set B'_k is defined by the composition of a fuzzy set $\boldsymbol{A'}$ and a relation $\boldsymbol{R_k}$, i.e.,

$$B'_k = \boldsymbol{A'} \circ (\boldsymbol{A_k} \to B_k)$$

or, at the level of membership functions,

$$\mu_{B'_k}(y|\boldsymbol{x'}) = \sup_{x \in X} \left\{ \mu_{A'}(\boldsymbol{x'}) \overset{T_2}{\star} I(\mu_{A_k}(\boldsymbol{x}), \mu_{B_k}(y)) \right\}. \tag{3}$$

In (3) conditional notation is applied, since input into a fuzzy system occurs at a certain value of $\boldsymbol{x}$, namely, $\boldsymbol{x'}$. The notation $\mu_{B'_k}(y|\boldsymbol{x'})$ shows that $\mu_{B'_k}$ changes with each value $\boldsymbol{x'}$. The computational complexity of expression (3) is $O(|X_1| \cdot |X_2| \cdot \ldots \cdot |X_n| \cdot |Y|)$.

3 A Method of Inference Using a Fuzzy Truth Value

Applying the truth modification rule [1]

$$\mu_{A'}(\boldsymbol{x}) = \tau_{A_k|A'}(\mu_{A_k}(\boldsymbol{x})),$$

where $\tau_{A_k|A'}$ is the fuzzy truth value of the fuzzy set $\boldsymbol{A_k}$ with respect to $\boldsymbol{A'}$, which is a compatibility function $CP(\boldsymbol{A_k}, \boldsymbol{A'})$ of membership function of $\boldsymbol{A_k}$ with respect to $\boldsymbol{A'}$, and $\boldsymbol{A'}$ is considered as reliable [2]:

$$\tau_{A_k|A'}(v) = \mu_{CP(A_k,A')}(v) = \sup_{\substack{\mu_{A_k}(\boldsymbol{x})=v \\ \boldsymbol{x} \in X}} \{\mu_{A'}(\boldsymbol{x})\}. \tag{4}$$

Let's move from variable $\boldsymbol{x}$ to variable v by denoting $\mu_{A_k}(\boldsymbol{X}) = v$. We get

$$\mu_{A'}(\boldsymbol{x}) = \tau_{A_k|A'}(\mu_{A_k}(\boldsymbol{x})) = \tau_{A_k|A'}(v), \tag{5}$$

then (3) will take the form:

$$\mu_{B'_k}(y|\boldsymbol{x}') = \sup_{v \in [0,1]} \left\{ \tau_{A_k|A'}(v) \overset{T_2}{\star} I(v, \mu_{B_k}(y)) \right\}. \tag{6}$$

When the implication is verbalized in (6), it will appear as:

$$\text{If } FTV \text{ is } true, \text{ then } y \text{ is } B'_k. \tag{7}$$

Thus, (7) represents another structure of rules in contrast to the canonical structures of Zadeh [15] and Takagi-Sugeno [14]. The application of this rule does not depend on the number of inputs in fuzzy systems.

Expression (6) is characterized by a complexity of the order $O(|v| \cdot |Y|)$. As follows from [12, 13],

$$\mu_{CP(A_k,A')}(v) = \underset{i=\overline{1,n}}{\tilde{T}_1} \mu_{CP(A_{ik},A'_i)}(v_i)$$

$$= (\ldots ((\mu_{CP(A_{1k},A'_1)}(v_1)\tilde{T}_1\mu_{CP(A_{2k},A'_2)}(v_2))\tilde{T}_1\mu_{CP(A_{3k},A'_3)}(v_3))\tilde{T}_1 \ldots)\tilde{T}_1\mu_{CP(A_{nk},A'_n)}(v_n), \tag{8}$$

where $\tilde{T}_1$ is a t-norm of n arguments extended by the generalization principle and

$$\mu_{CP(A_{ik},A'_i)}(v_i) = \sup_{\substack{\mu_{A_{ik}}(x_i)=v_i \\ x_i \in X_i}} \{\mu_{A'_i}(x_i)\}.$$

For example, an extended t-norm of 2 arguments has the form

$$\mu_{CP(A_k,A')}(v) = \underset{i=\overline{1,2}}{\tilde{T}_1} \mu_{CP(A_{ik},A'_i)}(v_i)$$

$$= \sup_{\substack{v_1 T_1 v_2 = v \\ (v_1,v_2) \in [0,1]^2}} \left\{ \mu_{CP(A_{1k},A'_1)}(v_1)\tilde{T}_3\mu_{CP(A_{2k},A'_2)}(v_2) \right\}. \tag{9}$$

The latter relation is characterized by a complexity of the order $O(|v|^2)$. The output value of the fuzzy system described by (1), when defuzzified by the center of gravity method taking into account (6), is determined by (see [10])

$$\overline{y}(\boldsymbol{x}') = \frac{\displaystyle\sum_{r=\overline{1,N}} \overline{y}_r \underset{k=\overline{1,N}}{T_4} \sup_{v \in [0,1]} \left\{ \tau_{A_k|A'}(v) \overset{T_2}{\star} I(v, \mu_{B_k}(\overline{y}_r)) \right\}}{\displaystyle\sum_{r=\overline{1,N}} \underset{k=\overline{1,N}}{T_4} \sup_{v \in [0,1]} \left\{ \tau_{A_k|A'}(v) \overset{T_2}{\star} I(v, \mu_{B_k}(\overline{y}_r)) \right\}}. \tag{10}$$

Since the implication in formula (10) does not depend on input data (2), then first, i.e. before using the compositional rule (6), $\tau_{k,r}(v) = I\big(v, \mu_{B_k}(\overline{y}_r)\big)$ is calculated for $k = \overline{1,N}$, $r = \overline{1,N}$. With this in mind, (10) takes the form

$$
\overline{y}(x') = \frac{\displaystyle\sum_{r=\overline{1,N}} \overline{y}_r \; T_4 \; \sup_{\substack{k=\overline{1,N} \\ v\in[0,1]}} \left\{ \tau_{A_k|A'}(v) \overset{T_2}{\star} \tau_{k,r}(v) \right\}}{\displaystyle\sum_{r=\overline{1,N}} T_4 \; \sup_{\substack{k=\overline{1,N} \\ v\in[0,1]}} \left\{ \tau_{A_k|A'}(v) \overset{T_2}{\star} \tau_{k,r}(v) \right\}}.
\tag{11}
$$

4 Features of the Inference Method Implementation Using a Fuzzy Truth Value

The figure below shows the flowchart of the fuzzy inference procedure.

Individual blocks in Fig. 1 correspond to various algorithmic tasks, therefore, when implementing each of these blocks, different implementation approaches can be used to organize efficient calculations. Further, the features of the application of these approaches in the implementation of the inference algorithm are considered.

4.1 Using OpenGL for the Fuzzy Truth Value Computing

Since in the software implementation of the proposed inference method in a generalized form, it is necessary to discretize the values of the membership function (m.f.) of fuzzy sets, when finding each fuzzy truth value at each grid point in the range $[0, 1]$, it is necessary to view the discretized values of the membership functions $\mu_{A_{ki}}(x_i)$ and $\mu_{A'_i}(x_i)$. Thus, the complexity of calculating the FTV for a given input for a given fuzzy set from the rule base is $O(D_{\text{ftv}} \times D_{\text{fset}})$, where D_{ftv} is the size of the sampling grid of the m.f. of the fuzzy truth value, and D_{fset} is the size of the sampling grid of the m.f. of the fuzzy set of the input or output variable. The calculation at different points of the sampling grid of the FTV can be distributed between the threads of the CUDA core block. With this approach, each thread will compute the fuzzy truth value for a given truth level by looking at all points of the sampling grid of the fuzzy set, and the computational complexity is reduced to $O(D_{\text{fset}})$. Another approach to implementing the calculation of the FTV at each point of the sampling grid is to use the hardware implementation of the internal mechanisms of OpenGL shaders instead of programming a streaming multiprocessor inside the CUDA core. Each shader is a custom or predefined program whose input and output data format is defined by the OpenGL standard specification. In this case, the process of calculating the FTV for all inputs and all rules consists in finding the intensity of the glow of single-channel pixels of an image of size $D_{\text{ftv}} \times (N \times n)$, where N is the number of rules in the rule base, n is the number of inputs. This image is saved to an internal buffer, the data from which is then copied to global memory for use

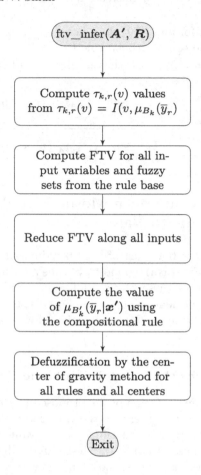

Fig. 1. Flowchart of the fuzzy inference procedure

inside the CUDA core at the next step of the inference algorithm. The calculation of the FTV by formula (4) is illustrated in Fig. 2. It is organized based on the specification of the pipeline for rendering three-dimensional graphics in OpenGL, according to which the calculation of the value of this formula is split into the vertex, geometry, rasterization, and fragment shaders. The vertex shader plots the graph of the membership function of the fuzzy set specified in the rule base; the ordinate in the graph is perpendicular to the pixel plane, and the range of abscissa values $[0, 1]$ is distributed over a column of D_{ftv} pixels. Each vertex has a value of the m.f. of the fuzzy set of the input variable attached to it as an attribute at the same point of the sampling grid. In the geometry shader, the vertices of the graph are connected by straight lines, forming a closed geometric shape in this graph. Then, during rasterization, rays from the pixel centers cross the straight lines of the graph, forming new vertices for the fragment shader, whose attributes are calculated using linear interpolation of the attributes of

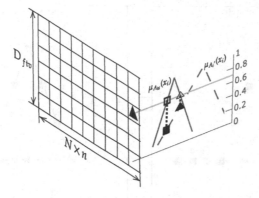

Fig. 2. Using OpenGL to calculate the FTV

the vertices of the crossed lines. Finally, in the fragment shader, the attached interpolated value of the m.f. of the fuzzy set of the input variable is taken as the value of the pixel channel intensity. If the ray originating from the pixel has crossed several straight lines of the graph, then the maximum intensity of the pixel channel is selected by specifying this intensity as the depth of the fragment using the built-in variable gl_Depth.

The described method involving OpenGL for the computation of the FTV is illustrated in Fig. 3. The shapes corresponding to the attribute values are given in gray. For the vertex shader, the figure shows the values of the m.f. of the fuzzy set in the rule base and in the input at all points of the sampling grid. In the geometry shader, these vertices are combined into a polyline graph of the corresponding membership function. During rasterization, the attribute values are interpolated at the points of the sampling grid of the FTV. The fragment shader is used to find the largest value of all candidates at a given point of the sampling grid of the FTV.

Double or triple buffering can be used when implementing the fuzzy output for data packets.

4.2 The Implementation of Efficient Convolution Inside the CUDA Kernel

After computing the FTV for all rules and all inputs, to compute the final inference result, we must first perform a reduction to obtain the T_1-norm of the calculated FTV for all inputs of each rule, according to formula (9), and then compute the value of formula (10) by performing a reduction for all rules and for all centers of the m.f. of the output variable using the results of the reduction. The reduction of the FTV across all inputs can be efficiently calculated, first by computing the T_3-norm of pairs, and then continue computing the pairwise T_3-norms until the result is obtained, resulting in a tree of intermediate T_3-norms of the FTVs. In this case, the computation of the reduction has complexity

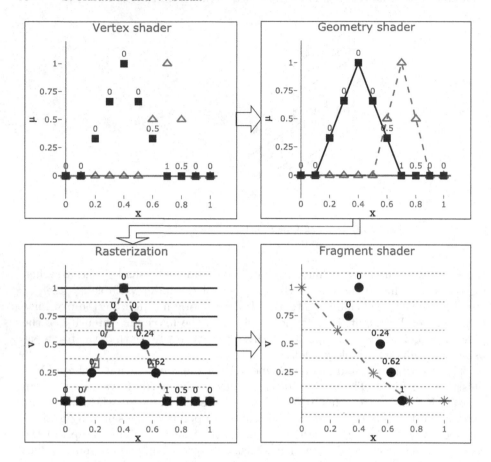

Fig. 3. Data flow along the OpenGL shader pipeline

$O(\log n \times D_{\mathrm{ftv}}^2)$. It is convenient to use dynamic CUDA kernels to implement this approach to reduction [11].

When implementing the convolution inside the CUDA core, it is important to take into account the specific details of calculations on streaming multiprocessors: one should avoid the inactivity of threads within one packet of 32 threads, as well as the occurrence of bank conflicts in data access [16,17].

4.3 Features of the Implementation of the FTV Convolution When $T_1 = min$

In the case when the *min* function is selected as T_1, and relying on the property of non-growing for both T_1 and T_3, it is possible to implement the calculation of (9) with complexity $O(D_{\mathrm{ftv}} \times \log n)$.

Algorithm 1. FTVs reduction when $T_1 = min$ and $T_3(a,b) \geq T_3(c,d)$ if $a > c$ or $b > d$

Require: ftv_i, $i = \overline{1,n}$

$\quad max\_ftv[i] = 0;$

$\quad$ **for** $v = 1 \ldots 0$ **do**

$\qquad s \leftarrow \{ftv_i[v] \mid ftv_i[v] >= max\_ftv[i]\}$;

$\qquad max\_ftv[i] \leftarrow max(max\_ftv[i], ftv_i[v]);$

$\qquad v\_max \leftarrow max_i\{ftv_i[v]\}$, $v\_max\_index \leftarrow \arg\max_i\{ftv_i[v]\}$;

$\qquad$ **if** $s = \emptyset$ & $i = v\_max\_index$ **then**

$\qquad\qquad r[i] \leftarrow v\_max;$

$\qquad$ **else**

$\qquad\qquad r[i] \leftarrow max\_ftv[i];$

$\qquad$ **end if**

$\qquad ftv[v] \leftarrow T_3\limits_i \{r[i]\};$

$\quad$ **end for**

$\quad$ **return** ftv

		$v\_min[1]=0.9$	$v\_min[2]=0.4$	$v\_max=0.7$ $v\_max\_index=3$	$v\_min[4]=0.6$	$v\_min[5]=0.4$	$v\_min[6]=1.0$			max_ftv			
		i=1	i=2	i=3	i=4	i=5	i=6	i=1	i=2	i=3	i=4	i=5	i=6
0.0	v=1.0	0.9	0.0	0.9	0.6	0.0	1.0	0.9	0.0	0.9	0.6	0.0	1.0
0.2	v=0.75	0.8	0.2	0.8	0.5	0.2	0.8	0.9	0.2	0.9	0.6	0.2	1.0
0.4 $\leftarrow min_i\{v\_min[i]\}$	v=0.5	0.6	0.4	0.7	0.4	0.4	0.6	0.9	0.4	0.9	0.6	0.4	1.0
	v=0.25	0.5	0.6	0.3	0.2	0.6	0.3						
	v=0.0	0.4	0.9	0.1	0.0	0.8	0.1						
$\uparrow$ ftv		ftv1	ftv2	ftv3	ftv4	ftv5	ftv6						

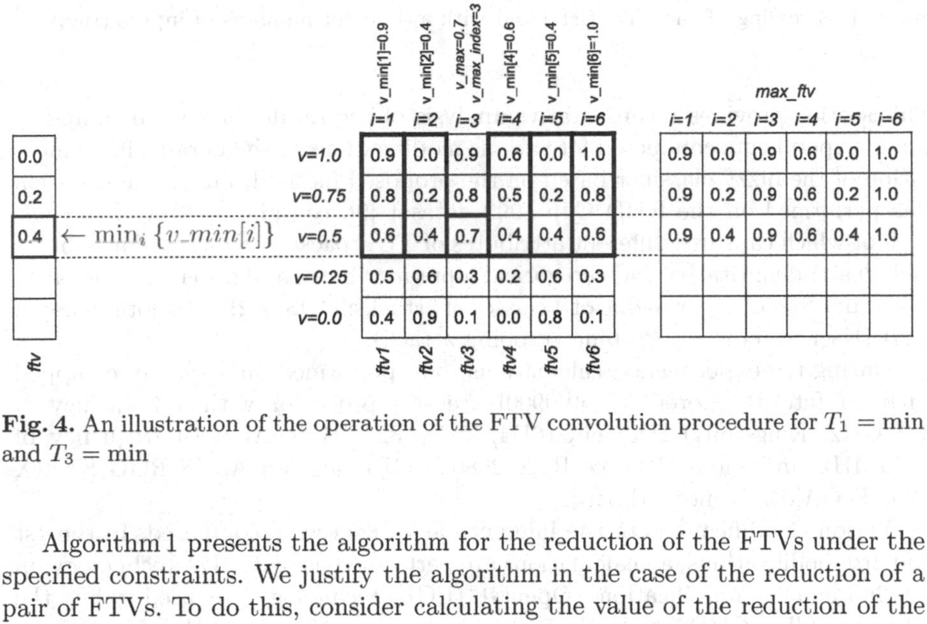

Fig. 4. An illustration of the operation of the FTV convolution procedure for $T_1 = min$ and $T_3 = min$

Algorithm 1 presents the algorithm for the reduction of the FTVs under the specified constraints. We justify the algorithm in the case of the reduction of a pair of FTVs. To do this, consider calculating the value of the reduction of the FTV at point v of the sampling grid. Since the value at that point is given by $\sup_{\substack{v_1 T_1 v_2 = v \\ v_1, v_2 \in [0,1]}} T_3(\tau_{A_{1k}/A_1'}(v_1), \tau_{A_{2k}/A_2'}(v_2))$, it is necessary to find such a pair of values $\tau_{A_{1k}/A_1'}(v_1)$ and $\tau_{A_{2k}/A_2'}(v_2)$ that maximize the value of the reduction of T_3. If either $v_1 = v$ or $v_2 = v$, then the optimal set of values of $\tau_{A_{ik}/A_i'}(v_i)$ is found. Otherwise, it is necessary to choose the largest of $\tau_{A_{ik}/A_i'}(v_i)$ for which $v_i = v$. Such reasoning can be extrapolated to the reduction of a larger number of FTVs. An example of the operation of the algorithm for $T_1 = min$, $T_3 = min$, $n = 6$, and a sampling grid of FTV of size 5 is given in Fig. 4.

5   A Comparative Analysis of Various Implementation Methods

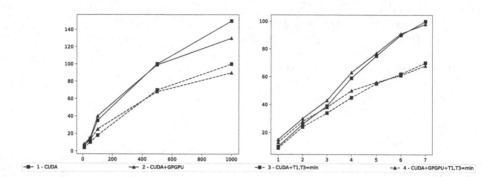

Fig. 5. Graphs of the operation time of various modifications at different values of the degree of sampling of the FTV (left) and with a different numbers of inputs (right)

This section provides a comparative analysis of the results of several computational experiments conducted for various modifications of the parallel implementation of the fuzzy classifier based on the proposed method. Fuzzy classification was performed on the KDD Cup 1999 dataset [9], containing 494 021 records; each of which captures different attributes of TCP packets. The set of attributes includes 41 quantitative and categorical input attributes and also refers the package either to normal or to one of 4 classes of attacks: DOS, R2L (Remote to user), U2R (User to root), or Probing (probing attack).

During the experiments, calculations were performed on a system equipped with an Intel(R) Core(TM) i9-9900K central processor with a frequency of 3.60 GHz, Kingston KHX2666C16D4/32GX 32 GB RAM with frequency of 2666 MHz, an Nvidia GeForce RTX 2080Ti GPU and an ASUS ROG STRIX Z390-E GAMING motherboard.

Various modifications of the inference algorithm were compared. In the 1st and 3rd modifications, all calculations are performed using CUDA technology; in the 2nd and 4th modifications, OpenGL (EGL) technology was used to find the FTV, as well as CUDA technology was also used for the rest of the calculations. In the 1st and 2nd modifications, there are no restrictions on the choice of T_1 and T_3, in the 3rd and 4th modifications, the min function is used as T_1 and T_3. In all modifications, the Lukashevich implication was used.

In the first series of computational experiments, the operating time of the algorithm is estimated at different sizes of the sampling grid of the FTV with the number of inputs equal to 7. In the second series of experiments, the operating time of the algorithm is compared with a different number of inputs and the sampling grid size equal to 500. Here we select a given number of the most significant quantitative features from the whole set of input ones. The list of selected features includes those with an acceptable degree of noise, allowing for the separation of a subset of classes.

According to the experimental results depicted in Fig. 5, it can be seen that the use of GPGPU becomes justified when the size of the computational grid is more than 500 and the number of inputs is more than 6, and the use of the optimal convolution algorithm of the FTV gives an advantage in computing time for almost the entire range of experimental parameter.

6 Conclusions

The calculation scheme proposed in this paper for the fuzzy inference method based on fuzzy truth value made it possible to achieve high performance for the fuzzy inference procedure using NS-fuzzification through the use of parallel computing technologies. The article describes the possibility of using OpenGL technology in the implementation of FTV calculation, as well as the key features of the implementation of effective convolution using CUDA technology. In this case when certain restrictions are imposed on the t-norms used in the reduction of the FTVs, an efficient algorithm for the reduction of the calculated FTVs for all inputs is proposed.

The computational experiments were carried out to estimate the time of computing of various modifications of the implementation of the fuzzy inference method described in this article using NS-fuzzification based on a fuzzy truth value. Based on the measurements obtained, conclusions were made about the expediency of using GPGPU to calculate the FTV and the efficiency of the reduction procedure achieved due to proposed optimization, with different sizes of the sampling grid and numbers of inputs in the fuzzy system.

References

1. Borisov, A.N., Krunberg, O.A., Fedorov, I.P.: Decision Making Based on Fuzzy Models: Application Examples. Zinatne Press (1990)
2. Dobua, D., Prad, A.: Theory of possiblities. Applications to knowledge representation in computer science, Radio i svyaz (1990)
3. Fu, C., Sarabakha, A., Kayacan, E., Wagner, C., John, R., Garibaldi, J.M.: Input uncertainty sensitivity enhanced nonsingleton fuzzy logic controllers for long-term navigation of quadrotor UAVs. IEEE/ASME Trans. Mechatron. 23(2), 725–734 (2018). https://doi.org/10.1109/TMECH.2018.2810947
4. Mamdani, E.H.: Applications of fuzzy algorithms for control of a simple dynamic plant. In: Proceedings of the IEEE (1974)
5. Mendel, J.M.: Non-singleton fuzzification made simpler. Inf. Sci. 559, 286–308 (2021). https://doi.org/10.1016/j.ins.2020.12.061. https://www.sciencedirect.com/science/article/pii/S0020025520312275
6. Mouzouris, G., Mendel, J.: Nonsingleton fuzzy logic systems: theory and application. IEEE Trans. Fuzzy Syst. 5(1), 56–71 (1997). https://doi.org/10.1109/91.554447

7. Piegat, A.: Fuzzy Modeling and Control. Studies in Fuzziness and Soft Computing. Physica-Verlag HD (2001). https://books.google.ru/books?id=329oSfh-vxsC
8. Pourabdollah, A., John, R., Garibaldi, J.: A new dynamic approach for non-singleton fuzzification in noisy time-series prediction, pp. 1–6 (2017). https://doi.org/10.1109/FUZZ-IEEE.2017.8015575
9. UML Repository: KDD cup 1999 data. https://archive.ics.uci.edu/ml/datasets/kdd+cup+1999+data. Accessed 1 Dec 2022
10. Rutkowski, L.: Computational intelligence - methods and techniques (2008)
11. Sanders, J., Kandrot, E.: CUDA by Example: An Introduction to General-Purpose GPU Programming, 1st edn. Addison-Wesley Professional (2010)
12. Sinuk, V., Polyakov, V., Kutsenko, D.: New fuzzy truth value based inference methods for non-singleton miso rule-based systems. In: Proceedings of the First International Scientific Conference "Intelligent Information Technologies for Industry" (IITI 2016) (2016)
13. Sinuk, V.G., Mikhelev, V.V.: Metody vivoda dlya sistem logicheskogo typa na osnove nechetkoy stepeni istinnosty. Izvestiya RAN. Teoriya i sistemy upravleniya (3), 1–8 (2018)
14. Takagi, T., Sugeno, M.: Fuzzy identification of systems and its applications to modeling and control. IEEE Trans. Syst. Man Cybern. **SMC-15**(1), 116–132 (1985). https://doi.org/10.1109/TSMC.1985.6313399
15. Zadeh, L.A.: Outline of a new approach to the analysis of complex systems and decision processes. IEEE Trans. Syst. Man Cybern. **SMC-3**(1), 28–44 (1973). https://doi.org/10.1109/TSMC.1973.5408575
16. Zone, N.D.: Cuda best practices guide (2020). https://docs.nvidia.com/cuda/cuda-c-best-practices-guide/index.html. Accessed 1 Dec 2022
17. Zone, N.D.: Cuda programming guide (2020). https://docs.nvidia.com/cuda/cuda-c-programming-guide/index.html. Accessed 1 Dec 2022

Solving the Three-Dimensional Faddeev–Merkuriev Equations via Spline Collocation and Tensor Product Preconditioning

V. A. Gradusov[✉], V. A. Roudnev, E. A. Yarevsky, and S. L. Yakovlev

Department of Computational Physics, Saint Petersburg State University,
Saint Petersburg 199034, Russian Federation
{v.gradusov,v.rudnev,e.yarevsky,s.yakovlev}@spbu.ru

Abstract. We present an efficient computational approach to solving the Faddeev-Merkuriev equations for quantum three-body systems. The efficiency of our approach stems from the following three key factors. The appropriate treatment of the three-body dynamics due to the use of the Faddeev-Merkuriev equations, which results in the simplification of the solution. The advanced partial-wave analysis based on the Wigner functions decomposition of the solutions that leads to a model-free reduction of the six dimensional problem to a three-dimensional one. The elaborated numerical scheme that makes extensive use of the structure of the equations. The numerical approach is based on the spline collocation method and uses the tensor product form of discretized operators. For solving the linear equations we worked out the preconditioning scheme which is based on the Matrix Decomposition Algorithm. We show that this numerical scheme outperforms the general-purpose direct sparse linear system solvers in both time and memory requirements. The numerical approach demonstrated also clear advantages over the generic scheme that we implemented in earlier research. The approach has been applied to high-precision calculations of bound states and scattering states of several three-body systems.

Keywords: Faddeev–Merkuriev equations · Spline collocation · Tensor product preconditioner

1 Introduction

Quantum three-body systems remain a source of challenges for both theoretical and experimental physicists. Calculations of some triatomic systems contribute to metrology, and quantum scattering of charged particles is used in antihydrogen formation experiments. Many of the applications require rather precise results about the systems studied.

We intend to create a computational framework applicable to various physical systems and states. Such a framework should be based on a mathematically sound

© The Author(s), under exclusive license to Springer Nature Switzerland AG 2023
L. Sokolinsky and M. Zymbler (Eds.): PCT 2023, CCIS 1868, pp. 63–77, 2023.
https://doi.org/10.1007/978-3-031-38864-4_5

problem formulation. One of the most established approaches to studying quantum three-body systems is based on the Faddeev–Merkuriev (FM) equations [8,16, 26] which can be applied to systems with short- and long-range (Coulomb) interactions.

A direct solution of the six-dimensional FM equations is hardly possible. We use the symmetries of the solutions to reduce the dimension of the configuration space. In the total-orbital-momentum representation [13], the FM equations are reduced to a finite system of three-dimensional partial differential equations. The numerical solution of such systems is still challenging.

Here we present a computational approach to solving the three-dimensional FM equations. The approach is based on the spline collocation method and makes intensive use of the tensor product form. The preconditioning scheme is based on the Matrix Decomposition Algorithm (tensor-trick algorithm). We show that the numerical scheme outperforms the general-purpose direct sparse linear system solvers in both time and memory requirements. We also discuss the parallel implementation of the scheme, its efficiency, and its limitations.

The paper is organized as follows. In Sect. 2 we describe the FM equation formalism. Section 3 is devoted to the description of our numerical scheme. In Sect. 4, we give some examples of high-precision calculations of three-body systems. We consider the atomic helium bound states and the multichannel scattering of the antiproton off the ground and excited states of the positronium with emphasis on the antihydrogen formation processes. Conclusion summarizes the study and points directions for further work.

2   The Theoretical Approach

2.1   The Faddeev–Merkuriev Equations

The quantum system consists of three charged particles with masses m_α and charges Z_α, $\alpha = 1, 2, 3$. In what follows, the set of indices $\{\alpha, \beta, \gamma\}$ runs over the set $\{1, 2, 3\}$ which enumerates particles. By the pair α, we denote a particle pair $\beta\gamma$ that is complementary to the particle α. Particle positions are described by sets of reduced Jacobi coordinates $(\boldsymbol{x}_\alpha, \boldsymbol{y}_\alpha)$ [8] (we use boldface for vectors). They are defined for a partition $\alpha(\beta\gamma)$ as scaled relative position vectors between the particles of the pair α and between their center of mass and the particle α. The reduced masses μ_α and $\mu_{\alpha(\beta\gamma)}$ are given in terms of particle masses m_α [8]. The reduced Jacobi vectors for various α are related by an orthogonal transformation $\boldsymbol{x}_\beta = c_{\beta\alpha}\boldsymbol{x}_\alpha + s_{\beta\alpha}\boldsymbol{y}_\alpha$, $\boldsymbol{y}_\beta = -s_{\beta\alpha}\boldsymbol{x}_\alpha + c_{\beta\alpha}\boldsymbol{y}_\alpha$ [8]. Further on, β Jacobi vectors are expressed through α.

The FM equations for three charged particles [8,16] can be written for the components ψ_α of the wave function as

$$\{T_\alpha + V_\alpha(x_\alpha) + \sum_{\beta \neq \alpha} V_\beta^{(1)}(x_\beta, y_\beta) - E\}\psi_\alpha(\boldsymbol{x}_\alpha, \boldsymbol{y}_\alpha)$$

$$= -V_\alpha^{(s)}(x_\alpha, y_\alpha) \sum_{\beta \neq \alpha} \psi_\beta(\boldsymbol{x}_\beta, \boldsymbol{y}_\beta), \quad \alpha \neq \beta, \quad \alpha, \beta = 1, 2, 3. \quad (1)$$

The kinetic energy operators T_α are defined as $T_\alpha \equiv -\Delta_{x_\alpha} - \Delta_{y_\alpha}$. The potentials V_α are the pairwise Coulomb interactions $V_\alpha(x_\alpha) = \sqrt{2\mu_\alpha} Z_\beta Z_\gamma / x_\alpha$ $(\beta, \gamma \neq \alpha)$. They are split into the interior (short-range) $V_\alpha^{(s)}$ and tail (long-range) $V_\alpha^{(l)}$ parts:

$$V_\alpha(x_\alpha) = V_\alpha^{(s)}(x_\alpha, y_\alpha) + V_\alpha^{(l)}(x_\alpha, y_\alpha). \tag{2}$$

Equations (1) can be summed up, thus resulting in the Schrödinger equation for the wave function $\Psi = \sum_\alpha \psi_\alpha$.

The splitting (2) is done by means of the Merkuriev cutoff function χ_α, $V_\alpha^{(s)}(x_\alpha, y_\alpha) = \chi_\alpha(x_\alpha, y_\alpha) V_\alpha(x_\alpha)$. This function confines the short-range part of the potential to a vicinity of the three-body collision point and the binary configuration ($x_\alpha \ll y_\alpha$ when $y_\alpha \to \infty$) [8]. We use the cutoff function from [10]:

$$\chi_\alpha(x_\alpha, y_\alpha) \equiv \chi_\alpha(x_\alpha) = 2\left(1 + \exp[(x_\alpha/x_{0\alpha})^{2.01}]\right)^{-1}. \tag{3}$$

In principle, the parameter $x_{0\alpha}$ can be chosen arbitrarily. It should be noted, however, that its choice changes the properties of the components ψ_α [10].

For scattering problems, the key property of FM Eqs. (1) is their asymptotic decoupling. This property means that, for energies below the breakup threshold, each component ψ_α at large distances behaves as a binary configuration of the pairing α [27]. For a total energy E of the system below the three-body ionization threshold, the asymptote is

$$\psi_\alpha(\boldsymbol{x}_\alpha, \boldsymbol{y}_\alpha) = \chi_{\mathbb{A}_0}(\boldsymbol{x}_\alpha, \boldsymbol{y}_\alpha)\delta_{\alpha\alpha_0} + \Xi_\alpha(\boldsymbol{x}_\alpha, \boldsymbol{y}_\alpha), \tag{4}$$

where the outgoing wave has the form

$$\Xi_\alpha(\boldsymbol{x}_\alpha, \boldsymbol{y}_\alpha)$$
$$= \sum_{n\ell m} \frac{\phi_A(x_\alpha)}{x_\alpha} Y_{\ell m}(\hat{\boldsymbol{x}}_\alpha) \sqrt{\frac{p_{n_0}}{p_n}} \widetilde{A}_{\mathbb{A},\mathbb{A}_0}(\hat{\boldsymbol{y}}_\alpha, \boldsymbol{p}_{n_0}) \frac{e^{i(p_n y_\alpha - \eta_n \log(2p_n y_\alpha))}}{y_\alpha}. \tag{5}$$

Here $Y_{\ell m}$ is a spherical harmonic function. The multi-index $\mathbb{A} = \{Am\} = \{\alpha n\ell m\}$ specifies the scattering channel, i.e., the two-body bound state in the pair α with wave function $\phi_A(x_\alpha)Y_{\ell m}(\hat{\boldsymbol{x}}_\alpha)/x_\alpha$ and energy ε_n. The momentum p_n of the outgoing particle is determined by the energy conservation condition $E = p_n^2 + \varepsilon_n$. The Sommerfeld parameter is defined as $\eta_n \equiv Z_\alpha(Z_\beta + Z_\gamma)\sqrt{2m_{\alpha(\beta\gamma)}}/(2p_n)$. The initial channel is defined by the incoming wave $\chi_{\mathbb{A}_0}(\boldsymbol{x}_\alpha, \boldsymbol{y}_\alpha)$, whose exact expression is given in [12].

The binary scattering amplitude

$$\mathcal{A}_{\mathbb{A}\mathbb{A}_0}(\hat{\boldsymbol{y}}_\alpha, \boldsymbol{p}_{n_0}) = \mathcal{A}_C(\hat{\boldsymbol{y}}_\alpha, \boldsymbol{p}_{n_0}) + \widetilde{\mathcal{A}}_{\mathbb{A},\mathbb{A}_0}(\hat{\boldsymbol{y}}_\alpha, \boldsymbol{p}_{n_0}) \tag{6}$$

describes the transition from the initial channel $\mathbb{A}_0$ to the channel $\mathbb{A}$. Here $\mathcal{A}_C$ is the two-body Coulomb scattering amplitude [17]. The amplitude $\mathcal{A}_{\mathbb{A}\mathbb{A}_0}$ is the final result of calculations. Then the scattering cross section $\sigma_{\mathcal{A}\mathcal{A}_0}$, which can be compared directly against experimental data, is expressed in terms of this amplitude [17].

FM Eq. (1) and boundary conditions (4), (5) form the boundary-value representation of the scattering problem, which can be solved numerically.

2.2   The Total-Orbital-Momentum Representation

Each Eq. (1) is a six-dimensional partial differential equation. We introduce the six-dimensional kinematic coordinates $(X_\alpha, \Omega_\alpha)$. The coordinates $X_\alpha = \{x_\alpha, y_\alpha, z_\alpha \equiv (\boldsymbol{x}_\alpha, \boldsymbol{y}_\alpha)/(x_\alpha y_\alpha)\}$ determine the positions of the particles in the plane containing them. The three Euler angles $\Omega_\alpha = \{\phi_\alpha, \vartheta_\alpha, \varphi_\alpha\}$ specify the position of the plane in space. The FM components are expressed in the coordinates $(X_\alpha, \Omega_\alpha)$ as

$$\psi_\alpha(X_\alpha, \Omega_\alpha) = \sum_{L=0}^{+\infty} \sum_{\tau=\pm 1} \sum_{M=-L}^{L} \sum_{M'=M_0}^{L} (1-z_\alpha^2)^{M'/2} \frac{\psi_{\alpha M M'}^{L\tau}(X_\alpha)}{x_\alpha y_\alpha} F_{MM'}^{L\tau}(\Omega_\alpha), \quad (7)$$

where $M_0 = (1-\tau)/2$, and the functions $F_{MM'}^{L\tau}(\Omega_\alpha)$ are expressed in terms of the Wigner D-functions $D_{MM'}^{L}$ [25]. The function $F_{MM'}^{L\tau}$ is the common eigenfunction of the squared total orbital momentum, its projection, and the spatial inversion operators [6,13]. The factor $(1-z_\alpha^2)^{M'/2}$ makes the partial components $\psi_{\alpha M M'}^{L\tau}$ and its derivatives nonsingular at $z_\alpha = \pm 1$ [11,23].

By plugging (7) into FM Eqs. (1) and projecting the result onto the functions $F_{MM'}^{L\tau}$, we obtain a finite set of three-dimensional equations for the partial components $\psi_{\alpha M M'}^{L\tau}(X_\alpha)$:

$$\left[T_{\alpha M M'}^{L\tau} + V_\alpha(x_\alpha) + \widehat{V}_\alpha(y_\alpha) - E\right]\psi_{\alpha M M'}^{L\tau}(X_\alpha)$$

$$+ T_{\alpha M, M'-1}^{L\tau -}\psi_{\alpha M, M'-1}^{L\tau}(X_\alpha) + T_{\alpha M, M'+1}^{L\tau +}\psi_{\alpha M, M'+1}^{L\tau}(X_\alpha) = -\frac{V_\alpha^{(s)}(x_\alpha, y_\alpha)}{(1-z_\alpha^2)^{\frac{M'}{2}}}$$

$$\times \frac{x_\alpha y_\alpha}{x_\beta y_\beta} \sum_{M''=M_0}^{L} \frac{2(-1)^{M''-M'}}{\sqrt{2+2\delta_{M''0}}} F_{M''M'}^{L\tau}(0, w_{\beta\alpha}, 0)(1-z_\beta^2)^{\frac{M''}{2}} \psi_{\beta M M''}^{L\tau}(X_\beta)$$

$$- \left(\sum_{\beta\neq\alpha} V_\beta^{(l)}(x_\beta, y_\beta) - \widehat{V}_\alpha(y_\alpha)\right)\psi_{\alpha M, M'}^{J\tau}(X_\alpha). \quad (8)$$

The kinetic part is of the form

$$T_{\alpha M M'}^{L\tau} = -\frac{\partial^2}{\partial y_\alpha^2} + \frac{1}{x_\alpha^2}\left(L(L+1) - 2M'^2\right) - \frac{\partial^2}{\partial x_\alpha^2} - \left(\frac{1}{y_\alpha^2} + \frac{1}{x_\alpha^2}\right)d_{z_\alpha}^{M'}, \quad (9)$$

$$T_{\alpha M, M'+1}^{L\tau +} = \frac{1}{x_\alpha^2}\lambda^{L,M'}\sqrt{1+\delta_{M'0}}d_{z_\alpha}^{M'+},$$

$$T_{\alpha M, M'-1}^{L\tau -} = -\frac{1}{x_\alpha^2}\lambda^{L,-M'}\sqrt{1+\delta_{M'1}}d_{z_\alpha}^{M'-}, \quad (10)$$

where $\lambda^{LM'} = \sqrt{L(L+1) - M'(M'+1)}$. Here we have introduced the operators

$$d_{z_\alpha}^{M'} = \left(1-z_\alpha^2\right)\frac{\partial^2}{\partial z_\alpha^2} - 2(M'+1)z_\alpha\frac{\partial}{\partial z_\alpha} - M'(M'+1),$$

$$d_{z_\alpha}^{M'+} = -\left(1-z_\alpha^2\right)\frac{\partial}{\partial z_\alpha} + 2(M'+1)z_\alpha, \quad d_{z_\alpha}^{M'-} = -\frac{\partial}{\partial z_\alpha}. \quad (11)$$

The explicit expression of the kinematic angle $w_{\beta\alpha}$ can be found in [13].

The potential terms in the 3D equations are rearranged using the representation of the tail parts of potentials:

$$\sum_{\beta\neq\alpha} V_\beta^{(1)}(x_\beta, y_\beta) = \widehat{V}_\alpha(y_\alpha) + \left(\sum_{\beta\neq\alpha} V_\beta^{(1)}(x_\beta, y_\beta) - \widehat{V}_\alpha(y_\alpha)\right). \tag{12}$$

The potential $\widehat{V}_\alpha$ is an approximation of $\sum_{\beta\neq\alpha} V_\beta^{(1)}$ that minimizes the new right-hand-side term $(\sum_{\beta\neq\alpha} V_\beta^{(1)} - \widehat{V}_\alpha)\psi_{\alpha M, M'}^{J\tau}$.

The choice of the potential $\widehat{V}_\alpha$ must ensure the square integrability of this term. The reason for the rearrangement is that the variables are now "almost separate" in the operator on the left. This separability is used to construct an effective preconditioner for the computational scheme.

Equations (8) are the three-dimensional FM equations in the total-orbital-momentum representation. The equations on partial components $\psi_{\alpha MM'}^{L\tau}$ with different indices L, M, and τ give rise to independent sets of equations. This is a direct consequence of the fact that the total orbital momentum, its projection, and the spatial parity are conserved for the three-body systems considered here. Given L, M, and τ, system (8) consists of $3n_M$ three-dimensional PDEs, where $n_M = (L - M_0 + 1)$. Owing to the symmetry (antisymmetry) of the wave function in the presence of identical particles, the number of coupled equations is reduced to $2n_M$ or n_M in the case of two or three identical particles, respectively [11].

The system (8) must be supplemented with asymptotic boundary conditions. For the bound state problem, the partial components $\psi_{\alpha MM'}^{L\tau}$ are required to be zero at a sufficiently large distance. For the scattering problem, the asymptotic boundary conditions on $\psi_{\alpha MM'}^{L\tau}(X_\alpha)$ are formulated as the sum

$$\psi_{\alpha MM'}^{L\tau}(X_\alpha) = \chi_{A_0 MM'}^{L\tau}(X_\alpha)\delta_{\alpha\alpha_0} + \Xi_{\alpha MM'}^{L\tau}(X_\alpha) \tag{13}$$

of the partial components of the incoming and outgoing waves (4), (5). They are obtained by projecting these waves onto the functions $F_{MM'}^{L\tau}$. Their explicit expressions can be found in [12].

The partial amplitude $\widetilde{\mathcal{A}}_{AA_0}^{L\lambda}$, extracted from $\Xi_{\alpha MM'}^{L\tau}$, is related to the coefficients of the spherical harmonics in the expansion of the amplitude $\widetilde{\mathcal{A}}_{AA_0}(\hat{\boldsymbol{y}}_\alpha)$. The scattering cross section σ_{AA_0} is the sum over L of the partial cross sections $\sigma_{AA_0}^L$, which are expressed in terms of the partial amplitudes $\widetilde{\mathcal{A}}_{AA_0}^{L\lambda}$.

By subtracting the incoming wave from the FM components, we obtain Eqs. (8) with an inhomogeneous term. Their solution satisfies a zero Dirichlet boundary condition at the origin and is asymptotically equal to the outgoing wave.

3 The Computational Scheme

3.1 The Basic Scheme

Assume that the spaces of basis functions consist of the functions $S_\alpha^i(x)$, $S_\alpha^j(y)$, and $S_\alpha^k(z)$. These functions are defined on the given intervals $[0, R_{x_\alpha}]$, $[0, R_{y_\alpha}]$, and $[-1, 1]$, respectively, and are supposed to be local; moreover, $S_\alpha^i(x)$ and $S_\alpha^j(y)$ satisfy the boundary conditions specified below. The three-dimensional tensor product basis is used then to expand the solutions $\psi_{\alpha MM'}^{J\tau}$ of Eqs. (8) in the cubes $[0, R_{x_\alpha}] \times [0, R_{y_\alpha}] \times [-1, 1]$:

$$\psi_{\alpha MM'}^{J\tau}(x_\alpha, y_\alpha, z_\alpha) = \sum_{i,j,k=1}^{n_{x_\alpha}, n_{y_\alpha}, n_{z_\alpha}} c_{ijk}^{M'} S_\alpha^i(x_\alpha) S_\alpha^j(y_\alpha) S_\alpha^k(z_\alpha). \tag{14}$$

Assume also that $(x_\alpha^\xi, y_\alpha^\eta, z_\alpha^\zeta)$, $\xi = 1, \ldots, n_{x_\alpha}$, $\eta = 1, \ldots, n_{y_\alpha}$, $\zeta = 1, \ldots, n_{z_\alpha}$, are regular grids of points. The choice of identical basis spaces for expanding the partial components $\psi_{\alpha MM'}^{J\tau}$ and sets of collocation points for Eqs. (8) with different indices M' is not used explicitly in the construction of the scheme. However, it simplifies the notations and can be used efficiently in the storage scheme, as explained below.

The basis functions $S_\alpha^i(x)$ and $S_\alpha^j(y)$ satisfy zero Dirichlet-type boundary conditions on the lines $x_\alpha = 0$ and $y_\alpha = 0$, and so does $S_\alpha^i(x)$ on the line $x_\alpha = R_{x_\alpha}$. The boundary condition satisfied by $S_\alpha^j(y)$ at the right endpoint depends on the type of problem solved. For bound state calculations, the zero Dirichlet-type boundary conditions are still relevant. In scattering calculations, for implementing the asymptotic boundary conditions (13), we use a hybrid basis consisting of the local functions that describe the solution in the nonasymptotic region and a few additional nonlocal basis functions. Each additional basis function has the form of the irregular Coulomb function $u_\ell^+(\eta_n, p_n y_\alpha)$ [17] in the asymptotic region. In the remaining part of the space, it is a polynomial chosen to satisfy the zero Dirichlet-type boundary condition at the origin and to ensure the required continuity of the basis function in the solution interval. The so chosen basis functions ensure the fulfillment of outgoing boundary conditions.

Applying the collocation method, i.e., requiring Eqs. (8) to be satisfied at the points of the grid, we obtain either inhomogeneous matrix equations of the form $(H - E^* S)c = f$ for the scattering problem or the generalized eigenvalue problem $Hc = ESc$ for the problem of bound states. The generalized eigenvalue problem can be rewritten as

$$S(H - E^* S)^{-1} \tilde{c} = \frac{1}{E - E^*} \tilde{c}, \tag{15}$$

where $\tilde{c} = (H - E^* S)c$, to find the eigenvalues in a vicinity of a given $E = E^*$. Here the matrix H is the discretized version of the operator in the 3D FM Eqs. (8) with $E = 0$ and has linear dimension $n_M \sum_\alpha n_{x_\alpha} n_{y_\alpha} n_{z_\alpha}$. It is sparse and has only $O(n_M^2 \sum_\alpha n_{x_\alpha} n_{y_\alpha} n_{z_\alpha})$ nonzero elements. The matrix S has elements $S_\alpha^i(x_\alpha^\xi) S_\alpha^j(y_\alpha^\eta) S_\alpha^k(z_\alpha^\zeta)$.

In the spirit of [14, 22], and [19], the arising systems of linear equations with matrix $(H - E^* S)$ are preconditioned by inverting approximately the operator on the left-hand side of Eqs. (8) with $E = E^*$.

3.2   The Preconditioner

The efficient inversion of the matrix of the operator on the left-hand side of Eqs. (8) is based on a technique known as Matrix Decomposition Algorithm (MDA) [5] or Tensor Trick (TT) [22]. The following model example illustrates it. Let $A_{1,2}$ and $B_{1,2}$ be matrices of dimensions $n \times n$ and $m \times m$, respectively. Suppose now that we need to invert an $(nm) \times (nm)$ matrix of the form

$$A_1 \otimes B_1 + A_2 \otimes B_2, \qquad (16)$$

where $\otimes$ denotes the Kronecker tensor product of matrices [9]. Let us introduce the operation $\mathfrak{D}$

$$(\overline{W}_A, W_A, \Lambda_A) = \mathfrak{D}(A_1, A_2) \qquad (17)$$

of finding (if they exist) the nonsingular complex matrices $\overline{W}_A$, W_A (and the diagonal matrix Λ_A) that simultaneously diagonalize the matrices A_1 and A_2 in the sense of the equalities $\overline{W}_A A_1 W_A = \Lambda_A$ and $\overline{W}_A A_2 W_A = I$. It is easy to show that the operation $\mathfrak{D}$ can be accomplished by solving the left and right generalized eigenvalue problems $\overline{W}_A A_1 = \Lambda_A \overline{W}_A A_2$ and $A_1 W_A = A_2 W_A \Lambda_A$. Let us assume that $(\overline{W}_B, W_B, \Lambda_B) = \mathfrak{D}(B_1, B_2)$. Then, according to the well-known basic properties of the Kronecker product [9] (namely, $(A_1 \otimes B_1)(A_2 \otimes B_2) = (A_1 A_2) \otimes (B_1 B_2)$ and $(A \otimes B)^{-1} = A^{-1} \otimes B^{-1}$), we can prove that

$$(A_1 \otimes B_1 + A_2 \otimes B_2)^{-1} = (W_A \otimes W_B)(\Lambda_A \otimes \Lambda_B + I \otimes I)^{-1}(\overline{W}_A \otimes \overline{W}_B). \quad (18)$$

The matrix $\Lambda_A \otimes \Lambda_B + I \otimes I$ is diagonal and can be inverted quickly. With the use of (18), the factorization of the matrix requires $O(n^3 + m^3)$ instead of $O(n^3 m^3)$ operations if we treat it as a matrix of the general form. The matrix-vector product with a factorized matrix of the form (18) requires $O(nm(n+m))$ multiplications instead of the ordinary $O(n^2 m^2)$. The algorithm given in the example (16)–(18) can be generalized in an obvious way to the case of sum of Kronecker products of more than two matrices.

The result of the discretization of a partial differential operator in a tensor product basis can be a matrix with a tensor structure of type (16), which is suitable for applying the MDA, only if the operator has a specific structure. This is not the case for the operator on the left-hand side of Eqs. (8) because of the terms containing the operators $\boldsymbol{d}_{z_\alpha}^{M'}$, $\boldsymbol{d}_{z_\alpha}^{M'+}$, and $\boldsymbol{d}_{z_\alpha}^{M'-}$, which, at first sight, can not be diagonalized simultaneously. We can construct, however, a basis of functions in which the diagonalization can be accomplished. These are the eigenfunctions of the operator $\boldsymbol{d}_{z_\alpha}^{M'}$ defined in (11):

$$g_\ell^{M'}(z_\alpha) = \sqrt{\frac{2\ell+1}{2} \frac{(\ell - M')!}{(\ell + M')!}} \frac{P_\ell^{M'}(z_\alpha)}{(1 - z_\alpha^2)^{M'/2}}, \qquad (19)$$

where $P_\ell^{M'}$ are the associated Legendre polynomials [2]. From their properties, it follows that $g_\ell^{M'} \equiv 0$ when $\ell < M'$; otherwise $g_\ell^{M'}$ is a polynomial of degree $\ell - M'$. They satisfy the relations

$$\boldsymbol{d}_{z_\alpha}^{M'} g_\ell^{M'}(z_\alpha) = -\ell(\ell+1) g_\ell^{M'}(z_\alpha), \qquad (20)$$

$$d_{z_\alpha}^{M'\pm} g_\ell^{M'\pm1}(z_\alpha) = \mp\lambda^{\ell,\pm M'} g_\ell^{M'}(z_\alpha), \tag{21}$$

with the operators $d_{z_\alpha}^{M'\pm}$ from (11) and orthonormality conditions with weight $(1 - z_\alpha^2)^{M'}$. By using these properties, it is straightforward to show that the matrix element of the operator on the left-hand side of Eqs. (8) in the basis of polynomial functions $g_\ell^{M'}$ is diagonal in ℓ. In other words, if we plug the expansion $\psi_{\alpha M M'}^{J\tau}(X_\alpha) = \sum_\ell \psi_{\alpha M M'\ell}^{J\tau}(x_\alpha, y_\alpha) g_\ell^{M'}(z_\alpha)$ into Eqs. (8) and project the resulting equations on the polynomial functions $g_\ell^{M'}$, we obtain a set of equations with a left-hand side of the form

$$\left[-\frac{\partial^2}{\partial y_\alpha^2} + \frac{1}{x_\alpha^2}(J(J+1) - 2M'^2) - \frac{\partial^2}{\partial x_\alpha^2} \right.$$
$$\left. + \frac{\ell(\ell+1)}{y_\alpha^2} + \frac{\ell(\ell+1)}{x_\alpha^2} + V_\alpha(x_\alpha) + \hat{V}_\alpha(y_\alpha) - E \right] \psi_{\alpha M M'\ell}^{J\tau}(x_\alpha, y_\alpha)$$
$$+ \frac{\hat{\lambda}^{J,-M'}\lambda^{\ell,-M'}}{x_\alpha^2} \psi_{\alpha M M'-1\ell}^{J\tau}(x_\alpha, y_\alpha) - \frac{\hat{\lambda}^{J,M'}\lambda^{\ell,M'}}{x_\alpha^2} \psi_{\alpha M M'+1\ell}^{J\tau}(x_\alpha, y_\alpha), \tag{22}$$

where $\hat{\lambda}^{J,\pm M'} = \lambda^{J,\pm M'}\sqrt{1 + \delta_{M'0(1)}}$. Now it is not difficult to show that, for every ℓ, the operator (22) can be inverted by a formula similar to (18) but with a tridiagonal matrix on the right-hand side to be inverted in this case.

Nevertheless, the use of the basis of functions $g_\ell^{M'}$ in the solution expansion (14) is undesirable since these functions are not local. This leads to a substantial increase in the size of the matrices involved. Let us show that the diagonalization of the operators $d_{z_\alpha}^{M'}, d_{z_\alpha}^{M'\pm}$ can be in fact accomplished in other—even local—bases of functions $S_\alpha^k(z_\alpha)$. Denote by $D_{z_\alpha}^{M'}$ and $D_{z_\alpha}^{M'\pm}$ the discretized versions of the operators $d_{z_\alpha}^{M'}$ and $d_{z_\alpha}^{M'\pm}$:

$$(D_{z_\alpha}^{M'})_{\zeta k} = (d_{z_\alpha}^{M'} S_\alpha^k)(z_\alpha^\zeta), \quad (D_{z_\alpha}^{M'\pm})_{\zeta k} = (d_{z_\alpha}^{M'\pm} S_\alpha^k)(z_\alpha^\zeta). \tag{23}$$

Find the diagonal representations

$$(\overline{W}_{z_\alpha}^{M'}, W_{z_\alpha}^{M'}, \tilde{\Lambda}_{z_\alpha}^{M'}) = \mathfrak{D}(D_{z_\alpha}^{M'}, S_{z_\alpha}), \quad M' = M_0, \ldots, J, \tag{24}$$

of the matrices $D_{z_\alpha}^{M'}$. If we assume that the basis of functions $S_\alpha^k(z)$ is chosen in such a manner that the first n_{z_α} eigenfunctions $g_\ell^{M'}$ can be approximated with good accuracy and the grid of collocation points z_α^ζ is chosen close to roots of $g_{M'+n_{z_\alpha}}^{M'}$, then the following approximate equalities hold:

$$\tilde{\Lambda}_{z_\alpha}^{M'} \approx \Lambda_{z_\alpha}^{M'} \equiv \text{diag}\{ - M'(M'+1), -(M'+1)(M'+2),$$
$$\ldots, -(M'+n_{z_\alpha}-1)(M'+n_{z_\alpha})\}, \tag{25}$$
$$\overline{W}_{z_\alpha}^{M'} D_{z_\alpha}^{M'\pm} W_{z_\alpha}^{M'\pm1} \approx \Lambda_{z_\alpha}^{M'\pm},$$

where

$$
\Lambda_{z_\alpha}^{M'+} = \begin{pmatrix} 0 & & & \\ -\lambda^{M'+1,M'} & 0 & & \\ & -\lambda^{M'+2,M'} & 0 & \\ & & \ddots & \\ & & & -\lambda^{M'+n_{z_\alpha}-1,M'} & 0 \end{pmatrix} \tag{26}
$$

and

$$
\Lambda_{z_\alpha}^{M'-} = \begin{pmatrix} 0 & \lambda^{M',-M'} & & \\ & 0 & \lambda^{M'+1,-M'} & \\ & & \ddots & \\ & & 0 & \lambda^{M'+n_{z_\alpha}-2,-M'} \\ & & & 0 \end{pmatrix}. \tag{27}
$$

The proof of approximate equalities (25) is given in the Appendix in [11]. As is shown there, the columns of the matrix $W_{z_\alpha}^{M'}$ are the expansion coefficients of the functions $g_\ell^{M'}$ with respect to the basis of functions S_α^k. The equalities (25) are approximate, but we regard them as exact in the construction of the preconditioner.

The construction of the preconditioner $\mathcal{L}^{-1}$ can be found in [11]. Note, however, that in the presented here formalism the roles of the variables x_α and y_α are interchanged relative to those in [11]. This change makes the numerical scheme more suitable for scattering calculations, which imply large values of n_{y_α}.

If we denote by L the discretized version of the operator on the left-hand side of Eqs. (8) with $E = E^*$, then $\mathcal{L}^{-1} \approx L^{-1}$. Note that the only sources of imprecision for the last equality are the approximate equalities (25). The preconditioner has the form

$$
\mathcal{L}^{-1} = \mathrm{diag}\{\mathcal{L}_1^{-1}, \mathcal{L}_2^{-1}, \mathcal{L}_3^{-1}\}, \tag{28}
$$

with

$$
\mathcal{L}_\alpha^{-1} = W_{z_\alpha} W_{y_\alpha} W_{x_\alpha} P \left(\widetilde{\mathcal{L}}_\alpha^0\right)^{-1} P \overline{W}_{x_\alpha} \overline{W}_{y_\alpha} \overline{W}_{z_\alpha}. \tag{29}
$$

Formulae (28) and (29) are the analogues of formula (18). The matrices $W_{x_\alpha(y_\alpha, z_\alpha)}$ and $\overline{W}_{x_\alpha(y_\alpha, z_\alpha)}$ are block diagonal with blocks that have the structure of the Kronecker tensor product of the "one-dimensional" matrices associated with the variables $x_\alpha, y_\alpha, z_\alpha$. The matrix $\widetilde{\mathcal{L}}_\alpha^0$ is block diagonal with blocks that are tridiagonal matrices of size $n_{x_\alpha} n_{y_\alpha} n_{z_\alpha}$. Lastly, P is the permutation matrix.

3.3 Algorithm Complexity and Parallelization

The construction of the tensor factorization is the most time-consuming and memory-intensive operation when calculating and storing the preconditioner. It is necessary to perform the diagonalization operation $\mathcal{D}$ and simultaneously store a total of $\sum_\alpha (n_M + n_{z_\alpha} - 1) n_{y_\alpha}$ pairs of matrices of general form and size n_{x_α}. Thus the estimated memory requirements are $2 \sum_\alpha (n_{z_\alpha} + n_M) n_{y_\alpha} n_{x_\alpha}^2$

numbers, and the computational cost scales as $O(\sum_\alpha (n_{z_\alpha} + n_M) n_{y_\alpha} n_{x_\alpha}^3)$. Finally, each matrix-vector product with the preconditioner $\mathcal{L}^{-1}$ requires $O(n_M \sum_\alpha n_{x_\alpha} n_{z_\alpha} n_{y_\alpha} (n_{x_\alpha} + n_{z_\alpha} + n_{y_\alpha}))$ operations.

Another time-consuming and memory-intensive part of the scheme is associated with the whole matrix H. Let us express it as $H = \widetilde{L} + \widetilde{R}$, where the matrices $\widetilde{L}$ and $\widetilde{R}$ contain, correspondingly, the diagonal and off-diagonal parts with respect to the blocks of the whole matrix H that are enumerated by the indices α of the FM components and Eqs. (8). The matrix $\widetilde{L}$ is less memory-intensive and can be efficiently stored as a sum of tensor products similar to (16). The exact description of the storage scheme can be found in [11].

Let us turn now to the matrix $\widetilde{R}$. We can show that the storage size and computational cost of the matrix-vector product implied by keeping this sparse matrix in the memory in the common CSR format [20] scales as $2n_M^2 r^3 \sum_\alpha n_{x_\alpha} n_{y_\alpha} n_{z_\alpha}$, where r is the overlap rate, which is defined as the maximum number of basis functions that are nonzero at any point of the interval of definition over all basis sets.

Consider now the use of the same basis set for expanding the components $\psi_{\alpha MM'}^{JT}$ with different indices M' and identical sets of collocation points for Eqs. (8) with different indices M'. Consider also the matrix $\widetilde{R}$ as a block matrix with blocks $\widetilde{R}_{\alpha\beta}$ enumerated by the indices of the FM components. Some of these blocks may be trivial depending on the permutational symmetry of the considered system. The nonzero blocks $\widetilde{R}_{\alpha\beta}$ can be expressed and stored in the form $\widetilde{R}_{\alpha\beta} = F_{\alpha\beta} \widetilde{S}_{\alpha\beta}$, with $\widetilde{S}_{\alpha\beta} = I_M \otimes S_{\alpha\beta}$. Here the elements of the "three-dimensional" matrix $S_{\alpha\beta}$ are

$$(S_{\alpha\beta})_{\zeta\xi\eta,kij} = S_\beta^k(z_\beta(x_\alpha^\xi, y_\alpha^\eta, z_\alpha^\zeta)) S_\beta^i(x_\beta(x_\alpha^\xi, y_\alpha^\eta, z_\alpha^\zeta)) S_\beta^j(y_\beta(x_\alpha^\xi, y_\alpha^\eta, z_\alpha^\zeta)). \quad (30)$$

This matrix is stored in memory in the CSR sparse matrix format. Each matrix $F_{\alpha\beta}$ stored in memory is a block matrix with blocks $F_{\alpha\beta}^{M'M''}$, $M', M'' = M_0, \ldots, J$. Each block is a "three-dimensional" diagonal matrix representing a function-multiplication operator acting on the partial component $\psi_{\beta MM''}^{LT}$ on the right-hand side of Eqs. (8). Storing the blocks of the matrix $\widetilde{R}$ in the form $\widetilde{R}_{\alpha\beta} = F_{\alpha\beta} \widetilde{S}_{\alpha\beta}$ requires saving $O\left((n_M^2 + r^3) \sum_\alpha n_{x_\alpha} n_{y_\alpha} n_{z_\alpha}\right)$ numbers and performing the same number of multiplication operations for matrix-vector products. This is drastic progress compared to storing $\widetilde{R}$ in the CSR format when $n_M > 1$.

Fortunately, both the simultaneous diagonalization operations involved in the construction of the preconditioner and the matrix-vector product with the matrix $\widetilde{R}$, which consists of sparse matrices $F_{\alpha\beta}$ and $S_{\alpha\beta}$ stored in the CSR format, can be decomposed into a set of independent calculations. The storage of the matrices that diagonalize the preconditioner, $F_{\alpha\beta}$ and $S_{\alpha\beta}$, using distributed memory is also straightforward. Thus the most time-consuming and memory-intensive parts of the considered algorithm are highly parallelizable.

4   The Results

We use the quintic Hermite splines S_5^3 as a basis. The overlap rate (defined in the previous section) $r = 6$ as there are six nonzero functions in each grid interval. The spline nodes in the solution interval are chosen by mapping an equidistant grid [18] with some empirically selected function. The details can be found in [11]. We use the collocation at Gaussian points [4,7]. The code is written in C++. The parallelization of the program is achieved by using functions from the Intel MKL [1] mathematical library, which is a part of the Intel Parallel Studio XE 2019 Update 4 software package. The largest modulus eigenvalues in eigenvalue problem (15) are obtained by the ARPACK [15] implementation of the Implicitly Restarted Arnoldi Method (IRAM) [21,24]. The preconditioned GMRES algorithm [20] is used to solve the system of linear algebraic equations (SLAE) with matrix $H - E^* S$. The computations use complex arithmetic and are done on a six-core machine with an Intel Xeon X5675 processor and 32 GB of RAM. In the tables and figures, we use the notations

$$(\alpha\colon n_{x_\alpha}, n_{y_\alpha}, n_{z_\alpha};\ \beta\colon n_{x_\beta}, n_{y_\beta}, n_{z_\beta}),\quad (\alpha\colon R_{x_\alpha}, R_{y_\alpha};\ \beta\colon R_{x_\beta}, R_{y_\beta}) \tag{31}$$

for the basis space parameters, which are the number of basis functions and the lengths of the intervals they are defined on.

We used the helium atom system for test calculations of bound state energies and the positron-antiproton-electron $e^+ \bar{p} e^-$ system for scattering calculations. All calculations were done in atomic units.

The calculations of the bound states of atomic helium have a long history. Many methods specifically developed for this system give very accurate energy values. In our calculations, we treated this system in general as an ordinary three-body system. The results for the energy of the atomic helium were regarded as a benchmark. For this reason, the mass of the helium nucleus was considered infinite in the calculations to mimic the benchmark results [3]. There was a good agreement with the benchmark values; even more, our universal code did converge to these values. A relative error of the order of 10^{-8} was reached with a basis much smaller than the maximal possible size available on the used hardware.

Table 1 compares the approach suggested in the present paper with the straightforward approach based on the application of the direct algorithm implemented in the Intel MKL Pardiso solver [1] for solving the SLAE with the matrix $(H - E^* S)$ from (15) at each IRAM iteration. We can see that the Pardiso approach uses much more memory and CPU time, and they grow much faster with the number of basis functions than in the approach using the tensor product preconditioner.

Table 2 shows the performance of the algorithm for the high case $J = 10$. In this case, a set of twenty coupled 3D PDEs (8) was solved. We see from this table that a relative error of approximately 10^{-5} is reached with relatively small computer resources.

The $e^+ \bar{p} e^-$ scattering problem is complicated by both elastic and rearrangement processes. It is much less studied and is an active field of current research

Table 1. Comparison of the tensor product preconditioner approach and the Pardiso-based approach. In each computational experiment, we calculate two lower energy levels 2^1P and 3^1P (i.e., $J = 1$ and $\tau = 1$ states, symmetric with respect to the exchange of electrons) of the helium atom. The benchmark energy values are -2.12384308649810135925 and -2.05514636209194353689 a.u. [3]

Basis sizes	Tensor product preconditioner		Pardiso		E, a.u.
	Total memory/ $H - E^*S/$ Preconditioner size, GB	Calculation of matrices/ IRAM wall time, minutes	Total memory/ $H - E^*S$ size, GB	Calculation of matrices/ IRAM wall time, minutes	
(1: 22, 22, 9; 3: 19, 19, 12)	0.14/0.09/0.01	0.01/0.3	2.29/0.28	0.05/0.6	−2.12524 −2.05654
(1: 31, 31, 9; 3: 22, 22, 15)	0.25/0.16/0.02	0.02/0.7	5.31/0.55	0.04/1.9	−2.12365 −2.05495
(1: 40, 40, 12; 3: 25, 25, 18)	0.45/0.30/0.04	0.05/1.2	12.5/1.07	0.1/6.9	−2.12378 −2.05508
(1: 49, 49, 12; 3: 28, 28, 21)	0.68/0.45/0.06	0.08/1.9	21.3/1.62	0.1/14	−2.12385 −2.05513
(1: 58, 58, 12; 3: 28, 28, 21)	0.85/0.56/0.10	0.1/2.3	29.4/2.04	0.2/22	−2.12384 −2.05514

Table 2. The performance of the algorithm for the high-J case. We request in each computational experiment the ground and first excited state energies of the helium atom with $J = 10$ and $\tau = 1$, symmetric with respect to the exchange of electrons. The solution domains are (1: 280.0, 280.0; 3: 2.0, 2.0) a.u.

Basis sizes	Matrix linear size	Total memory/ $H - E^*S/$ Preconditioner size, GB	Calculation of matrices/ IRAM wall time, minutes	E, a.u
(1: 58, 58, 6; 3: 4, 4, 6)	223 080	0.62/0.17/0.11	0.1/6.3	−2.00398 −2.00332
(1: 88, 88, 9; 3: 7, 7, 9)	771 507	2.2/0.59/0.43	0.7/33	−2.00412 −2.00346
(1: 118, 118, 9; 3: 7, 7, 9)	1 383 327	4.1/1.06/1.01	1.9/60	−2.00413 −2.00347
(1: 118, 118, 12; 3: 7, 7, 12)	1 844 436	7.3/1.41/1.18	2.4/280	−2.00413 −2.00347

with significant applications in ongoing experiments (see [12] and references therein). In the calculations presented here, we keep the accuracy of cross sections within 1%.

Table 3. The performance of the algorithm for calculations of the scattering of antiproton $\bar{p}$ on positronium e^+e^- with total energy $E = -0.13828$. The solution domains are (1: 25.0, 110.0; 2: 30.0, 100.0) a.u.

Basis sizes	Matrix linear size	Total memory/ $H - E^*S$/ Preconditioner size, GB	Calculation of matrices/ Equation solution wall time, seconds
(1: 10,50,4; 2: 8,38,3)	287 616	0.92/0.44/0.10	7/22
(1: 15,75,4; 2: 12,55,3)	659 784	2.2/1.03/0.31	23/61
(1: 15,75,6; 2: 12,55,5)	1 022 928	4.4/1.58/0.45	34/299
(1: 20,100,6; 2: 15,70,5)	1 781 088	8.0/2.78/0.99	79/588
(1: 20,100,8; 2: 15,70,6)	2 303 232	8.4/3.58/1.25	100/373

Table 3 and Fig. 1 show the performance of the algorithm for scattering calculations in the system $e^+\bar{p}e^-$ in the Ore energy gap.

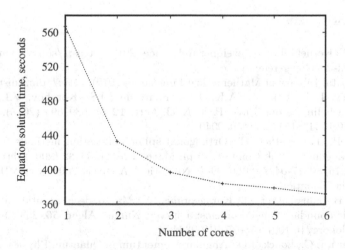

Fig. 1. The performance of the program for calculations of scattering of antiproton $\bar{p}$ on positronium e^+e^- with total energy $E = -0.13828$, with respect to the number of cores. The basis sizes are (1:20,100,8; 2:15,70,6). The solution domains are (1: 25.0, 110.0; 2: 30.0, 100.0) a.u.

5   Conclusions

We developed and implemented a highly efficient numerical scheme to solve the quantum three-body problem. The efficiency of our approach stems from the following factors: (1) the use of the Faddeev–Merkuriev equations, which allows for the simplification of the solution numerical approximation; (2) an advanced partial analysis that leads to a model-free reduction of the six-dimensional problem to a three-dimensional one; and (3) an elaborated numerical scheme that makes extensive use of the structure of the equations.

The numerical approach demonstrated clear advantages over the generic scheme that we implemented in earlier research. For example, as we can see from Table 1, the new approach uses only 1/20 of the memory required by the generic one, and this advantage becomes even more noticeable as the number of grid points increases.

However, our implementation of the scheme on parallel architectures has some shortcomings. Although the used operations are highly parallelizable, the performance saturates around six cores, as seen in Fig. 1. This limitation arises from the lack of a parallel implementation of the Arnoldi algorithm. In order to take full advantage of our numerical scheme, a parallelizable Krylov method is strongly needed.

Acknowledgments. The work of V. A. Gradusov and S. L. Yakovlev was supported by the Russian Science Foundation (grant № 23-22-00109). The research was carried out on the computational resources of the "Computer Center of SPbU" (http://cc.spbu.ru).

References

1. Intel Math Kernel Library Developer Reference (2019). https://software.intel.com/en-us/mkl-developer-reference-c
2. NIST Digital Library of Mathematical Functions (2019). http://dlmf.nist.gov/
3. Aznabayev, D.T., Bekbaev, A.K., Ishmukhamedov, I.S., Korobov, V.I.: Energy levels of a helium atom. Phys. Part. Nucl. Lett. **12**(5), 689–694 (2015). https://doi.org/10.1134/S1547477115050040
4. Bialecki, B., Fairweather, G.: Orthogonal spline collocation methods for partial differential equations. J. Comput. Appl. Math. **128**(1), 55–82 (2001). https://doi.org/10.1016/S0377-0427(00)00509-4. Numerical Analysis 2000, vol. VII: Partial Differential Equations
5. Bialecki, B., Fairweather, G., Karageorghis, A.: Matrix decomposition algorithms for elliptic boundary value problems: a survey. Numer. Algor. **56**, 253–295 (2011). https://doi.org/10.1007/s11075-010-9384-y
6. Biedenharn, L.C., Louck, J.D.: Angular Momentum in Quantum Physics. Addison-Wesley, Reading (1981)
7. de Boor, C., Swartz, B.: Collocation at Gaussian points. SIAM J. Numer. Anal. **10**(4), 582–606 (1973). https://doi.org/10.1137/0710052
8. Faddeev, L.D., Merkuriev, S.P.: Quantum Scattering Theory for Several Particle Systems. Kluwer, Dordrecht (1993)

9. Golub, G.H., Van Loan, C.F.: Matrix Computations. The Johns Hopkings University Press, Baltimore (2013)
10. Gradusov, V.A., Roudnev, V.A., Yarevsky, E.A., Yakovlev, S.L.: High resolution calculations of low energy scattering in $e^-e^+\bar{p}$ and $e^+e^-He^{++}$ systems via Faddeev-Merkuriev equations. J. Phys. B: At. Mol. Opt. Phys. **52**(5), 055,202 (2019). https://doi.org/10.1088/1361-6455/ab0143
11. Gradusov, V.A., Roudnev, V.A., Yarevsky, E.A., Yakovlev, S.L.: Solving the Faddeev-Merkuriev equations in total orbital momentum representation via spline collocation and tensor product preconditioning. Commun. Comput. Phys. **30**(1), 255–287 (2021). https://doi.org/10.4208/cicp.OA-2020-0097
12. Gradusov, V.A., Roudnev, V.A., Yarevsky, E.A., Yakovlev, S.L.: Theoretical study of reactions in the $e^-e^+\bar{p}$ three body system and antihydrogen formation cross sections. JETP Lett. **114**(1), 11–17 (2021). https://doi.org/10.1134/S0021364021130026
13. Kostrykin, V.V., Kvitsinsky, A.A., Merkuriev, S.P.: Faddeev approach to the three-body problem in total-angular-momentum representation. Few Body Syst. **6**, 97–113 (1989). https://doi.org/10.1007/BF01080553
14. Lazauskas, R.: Etude de la diffusion de particules lourdes sur des systèmes atomiques et nucléaires. Ph.D. thesis (2003). https://hal.archives-ouvertes.fr/tel-00004178
15. Lehoucq, R.B., Sorensen, D.C., Yang, C.: ARPACK Users Guide: Solution of Large Scale Eigenvalue Problems by Implicitly Restarted Arnoldi Methods. SIAM, Philadelphia (1998)
16. Merkuriev, S.P.: On the three-body Coulomb scattering problem. Ann. Phys. **130**(2), 395–426 (1980). https://doi.org/10.1016/0003-4916(80)90344-9
17. Messiah, A.: Quantum Mechanics. North-Holland, Amsterdam (1961)
18. Roudnev, V., Cavagnero, M.: Automatic grid construction for few-body quantum mechanical calculations. Comput. Phys. Commun. **182**(10), 2099 (2011). https://doi.org/10.1016/j.cpc.2011.05.003
19. Roudnev, V., Yakovlev, S.: Improved tensor-trick algorithm: application to helium trimer. Comput. Phys. Commun. **126**(1), 162–164 (2000). https://doi.org/10.1016/S0010-4655(00)00002-3
20. Saad, Y.: Iterative Methods for Sparse Linear Systems. SIAM, Philadelphia (2003)
21. Saad, Y.: Numerical Methods for Large Eigenvalue Problems. SIAM, Philadelphia (2011)
22. Schellingerhout, N.W., Kok, L.P., Bosveld, G.D.: Configuration-space Faddeev calculations: supercomputer accuracy on a personal computer. Phys. Rev. A **40**, 5568–5576 (1989). https://doi.org/10.1103/PhysRevA.40.5568
23. Scrinzi, A.: Helium in a cylindrically symmetric field. J. Phys. B: At. Mol. Opt. Phys. **29**(24), 6055–6068 (1996). https://doi.org/10.1088/0953-4075/29/24/012
24. Sorensen, D.C.: Implicit application of polynomial filters in a k-step Arnoldi method. SIAM J. Matrix Anal. Appl. **13**, 357–385 (1992). https://doi.org/10.1137/0613025
25. Varshalovich, D.A., Moskalev, A.N., Khersonsky, V.K.: Quantum Theory of Angular Momentum. World Scientific, Singapore (1989)
26. Yakovlev, S.L.: Quantum N-body problem: matrix structures and equations. Theor. Math. Phys. **181**(1), 1317–1338 (2014). https://doi.org/10.1007/s11232-014-0215-5
27. Yakovlev, S.L., Papp, Z.: The three-body Coulomb scattering problem in a discrete Hilbert-space basis representation. Theor. Math. Phys. **163**, 666–676 (2010). https://doi.org/10.1007/s11232-010-0049-8

Monitoring and Forecasting Crop Yields

Tatiana Makarovskikh$^{(\boxtimes)}$ ⓘ, Anatoly Panyukov ⓘ, and Mostafa Abotaleb ⓘ

South Ural State University, Chelyabinsk, Russian Federation
{Makarovskikh.T.A,paniukovav}@susu.ru

Abstract. We consider in this paper the problem of monitoring agricultural lands. The initial data for this are raster aerial photographs from a satellite or drone. Each tile of an image corresponds to a field area. The object under study corresponds to a certain set of tiles saved in seven bands (each band is saved in a separate raster file, and each tile has a value from 0 to 255). Satellite information is updated every 3–5 days. To monitor and forecast crop yields in the field, a time series for each tile is considered. The initial data consist of a list of vectors with lengths of about 100 elements (so many images can be obtained in one season). The number of vectors is arbitrary and depends on the size of the studied areas; moreover, it can vary. In this study, we consider (1) the application of an algorithm for finding a quasilinear autoregression equation with interdependent observable variables based on the generalized method of least deviations for a single tile or a set of tiles, and (2) the solution of the task flow for the entire population of tiles. This requires the parallel organization of the cache memory and the design of a database with the obtained characteristics for each considered object. We consider the scheme of this process parallelization and conduct experiments showing a 5- to 6-fold speedup on personal computers.

Keywords: Data analysis · Big data · Aerial monitoring · Parallel database · Forecasting algorithm · General least deviation method · Forecasting crops · Precision farming

1 Introduction

At present, our country is dealing with many imperative tasks related to the improvement of its security, competitiveness, and independence of production and products. Agriculture is one of such strategically important industries. Starting in the 2010s, digital technologies for precision farming (PF) have been gradually introduced into agriculture. The PF is multidisciplinary field of knowledge, so it is characterized by the complexity of scientific, engineering, agronomic, and management tasks. The existing methods and tools of PF have allowed some countries to quickly introduce an innovative development path to agriculture. The management of agricultural production with the help of computer technology, geoinformation technologies, and modern means of communication

© The Author(s), under exclusive license to Springer Nature Switzerland AG 2023
L. Sokolinsky and M. Zymbler (Eds.): PCT 2023, CCIS 1868, pp. 78–92, 2023.
https://doi.org/10.1007/978-3-031-38864-4_6

began to develop rapidly [21]. The implementation of PF is actively developing in Australia, Japan, Canada, Europe (in particular, Germany, Sweden, France, Spain, Denmark, and the UK), Argentina, Brazil, China, India, Malaysia, and Chile [11].

Most publications on PF in the world are devoted to the analysis of crop quality, the recognition of infected areas, etc. These articles usually present the results of experiments, however, it is not possible to make any comparison with developed approaches since the analysis deals with crops that are not cultivated in Russia, such as mango, orange, and kiwi, although tomatoes, potatoes, and corn, which are cultivated in our country, have also been considered. For example, the authors of [2] use the least mean square error (LMSE) on their data sets for recognition (healthy and decaying crops) and get an unprecedented analysis accuracy of 100%. However, after adding 10%, 20%, and 30% Gaussian noise, the resulting average recognition rates dropped significantly to 85%, 70%, and 25%, respectively. In [20], training samples were created for some areas in China by using historical maps of corn crops. The authors applied the feature optimization method to their data sets and obtained optimal characteristics at different stages of crop development. They also provided the structure schemes of the developed algorithms, therefore it seems possible to use their experience in the development of other algorithms and try to reproduce their algorithm for comparative analysis. Based on the results of computational experiments, we can assume that the described approach is quite flexible, and similar methods can be tested when analyzing the objects of our study (buckwheat and wheat crops). Nevertheless, this research is devoted only to recognition and classification and does not consider the dynamics of crop development.

A great deal of research on the dynamics of crop development both in Russia and in the rest of the world is conducted using machine-learning methods since they can catch the nonlinear relationships between predictors and yield on the regional level [16]. However, the main disadvantage of these methods is that they cannot produce adequate equations for the description of the examined process, and therefore the obtained results can only be applied to the examined area, so their use for another area requires neural network retraining. These papers present outstanding results for specified areas but do not suggest any general approach that can be used for other areas. There are several studies (see, for instance, [18]) that investigate the change of yield explanatory power of satellite-derived indicators but do not propose any models and do not present any original general approach that can be applied to any region, aside from the considered one, even after retraining.

Thus the tasks of image recognition and analysis of aerial photographs and datasets are not only a popular research topic but also an area that requires the development of new algorithms, high-quality computational experiments, and the creation of flexible algorithms that can be adapted to various shooting conditions, diverse crops, and different objects in the images. For example, to explore the possibility of retraining and using the developed model for the analysis of different types of objects. Moreover, in the context of this task, we deal with big data, but neither the problem of parallelization of computations nor its possibilities are considered in most papers. Thus all the papers on crop-yield forecasting and analysis can be divided into the following types: statistical studies using and representing different combinations of classical approaches (for instance, [16,18]), machine learning models mostly used for recognition of some information (for example, [2,19,20]), and mathematical models, in particular those dealing with elementary ordinary differential equations [6]. We see that there is a lack of research containing the complex approach with the development and analysis of the applied software suitable for solving the crop yield forecasting task.

For that reason, we do not speak in our paper about the recognition process itself and focus instead on the analysis of the collected data and consider one of the ways to save data about different agricultural objects in a database used for providing the quasilinear recurrence equations that describe and forecast the crop development. In the first section of the paper, we discuss the data representation suitable for running our modeling algorithm. The second section is devoted to the presentation of our general least deviation method, which produces high-quality quasilinear difference equations adequately describing the process under consideration. In the third section, we consider the identification of the general least deviation model (GLDM) for large task flows, which can be used for obtaining the model coefficients for large numbers of objects simultaneously. The last section of the paper is devoted to computational experiments aimed at exploring the speedup of calculations for datasets of different sizes. This approach makes it possible to analyze large numbers of objects simultaneously and get the model coefficients using numerical information obtained from aerial photographs.

2   Data Organization

A concept of data organization somewhat similar to the one used in our approach is considered in [3–5]. The authors of these papers propose a method of element-by-element image analysis for the formation of the linear contour of objects depicted in aerial photographs. The method makes it possible to recognize objects by their formal features, allows the analysis of more details and properties of the objects during the process of recognition, and also improves the quality and accuracy of the recognition. Unfortunately, aside from the algorithm itself, the authors do not provide any additional but very important information. There are no data on the efficiency of the algorithm, nor do the authors supply information on the time of work with graphic files of large dimensions, the results of computational experiments, or the accuracy of the detection of objects. Like many other authors, they restrict themselves to recognition and do not conduct further analysis of the state of the recognized objects depending on the time.

2.1   The Data Structure for Aerial Photography Representation

The data used in the analysis is obtained from the process shown in Fig. 1. In this paper, we discuss the last three blocks of the scheme, which involve time series analysis.

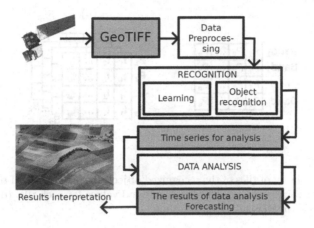

Fig. 1. The scheme of execution of the analysis system

We can use an image made by a satellite or a drone. It may be saved using a set of bands or it may be a single image. In any case, it is a single raster image or a set of raster images. In our approach to data organization, we consider the general case. Assume we have a satellite image. In our example, we use Sentinel free images from [1]. This web service offers images from all over the world, taken from January 2017 until the present day. This means that by saving images for the same object we can explore its state over the course of five years. Once we know the boundary of one object, we can save the vector of tiles belonging to the interior of the outer contour (lake or field) and the exterior of the inner contour (islands), starting from the upper left corner. Figure 2(a) shows how the tiles are numbered. The grey tiles do not belong to the recognized image. This data organization may be implemented for different types of objects such as lakes and islands, crop fields and forests, etc. As soon as the information from a multispectral camera mounted on a satellite or unmanned aerial vehicle (UAV) is saved in several bands (seven bands in total), we should save the vectors of tiles belonging to the considered object as follows (see Fig. 2(b)). Let P_i be the value of the color for a single tile i and assume it can vary from 0 to 255. We can normalize these data according to the formula $p_i = P_i/255$, so we obtain a number $p_i \in [0; 1]$. After obtaining these vectors, we can construct the vectors of color values each tile, the separate vector for each band (Fig. 2(c)). Thus we obtain a large number of very short vectors since the number of bands $k \approx 7$. If we use a 4K or 12K one-band camera for UAV, then $k = 1$.

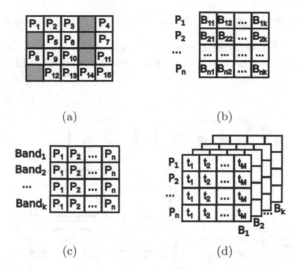

Fig. 2. (a) Numbering of tiles of the recognized object. (b) The vector of tiles belonging to the object for each band. (c) The vector of band values for each tile. (d) The matrix of values for each tile depending on the time

Proceeding this way, we obtain the values of each band for each tile. So, we have the spectral information for each area corresponding to each tile. If we need to consider the process over time, we can construct a three-dimensional matrix as follows (see Fig. 2(d)): for each tile of the recognized image, we save the time values $t_1, t_2, \ldots, t_M$.

Since the satellite images are provided every 3–5 days, the total number M of images is approximately 100–150 per year, provided that the images are taken independently of the season (for example, for the recognition of waterlogged lands), and 30–40 if we speak of seasonal research (for example, the vegetation of crops, deciduous-forest research, etc.) The number of tiles N depends on the real size of the recognized object and may vary from 1 to 10^6. Thus, to describe the dynamic process for each tile of the recognized object, we need the coefficients for N models. Since $N = \overline{1, 10^6}$, the calculation of model coefficients is a time-consuming process. To save time, we can run this process in parallel. In the section of this paper devoted to the experiments, we explore this case.

2.2   The Database of Objects Under Consideration

To save the data about the recognized geographical objects (lakes, crops, forests), we designed a database consisting of two tables (see Fig. 3).

The table OBJECT contains information about a single object, for example, a field, forest, lake, or road. It has a vector of Pixels belonging to the object and some additional information INFO, saved in a separate table or database. This information is very important for consumers but has no value for the execution of the model identification algorithm or forecasting functions. This INFO contains

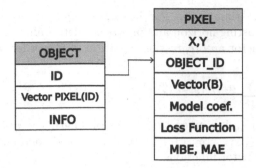

Fig. 3. The structure of the database for saving the information about the objects under consideration

such data as the owner of the object, some legal and economic data, values identifying the quality of the object, and so on. If we need any information from this set for further research, we transfer it to the tables under consideration or construct additional tables.

The table PIXEL contains numerical information about a single tile of an object. The table OBJECT is connected to this table through the field Object_ID, which identifies the object to which the tile belongs. One tile belongs to one object, an object may have many tiles. Each tile has a vector B of values for each band; we save Model coefficients, the value of the Loss function, the errors of modeling MBE and MAE, and the GPS coordinates (X,Y) of the tile.

Let us discuss the method used for obtaining the model coefficients, the loss function, and the errors of modeling.

3   Generalized Least Deviation Method (GLDM)

Let us consider the time series describing a dynamic process. We aim to construct the determinate quasilinear model adequately representing the considered process. This model can be used in the analysis of the same events in the future and for defining some dependencies of the investigated process. In terms of crop yield forecasting, we can explore a time series consisting of 10–100 points during one vegetation period to obtain the model of crop development in a specified area. Using this model, we can analyze and forecast crop yields for future periods to optimize their quality and quantity. In this section, we consider a model for a single time series.

There are many known classical approaches to the analysis of time series: ARIMA, Holt's method, BATS, etc. A large number of researchers prefer various machine-learning approaches. It should be noted that linear autoregressive models have a small forecasting horizon, and the construction of adequate non-linear models and/or neural networks may not be possible for technical reasons (such as very short time series, for instance). Quasilinear models allow for increasing the forecasting horizon and produce a determinate model. In general, the quasilinear n-factor autoregression equation of the order m can be written as

$$\sum_{j=1}^{n} a_j g_j(\{y_{t-k}\}_{k=1}^{m}) = y_t, \quad \{a_j\}_{j=1}^{n} \in \mathbb{R}^n, \tag{1}$$

where $\{y_t \in \mathbb{R}\}_{t=-1-m}^{T}$ is a given time series of length $T + m \geq (1 + 3m + m^2)$ (input data); $a_1, a_2, a_3 \ldots, a_m \in \mathbb{R}$ are determined factors, and $g_j(\cdot)$, $j = 1, 2, \ldots n$ are given factor functions.

The details of the considered approach are given in [13]. It consists in determining the parameters of the recurrence Eq. 1. The algorithm works as follows. The GLDM algorithm [15] takes a time series $\{y_t \in \mathbb{R}\}_{t=-1-m}^{T}$ of length $T + m \geq (1 + 3m + m^2)$ as input data and determines the factors $a_1, a_2, a_3 \ldots, a_m \in \mathbb{R}$ by solving the optimization problem

$$\sum_{t=1}^{T} \arctan \left| \sum_{j=1}^{n(m)} a_j g_j(\{y_{t-k}\}_{k=1}^{m}) - y_t \right| \rightarrow \min_{\{a_j\}_{j-1}^{n(m)} \subset \mathbb{R}} \tag{2}$$

The Cauchy distribution

$$F(\xi) = \frac{1}{\pi} \arctan(\xi) + \frac{1}{2}$$

has the maximum entropy among the distributions of random variables without mathematical expectation and variance. It is for this reason that the function $\arctan(\cdot)$ is used as the loss function.

Let us consider an m-th order model with a quadratic nonlinearity. Then the basic set $g_j(\cdot)$ may contain the following functions:

$$\begin{aligned} g_{(k)}(\{y_{t-k}\}_{k=1}^{m}) &= y_{t-k}, \\ g_{(kl)}(\{y_{t-k}\}_{k=1}^{m}) &= y_{t-k} \cdot y_{t-l}, \end{aligned} \quad k = 1, 2, \ldots, m; \ l = k, k+1, \ldots, m. \tag{3}$$

In this case, it is obvious that $n(m) = 2m + C_m^2 = m(m+3)/2$, and the number of $g(\cdot)$ functions can be arbitrary.

The predictor produces a family of difference equations of order m with indices $t = 1, 2, \ldots, T - 1, T$,

$$\overline{y[t]}_\tau = \sum_{j=1}^{n(m)} a_j^* g_j \left(\{\overline{y[t]}_{\tau-k}\}_{k=1}^{m} \right), \\ \tau = t, t+1, t+2, t+3, \ldots, T-1, T, T+1, \ldots, \tag{4}$$

for lattice functions $\overline{y[t]}$ with values $\overline{y[t]}_\tau$, which are interpreted as the forecasts for y_τ constructed at time moment t. To find the values of the function $\overline{y[t]}$, we use the solution of the Cauchy problem for Eq. (4) with initial conditions

$$\overline{y[t]}_{t-1} = y_{t-1}, \ \overline{y[t]}_{t-2} = y_{t-2}, \ldots, \ \overline{y[t]}_{t-m} = y_{t-m} \\ t = 1, 2, \ldots, T-1, T. \tag{5}$$

So we have the set $\overline{Y}_\tau = \left\{ \overline{y[t]}_\tau \right\}_{t=1}^{T}$ of possible prediction values of y_τ. Later we use this set to estimate the probabilistic characteristics of the y_τ value.

Problem (2) of GLDM estimation is a concave optimization problem. GLDM estimates are robust to the presence of correlation of values in $\{y_t \in \mathbb{R}\}_{t=-1-m}^{T}$, and (with appropriate settings) are the best for probability distributions of errors with heavier (than the normal distribution) tails [12]. All the above shows that the algorithm of WLDM estimation can be used to solve the identification problem. The results established in [14] allow us to reduce the problem of GLDM estimation to an iterative procedure with WLDM estimates [13].

Theorem 1. *The sequence* $\{(A^{(k)}, z^{(k)})\}_{k=1}^{\infty}$ *constructed by the GLDM-estimator algorithm converges to the global minimum* (a^*, z^*) *of problem (2).*

The description of the GLDM-estimator algorithm shows that its computational complexity is proportional to that of the algorithm for solving primal and/or dual WLDM problems. Numerous computational experiments show that the average number of iterations of the GLDM-estimator algorithm is equal to the number of coefficients in the identified equation. If this hypothesis turns out to be true, then the computational complexity of the solution to practical problems cannot exceed

$$O\big((n(m))^3\, T + n(m) \cdot T^2\big).$$

It is necessary to take into account that the search for and the finding of the high-order autoregression equation come with their own specific conditions. One of these conditions, in particular, is the high sensitivity of the algorithm to rounding errors. To eliminate the possibility of error in the calculations, it is necessary to accurately perform the basic arithmetic operations in the field of rational numbers and supplement them with parallelization.

The suggested predictor produces the family of difference equations (4) of the order m with indices $t = 1, 2, \ldots, T-1, T$ for the lattice functions $\overline{y[t]}$ with values $\overline{y[t]}_\tau$, which are interpreted as the forecasts for y_τ constructed at time moment t. To find the values of the function $\overline{y[t]}$, we rely on the solution of the Cauchy problem for Eq. (4) with initial conditions (5). So we have the set $\overline{Y}_\tau = \left\{ \overline{y[t]}_\tau \right\}_{t=1}^{T}$ of possible prediction values of y_τ. Later we use this set to estimate the probabilistic characteristics of the y_τ value.

To assess the quality of the obtained coefficients, we use two errors: MAE and MBE. In the realm of statistics, the mean absolute error (MAE) is a measure of the errors between paired observations expressing the same time series:

$$\text{MAE} = \frac{\sum_{t=3}^{\text{minFH}} \left| y[t] - \overline{y[t]} \right|}{\text{minFH}},$$

where minFH is a reasonable forecasting horizon. The mean bias error (MBE) is the exact difference between the predicted value and the actual value without any math function as the absolute value or square root applied to it:

$$\text{MBE} = \frac{\sum_{t=3}^{\text{minFH}} \left(y[t] - \overline{y[t]} \right)}{\text{minFH}}.$$

Thus, in terms of the analysis of aerial photographs, the suggested algorithm produces a mathematical model describing the process development for each tile. This is useful if we compare a set of models with each other and then detect those corresponding to areas with well-developed crops. Moreover, using model data from previous periods, we can compare them with data for the current period and forecast the development of the crops in the current vegetation period.

4   Parallel Prospects of the GLDM

Various parallel approaches to the parallelization of different least squares methods using multicore architectures are discussed in [9]. The authors of this paper present an efficient procedure for solving least squares sub-problems by the active-set algorithm. The authors of [17] discuss how to employ special features of ARIMA and multilayer perceptron (MLPs) models to model linear and nonlinear patterns in the data simultaneously and to yield the best performance with reasonable computational costs. Most papers considering parallelization, for example, [8], discuss the problem with long time series. The same task is considered in [10], where we explored the parallelization process for a single GLDM algorithm working with a single time series (for example, the time series for epidemic spreading, weather data, and others). We show that this task is poorly parallelized when using the OpenMP approach.

In the present paper, we consider one or more time series for each tile, therefore the initial data is a list of vectors of lengths less than 100 elements (so many images can be obtained in a year). The number of vectors is arbitrary and depends on the size of the studied areas; moreover, it can vary from 1 to about 10^6. In this case, the technology of parallelization is different. We parallelize the calculations for different tiles, so there is no need to run the GLDM algorithm itself in parallel for short time series. Thus we parallelize the calculations using the algorithm for different vectors. Both technologies, OpenMP and MPI, can be used for this.

The scheme of the organization of parallel calculations is shown in Fig. 4. In general, the number of vectors n is greater than the number of threads (or parallel processes) t. Then the next process to be evaluated is passed to the first free process. We have one level of parallelization with t processes. For calculations, we use the asynchronous version of the calculation scheme. A significant disadvantage of the synchronous version of the flowchart is the possible downtime of all process nodes, except for the root one. Downtime can occur if some of the processes finish solving their subtasks and send data to the parent before

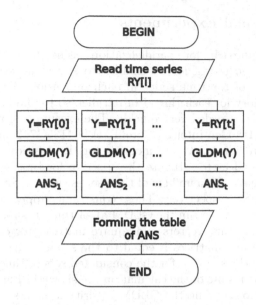

Fig. 4. The scheme of running identification of model parameters in parallel

the rest since the parent will create new subtasks for these processes only after receiving solutions from all processes.

Algorithm for the Root Process

Step 1. Select an array of vectors of the initial time series RY.

Step 2. Send one RY[i] vector to each of the free subordinate processes.

Step 3. Wait for a decision from each of the subtasks generated by the subordinate processes and receive data from each of them (an ANS array consisting of the model coefficients a_i, the loss function L values, and the errors MAE and MBE). Accept the subtask solution ANS from any process that sent data.

Step 4. Check if all subtasks are solved. If solved, finish running the algorithm. Otherwise, go to step 2.

Algorithm for the Subordinate Process

Step 0. Take from the parent process a point with the time series vector Y.

Step 1. Solve the task using the GLDM-estimator algorithm:

1.1. Generate the basic set of $g_{(*)}$ functions.

1.2. Form the projection matrix SST.

1.3. Perform the Jordan–Gauss transformation.

1.4. Run the procedure of estimation using the Generalized Least Deviation Method. Save the model coefficients a_i and the value of the loss function L to the ANS structure.

1.5. Calculate the average prediction errors MAE and MBA and save the values to the ANS structure.

Step 2. Pass the calculation result (i.e., the ANS structure) to the parent process.

5   Computational Experiments

The considered approach for parallelization using OpenMP is memory-consuming due to the use of local variables to store the vectors and square matrices of the size of the time series in each dimension. These variables are created in the memory for each thread in parallel, so the limit of memory used by the application is exceeded very quickly. The execution of the algorithm on a local computer (11th Gen Intel(R) Core(TM) i5-1135G7, 2.40 GHz, 2.42 GHz, 16 GB of RAM) providing 2 GB of memory for the solutions with the Visual C++ compiler allowed us to estimate the speedup for time series of 100, 300, 500, and 1000 elements. The numbers of time series suitable for calculation were 1000, 300, 200, and 80, respectively. These constraints appear due to the limits of the used heap memory. To run the GLDM algorithm, it is required to allocate memory for supplementary vectors and square matrices for each thread separately. The size of these matrices is equal to the squared size of the examined vector. We examine the speedup for the considered sets of time series on a personal computer. The results of the calculation are shown in Fig. 5. We count the time required only for running the GLDM algorithm for a set of data vectors, without considering input and output functions. The speedup value in this case is obtained by the following formula:

$$S = \frac{T_1}{T_n},$$

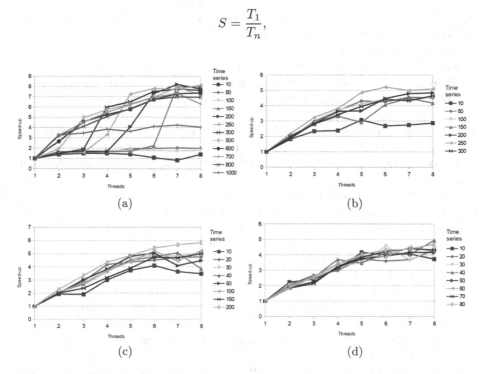

Fig. 5. The graph of speedup for time series: (a) length 100; (b) length 300; (c) length 500; (d) length 1000

where S is the speedup, T_1 is the calculation time when using only one thread, and T_n is the calculation time for n threads, $n = \overline{2,8}$. It is easy to see that the growth of the length of the time series makes the speedup value almost constant for any number of time series vectors in the initial data. On the other hand, the best results for short time series (of length 100 in the considered case) are obtained for 500–800 time series vectors; then, after increasing the number of vectors, the speedup significantly drops (because the memory is used at its limits in this case). These fluctuations can be explained by the size of the single task. It is very short and takes a very short time for solving, but the solution leads to heavy time overheads; this fact is also taken into account when calculating the performance. This assumption is confirmed by Figs. 5(b) and 5(c) with the longer time series. We see that the fluctuations of speedup become smaller with the growth of the time series length.

Considering the specific meaning of the problem statement, we see that time series of length less than 100 can appear in processes related to the development of crops because the vegetation period in the Russian Federation starts in March or April and ends in September or October (in some regions), so its length spans approximately 100 days. To obtain the model of crop development, we need to get the data on a daily basis. As for time series of length 300, they correspond to events observed during one year. Such data are used, for example, in the study of waterlogged lands, if the information about this can be observed without any dependency on the time of the year and weather, using images with calculated NDVI[1] for it.

Thus the experiment shows that the OpenMP approach is suitable for small sets of time series, whereas the MPI approach should be considered for more efficient use of the application memory. The task of efficiently using the cache memory is an open question and a topic for further research. Since the application running on a personal computer copes with 50–150 time series (remember that each time series corresponds to one tile) during one run, some additional approaches for memory use should be developed to analyze all the considered tiles. Perhaps there are some techniques for merging and classifying tiles with similar model parameters in one cluster. These will be the topics of future research devoted to the optimization of resources.

The results obtained in the experiment show that it is possible to develop a parallel personal application for laptops and/or mobile phones using the resources of these devices at maximum and to get the result faster by a factor of 5–6 since the time difference when using a personal computer for the calculation of large datasets will be essential. Taking into account that we obtain new data for the considered dynamical process in 24–72 h, this time is the limit for calculations, and this limit is achieved for 10^7 time series when using one thread, and

---

[1] The normalized difference vegetation index (NDVI) is a numerical indicator of the quality and quantity of vegetation in a field area. It is calculated from satellite images and depends on how plants reflect and absorb light waves of different wavelengths. This index can also be calculated for images from a 4K or 12K camera or a special NDVI camera.

for $(5 \cdot 10^7)$ objects when using 7–8 threads on a personal computer. This amount of data is enough for analysis on a personal computer. As for corporations considering far more objects, it is reasonable to use the resources of supercomputers (see, for example, [7]).

6   Conclusions

The computational experiments have shown that the GLDM-estimator algorithm we have considered in this research can be either parallelized or used for calculations with sets of large numbers of time series. In the last case, we parallelized the processes one by one. This approach may be used in real-life cases to construct models for the forecast of crops for sets of agricultural lands or areas with different properties and vegetation dynamics. As we see from the experiments, even in the case of modern personal computers, the numbers of objects under consideration may vary from 1000 for time series of length 100 to 80 for time series of length 1000. This means that our approach can be used by rather large companies dealing with 100–1000 agricultural objects in the course of one season. If the length of time series for one vegetation period is short, then we can rapidly calculate the model coefficients even using a PC or mobile phone without remote servers.

We obtained a 5- to 6-fold speedup using a personal computer. This is an indication that the algorithm can be implemented for desktop solutions using approximately 10^3 time series. Nevertheless, this solution requires very careful handling of heap memory because it is used at its upper limits. Thus we can anticipate the following directions for further research: (1) explore the possibilities and efficiency of the use of MPI (see algorithms in Sect. 4) and conduct computational experiments on the use of this technology and, possibly, the hybrid technology MPI+OpenMP; (2) develop a data clusterization algorithm to reduce the number of time series.

It should be noted that the images from which the initial data is obtained can be periodically characterized by high levels of cloudiness. Filtering cloudy images results in insufficient data for most Russian regions and does not solve the problem of missing data in some images. Therefore, it is possible that algorithms for recovering missing data in cloudy images will be required at further stages of research. Some related approaches are considered in [22].

References

1. Sentinel hub EO browser (2023). https://apps.sentinel-hub.com/eo-browser
2. Alshahrani, A., Manal, A., Al-Abadi, A., Al-Malki, A.: Ashour Automated System for Crops Recognition and Classification. In book. https://doi.org/10.4018/978-1-5225-1022-2.ch003
3. Burmistrov, A., Salnikov, I.: Information model of the distinguishing features of images on aerial photographs of rural areas. In: XXI Century: Results of the Past and Problems of the Present Plus, vol. 3, no. (19), pp. 41–45 (2014). (in Russian)

4. Burmistrov, A., Salnikov, I.: Method of element-by-element analysis of color images for the formation of distinctive features in the form of linear contours. In: XXI Century: Results of the Past and Problems of the Present Plus, vol. 1, no. 3(25), pp. 29–34 (2015). (in Russian)
5. Burmistrov, A., Salnikov, I.: The method of forming linear contours on aerial photographs of rural areas. Mod. Probl. Sci. Educ. **5**, 152–157 (2013). (in Russian)
6. Bukhovets, A.G., Semin, E.A., Kostenko, E.I., Yablonovskaya, S.I.: Modelling of the dynamics of the NDVI vegetation index of winter wheat under the conditions of the CFD. Bull. Voronezh State Agrarian Univ. **2**, 186–199 (2018). https://doi.org/10.17238/issn2071-2243.2018.2.186. (in Russian)
7. Dolganina, N., Ivanova, E., Bilenko, R., Rekachinsky, A.: HPC resources of south ural state university. In: Sokolinsky, L., Zymbler, M. (eds.) PCT 2022. Communications in Computer and Information Science, vol. 1618, pp. 43–55. Springer, Cham (2022). https://doi.org/10.1007/978-3-031-11623-0_4
8. Galicia, A., Talavera-Llames, R., Troncoso, A., Koprinska, I., Martínez-Álvarez, F.: Multi-step forecasting for big data time series based on ensemble learning. Knowl.-Based Syst. **163**, 830–841 (2019). https://doi.org/10.1016/j.knosys.2018.10.009
9. Luo, Y., Duraiswami, R.: Efficient parallel nonnegative least squares on multicore architectures. SIAM J. Sci. Comput. **33**(5), 2848–2863 (2011). https://doi.org/10.1137/100799083
10. Makarovskikh, T., Abotaleb, M.: Investigation of parallelism possibilities for forecasting using quasilinear recurrence equation, pp. 49–62 (2022)
11. Mondal, P., Basu, M.: Adoption of precision agriculture technologies in India and in some developing countries: scope, present status and strategies. Progr. Nat. Sci. **19**(6), 659–666 (2009). https://doi.org/10.1016/j.pnsc.2008.07.020
12. Panyukov, A., Tyrsin, A.: Stable parametric identification of vibratory diagnostics objects. J. Vibroeng. **10**(2), 142–146 (2008). http://elibrary.ru/item.asp?id=14876532
13. Panyukov, A.V., Makarovskikh, T.A., Abotaleb, M.S.: Forecasting with using quasilinear recurrence equation. In: Olenev, N., Evtushenko, Y., Khachay, M., Malkova, V. (eds.) OPTIMA 2022. CCIS, vol. 1739, pp. 183–195. Springer, Cham (2022). https://doi.org/10.1007/978-3-031-22990-9_13
14. Panyukov, A.V., Mezaal, Y.A.: Stable estimation of autoregressive model parameters with exogenous variables on the basis of the generalized least absolute deviation method. In: IFAC-PapersOnLine, vol. 51, pp. 1666–1669 (2018). https://doi.org/10.1016/j.ifacol.2018.08.217. Open access
15. Panyukov, A.V., Mezaal, Y.A.: Improving of the identification algorithm for a quasilinear recurrence equation. In: Olenev, N., Evtushenko, Y., Khachay, M., Malkova, V. (eds.) OPTIMA 2020. CCIS, vol. 1340, pp. 15–26. Springer, Cham (2020). https://doi.org/10.1007/978-3-030-65739-0_2
16. Paudel, D., et al.: Machine learning for regional crop yield forecasting in Europe. Field Crops Res. **276**, 108377 (2022). https://doi.org/10.1016/j.fcr.2021.108377
17. Rahimi, Z., Khashei, M.: A least squares-based parallel hybridization of statistical and intelligent models for time series forecasting. Comput. Ind. Eng. **118**, 44–53 (2018). https://doi.org/10.1016/j.cie.2018.02.023
18. Ronchetti, G., et al.: Remote sensing crop group-specific indicators to support regional yield forecasting in Europe, agriculture (2023). https://doi.org/10.1016/j.compag.2023.107633

19. Tokarev, K.E., Lebed, N.I., Kuzmin, V.A., Chernyavsky, A.N.: Theory and technologies of irrigation control for crops based on information technologies decision support and mathematical modelling. News of the Nizhnevolzhsky Agro-University Complex: Science and Higher Professional Education. Technical Science. Agricultural Engineering 4(60), 433–448, (2020). (in Russian)
20. Wei, M., et al.: Investigating the potential of sentinel-2 MSI in early crop identification in northeast china. Remote Sens. 14(8), 1928 (2022). https://doi.org/10.3390/rs14081928
21. Yakushev, V., Yakushev, V.: Mathematical models and methods of realizing information technology procedures in precision agriculture. Russ. Agric. Sci. 34(4), 280–283 (2008). https://doi.org/10.3103/s1068367408040216
22. Zymbler, M., Polonsky, V., Yurtin, A.: On one method of imputation missing values of a streaming time series in real time. Bull. South Ural State Univ. Ser.: Comput. Math. Softw. Eng. 10(4), 5–25 (2021). https://doi.org/10.14529/cmse210401

On Parallel Multigrid Methods for Solving Systems of Linear Algebraic Equations

Maxim Batalov[1,2]([✉]), Yana Gurieva[1], Valery Ilyin[1], and Artyom Petukhov[1]

[1] Institute of Computational Mathematics and Mathematical Geophysics,
Siberian Branch of the Russian Academy of Sciences, Novosibirsk, Russia
makcum1990@list.ru, {yana,petukhov}@lapasrv.sscc.ru, ilin@sscc.ru
[2] Novosibirsk State University, Novosibirsk, Russia

Abstract. In this paper, we consider algebraic multigrid methods (AMG) for solving symmetric positive-definite systems of linear algebraic equations (SLAE) with sparse high-order matrices arising from finite difference approximations of two- and three-dimensional boundary value problems on regular grids. Also, we investigate iterative algorithms in Krylov subspaces with preconditioning based on incomplete factorization with recursive ordering of variables defined on a sequence of embedded grids. We use the conjugate direction method, in which the solution of the auxiliary SLAE with its preconditioning matrix includes the conventional stages of restriction, coarse-grid correction, and prolongation. We show how additional preconditioning based on the principles of symmetric successive over-relaxation (SSOR) allows carrying out *presmoothing* and *postsmoothing* operations. Also, we discuss the parallelization effectiveness of the proposed algorithms with different numbers of embedded grids. Furthermore, we present the results of preliminary experimental investigations demonstrating the efficiency of the implemented methods and analyze the possibilities of generalizing the developed approaches to solving a wider class of problems.

Keywords: Large sparse SLAE · Algebraic multigrid method · Krylov subspace · Incomplete factorization algorithm · Recursive ordering · Parallelization of algorithms

1 Introduction

Multigrid methods for solving systems of linear algebraic equations are a specialized class of algorithms oriented to the fast implementation of iterative processes for discrete problems with large sparse matrices. Such matrices often arise from the approximation of multidimensional boundary value problems for partial differential equations by the finite-volume or finite-element methods on a sequence of embedded grids. Such approaches theoretically provide asymptotically optimal order efficiency and also demonstrate a record performance in solving many

© The Author(s), under exclusive license to Springer Nature Switzerland AG 2023
L. Sokolinsky and M. Zymbler (Eds.): PCT 2023, CCIS 1868, pp. 93–109, 2023.
https://doi.org/10.1007/978-3-031-38864-4_7

practical problems using existing software packages (see [1–20] and the literature cited there). However, the computational principles applied in these cases are poorly adapted for scalable parallelization since they are based on the sequential solution of problems with recursively decreasing dimensionality, which causes idle time of a large number of processors at certain stages. This factor allegedly confirms a well-known pessimistic thesis that good algorithms are poorly parallelizable. Nevertheless, experimental research in this direction is constantly going on (see, for instance, [15,19]).

The traditional interpretation of algebraic multigrid methods as a recursive application of two-grid methods was developed during the last decades. Many of these methods are determined by different types of smoothing, restriction, coarse-grid correction, and prolongation operators, with the possible use of so-called V-loops or W-loops and with the formation of preconditioned iterative processes in Krylov subspaces (see, e.g., [7,21,22]).

This paper is devoted to the performance analysis of some parallel multigrid techniques for solving two- and three-dimensional boundary value problems formulated for second-order elliptic differential equations on regular embedded grids (see [23]). The algorithms we propose are based on a recursive ordering of the variables admitting a block triangular representation of the generated SLAEs, with solutions produced by conjugate direction methods with different types of preconditioning.

The paper is structured as follows. In Sect. 2, we describe multigrid methods for two-dimensional problems on rectangular grids. Section 3 is devoted to three-dimensional problems. In Sect. 4, we outline the parallelization efficiency of the proposed algorithms. Section 5 presents a discussion of the results of preliminary numerical experiments on a representative series of methodical two- and three-dimensional examples. Finally, we consider the issues associated with generalizing the obtained results to a wider class of problems.

2   Some Variants of Multigrid Approaches for Solving Two-Dimensional Problems

Let $\Omega = (x_0, x_{N^x+1}) \times (y_0, y_{N^y+1})$ be a computational rectangular domain equipped with a rectangular grid Ω^h:

$$\Omega^h : x = x_i, \quad i = 1, \ldots, N^x, \quad y = y_j, \quad j = 1, \ldots, N^y.$$

On this grid, consider a system of $N = N^x N^y$ five-point equations

$$(Au)_{i,j} = a_{i,j}^{(0)} u_{i,j} - a_{i,j}^{(1)} u_{i-1,j} - a_{i,j}^{(2)} u_{i,j-1} - a_{i,j}^{(3)} u_{i+1,j} - a_{i,j}^{(4)} u_{i,j+1} = f_{i,j}, \quad i,j \in \Omega^h,$$
$$a_{1,j}^{(1)} = a_{i,1}^{(2)} = a_{N^x,j}^{(3)} = a_{i,N^y}^{(4)} = 0, \tag{1}$$

which approximate a boundary value problem in $\bar{\Omega} \in \Omega \cup \Gamma$ with some boundary conditions (for example, Dirichlet ones) for a second-order elliptic differential equation (see examples in [23]). In the case of natural ordering of the nodes, the numbers of the components of the vector $u = \{u_k\}$ can be linked with i and j

indices by the relation $k = i + (j-1)N^x$. We assume that the matrix A in (4) is a Stieltjes one, i.e., a symmetric positive-definite matrix with nonnegative elements $a_{i,j}^{(0)}, \ldots, a_{i,j}^{(4)}$ (it also has the monotonicity property $A^{-1} \geq 0$; the inequality is understood as it holds in an element-by-element manner). To solve SLAE (1), we construct a sequence of m embedded rectangular grids $\Omega^h = \Omega_1^h \supset \Omega_2^h \supset \ldots \supset \Omega_m^h$ so that each grid Ω_l^h at the l-th level is obtained by adding the coordinate lines that divide into half the steps of the sparser grid at the level $(l+1)$. The boundaries of the initial grid along the coordinate lines x_0, y_0, x_{N^x+1}, and y_{N^v+1} remain the boundaries for the grids of all levels, and the number of internal nodes within each of them equals $N_l = N_l^x N_l^y$, $N_{l+1}^x = N^x/2^l$, and $N_{l+1}^y = N^y/2^l$.

The set of grid nodes of each l-th level and the sets of corresponding vector components are decomposed into two subsets, one of which is the set of the next $(l+1)$-th level, resulting in recursive structures of the following kind:

$$\Omega_1^h = \bar{\Omega}_1^h \supset \Omega_2^h = \bar{\Omega}_1^h \supset \bar{\Omega}_2^h \ldots \supset \bar{\Omega}_{m-1}^h \supset \Omega_m^h,$$
$$u = u_1 = (\bar{u}_1^\mathsf{T} u_2^\mathsf{T})^\mathsf{T} = (\bar{u}_1^\mathsf{T} \bar{u}_2^\mathsf{T} \ldots \bar{u}_{m-1}^\mathsf{T} u_m^\mathsf{T})^\mathsf{T},$$
$$\Omega_l^h = \bar{\Omega}_l^h \supset \Omega_{l+1}^h, \quad u_l = (\bar{u}_l^\mathsf{T} u_{l+1}^\mathsf{T}), \tag{2}$$
$$u_l \in \mathcal{R}^{N_l}, \quad \bar{u}_l \in \mathcal{R}^{\bar{N}_l}, \quad N_l = \bar{N}_l + N_{l+1},$$
$$N = N_1 = \bar{N}_1 + N_2 = \bar{N}_1 + \bar{N}_2 + \ldots + \bar{N}_{m-1} + N_m.$$

Grid nodes and vector components are numbered (ordered recursively) uniformly for each l-th level: first, the components $\bar{\Omega}_l^h$ and $\bar{u}_l$, and then Ω_{l+1}^h and u_{l+1}. Taking into account that the nodes of Ω_l^h for all $l \geq 2$ are connected by grid edges only to nodes from Ω_1^h, the block structure of SLAE (1) is written as follows:

$$Au = A^{(1)}u_1 = \begin{bmatrix} A_{1,1}^{(1)} & A_{1,2}^{(1)} \\ A_{2,1}^{(1)} & A_{2,2}^{(1)} \end{bmatrix} \begin{bmatrix} \bar{u}_1 \\ u_2 \end{bmatrix} = \begin{bmatrix} \bar{f}_1 \\ f_2 \end{bmatrix},$$
$$A_{1,1}^{(1)} \in \mathfrak{R}^{\bar{N}_1, \bar{N}_1}, \quad A_{2,1}^{(1)} = (A_{1,2}^{(1)})^\mathsf{T} \in \mathfrak{R}^{N_2, \bar{N}_1}, \tag{3}$$

where $A_{2,2}^{(1)}$ is a diagonal matrix. As the number of nesting levels increases, the matrix A becomes arrow-shaped. For example, for $m = 3$ we have

$$Au = \begin{bmatrix} A_{1,1}^{(1)} & A_{1,2}^{(2)} & A_{1,3}^{(3)} \\ A_{2,1}^{(2)} & A_{2,2}^{(2)} & 0 \\ A_{3,1}^{(3)} & 0 & A_{3,3}^{(3)} \end{bmatrix} \begin{bmatrix} \bar{u}_1 \\ \bar{u}_2 \\ u_3 \end{bmatrix} = \begin{bmatrix} \bar{f}_1 \\ \bar{f}_2 \\ f_3 \end{bmatrix}. \tag{4}$$

Let us now consider the internal structure of the matrix $A_{1,1}^{(1)}$ in (3) and (4). We partition the set of nodes of the fine grid into three subsets: $\Omega_1^h = \Omega_1^{(1)} \cup \Omega_2^{(1)} \cup \Omega_3^{(1)}$. In Fig. 1, these sets are denoted by the symbols $\circ$, $\times$, and $\bullet$, respectively.

The last subset constitutes the coarse grid; the nodes of type "$\times$" belong to the midpoints of its edges, while the nodes of type "$\circ$" belong to the cell centers.

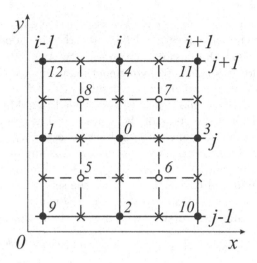

Fig. 1. Local numbering and node designations for the two-dimensional multigrid method

Let us rewrite SLAE (4) using appropriate notations for subvectors and taking into account the local relations between grid nodes of different types:

$$A^{(1)}u^{(1)} = \begin{bmatrix} A_{1,1}^{(1)} & A_{1,2}^{(1)} & 0 \\ A_{2,1}^{(1)} & A_{2,2}^{(1)} & A_{2,3}^{(1)} \\ 0 & A_{3,2}^{(1)} & A_{3,3}^{(1)} \end{bmatrix} \begin{bmatrix} \bar{u}_1^{(1)} \\ \bar{u}_2^{(1)} \\ \bar{u}_3^{(1)} \end{bmatrix} = f^{(1)} = \begin{bmatrix} \bar{f}_1^{(1)} \\ \bar{f}_2^{(1)} \\ \bar{f}_3^{(1)} \end{bmatrix}, \tag{5}$$

$$A^{(1)} = D^{(1)} + L^{(1)} + U^{(1)}.$$

Here we use the notations $D^{(1)} = \{A_{k,k}^{(1)}\}$, $L^{(1)} = \{A_{k,k-1}\}$, and $U^{(1)} = \{A_{k,k+1}^{(1)}\}$ for, respectively, the block diagonal part, the lower triangular, and the upper triangular parts of matrix A; the subvector $u_3^{(1)} = u_2$ corresponds to the coarse grid variables Ω_2^h. To solve SLAE (5), we apply any of the preconditioned methods of conjugate directions in Krylov subspaces, for example, the conjugate gradient algorithm:

$$r^0 = f - Au^0, \quad p^0 = B^{-1}r^n, \quad n = 0, 1, \ldots,$$
$$u^{n+1} = u^n + \alpha_n p^n, \quad r^{n+1} = r^n - \alpha_n Ap^n,$$
$$p^{n+1} = B^{-1}r^{n+1} + \beta_n p^n, \quad \alpha_n = \sigma_n/\rho_n, \tag{6}$$
$$\beta_n = \sigma_{n+1}/\sigma_n, \quad \sigma_n = (r^n, B^{-1}r^n), \quad \rho_n = (p^0, Ap^n).$$

The preconditioning matrix for the block tridiagonal SLAE (5) is obtained by the incomplete factorization method [21] (below, the upper indices are omitted for the sake of brevity):

$$B = (G + L)G^{-1}(G + U) = G + L + U + LG^{-1}U. \tag{7}$$

From the general requirement $B \approx A$, we construct the block diagonal matrix G using the relation $G = D - \overline{LG^{-1}U} - \theta S$, $Se = (LG^{-1}U - \overline{LG^{-1}U})e$, where the line above the matrix means a certain approximation, and the matrix G is chosen according to the compensation principle or the condition of coincidence of the row sums of the original and preconditioned matrices $Be = Ae$ for the compensation parameter value $\theta = 1$ (e is the vector with all components equal to 1, and S is a diagonal matrix).

Using representation (7) and introducing the renumbering for the preconditioner $B = B^{(1)}$, we obtain the following formulas:

$$B^{(1)} = \begin{bmatrix} G_1^{(1)} & 0 & 0 \\ A_{2,1}^{(1)} & G_2^{(1)} & 0 \\ 0 & A_{3,2}^{(1)} & G_3^{(1)} \end{bmatrix} (G^{(1)})^{-1} \begin{bmatrix} G_1^{(1)} & A_{1,2}^{(1)} & 0 \\ 0 & G_2^{(1)} & A_{2,3}^{(1)} \\ 0 & 0 & G_3^{(1)} \end{bmatrix}, \tag{8}$$

$$G_1^{(1)} = A_{1,1}^{(1)}, \quad G_2^{(1)} = A_{2,2}^{(1)} - (A_{2,1}^{(1)}(G_1^{(1)})^{-1}A_{1,2}^{(1)})_1 - \theta S^{(1)},$$

$$S^{(1)}e = \left[A_{2,1}^{(l)}(G_1^{(1)})^{-1}A_{1,2}^{(1)} - (A_{2,1}^{(1)}(G_1^{(1)})^{-1}A_{1,2}^{(1)})_1 \right] e,$$

$$G_3^{(1)} = A_{3,3}^{(1)} - A_{3,2}^{(1)}(G_2^{(1)})^{-1}A_{2,3}^{(1)},$$

where $(M)_1$ stands for the diagonal part of matrix M; G_1 and G_2 are diagonal matrices, and G_3 is a pentadiagonal matrix of the same structure as $A^{(1)}$ but on the sparse grid Ω_2^h. Accordingly, we assume that G_3 represents the reduced form of the original matrix $A^{(1)}$ on the coarse grid and denote $G_3 = A^{(2)} \in \mathfrak{R}^{N_2,N_2}$.

The preconditioned conjugate gradient method requires computing the vector $q^n = (B^{(1)})^{-1}r^n$ at each iteration, which results in implementing the following relations:

$$B^{(1)}q^n = r^n, \quad (G^{(1)} + L^{(1)})v^n = r^n, \quad (G^{(1)} + U^{(1)})q^n = G^{(1)}v^n. \tag{9}$$

In the block component form, it is written as

$$G_1^{(1)}v_1 = r_1, \quad G_2^{(1)}v_2 = r_2 - A_{2,1}^{(1)}v_1, \quad G_3^{(1)}v_3 = r_3 - A_{3,2}^{(1)}v_2,$$

$$q_3 = v_3, \quad G_2^{(1)}w_2 = A_{2,3}^{(1)}q_3, \quad q_2 = v_2 - w_2, \quad q_1 = v_1 - (G_1^{(1)})^{-1}A_{1,2}^{(1)}q_2, \tag{10}$$

where the notation of subvectors corresponds to (5), and the index n is omitted for brevity. Since $G_1^{(1)}$ and $G_2^{(1)}$ are diagonal matrices, the most resource-intensive operation in (10) is the solution of the auxiliary SLAE with matrix $G_3 = A^{(2)}$ on the coarse grid Ω_2^h. Since $q_3^{(1)} = q^{(2)} \in \mathfrak{R}^{N_2}$, according to the notations used in (5), the resulting five-point system can be written in the form

$$A^{(2)}q^{(2)} = f^{(2)} = r_1^{(1)} - A_{3,2}^{(1)}v_2^{(1)}. \tag{11}$$

If we solve this vector equation by the direct method, we come to the two-grid preconditioned method of conjugate gradients, in other words, to the implicit algorithm of Implicit Incomplete Factorization (IMIF) in Krylov subspaces. Having formulas (5) and (10), to determine the matrix G, we can use the relation

$$G = \frac{1}{\omega}D \tag{12}$$

instead of (8), where $\omega \in [0, 2]$ is the relaxation parameter corresponding to the two-grid SSOR (Symmetric Successive Over-Relaxation) [21] method in Krylov subspaces. In this case, G_3 as well as G_1 and G_2 are diagonal matrices, and we obtain a single-grid algorithm but with a special ordering of the nodes and the corresponding vector variables.

Based on the considered approaches, we formulate the multigrid algorithms as a recursive application of the two-grid algorithm. Namely, to solve SLAE (11) with a pentadiagonal matrix, we use its block representation of the form (5),

$$A^{(2)}q^{(2)} = \begin{bmatrix} A_{1,1}^{(2)} & A_{1,2}^{(2)} & 0 \\ A_{2,1}^{(2)} & A_{2,2}^{(2)} & A_{2,3}^{(2)} \\ 0 & A_{3,2}^{(2)} & A_{3,3}^{(2)} \end{bmatrix} \begin{bmatrix} q_1^{(2)} \\ q_2^{(2)} \\ q_3^{(2)} \end{bmatrix} = f^{(2)} = \begin{bmatrix} f_1^{(2)} \\ f_2^{(2)} \\ f_3^{(2)} \end{bmatrix}, \tag{13}$$

and construct a preconditioning matrix $B^{(2)} \in \mathfrak{R}^{N_2, N_2}$ by analogy with (8). These formulas remain valid, we only need to replace the upper indices (1) with (2). The matrix $G_3^{(2)}$ becomes pentadiagonal. Let us rename it: $G_3^{(2)} = A^{(3)}$. If $m = 3$, we invert it by a direct method, and if $m > 3$, we continue the process of recursive construction.

The considered multigrid algorithms for five-point SLAE (1) are not the only possible. Their structure essentially depends on the way of ordering the unknowns and the corresponding vector components and also on the way of performing the required vector-matrix operations.

One alternative approach is to initially exclude from system (5) the vector $u_2^{(1)}$, whose components correspond to the edge nodes of the grid Ω_2^h, denoted by the symbol $\times$ in Fig. 1. As a result, we obtain the SLAE in the form

$$\begin{bmatrix} \bar{A}_{1,1} & \bar{A}_{1,2}^{(2)} \\ \bar{A}_{2,1} & \bar{A}_{2,2}^{(2)} \end{bmatrix} \begin{bmatrix} u_1 \\ u_2 \end{bmatrix} = f^{(2)} = \begin{bmatrix} \bar{f}_1 \\ \bar{f}_2 \end{bmatrix}, \tag{14}$$

where the subvectors u_1 and u_2 correspond to the nodes of type "o" and "•", and the matrices and right-hand side vectors are given by the formulas

$$\bar{A}_{1,1} = A_{1,1}^{(1)} - A_{1,2}^{(1)}(A_{2,2}^{(1)})^{-1}A_{2,1}^{(1)}, \quad \bar{A}_{1,2} = -A_{1,2}^{(1)}(A_{2,2}^{(1)})^{-1}A_{3,1}^{(1)},$$
$$\bar{A}_{2,2} = A_{3,3}^{(1)} - A_{3,2}^{(1)}(A_{2,2}^{(1)})^{-1}A_{2,3}^{(1)}, \quad \bar{A}_{1,2} = -A_{3,2}^{(1)}(A_{2,2}^{(1)})^{-1}A_{3,1}^{(1)}, \tag{15}$$
$$\bar{f}_1 = f_1^{(1)} - A_{1,2}^{(1)}(A_{2,2}^{(1)})^{-1}f_2^{(1)}, \quad \bar{f}_3 = f_3^{(1)} - A_{3,2}^{(1)}(A_{2,2}^{(1)})^{-1}f_2^{(1)}.$$

Note that the diagonal blocks $\bar{A}_{1,1}$ and $\bar{A}_{2,2}$ are five-diagonal matrices but on coarse grids composed of nodes of types "o" and "•", while the off-diagonal blocks $\bar{A}_{1,2}$ and $\bar{A}_{2,1}$ are four-diagonal matrices.

To solve SLAE (14), we apply the multigrid method by constructing an auxiliary reduced system for the subvector u_2. This solution can be found by iteratively applying the compensation principle in the following manner:

$$\bar{A}_2 u_2^{n+1} = (\bar{A}_{2,2}^{(2)} - \theta S)u_2^{n+1} = \bar{f}^{(2)} = \bar{f}_2 - \theta S u_2^n - \bar{A}_{2,1}u_1^n, \tag{16}$$

where $\theta \in (0,1]$ is the iterative (compensating) parameter, and S is a diagonal matrix determined by the row sums criterion according to the formula

$$Se = \bar{A}_{2,1}e, \quad e = 1. \tag{17}$$

In the case of the two-grid method, SLAE (16), with the pentagonal matrix $\bar{A}_2$ of the same structure as A in (2) and the indices $i \pm 1$ and $j \pm 1$ replaced with $i \pm 2$ and $j \pm 2$, is solved by the direct method. Then, plugging the resulting solution into the first block row of Eq. (14), we arrive at an iterative process of the form

$$\bar{A}_{1,1}u_1^{n+1} = \bar{f}_1^n = \bar{A}_{1,2}^{(2)}(\bar{A}_2)^{-1}(\bar{A}_{(2,1)}u_1^n + \theta S u_2^n) + g, \quad g = \bar{f}_1 + (\bar{A}_{2,2}^{(2)} - \theta S)^{-1}\bar{f}_2. \tag{18}$$

It can be shown that if the matrix A of the original algebraic system (1) is of the positive type (we mean the property of nonfactorizability, diagonal dominance, positive definiteness of the diagonal elements, and nonpositive definiteness of the off-diagonal ones; see [22]), then the matrix $\bar{A}_{1,1}$ from (18) has strict diagonal dominance, and therefore its condition number

$$\operatorname{cond}(A) = M/m, \quad M = \max_p\{|\lambda_p|\}, \quad m = \min_p\{|\lambda_p|\},$$

is finite, i.e., it does not depend on the SLAE dimension, and the spectrum bounds m and M can be easily estimated. From here it follows that an economical Chebyshev acceleration method can be applied to solve (18). This iterative process for an arbitrary initial guess u_1^0 is described by the formulas

$$r^0 = g - \bar{A}_{1,1}u^0, \qquad p^0 = r^0, \quad k = 0, 1, \dots :$$
$$u^{k+1} = u^k + \alpha_k p^k, \qquad r^{k+1} = r^k - \alpha_k \bar{A}_{1,1}p^k, \tag{19}$$
$$p^{k+1} = r^{k+1} + \beta_k p^k, \qquad \beta_k = \gamma_k \alpha_{k-1}/\alpha_k$$

(the subscript n is omitted for the sake of brevity), and the numerical parameters are calculated using the recursions

$$\gamma_0 = 0, \; \delta_0 = \gamma^{-1} = \frac{M-m}{M+m}, \; \delta_{n+1} = (2\gamma - \delta_k)^{-1}, \; \gamma_{k+1} = \delta_{k+1}\delta_k.$$

The iterations in (19) continue until the condition

$$(r^k, r^k) \le \epsilon_i^2(g, g), \; \epsilon_i \ll 1, \tag{20}$$

holds, with the following number of iterations being sufficient:

$$\kappa(\epsilon_i) \le \ln \frac{1 + \sqrt{1 - \epsilon_i^2}}{\epsilon_i} \Big/ \ln \frac{1 + \sqrt{m/M}}{1 - \sqrt{m/M}} + 1. \tag{21}$$

If we neglect the error of inversion of matrix $A_{1,1}$ within the external iteration process (16), (18), then we can write it as

$$\bar{u}^{n+1} = T\bar{u}^n + \phi, \tag{22}$$

where $\bar{u} = (u_1^n, u_2^n)^\top$, and the formulas for Tu^n and ϕ can be deduced easily from the previous relations. It is obvious that if the sequence $\bar{u}^n$ converges in the limit to a vector $\bar{u}$, then it is a solution of the "preconditioned" (nonsingular) SLAE

$$\bar{A}\bar{u} \equiv (I - T)\bar{u} = \phi. \tag{23}$$

We can apply any iterative method in the Krylov subspaces for its fast solving. Since the matrix $\bar{A}_1$ is not symmetric, we can apply such algorithms as GMRES (generalized minimal residual) or SCR (semiconjugate residual), which are equivalent in their variational properties (see the review [22] and the references given in it). However, we have to face the weak side of this approach: a long recursion that requires storing all directional vectors. Alternatively, there are biorthogonalization methods (such as BiCGStab) that use short recursions but do not have minimalizing properties. A compromise variant here can be the transformed conjugate residual method CR$A^\top$ [22], that is, the CR algorithm (formally) with a preconditioning matrix $A^\top$ whose residual norm is minimized at each iteration:

$$
\begin{aligned}
r^0 &= \phi - \bar{A}\bar{u}^0, & p^0 &= \bar{A}^\top r^0, \\
\bar{u}^{n+1} &= \bar{u}^n + \alpha_n p^n, & r^{n+1} &= r^n - \alpha_n \bar{A} p^n, \\
p^{n+1} &= \bar{A}^\top r^{n+1} + \beta_n p^n, & \alpha_n &= \gamma_n/\rho_n, \quad \beta_n = \gamma_{n+1}/\gamma_n, \\
\rho_n &= (\bar{A}p^n, \bar{A}p^n), & \gamma_n &= (\bar{A}^\top r^n, \bar{A}^\top r^n).
\end{aligned} \tag{24}
$$

Note that the multiplication by the matrix $\bar{A}$ in these formulas is actually reduced to one "simple" iteration of the form (23). For example, the calculation of the initial residual is done as follows:

$$r^0 = \phi - (I - T)\bar{u}^0 = T\bar{u}^0 + \phi - \bar{u}^0 = \hat{u}^1 - \bar{u}^0,$$

where $\hat{u}^1$ is the vector obtained from (22) for $n = 0$.

3   Multigrid Methods of Incomplete Factorization for Three-Dimensional Problems

In this section, we consider a direct generalization of the presented algorithms to the case of regular embedded parallelepiped grids. Here we assume for simplicity that the boundary of the computational domain (a parallelepiped) contains or runs along the nodes of the coarse grid Ω_l^h. An example of such a pattern for the grids of two neighboring levels Ω_{l-1}^h and Ω_l^h is shown in Fig. 2.

SLAE (1) is assumed to be a seven-point Stieltjes system. Its grid pattern nodes with local numbers $1, 2, \ldots, 6$ are shown in Fig. 2.

Here we describe in more detail the developed algorithms in the case of a two-grid algorithm. The set of nodes of the original fine grid $\bar{\Omega}_1^h \subset \Omega^h$, which does not overlap with the set $\Omega_2^h \subset \Omega_1^h = \Omega^h$ of the coarse grid, is partitioned in such a way that we can distinguish four node types:

$$\Omega^h = \Omega_1^h = \bar{\Omega}_1^h \cup \Omega_2^h = \Omega_1^1 \cup \Omega_1^2 \cup \Omega_1^3 \cup \Omega_1^4, \tag{25}$$

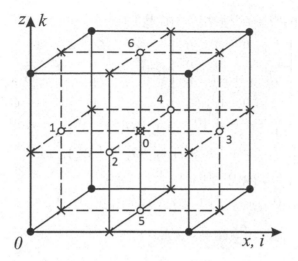

Fig. 2. Node notations of the two-level method on cubic nested grids

where $\Omega_1^4 = \Omega_2^h$. The introduced subsets successively correspond to the centers of the elementary volumes, faces, midpoints of the edges, and nodes of the coarse grid, denoted in Fig. 2 by the symbols $\otimes$, $\circ$, $\times$, and $\bullet$, respectively. We do a global numbering of nodes Ω^h according to ordering (17) (all nodes from Ω_1^1 go first, then the nodes from Ω_1^2, and so on). If we denote the associated subvectors (of the dimensions $N_1^{(1)}$, $N_2^{(1)}$, $N_3^{(1)}$, and $N_4^{(1)}$) in the original SLAE by $\bar{u}_1^{(1)}, \bar{u}_2^{(1)}, \bar{u}_3^{(1)}, \bar{u}_4^{(1)}$ and $\bar{f}_1^{(1)}, \bar{f}_2^{(1)}, \bar{f}_3^{(1)}, \bar{f}_4^{(1)}$, then we can rewrite it in a block tridiagonal form:

$$
Au = \begin{bmatrix} A_{1,1}^{(1)} & A_{1,2}^{(1)} & 0 & 0 \\ A_{2,1}^{(1)} & A_{2,2}^{(1)} & A_{2,3}^{(1)} & 0 \\ 0 & A_{3,2}^{(1)} & A_{3,3}^{(1)} & A_{3,4}^{(1)} \\ 0 & 0 & A_{4,3}^{(1)} & A_{4,4}^{(1)} \end{bmatrix} \begin{bmatrix} u_1^{(1)} \\ u_2^{(1)} \\ u_3^{(1)} \\ u_4^{(1)} \end{bmatrix} = \begin{bmatrix} f_1^{(1)} \\ f_2^{(1)} \\ f_3^{(1)} \\ f_4^{(1)} \end{bmatrix}, \tag{26}
$$

where all diagonal blocks are diagonal matrices, as follows from the local relationships of the nodes of different types in Fig. 2. For SLAE (18) with matrix $A^{(1)} = D^{(1)} + L^{(1)} + U^{(1)}$, we define the preconditioner in the following factorized form (recall that $(M)_1$ stands for the diagonal part of matrix M):

$$B^{(1)} = (G^{(1)} + L^{(1)})(G^{(1)})^{-1}(G^{(1)} + U^{(1)})$$

$$= \begin{bmatrix} G_{1,1}^{(1)} & 0 & 0 & 0 \\ A_{2,1}^{(1)} & G_2^{(1)} & 0 & 0 \\ 0 & A_{3,2}^{(1)} & G_3^{(1)} & 0 \\ 0 & 0 & A_{4,3}^{(1)} & G_4^{(1)} \end{bmatrix} (G^{(1)})^{-1} \begin{bmatrix} G_1^{(1)} & A_{1,2}^{(1)} & 0 & 0 \\ 0 & G_2 & A_{2,3}^{(1)} & 0 \\ 0 & 0 & G_3^{(1)} & A_{3,4}^{(1)} \\ 0 & 0 & 0 & G_4^{(1)} \end{bmatrix}, \qquad (27)$$

$$G_1^{(1)} = A_{1,1}^{(1)}, \quad G_2^{(1)} = A_{2,2}^{(1)} - (A_{2,1}^{(1)}(G_1^{(1)})^{-1}A_{1,2}^{(1)})_1 - \theta_2 S_2^{(1)},$$

$$S_2^{(1)} e_2 = \left[A_{2,1}^{(1)}(G_1^{(1)})^{-1}A_{1,2}^{(1)} - (A_{2,1}^{(1)}(G_1^{(1)})^{-1}A_{1,2}^{(1)})_1 \right] e_2,$$

$$G_3^{(1)} = A_{3,3}^{(1)} - (A_{3,2}^{(1)}(G_2^{(1)})^{-1}A_{2,3}^{(1)})_1 - \theta_3 S_3^{(1)},$$

$$S_3^{(1)} e_3 = \left[A_{3,2}^{(1)}(G_3^{(1)})^{-1}A_{2,3}^{(1)} - (A_{3,2}^{(1)}(G_2^{(1)})^{-1}A_{3,2}^{(1)})_1 \right] e_3,$$

$$G_4^{(1)} = A_{4,4}^{(1)} - A_{4,3}^{(1)}(G_3^{(1)})^{-1}A_{3,4}^{(1)}.$$

Here $S_1^{(1)}$, $S_2^{(1)}$, and $S_3^{(1)}$ are diagonal matrices; $G_4^{(1)}$ is a seven-diagonal matrix with a portrait of the same type as $A^{(1)}$, and it will be considered as matrix $A^{(2)}$ in the SLAE for the grid Ω^{2h} of the next grid level. The compensation parameters $\theta_2^{(1)}, \theta_3^{(1)} \in [0, 1]$ are in general different, and the trial vectors $e_2^{(1)}, e_3^{(1)}$ are of the dimensions $N_2^{(1)}$ and $N_3^{(1)}$, respectively.

To solve SLAE (18) with the preconditioner $B^{(1)}$ from (19), as in the two-dimensional case, we apply the conjugate gradient method with incomplete factorization, according to formulas (6)–(9). To solve the auxiliary equation $B^{(1)}q^n = r^n$ at each iteration, we obtain the following formulas in a block component form (we omit the index n for the sake of brevity) instead of (10):

$$G_1^{(1)} v_1^{(1)} = r_1^{(1)}, \quad G_2^{(1)} v_2^{(1)} = r_2^{(1)} - A_{2,1}^{(1)} v_1^{(1)}, \quad G_3^{(1)} v_3^{(1)} = r_3^{(1)} - A_{3,2}^{(1)} v_2^{(1)},$$

$$G_4^{(1)} v_4^{(1)} = r_4^{(1)} - A_{4,3}^{(1)} v_3^{(1)}, q_4^{(1)} v_2^{(1)} = v_4^{(1)}, G_3^{(1)} w_3^{(1)} = A_{3,4}^{(1)} q_4^{(1)}, q_3^{(1)} = v_3^{(1)} - w_3^{(1)},$$

$$G_2^{(1)} w_2^{(1)} = t A_{2,3}^{(1)} q_3^{(1)}, \ q_2^{(1)} = v_2^{(1)} - w_2^{(1)}, \ q_1^{(1)} = v_1^{(1)} - (G_1^{(1)})^{(-1)} A_{1,2}^{(1)} q_2^{(1)}, \qquad (28)$$

where the subvector $q_4^{(1)}$ is in fact the vector $q^2 \in \mathfrak{R}^{N_2}$, defined on the coarse grid Ω_2^h. The computation of the matrices $G_1^{(1)}, G_2^{(1)}, G_3^{(1)}, G_4^{(1)}$ and the subvectors $v_1^{(1)}, v_2^{(1)}, v_3^{(1)}$ in formulas (18) and (19) can be interpreted as a stage of reduction of the original SLAE on the fine grid to a system of equations with a seven-diagonal matrix $G_4^{(1)} = A^{(2)}$ on the coarse grid, namely

$$A^{(2)}q^{(2)} = f^{(2)} = r_4^{(1)} - A_{4,3}^{(1)}v_3^{(1)}.$$

If the vector $q^{(2)}$ is computed (this operation represents a coarse-grid correction) using a direct method, then we come to a two-grid algorithm. Otherwise, an m-grid method is implemented by recursive application of the two-grid method. Reverse calculations in formulas (20), where the subvectors $q_3^{(1)}, q_2^{(1)}, q_1^{(1)}$ are obtained, represent the stage of continuation of the solution from Ω_2^h to $\bar{\Omega}_1^h$. When constructing the multigrid algorithm, the set of nodes of the three-dimensional grid Ω_2^h is also split into four types; this approach is repeated for the embedded grid Ω_l^h of any level $l = 2, 3, \ldots, m$. For the corresponding block diagonal matrices A^l of the form (18), the preconditioners $B^{(l)}$ are sequentially constructed (as the matrices) and embedded in each other according to formulas (18) and (19), where the top index 1 is replaced by l.

The external iterative process of conjugate directions is constructed in exactly the same manner as in the two-grid version, with the only difference being that there are some difficulties in the implementation of the preconditioner, i.e., the solution of the auxiliary SLAE $B^{(l)}q^n = r^n$.

4 Parallelization of Multigrid Methods

To evaluate the quality of parallelization of the algorithms, we relied on such classical criteria as computational acceleration and processor efficiency, namely

$$S_p(A) = T_1(A)/T_p(A), \quad E_p(A) = S_p(A)/p, \tag{29}$$

where A denotes the problem or algorithm under investigation, p is the number of processors, and $T_p(A)$ is the execution time of A on p processors. Moreover, the execution time of A on a single processor consists of the duration of arithmetic operations and data transfer, i.e.,

$$T_1(A) = T_a + T_c = \tau_a N_a + (\tau_0 + \tau_c N_c)N_t, \tag{30}$$

where τ_a, τ_c, and τ_0, $\tau_a \ll \tau_c \ll \tau_0$, are, respectively, the average time per arithmetic operation, the average time per number transaction, and the transaction latency; N_a, N_c, and N_t are, respectively, the number of arithmetic operations, the volume of data transferred, and the number of information arrays or data packages forwarded. We assume conventionally (although (23) does not reflect this) that all operations are performed on real numbers with standard double precision (64-bit machine words). Obviously, the application of averaged characteristics of computer devices to formula (23) is a rather rough model of calculations, very much like "the average temperature per patient of a hospital". However, we can arrive at several conclusions and recommendations about the technology of high-performance and/or scalable parallelization on this basis. On the other hand, a detailed analysis of a supercomputer with a heterogeneous architecture using real-time simulation requires an even more powerful computer.

We will focus on a compromise representation of the multiprocessor computing system (MPS) as a cluster of computing nodes with a distributed memory, which implements the transfer of information messages via connecting buses (MPI interface). In this case, each node has multiple CPUs with common hierarchical memory and supports multithread computations (OpenMP system). Such two-level parallelism is controlled with hybrid programming tools.

The concept of scalable parallelism is defined ambiguously and is considered in two senses: strong and weak. The first means the linear acceleration of computations for a fixed task as the number of processor devices increases; the second is defined as the economy of computational time for the task or algorithm under the assumption of a proportionate growth in the number of processors and resource intensity. The problem of parallelizing a computational task comprising multiple solutions of algebraic systems with identical matrices but sequentially or simultaneously determined right-hand sides is one having particular methodical interest.

To analyze the parallelization effectiveness of the proposed algorithms, we focus on the three-dimensional case as the most interesting from a practical point of view. Let the initial Ω_1^h (fine grid) be a parallelepipedal grid containing $N^{(1)} = N_x^{(1)} N_y^{(1)} N_z^{(1)}$ nodes. Consider for simplicity a three-grid version of the algorithm, where the coarsest grid has $N^{(3)} = N_x^{(3)} N_y^{(3)} N_z^{(3)}$ nodes, and the numbers of nodes for embedded grids are determined by the formula

$$N^{(l)} = (2N_x^{(l+1)} - 1)(2N_y^{(l+1)} - 1)(2N_z^{(l+1)} - 1), \quad l = 1, 2. \tag{31}$$

This corresponds to the fact that a finer grid Ω_l^h is constructed by adding coordinate planes passing through the middle (possibly approximately) of the edges of the refined grid Ω_{l+1}^h. Applying more than $m = 3$ levels seems impractical since Ω_3^h contains about 64 times fewer nodes than Ω_1^h and further grids would only give a small gain in algorithm performance.

To quantify a possible speedup, we split the entire computational process under study into the following main characteristic stages:

a. Creation of vector-matrix data structures that correspond to the application of hierarchical (recursive) ordering of nodes in embedded grids.
b. Computation of the matrix elements in (18), once before iterations.
c. Performing the operations to start the preconditioned conjugate gradient method (6). This includes finding r^0 and carrying out the forward pass in (19), as well as determining the vectors $v_1(0)$, $v_2(0)$, and $v_3(0)$, which is actually a stage of SLAE reduction. It is followed by the computation of $v_4(0) = q_4(0)$ (the coarse-grid correction stage) and the determination of the subvectors $q_3(0)$, $q_2(0)$, and $q_1(0)$ (the back pass in (19), representing the extension of these vectors from the coarse grid to the fine grid). This stage ends with the determination of the initial guiding vector p^0.
d. Consecutive iterations to perform the vector-matrix multiplication Ap^n and solve the SLAE $Bq^n = r^n$ (in other words, to compute the vector $q^n = B^{-1}r^n$, formally related to the preconditioning matrix inversion) on each of them, and carry out simpler vector operations of the conjugate gradient method (the latter include two scalar vector products, which are relatively worse parallelizable).

Obviously, to evaluate qualitatively the acceleration in parallel computations, it is sufficient to consider the most resource-intensive stage, which is the last one (d), since it requires a high number of iterations, namely $n(\epsilon) \leq \frac{1}{2}\sqrt{\kappa}\ln\frac{2}{\epsilon}$, where $\kappa = \lambda_{\max}/\lambda_{\min}$; κ is generally the effective conditional number, expressed in the case of degenerate matrices through $\lambda_{\min}$, i.e., the minimal nonzero eigenvalue. Operations related directly to the conjugate gradient method are parallelized through a common approach. If the SLAE exceeds the resources of one computational node, the two-level technology with algebraic domain decomposition into approximately equal nonintersecting subdomains is used for enhancing the computation acceleration. In this case, calculations for the corresponding subdomain are implemented synchronously on each multicore node, and information messages are exchanged between them with the help of an MPI library. At the same time, the computations in each subdomain are performed in parallel with the help of multithreaded arithmetics. Actually, this type of operation does not relate to the specifics of multigrid algorithms and allows achieving a high (almost linear) scalability.

Another situation arises in the implementation of the preconditioner for the recursive structure described above. In this situation, the matrix blocks corresponding to subsets $\bar{\Omega}_l^h$ (belonging to the same embedding level) have a block tridiagonal third-order form (while the fourth block belongs to the Ω_{l+1}^h grid). Therefore, the implementation of the corresponding formulas (19) in the restriction and prolongation phases should be performed sequentially in three stages. Here each stage is associated with calculations for different types of nodes (edge, face, and volume nodes in the l-th grid). It should be noted that the calculations for each l-th grid can be performed only in a consecutive manner. Moreover, since each grid-refining step increases the number of nodes by a factor of about 8, the greatest contribution to the speedup is made by the parallelization of the original grid Ω_1^h. Although most processors are idle while processing the nodes of coarser grids, the resulting slowdown is relatively negligible since the total number of arithmetic steps in these stages is rather small.

5   Numerical Experiments

To illustrate the effectiveness of the proposed algorithms, we present the results of preliminary experimental studies on a series of methodical SLAEs obtained from finite-difference standard approximations of 2D and 3D Dirichlet boundary value problems for the Poisson equation in square or cubic computational domains with square and cubic grids and different numbers of grid steps. The matrices of the algebraic systems are five-diagonal or seven-diagonal, with the constant entry $(4, -1, -1, -1, -1)$ or $(6, -1, -1, -1, -1, -1, -1)$, depending on the problem dimension. We employed the preconditioned iterative conjugate gradient method with the criterion for stopping iterations given as $r^n, r^n) \le \epsilon^2(f, f)$, $\epsilon \ll 1$. The computations were performed with different numbers of embedded grids: $m = 1, 2, 3, 4$, where $m = 1$ corresponds to the "usual" single-grid method. All arithmetic operations were performed with standard double precision.

Table 1 shows the computation results for the 2D Dirichlet problem in the square domain $\Omega = [0, 1]^2$ with square grids and SLAE dimensions $N = 511^2, 1023^2, 2047^2$. The iterative process was implemented via formulas (6)–(10) for the preconditioned conjugate gradient method with the threshold $\epsilon = 10^{-7}$ in the criterion for terminating the iterations. The value of the iterative (compensating) parameter was chosen everywhere as $\theta = 1$. All experiments confirmed

Table 1. Data from computational experiments for the 2D problem solved by the preconditioned conjugate gradient method

N/m	1	2	3	4
511^2	836	9	14	20
	34	$0.42 + 1.41$	$0.16 + 1.60$	$0.10 + 1.76$
	$1.4 \cdot 10^{-6}$	$5.6 \cdot 10^{-8}$	$2.2 \cdot 10^{-8}$	$6.7 \cdot 10^{-8}$
1023^2	1635	8	13	19
	303	$1.59 + 3.97$	$0.55 + 6.38$	$0.30 + 8.09$
	$3.0 \cdot 10^{-6}$	$7.9 \cdot 10^{-8}$	$8.7 \cdot 10^{-8}$	$9.9 \cdot 10^{-8}$
2047^2	3197	8	12	18
	2750	$5.54 + 18.64$	$1.82 + 29.96$	$1.21 + 37.98$
	$5.2 \cdot 10^{-6}$	$3.2 \cdot 10^{-8}$	$3.0 \cdot 10^{-8}$	$3.8 \cdot 10^{-8}$

the optimality of this value. Problems with the exact solution $u(x, y) = 1$ and initial guess $u(x, y) = \sin \pi x \sin \pi y$ were used as test examples. Each cell of the table contains the following data (from top to bottom): the number of iterations n, the time to solve the SLAE (the number on the left is the time for preparatory operations performed only once before iterations when solving the system with the same matrix and successively defined right-hand sides; the number on the right is the iteration time), and the resulting maximum absolute error of the numerical solution, defined as $\delta = \|u - u^n\|_\infty$.

We can see from these results that the number of iterations is almost independent of the number of grid nodes (experiments with other data confirmed this conclusion). Note that if the initial error $u - u^0$ is constant, the process converges at $\theta = 1$ in one iteration, as it should be according to a simple theoretical analysis. As for the optimal number of embedded grids, it corresponds to the value $m = 2$ or 3, which is to be expected according to the estimates of the total volume of computations. The authors carried out the computational experiments on a node of the NKS-1P cluster, installed at the Siberian Supercomputer Center of the Institute of Computational Mathematics and Mathematical Geophysics, SB RAS [25]. The node is equipped with processors Intel® Xeon® E5-2630v4 (2.2 GHz, 10 cores) and 128 GB RAM.

In Table 2, we present the results of the solution of the same series of two-dimensional problems but the operation of extending the approximate solutions from a coarse to a fine grid was done by Chebyshev acceleration using formulas (19)–(22). The number of external iterations, in this case, is larger than that in Table 1 because the iterations were done according to a simple algorithm, without acceleration employing (24) in Krylov subspaces. The runs were carried out on a home PC with an Intel® Core™ i7-4770 CPU at 3.40 GHz and 16.0 GB RAM aboard.

Table 2. Data of computational experiments for the 2D problem solved by simple iteration

$N \ / \ m$	1	2	3	4
511^2	897	11	16	23
	39	$0.51 + 1.93$	$0.35 + 2.11$	$0.19 + 2.27$
	$1.9 \cdot 10^{-6}$	$9.1 \cdot 10^{-8}$	$3.5 \cdot 10^{-8}$	$7.2 \cdot 10^{-8}$
1023^2	1893	10	16	23
	420	$1.87 + 4.35$	$0.97 + 7.63$	$0.54 + 9.34$
	$9.5 \cdot 10^{-6}$	$3.4 \cdot 10^{-8}$	$5.1 \cdot 10^{-8}$	$6.7 \cdot 10^{-8}$
2047^2	3721	9	15	21
	4398	$8.74 + 23.03$	$3.54 + 41.39$	$2.01 + 53.13$
	$3.4 \cdot 10^{-6}$	$6.1 \cdot 10^{-8}$	$6.9 \cdot 10^{-8}$	$4.5 \cdot 10^{-8}$

Table 3 shows the results of numerical experiments conducted to solve 3D problems using formulas (27), (29), and the preconditioned conjugate residual method (this algorithm without preconditioning was also applied to solve the obtained algebraic systems on the coarsest grids; the threshold $\epsilon = 10^{-8}$ in the stopping criterion was used in both external and internal iterations). In the computational domain $\Omega = [0, 1]^3$ (unit cube), we solved SLAEs approximating the Poisson equation with Dirichlet boundary conditions and the exact solution $u = \sin \pi x$ on cubic grids with $N = 127^3$ and $N = 255^3$ inner nodes. The computations were performed with different numbers of embedded grids: $m = 1, 2, 3, 4, 5$ ($m = 1$ corresponds to the usual single-grid method without preconditioning). In each cell of Table 3, the upper figure is the number of iterations and the lower is the total computational time in seconds. Both numbers correspond to the value $\theta = 1$ of the compensating parameter; moreover, $u^0 = 0$ was the initial guess. The computations were performed on a laptop with an Intel® Core™ i7-7700HQ processor at 2.80 GHz and 8.00 GB RAM.

Table 3. Data of computational experiments for 3D problems

$N \ / \ m$	1	2	3	4	5
127^3	276	18	38	75	136
	11.9	13.3	3.81	5.99	10.4
255^3	529	18	37	74	143
	239	202	50.4	59	110

According to these results, the number of iterations of the multigrid method is practically independent of the number of nodes, that is, of the SLAE dimension. The optimal number of grids for the minimal number of iterations is $m = 2$. However, to achieve the fastest time, $m = 3$ is the preferred variant. Additional experiments (here we omit the corresponding data) demonstrated the existence of optimal values of the iterative parameter θ that are close to 1 ($\theta \approx 0.999$). Nevertheless, in this case, the number of iterations insignificantly decreases by about 10%.

6   Conclusions

In this paper, we considered efficient algebraic multigrid methods for solving large sparse SLAEs with symmetric positive-definite matrices arising from the approximation of two- and three-dimensional boundary value problems. Also, we proposed iterative methods of conjugate directions using large-block algorithms of incomplete factorization with a recursive ordering of variables. Some stages of the computational process can be interpreted as operations of restriction, coarse-grid correction, and prolongation of successive approximations from a coarse grid to a fine grid. We showed that additional preconditioning by the symmetric successive over-relaxation method allows us to carry out the procedures of preliminary and final smoothing at each iteration. The results of preliminary experimental research on test examples showed that the number of iterations in the developed approaches practically does not depend on the SLAE dimension. The suggested iterative processes can naturally be subject to scalable parallelization on multiprocessor computing architectures, as well as generalized to broader classes of problems with real data and implemented on unstructured grids. The main issues, in this case, lie in the technologies of both data structures and automation of algorithm constructions.

References

1. Fedorenko, R.P.: The speed of convergence of one iterative process. USSR Comput. Math. Math. Phys. **4**(3), 559–564 (1964). https://doi.org/10.1016/0041-5553(64)90253-8
2. Bakhvalov, N.S.: On the convergence of a relaxation method with natural constraints on the elliptic operator. USSR Comput. Math. Math. Phys. **6**(5), 101–135 (1966). https://doi.org/10.1016/0041-5553(66)90118-2
3. Bornemann, F.A., Deuflhard, P.: The cascadic multigrid methods for elliptic problems. Numer. Math. **75**(2), 135–152 (1996). https://doi.org/10.1007/S002110050234
4. Ilyin, V.P.: About one variant of multigrid method. Sib. Math. J. **26**(2), 102–107 (1985). https://doi.org/10.1007/BF00968767
5. Shaidurov, V.V.: Some estimates of the rate of convergence for the cascadic conjugate-gradient method. Comput. Math. Appl. **31**(4/5), 161–171 (1996). https://doi.org/10.1016/0898-1221(95)00228-6
6. Brandt, A.: Algebraic multigrid theory: the symmetric case. Appl. Math. Comput. **19**, 23–56 (1986). https://doi.org/10.1016/0096-3003(86)90095-0
7. Saad, Y.: Iterative Methods for Sparse Linear Systems, 2nd edn. SIAM (2003)
8. Olshansky, M.A.: Analysis of a multigrid method for convection-diffusion equations with Dirichlet boundary conditions. JVMiMF **44**(8), 1450–1479 (2004)

9. Notay, Y.: Algebraic multigrid and algebraic multilevel methods: a theoretical comparison. Numer. Linear Algebra Appl. **12**, 419–451 (2005). https://doi.org/10.1002/nla.435
10. Bank, R., Falgout, R., Jones, T., Manteuffel, T., McCormick, S., Ruge, J.: Algebraic multigrid domain and range decomposition (AMG-DD/AMG-RD). SIAM J. Sci. Comput. **37**(5) (2015). https://doi.org/10.1137/140974717
11. Vassilevski, Y.V., Olshanskii, M.A.: Short Course on Multi-grid and Domain Decomposition Methods. MAKS Press Publ., Moscow (2007)
12. Vanek, P.: Smoothed prolongation multigrid with rapid coarsening and massive smoothing. Appl. Math. **57**, 1–10 (2012). https://doi.org/10.1007/s10492-012-0001-3
13. Brezina, M., Falgout, R., Maclachlani, S., Manteuffel, T., McCormick, S., Ruge, J.: Adaptive smoothed aggregation (aSA) multigrid. SIAM Rev. **25**(6), 1896–1920 (2004). https://doi.org/10.1137/050626272
14. Notay, Y.: Analysis of two-grid methods: the nonnormal case. Report GANMN 18-01 (2018). https://doi.org/10.1090/mcom/3460
15. Notay, Y., Napov, A.: A massively parallel solver for discrete Poisson-like problems. J. Comput. Phys. **281**, 237–250 (2015). https://doi.org/10.1016/j.jcp.2014.10.043
16. Notay, Y., Napov, A.: An efficient multigrid method for graph Laplacian systems II: robust aggregation. SIAM J. Sci. Comput. **39**(5), 379–403 (2017). https://doi.org/10.1137/16M1071420
17. Xu, J., Zikatanov, L.: Algebraic Multigrid Methods. Acta Numerica. Cambridge University Press (2017). https://doi.org/10.1017/S0962492917000083
18. Gurieva, Y.L., Il'in, V.P., Petukhov, A.V.: On multigrid methods for solving two-dimensional boundary-value problems. J. Math. Sci. **249**(2), 118–127 (2020). https://doi.org/10.1007/s10958-020-04926-7
19. Demidov, D.: AMGCL: an efficient, flexible, and extensible algebraic multigrid implementation. Lobachevskii J. Math. **40**(5), 535–546 (2019). https://doi.org/10.1134/S1995080219050056
20. Ilyin, V.P.: Multigrid methods of incomplete factorization. Zapiski Nauchnykh Ceminarov POMI **514**, 61–76 (2022)
21. Ilyin, V.P.: Methods and Technologies of Finite Elements. IVMiMG SB RAS, Novosibirsk (2007)
22. Ilyin, V.P.: Iterative preconditioned methods in Krylov spaces: trends of the 21st century. Comput. Math. Math. Phys. **61**(11), 1750–1775 (2021). https://doi.org/10.1134/S0965542521110099
23. Ilyin, V. P.: Mathematical modeling. Part 1. Continuous and Discrete Models. Novosibirsk. SO RAN (2017)
24. Il'in, V. P., Kozlov, D. I., Petukhov, A. V.: On the minimal residual methods for solving diffusion-convection SLAEs. J. Phys.: Conf. Ser. **2099**, 012005 (2021). https://doi.org/10.1088/1742-6596/2099/1/012005
25. Super Siberian Computing Center ICMMG SB RAS. http://www.sscc.icmmg.nsc.ru

Optimized Relativistic Code for Massive Parallel Systems

Elena N. Akimova[1,2]([✉])(ⓘ), Vladimir E. Misilov[1,2](ⓘ), Igor M. Kulikov[3](ⓘ),
and Igor G. Chernykh[3](ⓘ)

[1] Krasovskii Institute of Mathematics and Mechanics, Ural Branch of the Russian Academy of Sciences, 16 S. Kovalevskaya Street, Ekaterinburg, Russian Federation
aen15@yandex.ru
[2] Ural Federal University, 19 Mira Street, Ekaterinburg, Russian Federation
v.e.misilov@urfu.ru
[3] Institute of Computational Mathematics and Mathematical Geophysics, Siberian Branch of the Russian Academy of Sciences, 6 Prospekt Ak. Lavrent'yeva, Novosibirsk, Russian Federation
kulikov@ssd.sscc.ru, chernykh@parbz.sscc.ru

Abstract. This paper introduces a code designed for the three-dimensional relativistic hydrodynamic simulation of astrophysical flows on massive parallel architectures. The code utilizes numerical techniques based on Godunov's method and the piecewise parabolic approximation with a local stencil to solve the equations of gravitational hydrodynamics. The implementation of the code leverages the hybrid use of MPI, OpenMP, and vectorization technologies. The collision of relativistic jets serves as a case study to evaluate the code. Experiments were conducted to assess its efficiency, performance, and scalability.

Keywords: Hydrodynamical model · High-performance computing · Massive parallel system · Hybrid MPI and OpenMP technologies · Scalability

1 Introduction

At present, relativistic jets are poorly studied objects [1]. The sources of such jets are accreting supermassive black holes in the centers of galaxies [2,3]. The basic accretion mechanism was described in [4] and further developed in [5–7]. Of particular interest is the interaction of relativistic flows [8–10], which are pretty well observed [11–14]. The problem of the interaction of wind from a relativistic jet with molecular clouds [15] is also worth noting.

The simulation of such processes requires the use of specialized relativistic hydrodynamics. Given the immense scale of these astrophysical objects, their simulation mandates the deployment of powerful supercomputers. Modern supercomputers predominantly adopt hybrid architectures, comprising clusters equipped with graphics processors and general-purpose multicore central processors. The development of codes tailored for these architectures poses a formidable

ⓒ The Author(s), under exclusive license to Springer Nature Switzerland AG 2023
L. Sokolinsky and M. Zymbler (Eds.): PCT 2023, CCIS 1868, pp. 110–122, 2023.
https://doi.org/10.1007/978-3-031-38864-4_8

challenge. It demands not only the utilization of appropriate technologies but also the formulation of a specialized numerical method and mathematical models. We present in this paper an enhanced version of the code introduced in [16,17], specifically tailored to efficiently leverage vectorization, OpenMP, and MPI technologies.

Several codes adapted for graphics processors (GPU) or the Intel Xeon Phi accelerators have been developed. We review the most interesting solutions.

In Sect. 2 we provide the mathematical model and numerical method for solving the hydrodynamical equations. Section 3 describes the architecture of the hybrid parallel code. Section 4 is devoted to the study of its performance in terms of speedup and scalability. Section 5 describes the model problem. Section 6 concludes the paper.

2 Mathematical Model and Numerical Method

Here we present a brief summary of the mathematical model and numerical method described in [16].

Let ρ, $\vec{v}$, and p represent physical variables, namely, density, velocity vector, and pressure. Assuming $c \equiv 1$, the Lorentz factor is defined as $\Gamma = 1/\sqrt{1 - v^2}$. The state of the ideal gas model is determined by the special enthalpy

$$h = 1 + \frac{\gamma}{\gamma - 1} \frac{p}{\rho},$$

where γ is the adiabatic index.

For the equations of special relativistic hydrodynamics, we introduce the following conservative variables: the relativistic density, $D = \Gamma \rho$, the relativistic momentum, $M_j = \Gamma^2 \rho h v_j$ (for the components $j = x, y, z$), and the total relativistic energy, $E = \Gamma^2 \rho h - p$.

The system of equations for the conservative variables is

$$\frac{\partial}{\partial t} \begin{pmatrix} \Gamma \rho \\ \Gamma^2 \rho h v_j \\ \Gamma^2 \rho h - p \end{pmatrix} + \sum_{k=1}^{3} \frac{\partial}{\partial x_k} \begin{pmatrix} \rho \Gamma v_k \\ \rho h \Gamma^2 v_j v_k + p \delta_{jk} \\ (\Gamma^2 \rho h - p) v_k + p v_k \end{pmatrix} = 0, \tag{1}$$

where δ_{jk} is the Kronecker delta.

This system can be rewritten in a vector form as follows:

$$\frac{\partial U}{\partial t} + \sum_{k=1}^{3} \frac{\partial F_k}{\partial x_k} = 0. \tag{2}$$

Then, for an arbitrary cell, the Godunov scheme has the form

$$\frac{U_{i+\frac{1}{2},k+\frac{1}{2},l+\frac{1}{2}}^{n+1} - U_{i+\frac{1}{2},k+\frac{1}{2},l+\frac{1}{2}}^{n}}{\tau} + \frac{F_{x,i+1,k+\frac{1}{2},l+\frac{1}{2}}^{*} - F_{x,i,k+\frac{1}{2},l+\frac{1}{2}}^{*}}{h_x}$$

$$+ \frac{F_{y,i+\frac{1}{2},k+1,l+\frac{1}{2}}^{*} - F_{y,i+\frac{1}{2},k,l+\frac{1}{2}}^{*}}{h_y} + \frac{F_{z,i+\frac{1}{2},k+\frac{1}{2},l+1}^{*} - F_{z,i+\frac{1}{2},k+\frac{1}{2},l}^{*}}{h_z} = 0, \tag{3}$$

where $h_{x,y,z}$ are the steps of the spatial grid and F^* are the fluxes of the corresponding variables through the cell boundary. These fluxes are obtained from solving the Riemann problem.

Note that the inverse transition from conservative variables to physical variables involves solving a nonlinear equation. To accomplish this, an iterative Newton's method is employed.

The numerical solver is based on the piecewise parabolic method on a local stencil (PPML) and is described in detail in [16,17].

3 Hybrid Parallel Implementation

In this section, we present a comprehensive description of the code developed for hydrodynamic simulation. Our implementation adopts a hybrid approach, incorporating both MPI and OpenMP technologies. Additionally, we leverage the Intel SIMD Data Layout Template (SDLT) library and the auto-vectorization directives provided by the Intel C++ Compiler Classic to enhance the code performance and efficiency.

3.1 The Domain Decomposition

Our implementation incorporates a domain decomposition approach that facilitates the efficient computation of the hydrodynamical equations. By utilizing a uniform grid in Cartesian coordinates and iterating over three nested loops, our code allows for using arbitrary Cartesian topologies for domain decomposition. This computational structure offers significant potential for scalability.

The domain decomposition in our code employs a multilevel multidimensional approach. Specifically, the outer one-dimensional decomposition is achieved using the MPI technology, as illustrated in Fig. 1. For the periodic boundary conditions, the leftmost and rightmost subdomains are considered adjacent.

Within each subdomain, the inner fine decomposition is done by vectorizing the inner loop, while the decomposition of the remaining two coordinates is achieved by using two collapsed OpenMP loops, as depicted in Fig. 2. This combination of parallelization techniques optimizes the code's performance and ensures efficient computations within each subdomain.

3.2 The Computational Algorithm

The code implements the following algorithm to compute a single time step utilizing the corresponding function names:

1. Determine the minimum time step across all spatial cells and MPI processes using the `computational_tau()` function.
2. Construct local parabolic approximations of the primitive variables for each cell, considering the boundary conditions, using the `build_parabola_sdlt()` function.

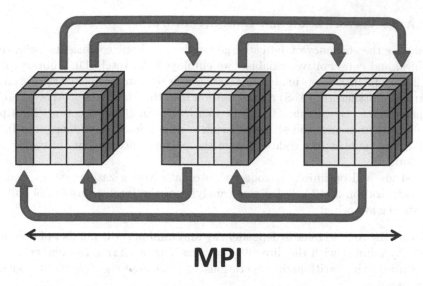

Fig. 1. Geometric domain decomposition using MPI technology

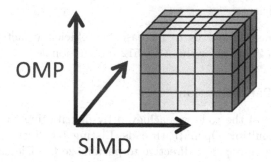

Fig. 2. Geometric domain decomposition using OpenMP and SIMD technologies

3. Transfer the coefficients of the parabolic approximations for the adjacent subdomain boundaries between MPI processes employing a ring topology.
4. Solve the Riemann problem for each cell (`eulerian_stage()`).
5. Handle the boundary conditions for the obtained conservative variables.
6. Transfer the values of the conservative variables for the adjacent subdomain boundaries between MPI processes.
7. Calculate the primitive variables for each cell.
8. Handle the boundary conditions for the primitive variables using the `boundary_mesh()` function.
9. Transfer the primitive variables for the adjacent subdomain boundaries between MPI processes.

3.3   Auto Vectorization and Data Structures

To enhance the efficiency of data storage for the parabolic coefficients, primitive variables, and conservative variables, we employed the Intel SDLT library [19]. This library facilitates optimal data organization by automatically transforming the Array of Structures (AoS) representation into the Structure of Arrays (SoA) internal format. By aligning the data to SIMD (Single Instruction, Multiple Data) words and cache lines, and offering n-dimensional containers, the Intel SDLT library enables the code to attain the performance benefits of vectorized C++ code.

To study and optimize the code for automatic vectorization, we referred to the "Vectorization and Code Insights" analysis of the Intel Advisor tool [20]. It suggests the following:

- Modify the code to remove dependencies and minimize the number of function calls by inlining with the directive `#pragma forceinline recursive`.
- Optimize the arithmetic operations by using the compiler option `\Qprec-div-`.
- Reduce the amount of branching in the procedures for computing the parabolic coefficients.

These modifications allowed us to increase the efficiency factor of automatic vectorization from 2.5 to 6 for the AVX-512 instruction set.

3.4   OpenMP Parallelization

The parallelization of the code was achieved by distributing the computational workload among multiple OpenMP threads. Listing 1.1 illustrates the common usage of the `#pragma omp for` directive to parallelize the Riemann solver loop. In this case, two outer loops were collapsed and parallelized using OpenMP, while the inner loop was vectorized. To provide flexibility in program optimization without the need for recompilation, the scheduling was set to `runtime`. This approach allowed for fine-tuning of the program's performance.

Listing 1.1. Parallel Riemann solver loop

```
#pragma omp for schedule(runtime) collapse(2)
        for (i = 1; i < NX - 1; i++)
                for (k = 1; k < NY - 1; k++)
#pragma ivdep
                        for (l = 1; l < NZ - 1; l++)
                        {
//Riemann solver
#pragma forceinline recursive
                                SRHD_Lamberts_Riemann(
                                        ...
```

3.5   MPI Parallelization

The data exchange is carried out in such a way that neighboring processes exchange boundary values twice. All processes send the single rightmost layer of their subdomain to their right neighbor. Then they receive the leftmost layer of the right neighbor. After that, there is a similar exchange with the left neighbors.

Functions `serialize_sdlt_data()` and `deserialize_sdlt_data()` serialize and deserialize the data from SDLT containers to and from the "flat" buffer for transferring via the MPI.

Listing 1.2. MPI communication code

```
// Communications to right
if (rank == 0)
{
        serialize_sdlt_data(parabola_container, buffer, NX - 2);
        MPI_Send(buffer, buffer_size, MPI_DOUBLE, rank_right,
                TAGTORIGHT, MPI_COMM_WORLD);
        MPI_Recv(buffer, buffer_size, MPI_DOUBLE, rank_left,
                TAGTORIGHT, MPI_COMM_WORLD, MPI_STATUS_IGNORE);
        deserialize_sdlt_data(parabola_container, buffer, 0);
}
else
{
        MPI_Recv(buffer, buffer_size, MPI_DOUBLE, rank_left,
                TAGTORIGHT, MPI_COMM_WORLD, MPI_STATUS_IGNORE);
        deserialize_sdlt_data(parabola_container, buffer, 0);
        serialize_sdlt_data(parabola_container, buffer, NX - 2);
        MPI_Send(buffer, buffer_size, MPI_DOUBLE, rank_right,
                TAGTORIGHT, MPI_COMM_WORLD);
}
// Communications to left
if (rank == size - 1)
{
        serialize_sdlt_data(parabola_container, buffer, 1);
        MPI_Send(buffer, buffer_size, MPI_DOUBLE, rank_left,
                TAGTOLEFT, MPI_COMM_WORLD);
        MPI_Recv(buffer, buffer_size, MPI_DOUBLE, rank_right,
                TAGTOLEFT, MPI_COMM_WORLD, MPI_STATUS_IGNORE);
        deserialize_sdlt_data(parabola_container, buffer, NX - 1);
}
else
{
        MPI_Recv(buffer, buffer_size, MPI_DOUBLE, rank_right,
                TAGTOLEFT, MPI_COMM_WORLD, MPI_STATUS_IGNORE);
        deserialize_sdlt_data(parabola_container, buffer, NX - 1);
        serialize_sdlt_data(parabola_container, buffer, 1);
        MPI_Send(buffer, buffer_size, MPI_DOUBLE, rank_left,
                TAGTOLEFT, MPI_COMM_WORLD);
}
```

4   Code Research

In the context of a hybrid implementation, it is important to consider two types of scalability:

1. Strong scalability. This refers to the ability to reduce the computation time of a single step for a given problem as the number of devices utilized increases. In other words, strong scalability measures the efficiency of parallelization when distributing the workload across a varying number of devices. The goal is to achieve a proportional reduction in computation time as more devices are added.
2. Weak scalability. This concept involves maintaining a constant single-step computation time and an equivalent workload per device while simultaneously increasing the number of devices employed. The objective is to assess the scalability of the system as the problem size expands alongside the number of devices. Achieving good weak scalability implies that the computational resources can be efficiently utilized to handle larger and more complex problems without a significant increase in the computation time per device.

By considering both strong and weak scalability, one can comprehensively evaluate the performance and efficiency of the hybrid implementation across different computational scenarios.

The experiments were performed on the Uran supercomputer of the Krasovskii Institute of Mathematics and Mechanics, Ural Branch of RAS. The nodes used have a pair of 18-core Intel Xeon Gold 6254 processors and 384 GB of RAM. A mesh with a size of $512 \times 512 \times 512$ points was used for the model problem. The computing times given below represent a single time step and exclude the time spent on initialization, finalizing, and file operations.

4.1   OpenMP Threading Performance: Strong Scalability

To assess the threading performance, we utilized the speedup coefficient $S_m = T_1/T_m$ and the efficiency coefficient $E_m = S_m/m$), where T_m represents the computing time on m OpenMP threads for the same problem.

Table 1 presents the results obtained from solving the problem with a grid size of $512 \times 512 \times 512$ points using varying numbers of OpenMP threads. The table includes the computation time for a single time step, as well as the corresponding speedup and efficiency coefficients. Figures 3 and 4 show the graphs of the speedup and efficiency.

Table 1. Threading performance for the test problem

Number m of OpenMP threads	Time T_m (seconds)	Speedup S_m	Efficiency E_m
1	89.7	–	–
2	46.2	1.94	0.97
4	24.1	3.72	0.93
8	15.2	5.90	0.73
18	7.5	11.96	0.66

A 12-fold speedup on the 18-core processor was achieved.

4.2 MPI Performance: Weak Scalability

The scalability of the code was evaluated using a grid of size $p \cdot 512 \times 512 \times 512$, where p represents the number of nodes utilized. Consequently, each node's subdomain has size $512 \times 512 \times 512$ points. The scalability, denoted as F_p, was calculated using the formula $F_p = T_1/T_p$, where T_p represents the computation time on p nodes.

Table 2 contains the results obtained from the scaling experiments. It provides the computation times T_p for a single time step, the scalability values F_p corresponding to various numbers p of nodes, and the associated problem sizes. Figure 5 illustrates the graph displaying the scalability results.

Table 2. Scalability for the test problem

Number p of nodes	Grid size	Time T_p (seconds)	Scalability F_p
1	$512 \times 512 \times 512$	7.5	–
2	$1024 \times 512 \times 512$	8.1	0.93
4	$2048 \times 512 \times 512$	9.0	0.83
8	$4096 \times 512 \times 512$	9.3	0.81
16	$8192 \times 512 \times 512$	9.7	0.77

For these experiments, 1 to 16 nodes (18 to 288 cores of the Intel Xeon Gold 6254 processor) were used. The code used 18 OpenMP threads on each node. An 80% performance was reached.

There are several points to note.

- Despite the single node having two 18-core processors, the experiments were performed on a single processor, binding all threads to a single socket. No NUMA optimizations were implemented.

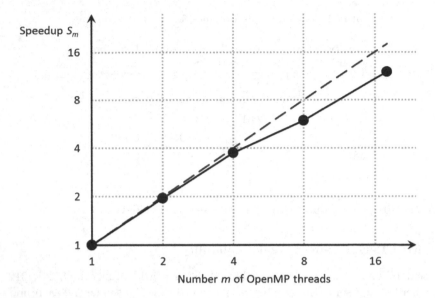

Fig. 3. The speedup of the parallel code on the 18-core Intel Xeon Gold 6254 processor. The dashed line represents the ideal speedup.

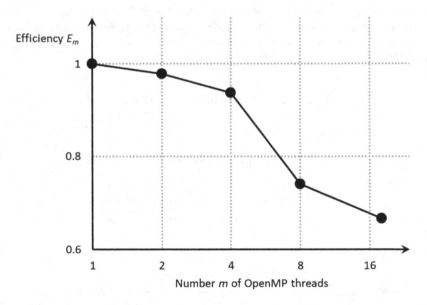

Fig. 4. The efficiency of the parallel code on the 18-core Intel Xeon Gold 6254 processor

- The algorithm is memory-bound, so the performance of the code on a single node is limited by the memory bandwidth [17].
- The speedup from vectorization is also limited by the memory bandwidth. When the bandwidth is saturated, the vectorized and unvectorized codes show similar times.
- The Coarray Fortran technology has been identified as a viable alternative to MPI for the development of parallel programs designed for distributed memory architectures [18].

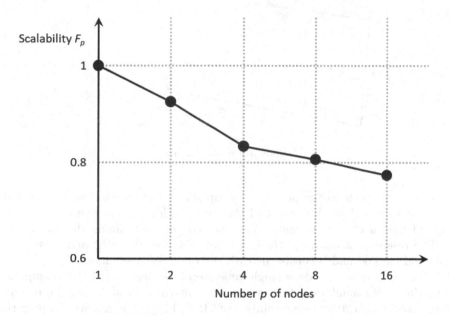

Fig. 5. Scalability of the code on the Uran supercomputer

5   Collision of Relativistic Jets

We consider the simulation of the interaction of two galactic jets. The formulation of the problem is described in detail in [18]. The simulation was performed using Algorithm 3.2. Figure 6 shows the density of the jets at a time point of 2000 years. The simulation requires a resolution of at least $512 \times 512 \times 512$ points and about 8000 time steps.

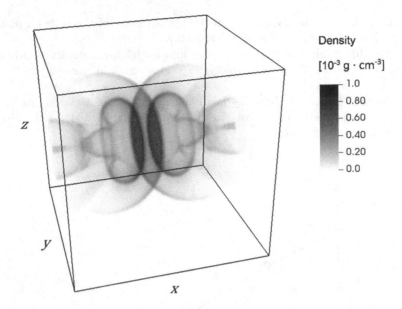

Fig. 6. Simulation of colliding jets

We do not dwell on the physical description of the interaction. Let us only note that spherical shock waves and their interaction can be well described in terms of spatial resolution, and so can the "cocoon" containing the relativistic jet. The resulting structure of the shock waves is free from the artifacts of the numerical method and is consistent with the observed phenomena.

With the developed code, a single time step takes less than 10 s to complete. Thus, the whole simulation, taking into account the cost of saving the results, requires more than 20 h. For a resolution of $512 \times 512 \times 512$ points, we can perform the simulation using only a single 18-core processor. If we use the $1024 \times 1024 \times 1024$ grid, we need eight nodes to obtain a similar computing time. Note that the larger grid also requires more memory. The $512 \times 512 \times 512$ grid requires about 140 GB, while the $1024 \times 1024 \times 1024$ grid takes eight times as much. A single node of the Uran supercomputer has only 384 GB. Thus, we need MPI parallelization so we can use a higher resolution.

6   Conclusions

We presented in this paper a hybrid parallel code for the hydrodynamical simulation of astrophysical flows on clusters with multicore processors. Vectorization and OpenMP technology allowed us to achieve a 12-fold speedup on a single node with an 18-core processor with AVX-512 instructions. The scalability of the MPI code reached 80% on 16 nodes (288 processor cores) of the Uran supercomputer. The numerical experiments focused on the simulation of the collision of two relativistic jets, which served as the model problem for the research.

Acknowledgments. The computations were performed on the Uran supercomputer at the Institute of Mathematics and Mechanics UB RAS, Ekaterinburg, Russian Federation.

The work of Igor Kulikov and Igor Chernykh was supported through the base-budget program of the Institute of Computational Mathematics and Mathematical Geophysics SB RAS (№ 0251-2021-0005).

References

1. Araudo, A., Bosch-Ramon, V., Romero, G.: Gamma rays from cloud penetration at the base of AGN jets. Astron. Astrophys. **522**, Article Number 522 (2010). https://doi.org/10.1051/0004-6361/201014660
2. Begelman, M., Blandford, R., Rees, M.: Theory of extragalactic radio sources. Rev. Mod. Phys. **56**, 255–351 (1984). https://doi.org/10.1103/RevModPhys.56.255
3. Laing, R.: The sidedness of jets and depolarization in powerful extragalactic radio sources. Nature **331**, 149–151 (1988). https://doi.org/10.1038/331149a0
4. Shakura, N., Sunyaev, R.: Black holes in binary systems. Observational appearance. Astron. Astrophys. **24**, 337–355 (1973)
5. Bisnovatyi-Kogan, G., Blinnikov, S.: A hot corona around a black-hole accretion disk as a model for CYG X-1. Sov. Astron. Lett. **2**, 191–193 (1976)
6. Artemova, Y., Bisnovatyi-Kogan, G., Igumenshchev, I., Novikov, I.: Black hole advective accretion disks with optical depth transition. Astrophys. J. **637**, 968–977 (2006). https://doi.org/10.1086/496964
7. Narayan, R., Yi, I.: Advection-dominated accretion: a self-similar solution. Astrophys. J. Lett. **428**, L13–L16 (1994). https://doi.org/10.1086/187381
8. Glushak, A.P.: Microquasar jets in the supernova remnant G11.2–0.3. Astron. Rep. **58**(1), 6–15 (2014). https://doi.org/10.1134/S1063772914010028
9. Barkov, M.V., Bisnovatyi-Kogan, G.S.: Interaction of a cosmological gamma-ray burst with a dense molecular cloud and the formation of jets. Astron. Rep. **49**, 24–35 (2005). https://doi.org/10.1134/1.1850203
10. Istomin, Ya.N., Komberg, B.V.: Gamma-ray bursts as a result of the interaction of a shock from a supernova and a neutron-star companion. Astron. Rep. **46**, 908–917 (2002). https://doi.org/10.1134/1.1522079
11. Artyukh, V.S.: Phenomenological model for the evolution of radio galaxies such as Cygnus A. Astron. Rep. **59**(6), 520–524 (2015). https://doi.org/10.1134/S1063772915060025
12. Artyukh, V.S.: Effect of aberration on the estimated parameters of relativistic radio jets. Astron. Rep. **62**(7), 436–439 (2018). https://doi.org/10.1134/S106377291806001X
13. Butuzova, M.S.: Search for differences in the velocities and directions of the kiloparsec-scale jets of quasars with and without X-ray emission. Astron. Rep. **60**(3), 313–321 (2016). https://doi.org/10.1134/S1063772916030033
14. Butuzova, M.S.: The blazar OJ 287 jet from parsec to kiloparsec scales. Astron. Rep. **65**(8), 635–644 (2021). https://doi.org/10.1134/S1063772921080023
15. Sotomayor, P., Romero, G.: Nonthermal radiation from the central region of super-accreting active galactic nuclei. Astron. Astrophys. **664**, Article Number A178 (2022). https://doi.org/10.1051/0004-6361/202243682
16. Kulikov, I.: A new code for the numerical simulation of relativistic flows on supercomputers by means of a low-dissipation scheme. Comput. Phys. Commun. **257**, Article Number 107532 (2020). https://doi.org/10.1016/j.cpc.2020.107532

17. Akimova, E.N., Misilov, V.E., Kulikov, I.M., Chernykh, I.G.: OMPEGAS: optimized relativistic code for multicore architecture. Mathematics **10**, Article Number 2546 (2022). https://doi.org/10.3390/math10142546
18. Kulikov, I., et al.: A new parallel code based on a simple piecewise parabolic method for numerical modeling of colliding flows in relativistic hydrodynamics. Mathematics **10**(11), Article Number 1865 (2022). https://doi.org/10.3390/math10111865
19. Intel Corporation. SIMD Data Layout Templates. https://www.intel.com/content/www/us/en/develop/documentation/oneapi-dpcpp-cpp-compiler-dev-guide-and-reference/top/compiler-reference/libraries/introduction-to-the-simd-data-layout-templates.html. Accessed 23 Feb 2022
20. Intel Corporation. Intel Advisor User Guide. https://www.intel.com/content/www/us/en/develop/documentation/advisor-user-guide/top.html. Accessed 23 Feb 2022

Using Parallel SAT Solving to Study Hard Combinatorial Problems Associated with Boolean Circuits

Victor Kondratiev[1]($\boxtimes$)(ID), Stepan Kochemazov[2](ID), and Alexander Semenov[1](ID)

[1] ITMO University, St. Petersburg, Russian Federation
vikseko@gmail.com
[2] ISDCT SB RAS, Irkutsk, Russian Federation

Abstract. We propose a family of parallel algorithms aimed at solving problems related to hardware verification. We consider the Logical Equivalence Checking problem (LEC) and a particular case known as Automated Test Pattern Generation (ATPG). The main algorithmic basis for solving LEC and ATPG consists of state-of-the-art SAT-solving algorithms. However, for extremely hard SAT instances, the situation often arises when we can say nothing about the runtime of the SAT solver on a considered instance. We can, nonetheless, estimate the runtime if we decompose the original instance into a family of simpler instances that can be solved in a reasonable time. As an additional bonus, this approach provides a means for solving a given problem in parallel. We exploit the described idea in some extremely hard ATPG instances in SAT form and demonstrate that parallel computing is essential for efficient ATPG solving.

Keywords: Boolean satisfiability · Parallel SAT solving algorithms · Electronic design automation · Logical equivalence checking · Automated test pattern generation

1 Introduction

The algorithms for solving the Boolean satisfiability problem (SAT) are successfully applied today to a vast spectrum of practical problems from diverse areas, such as software verification and program testing [4,8,19], computer security and cryptanalysis [2,9,29,30,34], combinatorics and Ramsey theory [14,15,18,35], and others. Hardware verification—in particular, Electronic Computer-Aided Design (ECAD) and Electronic Design Automation (EDA)—remains one of the major industrial areas where complete SAT solvers are employed. The SAT solvers based on the CDCL algorithm [20] are among the principal computational tools in EDA.

One of the particularly challenging problems related to SAT solvers is that, given a hard SAT instance, it is not known how long it will take a solver to solve it. To the best of our knowledge, this problem has not been systematically

© The Author(s), under exclusive license to Springer Nature Switzerland AG 2023
L. Sokolinsky and M. Zymbler (Eds.): PCT 2023, CCIS 1868, pp. 123–136, 2023.
https://doi.org/10.1007/978-3-031-38864-4_9

studied until recently, although it was mentioned in the studies of the so-called heavy-tailed behavior [13]. In [27], it was suggested to estimate the hardness of SAT instances with respect to some decomposition of an original formula into a family of simpler subproblems that can be (individually) solved relatively fast. The approach from [27] is based on those described in [33] and [1], and its founding ideas combine well with the parallel computing paradigm. Here and in what follows, we use methods similar to that proposed in [27] to solve extremely hard problems related to EDA.

In the present paper, the central object of study is the problem of Logical Equivalence Checking of Boolean circuits (LEC) and its special case related to the Automatic Test Pattern Generation (ATPG) in the context of the so-called *stuck-at-fault model*. We demonstrate that parallel computing is essential for successfully solving the considered problems. The main practical result of the paper is the implementation of several parallel algorithms for solving the problems outlined above. Note that the only publicly available software that can be used for solving problems of this kind is the well-known ABC tool [6]. However, it employs a deprecated embedded MiniSat SAT solver [12] and does not support parallel mode.

Thus, the main contributions of this paper are the following: 1) we show that it is possible to adapt the technique from [28] to estimate the time required for solving hard ATPG instances and to solve them in parallel; 2) we develop and implement parallel algorithms for solving hard ATPG instances; 3) we successfully use the developed algorithms to solve in parallel some extremely hard benchmarks.

The paper is organized as follows. Section 2 describes the basic concepts and terms used in the study. Section 3 provides a description of the method for estimating hardness of LEC with respect to the SAT partitioning. Section 4 describes the developed algorithm for parallel ATPG testing using the "stuck-at fault" model. Section 5 presents the results of computational experiments on the application of the developed methods for solving problems of constructing complete sets of ATPG tests for several multipliers. Conclusion summarizes the study and points directions for further work.

2 Preliminaries

Electronic Design Automation (EDA) is a critically important area of the modern computer industry. It studies the problems related to the development and testing of integrated circuits. In recent years, the number of combinatorial problems arising in the context of these research directions has steadily increased, emphasizing the relevance of developing algorithms for solving them.

Boolean circuits are among the simplest and most widely used models of digital circuits. The convenience of Boolean circuits as a model is determined by the fact that their primary properties can be formulated within the framework of well-developed mathematical formalisms from graph theory and the theory of Boolean functions. This fact makes it possible to directly express many properties of real-world digital circuits in the language of Boolean circuits.

2.1   Boolean Circuits

A *Boolean circuit* is a directed acyclic labeled graph, defined as an ordered pair (V, E), where V is a set of vertices and E is a set of directed edges, called *arcs*. This graph can be viewed as a method for defining a complex function that transforms binary words into binary words. The vertices from V denote the input and the elementary functions that compose the considered function. Elementary functions are called *gates* and correspond to the logical connectives from some predefined basis. The most widely used bases are $\{\wedge, \vee, \neg\}$, $\{\wedge, \neg\}$, $\{\oplus, \wedge, 1\}$, and so forth. Concerning the vertices from V, we will use the standard definitions from graph theory: for any arc $(u, v) \in E$, vertex u is called *parent*, and vertex v *child*. The vertices without parents form the set of *inputs* of a circuit, which we denote by V^{in}; the vertices without children correspond to the circuit *outputs*, and their set is denoted by V^{out}. Every vertex $v \in V \setminus V^{\text{in}}$ is called a *gate*. A logical connective from the considered basis is associated with each gate.

An example of a Boolean circuit implementing the function $f\colon \{0,1\}^3 \to \{0,1\}^2$ over the basis $\{\vee, \wedge, \neg, \oplus\}$ is given in Fig. 1.

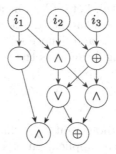

Fig. 1. An example of a Boolean circuit with three inputs (i_1, i_2, i_3) and seven gates

2.2   Boolean Satisfiability and Circuits

The *Boolean satisfiability problem* (SAT) is formulated as follows: for an arbitrary Boolean formula, determine whether it is satisfiable. Usually, it is assumed that the formula is in the Conjunctive Normal Form (CNF). Recall that (see, for example, [5]) a Boolean formula F is said to be *satisfiable* if there exists such an assignment of the variables occurring in F that the substitution of this assignment into F (see [7]) results in F taking the value 1 (True). We refer to such an *assignment* as a *satisfying* one. If there are no satisfying assignments for a given formula, then we say that the formula is *unsatisfiable*.

SAT is NP-complete in its decision variant and NP-hard when viewed as a search problem (i.e., when a formula is satisfiable, we should also provide a satisfying assignment). During recent years though, there have appeared many industrial problems in which the algorithms for solving SAT (SAT solvers) show good performance. Electronic Design Automation (EDA) is one of the areas where we can find many problems of this kind. Here we study a particular problem from EDA, called *Logical Equivalence Checking* (LEC). It can be stated as follows. For two different Boolean circuits S_f and S_h that define the functions $f, h \colon \{0,1\}^n \to \{0,1\}^m$, determine if it holds that $f \cong h$ (pointwise equivalence) or, put otherwise, S_f and S_h specify the same discrete function.

For two circuits S_f and S_h, we can efficiently (in polynomial time in the number of vertices in the circuits) construct a CNF that is unsatisfiable if and only if $f \cong h$. Below, we briefly describe the corresponding procedure.

Assume that B is a set of Boolean variables. Here and below, by $\{0,1\}^{|B|}$ we denote the set of all possible assignments of variables from B. Associate with each vertex $v \in V$ of circuit S_f a separate Boolean variable and denote the resulting set of variables by X. Assume that X is endowed with the same order relation as V. Let $X^{\text{in}} = \{x_1, \ldots, x_n\}$ be the set formed by all variables associated with the inputs of a circuit, and let $Y = \{y_1, \ldots, y_m\}$ be the set of variables associated with circuit outputs. Suppose that $v \in V \setminus V^{\text{in}}$ is an arbitrary gate, g_v is a logical connective corresponding to v, and x is a variable associated with v. Let $P(v)$ be the set of vertices that are the parents of v. By X_P we denote the set of variables associated with vertices from $P(v)$. Let $F(X_P)$ be an arbitrary formula over X_P that defines the function g_v. Consider the function $\phi_v \colon \{0,1\}^{|X_P \cup \{x\}|} \to \{0,1\}$ defined by the formula $F(X_p) \equiv x$ and denote by C_v the CNF representation of ϕ_v. We will refer to the following formula as the *template CNF* for the function $f \colon \{0,1\}^n \to \{0,1\}^m$:

$$C_f = \bigwedge_{v \in V \setminus V^{\text{in}}} C_v. \tag{1}$$

Note that the transition from the circuit S_f, which defines the function f, to CNF (1) consists of the sequential application of Tseitin transformations [31].

Recall that the notation x^σ, $\sigma \in \{0,1\}$, stands for the formula x when $\sigma = 1$ and the formula $\neg x$ when $\sigma = 0$. Both formulas are called *literals* for the variable x. Note that under this notation $\sigma^{\neg \sigma} = 0$ for any $\sigma \in \{0,1\}$. The following statement is very important for determining various properties of Boolean circuits. In its formulation, we refer to the well-known Unit Propagation rule [20], i.e., the main method for Boolean constraint propagation used in SAT solvers based on the CDCL algorithm.

Lemma 1. *For any $\alpha \in \{0,1\}^n$, $\alpha = (\alpha_1, \ldots, \alpha_n)$, the application of only the unit propagation rule to the formula $x_1^{\alpha_1} \wedge \ldots \wedge x_n^{\alpha_n} \wedge C_f$ results in the inference of values in the form of literals for all variables from $X \setminus X^{\text{in}}$, including the variables from $Y \colon y_1 = \gamma_1, \ldots, y_m = \gamma_m \colon f(\alpha) = \gamma, \gamma = (\gamma_1, \ldots, \gamma_m)$.*

This statement has appeared several times in papers related to Boolean circuits and SAT, e.g., [3, 11, 26].

2.3 Equivalence Checking for Boolean Circuits

Let us again consider the LEC problem for two circuits S_f and S_h such that $f, h \colon \{0,1\}^n \to \{0,1\}^m$. Assume that the same order is defined on the sets of inputs of S_f and S_h (which matches the order of bits of an input word from $\{0,1\}^n$) and glue the pairs of inputs of these two circuits having the same numbers. We denote the obtained circuit by $S_{f \triangle h}$. Note that it defines (in the sense described above) a function $f \triangle h \colon \{0,1\}^n \to \{0,1\}^{2m}$. Next, construct a template CNF $C_{f \triangle h}$ for $S_{f \triangle h}$ using the algorithm described in the previous subsection. Assume that $Y^f = \{y_1^f, \ldots, y_m^f\}$ and $Y^h = \{y_1^h, \ldots, y_m^h\}$ are the sets of variables associated with the outputs of the circuits. Consider the formula

$$\mathcal{M} = (y_1^f \oplus y_1^h \vee \ldots \vee y_m^f \oplus y_m^h),$$

which is called a *miter* [23], and construct an equisatisfiable CNF for it using Tseitin transformations. We denote the resulting CNF by $C(\mathcal{M})$. It is easy to show that the circuits S_f and S_h are equivalent ($f \cong h$) if and only if the CNF $C_{f \triangle h} \wedge C(\mathcal{M})$ is unsatisfiable.

2.4 Automatic Test Pattern Generation for Boolean Circuits

The following problem is of extreme importance for the microelectronic industry. Assume that there is some possibility of defects when manufacturing digital circuits. As a result of a defect, one (or more) nonconstant gate in a circuit becomes constant and outputs only 0 or only 1 on every input word. This type of defect is known as the *stuck-at-fault* model. The usual practice to check whether the circuits have stuck-at-fault defects is to test some control sample of randomly chosen designs from the manufactured products. In this context, it is important to have a technology that, based on the inputs given to a tested circuit and the output values obtained from it, makes it possible to understand that some gate does not satisfy the original specification due to being stuck at either 0 or 1. Naturally, a circuit with a stuck-at-fault gate is defective if it is not equivalent to an original correct circuit. Thus, in the context of this problem, for each gate $v \in V \setminus V^{\mathrm{in}}$ of a considered circuit, we need to find the assignments $(\alpha_0, \gamma_0, \gamma_0')$ and $(\alpha_1, \gamma_1, \gamma_1')$ that can be used to detect whether v is stuck at some value. For example, if gate v is stuck at constant 0 (and this fact does not agree with the design of the original circuit), then on some input α_0, an original circuit would produce the output γ_0, while a defective one would output γ_0'. Thus, to thoroughly test a circuit containing K gates for stuck-at-fault gates, we need $2K$ triplets of the kind indicated above, generated in advance. It is worth noting that a gate v stuck at some value may not influence the functionality of a circuit, i.e., a *faulty* circuit may be equivalent to an original one. That situation is not considered critical for obvious reasons. The problem of constructing a complete set of tests for all gates of S_f in the above context is known as the *Automated Test Pattern Generation* problem (ATPG) for the stuck-at-fault model.

3 Solving ATPG for Boolean Circuits Using Parallel SAT-Based Algorithms

In this section, we consider ATPG for two Boolean circuits over the basis $\{\wedge, \neg\}$. The corresponding circuits are known as And-Inverter Graphs (AIG) and are widely used in symbolic verification.

3.1 The Hardness of LEC with Respect to SAT Partitioning

An interesting fact is that modern SAT solvers based on the CDCL algorithm [20] often show good efficiency on the ATPG problem for many commercial digital circuits. This fact was one of the main reasons for the explosive growth of interest in the use of SAT solvers in EDA. However, for many functions specified by circuits, ATPG can be extremely hard, at least for some gates. In such a situation, a SAT solver may work with a corresponding LEC problem for hours or even days, and for standard sequential SAT solvers, there are no known ways to construct any prognosis regarding how long it will take to solve a problem. However, such a prognosis can be constructed if we split an original hard SAT instance into a family of simpler subproblems that can be solved in parallel. It was proposed in [27] to estimate the hardness of a Boolean formula with respect to its decomposition drawing on ideas from [33] and [1].

3.2 Exploiting the Structure of Circuits When Solving ATPG

Below we employ the approach described in [28] for estimating the hardness of the considered instances. In particular, we consider LEC for two Boolean circuits S_f and S_h. In the set of variables associated with the vertices of the circuit $S_{f\triangle h}$, we outline the set $X^{\text{in}} = \{x_1, \ldots, x_n\}$ of variables corresponding to the inputs of the circuits. Next, we split X^{in} into pairwise disjoint subsets $X^1, \ldots, X^q$ as described below. We choose some $1 < k < n$ and set $q = n/k$ if n is divisible by k. Otherwise, we set $q = \lceil n/k \rceil$. In the first case, each X^j, $j \in \{1, \ldots, q\}$, contains k variables from X^{in}. In the second case, each set $X^1, \ldots, X^{\lfloor n/k \rfloor}$ contains k variables, while the set X^q contains r variables, $n = \lfloor n/k \rfloor \cdot k + r$, $r \in \{1, \ldots, k - 1\}$. With each set X^j, $j \in \{1, \ldots, q\}$, we associate two Boolean functions $\lambda_1^j \colon \{0,1\}^{|X^j|} \rightarrow \{0,1\}$ and $\lambda_2^j \colon \{0,1\}^{|X^j|} \rightarrow \{0,1\}$ such that $\lambda_2^j = \neg\lambda_1^j$.

Recall that a SAT partitioning [16] of an arbitrary CNF formula C over variables X is a set of formulas $G_1, \ldots, G_s$ such that two conditions are satisfied:

1. C and $C \wedge (G_1 \vee \ldots \vee G_s)$ are equisatisfiable;
2. for any $i, l \in \{1, \ldots, s\}$, $i \neq l$, formula $C \wedge G_i \wedge G_l$ is unsatisfiable.

Denote by ϕ_1^j and ϕ_2^j the Boolean formulas in CNF that specify the functions λ_1^j and λ_2^j. It was shown in [28] that the set of all $s = 2^{\lceil n/k \rceil}$ formulas of the kind $\phi^1 \wedge \ldots \wedge \phi^{\lceil n/k \rceil}$, where ϕ^j, $j \in \{1, \ldots, \lceil n/k \rceil\}$, represents both ϕ_1^j and ϕ_2^j, defines a SAT partitioning of $C_{f\triangle h} \wedge C(\mathcal{M})$.

An important property of any SAT partitioning is that all problems of the kind $G_i \wedge C$, $i \in \{1, \ldots, s\}$, can be solved in parallel. That is why, using the SAT partitioning from [28], to solve SAT for $C_{f \Delta h} \wedge C(\mathcal{M})$ we need to determine the satisfiability of $2^{\lceil n/k \rceil}$ formulas of the kind

$$\phi^1 \wedge \ldots \wedge \phi^{\lceil n/k \rceil} \wedge C_{f \Delta h} \wedge C(\mathcal{M}),$$

and this can be done in parallel.

Another important property of the partitioning strategy from [28] is that the total time required to solve all $2^{\lceil n/k \rceil}$ subproblems of the described kind can be quite accurately estimated for some hard LEC instances using a simple probabilistic algorithm (related to the Monte Carlo method), described in [27] and [28]. For this purpose, it is sufficient to use a sample of N out of $2^{\lceil n/k \rceil}$ formulas of the kind $\phi^1 \wedge \ldots \wedge \phi^{\lceil n/k \rceil}$, chosen independently and uniformly from the set of all possible formulas of this kind, and calculate the following value:

$$\frac{1}{N} \sum_{j=1}^{N} t_A \left(\left(\phi^1 \wedge \ldots \wedge \phi^{\lceil n/k \rceil} \right)^j \wedge C_{f \Delta h} \wedge C(\mathcal{M}) \right). \tag{2}$$

In (2), we denote by $\left(\phi^1 \wedge \ldots \wedge \phi^{\lceil n/k \rceil} \right)^j$ the formula number j in the random sample of size N formed by formulas of the kind $\phi^1 \wedge \ldots \wedge \phi^{\lceil n/k \rceil}$ and by $t_A(C)$ the runtime of a complete SAT solver A on formula C. From the results in [27], it follows that the value (2) the better approximates the hardness of the formula $C_{f \Delta h} \wedge C(\mathcal{M})$ with respect to the SAT partitioning

$$\Pi = \left\{ \left(\phi^1 \wedge \ldots \wedge \phi^{\lceil n/k \rceil} \right)^l \right\}_{l=1}^{2^{\lceil n/k \rceil}},$$

the larger N is. However, it was shown in [28] that the estimate (2) can be accurate for some circuits, even if N is in the range of hundreds. We will use expressions of the kind (2) to estimate the hardness of some hard ATPG instances.

4   LEC and ATPG Using Parallel Computing

In this section, we describe the general strategy employed for solving ATPG instances in parallel. Parallel solving is relevant here because, to construct a complete set of ATPG tests, it is often necessary to solve tens of thousands of LEC instances. An important fact is that such problems are relatively simple for modern SAT solvers in most cases, even when we consider circuits specifying functions for which the inversion problems are well known to be hard, e.g., multiplication algorithms. However, there are no a priori known estimates for the runtime of a SAT solver, even for relatively simple ATPG instances. Aside from that, as we will see below, some ATPG instances are extremely hard for any state-of-the-art SAT solvers. Both reasons make an appealing case for solving ATPG in parallel.

Assume that we have the correct original circuit S_f and a circuit $S_{f'} = S_{(f,v',\delta)}$, constructed out from S_f by changing a gate v into a gate v' of the same arity that takes on the constant value $\delta \in \{0,1\}$. We refer to v' as the *stuck-at-fault image* of gate v. Next, fix some arbitrary $v' \in V \setminus V^{\text{in}}$ and $\delta \in \{0,1\}$ and consider the circuits S_f and $S_{f'}$. Note that the same order (described above) is defined on the sets of vertices of both circuits. We refer to vertices that have the same numbers under this order as *same-named vertices*.

First, glue the same-named inputs of circuits S_f and $S_{f'}$, thereby constructing a circuit $S_{f \triangle f'}$. Note, that the gluing procedure can be further extended to some of the gates from $S_{f \triangle f'}$. Ideologically, the corresponding procedure is similar to the one used to glue the vertices of a binary decision tree, by defining a Boolean function when constructing the corresponding Reduced Ordered Binary Decision Diagram (ROBDD) [22]. In particular, each gate v of the circuit $S_{f \triangle f'}$ is defined, depending on its arity, by three *coordinates*, which specify its parents (one or two) and the Boolean connective linked with v. If the two gates are specified by the same coordinates, then they can be glued. For an arbitrary gate $v \in V \setminus V^{\text{in}}$, consider all paths connecting v with vertices from Y. We denote by D_v the set of all vertices these paths pass through (including v) and refer to D_v as the *shadow* of the vertex v.

Let $v \in V \setminus V^{\text{in}}$ be an arbitrary gate and v' the stuck-at-fault image of gate v. It is easy to see that the following fact holds.

Statement 1. *When the gluing procedure described above is applied to circuits S_f and $S_{f'}$, it glues all same-named vertices, except for a (possible) set of same-named vertices that lie in the shadows D_v and D'_v.*

The proof of this statement follows directly from the definition of the gluing procedure and the fact that $v \neq v'$ in the sense of equivalence of the corresponding coordinates.

We denote by $\tilde{S}_{f \triangle f'}$ the circuit obtained from $S_{f \triangle f'}$ by gluing all possible vertices using the procedure described above. Note that some of the same-named outputs of circuits S_f and $S_{f'}$ can also be glued together. Let us construct for $\tilde{S}_{f \triangle f'}$ its template CNF $\tilde{C}_{f \triangle f'}$. We denote by $\tilde{C}(\mathcal{M})$ the CNF formula that represents (in the sense mentioned above) the miter of the same-named outputs of all output variables of S_f and $S_{f'}$ that have not been glued together. Then the following theorem holds.

Theorem 1. *If the CNF formula $\tilde{C}_{f \triangle f'} \wedge \tilde{C}(\mathcal{M})$ is satisfiable, then by solving SAT for this formula we get the triplet $(\alpha_\delta, \gamma_\delta, \gamma'_\delta)$ for detecting the corresponding fault in gate v.*

Proof Sketch. Similar to many other facts that establish the interconnection between the properties of circuits and that of the formulas constructed for those circuits, this proof is based on Lemma 1. It follows from the lemma that the number of assignments that satisfy the CNF $\tilde{C}_{f \triangle f'}$ is equal to 2^n since each input vector $\alpha \in \{0,1\}^n$ induces (in the sense of Lemma 1) a single assignment that satisfies $\tilde{C}_{f \Delta f'}$. It is easy to see that, for any assignment satisfying $\tilde{C}_{f \Delta f'}$, there exists a single input $\alpha \in \{0,1\}^n$ that induces it. Assume that some $\alpha \in \{0,1\}^n$ induces for the circuits S_f and $S_{f'}$ assignments in which the values of the variables $y \in D_v$ and $y' \in D_{v'}$ are different, where y and y' are output variables with the same number in both S_f and $S_{f'}$. In this case, it is clear that such an assignment also induces an assignment satisfying $\tilde{C}_{f \Delta f'} \wedge \tilde{C}(\mathcal{M})$, which yields the corresponding triplet $(\alpha_\delta, \gamma_\delta, \gamma'_\delta)$ for detecting the fault in the gate v. In the opposite case, i.e., if every $\alpha \in \{0,1\}^n$ induces an assignment in which all pairs of output gates with the same number have the same value, then the formula $\tilde{C}(\mathcal{M})$ takes on the value *False*, and therefore, $\tilde{C}_{f \Delta f'} \wedge \tilde{C}(\mathcal{M})$ is unsatisfiable.   □

We mentioned above that SAT for the CNF $\tilde{C}_{f \Delta f'} \wedge \tilde{C}(\mathcal{M})$ may be either simple or extremely hard for modern SAT solvers. Unfortunately, we cannot always estimate the hardness of an arbitrary problem quickly since the corresponding procedure may possibly require a lot of time, thus making its application unreasonable for simple problems. In this situation, we use the following approach. We denote by R the set of CNF formulas encoding all possible ATPG problems for the considered circuit S_f. Define some time limit t_1 and launch a SAT solver A on each formula $C \in R$ in parallel, with the time limit t_1 for each instance. If the solver A succeeds in proving the satisfiability of a formula, then we obtain the corresponding test of the kind $(\alpha_\delta, \gamma_\delta, \gamma'_\delta)$, $\delta \in \{0,1\}$. Otherwise, denote by R^{t_1} the set of all CNF formulas from R for which the unsatisfiability was proven in time $\leq t_1$. Consider the set $R_1 = R \setminus R^{t_1}$, fix a time limit t_2, $t_2 > t_1$, and repeat the operations above. Next, fix some k, $k \geq 1$, and perform k iterations of the described process. Let $R_k = R_{k-1} \setminus R^{t_k}$ be the final set. If $R_k = \emptyset$ and the unsatisfiability was proven for all formulas, then S_f and $S_{f'}$ are equivalent.

Otherwise, set R_k consists of hard CNF formulas, and we can consider SAT for each one separately. We refer to the described procedure as *k-step SAT filtering of* R. The algorithm in pseudocode is given in Algorithm 1.

5   Computational Experiments

Here we present the results of computational experiments on solving ATPG using the algorithms described above. In all experiments, as a computing environment, we used a Yandex Cloud machine based on the Intel Ice Lake platform with 96 CPU cores at a clock speed of 2 GHz and 288 GB of RAM. All algorithms were implemented as MPI applications using the Python programming language and the mpi4py library. For debugging, we employed the Academician V. M. Matrosov cluster of the Irkutsk Supercomputer Center [21]. In all experiments, we used the Kissat SAT solver[1] to solve ATPG instances in SAT form.

Note that the choice of the programming language here is mostly dictated by the fact that the presented results are considered a study. Of course, for industrial implementation, it makes sense to implement all considered algorithms in

---

[1] https://github.com/arminbiere/kissat.

Algorithm 1: Pseudocode of the algorithm of iterative sieving of ATPG instances for all gates in a circuit

---

Input   : Set of CNFs R; Number of steps $k \geq 0$; SAT-solver A; Set of time
            limits $T = \{t_1, t_2, \ldots, t_k\}$, $t_1 < t_2 < \ldots < t_k$.
Output: Set of CNFs R_k.
$R_0 \leftarrow R$;
for $i \leftarrow 1$ to k do
    for $C \in R_{i-1}$ do
        // Run A on CNF C with time limit t_i
        $result \leftarrow SolveProblem(A, C, t_i)$;
        if $result$ is $INDET$ then
            C add to R_i;
        end
    end
end

C/C++, for instance. It is also worth noting that the considered benchmarks are computationally quite hard. For this reason, the major portion of the program runtime was spent on invoking the Kissat solver (written in C). Compared to the total runtime of all Kissat runs, the time spent on executing the Python code was very small.

We used as benchmarks the problem of constructing complete sets of ATPG tests for several functions implementing algorithms for multiplying pairs of natural numbers. Specifically, the following multiplication algorithms were considered: standard *column* multiplier, *Wallace tree* algorithm [32], *Dadda* algorithm [10], and *Karatsuba decomposition* algorithm [17]. We considered the variants of the algorithms that multiply two Q-bit numbers, where $Q \in \{20, 32\}$. We refer to the corresponding benchmarks as C_Q, W_Q, D_Q, and K_Q for Column, Wallace, Dadda, and Karatsuba algorithms, respectively. For each algorithm, a Boolean circuit was constructed implementing the algorithm in the form of an And-Inverter Graph (AIG) (i.e., over the basis $\{\neg, \wedge\}$), using the Transalg program [24,25]. Furthermore, to construct a complete set of ATPG tests for the corresponding AIG, a specific tool was developed as a Python script.

In the first series of experiments, we used k-step SAT filtering (Algorithm 1). The results are given in Table 1. The column "Algorithm" shows the multiplication algorithm in question; "Number of problems" gives the total number of subproblems in the complete ATPG test suite for the considered algorithm, which is twice the number of gates in the corresponding circuit. The following columns indicate the number of subproblems solved and unsolved (INDET columns) at each step. At each filtering step, the algorithm attempts to solve all the subproblems remaining unsolved from the previous step but with a larger time limit. Thus, for problems with $Q = 20$, the time limit in the first step was 2 s, in the second step it was increased to 100 s, and in the third step, to 43 200 s (that is, 12 h). In the cases with $Q = 32$, since the corresponding problems were

Table 1. k-step SAT-filtering for ATPG testing of multipliers

Algorithm	Number of problems	First step		Second step		Third step	
		Solved	INDET	Solved	INDET	Solved	INDET
C_{20}	18592	18574	18	18	0	–	–
D_{20}	17038	17026	12	12	0	–	–
W_{20}	18034	18034	0	–	–	–	–
K_{20}	37726	39540	186	164	22	21	9
C_{32}	48962	48298	664	659	5	5	0
D_{32}	44926	44789	137	137	0	–	–
W_{32}	46978	46978	0	–	–	–	–
K_{32}	86826	83025	3801	3727	74	52	22

significantly harder, the time limit was increased for the first two steps, namely, to 3 s in the first step and to 1000 s seconds in the second.

Based on the results of the first part of the experiments, we can draw the following conclusions. All ATPG problems for C_Q, W_Q, and D_Q, $Q \in \{20, 32\}$, were easy for Kissat (the longest solving time was 2353 seconds for one of the problems for C_{32}). However, several tests for the algorithms K_{20} and K_{32} proved extremely hard: Kissat consistently failed to solve them in 12 h. Nevertheless, all such problems for K_{20} were solved in parallel using the technique described in Sect. 3.2. Specifically, the set of input variables X^{in} was split into subsets of four variables each. Thus the sets X^j, $j \in \{1, \ldots, 10\}$, were used for K_{20}, whereas the sets X^j, $j \in \{1, \ldots, 16\}$, were used for K_{32}. In each case, the function

$$\lambda^j = x_1{}^j \oplus x_2{}^j \oplus x_3{}^j \oplus x_4{}^j$$

and its negation were associated with the set X^j in the manner described in Sect. 3.2. The results of the second part of the experiments are given in Table 2.

Let us describe Table 2. In all columns concerning the time, it is given in seconds. The "Instance" column contains the name of the ATPG instance for K_{20}, which includes the number identifying the stuck-at-fault gate and its polarity ("n" for negative and "p" for positive). In "Total number of subproblems", we have the total number of subproblems in the partitioning. The column "Average time" shows the mean total time required to solve a subproblem. In "Total time", we see the total time required to solve all subproblems using one processor core. The "Wall-clock time (96 cores)" column shows the time it took to solve all subproblems from the corresponding partitioning; this time corresponds to the total time the user would need to solve the LEC instance using the given partitioning on 96 cores. Unfortunately, 22 similar problems for K_{32}, not solved by the 3-step filtering algorithm, proved very hard even to be solved with the described partitioning strategy; in this case, we have only their rather large hardness estimates. For example, in one of those problems, we estimated that the total time required

Table 2. Solving hard ATPG instances for K_{20} using Input Decomposition

Instance	Total number of subproblems	Average time	Total time	Wall-clock time (96 cores)
19187_n	1024	460.24	471285.76	5618
19188_n	1024	450.17	460974.08	5494
19189_p	1024	450.00	460800.00	5493
19192_p	1024	1681.61	1721968.64	19670
19193_n	1024	1685.78	1726238.72	19794
19648_n	1024	911.63	933509.12	10501
19649_p	1024	910.97	932833.28	10480
19656_n	1024	1399.76	1433354.24	16261
19657_n	1024	1402.14	1435791.36	16329

to completely solve the subproblems from the decomposition would be at least 1.54×10^8 s (almost 20 days of wall-clock time on 96 cores).

Thus, it is clear that, for all considered multiplication algorithms (except K_{32}), the proposed method made it possible to construct systems of ATPG tests that reveal a single fault of the specified kind for each gate in the corresponding circuit. In this sense, the constructed suites of tests can be regarded as complete.

6   Conclusion

In the paper, we studied extremely hard SAT instances that arise in the Automated Test Pattern Generation area of Electronic Design Automation. We showed that using a special form of SAT partitioning it is possible to decompose these problems and solve them in parallel. To improve the efficiency of parallel solving, we proposed an algorithm for filtering ATPG instances using a SAT solver, exploiting the fact that ATPG SAT instances for different gates have drastically different hardness. While the vast majority of such instances are relatively simple, their total number can be in the tens of thousands. This fact together with the existence of extremely hard instances, which can be tackled using the decomposition strategy, makes the use of parallel computing a requirement for efficient test generation, and the results of our experiments emphasize this conclusion.

Acknowledgments. Victor Kondratiev and Alexander Semenov were supported by the Russian Science Foundation (project 22-21-00583). They contributed to the theoretical foundations of the proposed method and developed the corresponding algorithms.

Stepan Kochemazov received support from the Ministry of Science and Higher Education of the Russian Federation (research project № 121041300065-9). He developed the benchmark sets used in the experimental part of the research.

References

1. Ansótegui, C., Bonet, M.L., Levy, J., Manyà, F.: Measuring the hardness of SAT instances. In: AAAI, pp. 222–228 (2008)
2. Bard, G.V.: Algebraic Cryptanalysis. Springer, USA (2009). https://doi.org/10.1007/978-0-387-88757-9
3. Bessière, C., Katsirelos, G., Narodytska, N., Walsh, T.: Circuit complexity and decompositions of global constraints. In: IJCAI, pp. 412–418 (2009)
4. Biere, A., Cimatti, A., Clarke, E., Zhu, Y.: Symbolic model checking without BDDs. In: Cleaveland, W.R. (ed.) TACAS 1999. LNCS, vol. 1579, pp. 193–207. Springer, Heidelberg (1999). https://doi.org/10.1007/3-540-49059-0_14
5. Biere, A., Heule, M., van Maaren, H., Walsh, T. (eds.): Handbook of Satisfiability. FAIA, 2nd edn., vol. 336. IOS Press (2021)
6. Brayton, R., Mishchenko, A.: ABC: an academic industrial-strength verification tool. In: Touili, T., Cook, B., Jackson, P. (eds.) CAV 2010. LNCS, vol. 6174, pp. 24–40. Springer, Heidelberg (2010). https://doi.org/10.1007/978-3-642-14295-6_5
7. Chang, C.L., Lee, R.C.T.: Symbolic Logic and Mechanical Theorem Proving. Computer Science Classics, Academic Press, Cambridge (1973)
8. Clarke, E., Kroening, D., Lerda, F.: A tool for checking ANSI-C programs. In: Jensen, K., Podelski, A. (eds.) TACAS 2004. LNCS, vol. 2988, pp. 168–176. Springer, Heidelberg (2004). https://doi.org/10.1007/978-3-540-24730-2_15
9. Courtois, N.T., Bard, G.V.: Algebraic cryptanalysis of the data encryption standard. In: Galbraith, S.D. (ed.) Cryptography and Coding 2007. LNCS, vol. 4887, pp. 152–169. Springer, Heidelberg (2007). https://doi.org/10.1007/978-3-540-77272-9_10
10. Dadda, L.: Some schemes for parallel multipliers. Alta Frequenza **34**(5), 349–356 (1965)
11. Drechsler, R., Junttila, T.A., Niemelä, I.: Non-clausal SAT and ATPG. In: Handbook of Satisfiability. FAIA, 2nd edn., vol. 336, pp. 1047–1086. IOS Press (2021)
12. Eén, N., Sörensson, N.: An extensible SAT-solver. In: Giunchiglia, E., Tacchella, A. (eds.) SAT 2003. LNCS, vol. 2919, pp. 502–518. Springer, Heidelberg (2004). https://doi.org/10.1007/978-3-540-24605-3_37
13. Gomes, C.P., Selman, B., Crato, N., Kautz, H.A.: Heavy-tailed phenomena in satisfiability and constraint satisfaction problems. J. Autom. Reason. **24**(1/2), 67–100 (2000)
14. Heule, M.J.H.: Schur number five. In: AAAI, pp. 6598–6606 (2018)
15. Heule, M.J.H., Kullmann, O., Marek, V.W.: Solving and verifying the Boolean Pythagorean triples problem via cube-and-conquer. In: Creignou, N., Le Berre, D. (eds.) SAT 2016. LNCS, vol. 9710, pp. 228–245. Springer, Cham (2016). https://doi.org/10.1007/978-3-319-40970-2_15
16. Hyvärinen, A.E.J.: Grid based propositional satisfiability solving. Ph.D. thesis. Aalto University Publication Series (2011)
17. Knuth, D.: The Art of Computer Programming, Volume 2: Seminumerical Algorithms. Addison-Wesley Series in Computer Science & Information Processing. Addison-Wesley (1969)
18. Konev, B., Lisitsa, A.: A SAT attack on the Erdős discrepancy conjecture. In: Sinz, C., Egly, U. (eds.) SAT 2014. LNCS, vol. 8561, pp. 219–226. Springer, Cham (2014). https://doi.org/10.1007/978-3-319-09284-3_17
19. Kroening, D.: Software verification. In: Handbook of Satisfiability. FAIA, 2nd edn., vol. 336, pp. 791–818. IOS Press (2021)

20. Marques-Silva, J., Lynce, I., Malik, S.: Conflict-driven clause learning SAT solvers. In: Handbook of Satisfiability. FAIA, 2nd edn., vol. 336, pp. 133–182. IOS Press (2021)
21. Irkutsk Supercomputer Center of SB RAS. http://hpc.icc.ru
22. Meinel, C., Theobald, T.: Algorithms and Data Structures in VLSI Design: OBDD - Foundations and Applications. Springer, Heidelberg (1998). https://doi.org/10.1007/978-3-642-58940-9
23. Molitor, P., Mohnke, J.: Equivalence Checking of Digital Circuits: Fundamentals, Principles, Methods. Kluwer Academic Publishers (2004)
24. Otpuschennikov, I., Semenov, A., Gribanova, I., Zaikin, O., Kochemazov, S.: Encoding cryptographic functions to SAT using TRANSALG system. In: ECAI, pp. 1594–1595 (2016)
25. Semenov, A., Otpuschennikov, I., Gribanova, I., Zaikin, O., Kochemazov, S.: Translation of algorithmic descriptions of discrete functions to SAT with applications to cryptanalysis problems. Log. Methods Comput. Sci. **16**(1), 1–42 (2020)
26. Semenov, A.A.: Decomposition representations of logical equations in problems of inversion of discrete functions. J. Comput. Syst. Sci. Int. **48**, 718–731 (2009)
27. Semenov, A.A., Chivilikhin, D., Pavlenko, A., Otpuschennikov, I.V., Ulyantsev, V., Ignatiev, A.: Evaluating the hardness of SAT instances using evolutionary optimization algorithms. In: CP, LIPIcs, vol. 210, pp. 47:1–47:18 (2021)
28. Semenov, A.A., Chukharev, K., Tarasov, E., Chivilikhin, D., Kondratiev, V.: Estimating the hardness of SAT encodings for logical equivalence checking of Boolean circuits. arXiv abs/2210.01484 (2022)
29. Semenov, A., Zaikin, O., Bespalov, D., Posypkin, M.: Parallel logical cryptanalysis of the generator A5/1 in BNB-grid system. In: Malyshkin, V. (ed.) PaCT 2011. LNCS, vol. 6873, pp. 473–483. Springer, Heidelberg (2011). https://doi.org/10.1007/978-3-642-23178-0_43
30. Semenov, A.A., Zaikin, O., Otpuschennikov, I.V., Kochemazov, S., Ignatiev, A.: On cryptographic attacks using backdoors for SAT. In: AAAI, pp. 6641–6648 (2018)
31. Tseitin, G.S.: On the complexity of derivation in propositional calculus. In: Studies in Constructive Mathematics and Mathematical Logic, Part II, pp. 115–125 (1970)
32. Wallace, C.S.: A suggestion for a fast multiplier. IEEE Trans. Electron. Comput. **EC-13**(1), 14–17 (1964)
33. Williams, R., Gomes, C.P., Selman, B.: Backdoors to typical case complexity. In: IJCAI, pp. 1173–1178 (2003)
34. Zaikin, O.: Inverting 43-step MD4 via cube-and-conquer. In: IJCAI, pp. 1894–1900 (2022)
35. Zhang, H.: Combinatorial designs by SAT solvers. In: Handbook of Satisfiability. FAIA, 2nd edn., vol. 336, pp. 819–858. IOS Press (2021)

Parallelization of the Generalized Multimode Nonlinear Schrödinger Equation Solver: A Performance Analysis

Evgeniy Kazakov, Jiexing Gao[✉], Pavel Anisimov, and Viacheslav Zemlyakov

Huawei Technologies Co., Ltd., Russian Research Institute,
Moscow, Russian Federation
gaojiexing@huawei.com

Abstract. The numerical modeling of optical signal propagation in fibers usually requires high-performance solvers for the nonlinear Schrödinger equation. Multicore CPUs and Graphical Processing Units (GPUs) are usually used for highly intensive parallel computations. We consider several implementations of solvers for the generalized multimode nonlinear Schrödinger equation. Reference MATLAB code (freely available at https://github.com/WiseLabAEP/GMMNLSE-Solver-FINAL) of the split-step Fourier method (SSFM) and the massively parallel algorithm (MPA) have been redesigned using the C++ OpenMP interface and C-oriented Compute Unified Device Architecture (CUDA) by Nvidia. Using this code, we explore several approaches for parallelization of computations. We show that, for small numbers of modes, the OpenMP implementation of the MPA is up to an order of magnitude faster than the GPU implementation owing to data transfer overheads, while the GPU implementation overperforms the CPU one starting from 10 modes. We also give several practical recommendations regarding the integration step size of the solvers.

Keywords: Nonlinear Schrödinger equation · Split step Fourier method · Massively parallel algorithm

1 Introduction

Optical fibers are widely used in telecommunication. The so-called multimode fibers enable the simultaneous propagation of multiple guided modes. Each mode can be encoded as an independent signal, increasing the throughput via spatial multiplexing. The propagation of light in such fibers is influenced by several physical phenomena (polarization effects, high-order dispersion, Kerr and Raman nonlinearities [1]) and can be described by the generalized multimode nonlinear Schrödinger equation (GMMNLSE) [10].

The GMMNLSE can be solved numerically by the split-step Fourier method (SSFM), in which the integration of the linear term of the GMMNLSE is done over the frequency domain, while that of the nonlinear term is done over the time

© The Author(s), under exclusive license to Springer Nature Switzerland AG 2023
L. Sokolinsky and M. Zymbler (Eds.): PCT 2023, CCIS 1868, pp. 137–151, 2023.
https://doi.org/10.1007/978-3-031-38864-4_10

domain. The complexity of the SSFM grows as $O(P^4)$, where P is the number of modes. That makes computations time-consuming in the case of multimode fibers.

The massively parallel algorithm (MPA) was introduced in [9]. Originally, the method was designed for multicore CPUs and allowed performing simulations $M/2$ times as fast as the SSFM, where M is the number of CPU cores. Later, a GPU implementation of the MPA was described in [13]. It provided orders-of-magnitude speedup over the SSFM executed on CPUs. A 30-fold speedup with respect to the single processor version of the code was reported in [7].

Owing to the high computational burden, it is very important to set the optimal parameters of the solvers to guarantee accurate results or, at least, to assess the accuracy of computations. The principal parameter controlling the computational time and accuracy is the integration step size, i.e., the spatial discretization step of the fiber along its length. So far, there is no well-established guide to choosing the optimal step size apart from empirical rules that are not fail-safe.

In this work, we develop parallelized C++ versions of the SSFM and MPA based on the MATLAB code from [12]. Section 2 provides short theoretical basics about GMMNLSE, SSFM and MPA. Section 3 presents C++ code implementations for both multicore CPU and GPU platforms. By using them, In Sect. 4 we explore performance issues, with a particular focus on how to maximize accuracy in a minimum time. Sections 4.2–4.5 formulates our practical recommendations on the platform to be used (i.e., CPU versus GPU), parallelization strategy, floating-point precision, integration step size and application adaptive step size. Conclusions are drawn in Sect. 5.

2   Theoretical Information

The GMMNLSE has been extensively described [1]. Here we briefly summarize the mathematical background to put the subsequent discussion into proper context. The GMMNLSE of the electric field temporal envelope $A_p(z,t)$ for the spatial mode p in time t at spatial position z can be written in an operator form as

$$\frac{\partial A_p}{\partial z} = \mathfrak{D} A_p + \mathfrak{N} A_p, \tag{1}$$

where $\mathfrak{D}$ is a linear (dispersion) operator involving the temporal derivatives of A_p,

$$\mathfrak{D} A_p = i\big(\beta_0^{(p)} - \operatorname{Re}\beta_0^{(0)}\big) A_p - i\big(\beta_1^{(p)} - \operatorname{Re}\beta_1^{(0)}\big)\frac{\partial A_p}{\partial t} + i\sum_{n\geq 2}\frac{\beta_n^{(p)}}{n!}\left(i\frac{\partial}{\partial t}\right)^n A_p, \tag{2}$$

and $\mathfrak{N}$ is a nonlinear operator of A_p involving also other modes $(A_q,\ q \neq p)$, namely,

$$\mathfrak{N}A_p = i\frac{n_2\omega_0}{c}\left(1 + \frac{i}{\omega_0}\frac{\partial}{\partial t}\right) \times$$

$$\times \sum_{l,m,n}\left\{(1 - f_R)\,S_{plmn}^K A_l A_m A_n^* + f_R S_{plmn}^R A_l\,[h \otimes (A_m A_n^*)]\right\};\qquad (3)$$

$\beta_j^{(p)}$ stands for the j-th-order dispersion coefficient of the p-th mode; n_2 is the nonlinear index coefficient; ω_0 is the center frequency; f_R denotes the fractional Raman contribution to nonlinearity; S_{plmn}^K and S_{plmn}^R are the modal overlap tensors for the Kerr and Raman terms, respectively; h is the Raman response function; $\otimes$ represents the convolution operator.

We consider the SSFM, that is, the spatial discretization of the fiber along its length. The integration step Δz along the z direction is chosen small enough so as to assume that operators $\mathfrak{D}$ and $\mathfrak{N}$ act independently. That is the so-called weak nonlinearity approximation. Then the integration of Eq. (1) can be decoupled with the operator $\mathfrak{N}$ integrated over the time domain and the operator $\mathfrak{D}$ integrated over the frequency domain using the Fourier transform. The SSFM algorithm can be summarized as follows:

1. Integrate Eq. (1) by setting $\mathfrak{D} = 0$ to compute $A_p^{\mathfrak{N}}(t, z)$.
2. Apply the Fourier transform to $A_p^{\mathfrak{N}}(t, z)$ to compute $A_p^{\mathfrak{N}}(\omega, z)$.
3. Integrate $\mathfrak{D}A_p^{\mathfrak{N}}(\omega, z)$ in the frequency domain to compute $A_p(\omega, z + \Delta z)$.
4. Take the inverse Fourier transform of $A_p(\omega, z + \Delta z)$ to obtain $A_p(t, z + \Delta z)$.

Note that all computations for the SSFM are performed sequentially.

In the MPA, computations are performed using M threads. Besides the fine discretization (as in the SSFM) with the step Δz, we consider the long step size $L = M\Delta z$, which incorporates M substeps of Δz. Computations are performed iteratively. For $i = 1, \ldots, M$, Eq. (1) is integrated by the SSFM with the integration step size equal to $i\Delta z$, thereby computing $A_p(t, z_i)$ for a given $A_p(t, z_0)$, where $z_i = z_0 + i\Delta z$. Note that this step is executed in parallel by M threads providing $A_p(t, z_i),\ i = 1, \ldots, M$. To perform step 3 of the SSFM algorithm, the values of $A_p(t, z_i),\ i = 1, \ldots, M$, are collected across M threads and summed using the trapezoidal rule. Since the points at the beginning of the interval L are computed more accurately than those at its end, iterations may be required. During the next iteration, the aforementioned steps are repeated but using now as initial values of A_p those found in the previous iteration. Once the difference between results in the current and previous iterations is below a given threshold, the process is deemed convergent.

Both SSFM and MPA require temporal and spatial discretization of the (z, t)-domain. It is a common practice to discretize the time domain by 2^N points and apply the fast Fourier transform (FFT). Depending on the application, the value of N is in the range 12 to 16. The optimal value of Δz is unknown beforehand. In [13] a rule of thumb is suggested, namely, Δz should be $\sim 10^{-2}L_{\mathfrak{N}}$, where $L_{\mathfrak{N}}$ is the characteristic nonlinear length. After traversing a distance $\sim L_{\mathfrak{N}}$, the impact of nonlinear effects incorporated in $\mathfrak{N}$ becomes significant. The value of $L_{\mathfrak{N}}$ is inversely proportional to the pulse power. Likewise, the dispersion length $L_{\mathfrak{D}}$ may correspond to dispersion effects in fibers. The value of $L_{\mathfrak{D}}$ does not depend on the pulse power but rather on the time window and fiber characteristics. Computational formulas for $L_{\mathfrak{N}}$ and $L_{\mathfrak{D}}$ can be found in [1].

3   The Implementations of SSFM and MPA

We used publicly available MATLAB implementations of SSFM and MPA from [12] as references. Based on them, we developed several C++-based codes, which we outline below.

Computations were performed on a server platform with thirty-two Intel Xeon Gold 6151 CPUs at 3.0 GHz, an Nvidia Tesla V100 graphics card with 16 GB graphics buffer, and 125 GB of DDR4 RAM.

3.1   The SSFM

The C++ implementation of the SSFM (referred to hereinafter as the CPU SSFM) is a serial implementation of the classical split-step method on a CPU platform. The code was validated against the reference MATLAB code. For all considered scenarios, we obtained an agreement up to the sixth digit.

The developed code was profiled to find the most time-consuming parts of the SSFM. We distinguished the time $t_{\mathfrak{N}A}$, required to compute the terms in $\mathfrak{N}A$, and the time t_{FFT}, required for performing forward and inverse FFTs. The results are shown in Table 1. For small numbers of modes, the FFT takes the principal portion of the computation time. As the number of modes increases, the computation of the nonlinear term becomes the performance bottleneck.

We consider two OpenMP implementations of the SSFM. The first one is straightforward and is based on parallelization across the modes. All four stages of the SSFM are performed independently for P modes. After making a step Δz, the values of the modes are exchanged between the threads (via the shared memory), and the integration along the z direction continues. Such a strategy decreases $t_{\mathfrak{N}A}$. Since the number of points along the t direction is large, the forward and inverse fast Fourier transforms are computed in parallel in the second implementation. For this, we used a parallelized library fftw3 [4], which allowed us to decrease t_{FFT}. We also give an estimate of the maximum speedup in conformity with Amdahl's law [2] assuming that the FFT elapsed time can be reduced to zero. We found out that the performance gain from parallelizing the FFT computation for $P = 3$ modes is 20% for $N_t = 2^{12}$ and 50% for $N_t = 2^{16}$. That agrees with estimates consistent with Amdahl's law. We conclude that the FFT parallelization on CPUs makes sense for small numbers of modes and large numbers of time points.

Table 1. The computation time of the $\mathfrak{N}A$ operator and FFT

Number of modes	Time, ms		
	$t_{\mathfrak{N}A}$	t_{FFT}	$\frac{t_{FFT}}{t_{\mathfrak{N}A}}$
1	0.02	0.36	15.53
6	8.60	7.44	0.86
10	90.01	20.18	0.22

3.2 The SSFM with GPU Support

We add GPU support to our code to accelerate the computation of $\mathfrak{N}A$ as the most time-consuming stage of the SSFM (as shown in the previous section). For a given z_i, a set of $\mathfrak{N}A_p(z_i, t_j)$, $p = 1, \ldots, P$, $j = 1, \ldots, N_t$, is computed by N_t threads. The required forward and inverse FFTs (see steps 2 and 4 of the SSFM) are computed by a single thread on a CPU. This approach is efficient only for large numbers of available threads. This is why we consider this implementation only for the GPU platform.

To take advantage of GPU capabilities, we should remember that the non-linear operator $\mathfrak{N}$ is applied to each point t_j in the profile $A_p(z, t_i)$. In this regard, the grid of threads on the GPU is set as follows. Given the amount of shared memory per block M_{shared} and the amount of memory required to process a single mode M_{mode}, the number of threads per block is estimated as $N_{threads} = M_{shared}/M_{mode}$. The number of blocks N_{blocks} is computed as $N_t/N_{threads}$.

3.3 The MPA with OpenMP Support

For the MPA, we use the OpenMP framework as the most straightforward option. The shared memory is exploited between threads to minimize the time required for collecting data across threads. The loop across M is executed in parallel. Parallelization is implemented in such a manner that each substep $i\Delta z$, $i = 1, \ldots, M$, is calculated by its own thread. Thus each thread gets the whole copy of the initial field $A_p(z_i, t_j)$, $p = 1, \ldots, P$, $j = 1, \ldots, N_t$, computes $\mathfrak{N}A$, and performs FFTs.

We can run the MPA code as a serial one. In this case, we obtain a serial SSFM with one extra loop across M substeps. Note that the SSFM and MPA use different integration methods. The SSFM relies on a Runge–Kutta solver of the fourth order, while the MPA adopts the Euler scheme (even though the MPA involves iterations). The computation time of SSFM and MPA executed on a single CPU and that of MPA with OpenMP support on 10 CPUs are shown in Table 2. Note that the serial MPA implementation is significantly faster than the SSFM, while the MPA with OpenMP is faster than both serial codes.

Table 2. The computation time of a single-threaded SSFM, single-threaded MPA, and multi-threaded MPA with $M = 10$

Number of modes	Time, s		
	SSFM	MPA	
	1 CPU	1 CPU	OMP M CPUs
1	3	2	1
3	24	14	5
6	122	89	20
10	912	639	86
15	3519	2529	275

3.4 The MPA with OpenMP and GPU Support

The MPA can be parallelized by GPU as described in Sect. 3.2. We consider a combined usage of OpenMP and GPU for accelerating the MPA. The idea of combining the GPU and OpenMP approaches in the MPA is illustrated in Fig. 1. On GPU, MN_t threads are used to compute $A_p(z_i, t_j)$, $i = 1, \ldots, M$, $j = 1, \ldots, N_t$, $p = 1, \ldots, P$. Thus each thread computes $A_p(z_i, t_j)$ for given z_i and t_j and all modes. The forward and inverse FFTs are performed on CPUs in parallel using OpenMP support from the fftw3 library. This implementation can be further improved by using CUDA streams, but we do not consider this approach in this paper.

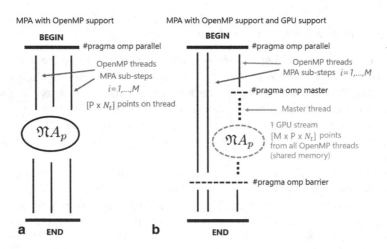

Fig. 1. One-iteration flowcharts of the MPA with OpenMP support without GPU (a) and with GPU (b) support

4   Numerical Results

4.1   Computation Time

In this section, we compare the corresponding computation times for various implementations of the SSFM and MPA. The computations correspond to a fiber length of 1 m. The integration step size Δz is set to 500 μm. The results for 1, 3, 6, 10, and 15 modes are summarized in Fig. 2. The GPU implementation of the SSFM is slower than the CPU implementation of the MPA (it was indeed expected since the SSFM is not a parallel algorithm, whereas using the GPU leads to additional overheads attributable to "host-device" data transfer). The GPU implementation of the MPA outruns the CPU implementation for $P \geq 10$ modes. However, the computation times corresponding to the GPU and CPU implementations of the MPA are close to each other.

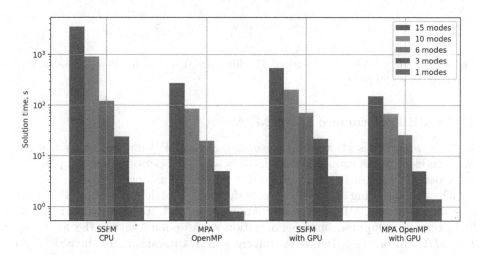

Fig. 2. The computation time of different implementations of the SSFM and MPA for 1, 3, 6, 10, and 15 modes

In Fig. 3, we replicate the results demonstrated in Fig. 3 from [13] and show how the computation time changes with respect to M for $P = 10$ modes in the CPU and GPU versions of the SSFM and MPA.

The largest gap in solution time is observed between the SSFM on CPUs and the MPA on CPUs (red lines) since the SSFM is executed on a single core, whereas the MPA utilizes M cores. Comparing the MPA implementations on GPU and CPU (solid lines), we can see that the gain in performance from GPUs is not significant.

We also note that the computation time quickly decreases when M increases from 1 to 5 and reaches a plateau at $M = 10$. Consequently, it is possible to obtain a maximal speedup gain through parallelism on widely available CPUs.

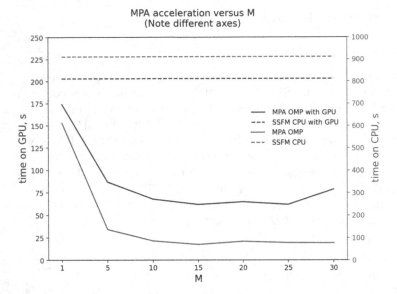

Fig. 3. The MPA M factor evolution. The fiber length $L = 1$ m, $P = 10$ modes, and step size $\Delta z = 500$ μm.

4.2   GPU Performance in the MPA

We analyze in this section the performance of the GPU implementation of the MPA to identify the causes of the relatively low GPU performance compared to the OpenMP implementation of the MPA for small numbers of modes.

The code profiling shows that the performance bottleneck in the GPU code of both SSFM and MPA is the evaluation of the $\mathfrak{N}A_p$ term. In the MPA, the $\mathfrak{N}A_p$ term is computed once per iteration at M points within the long step $L = M\Delta z$. In practice, the MPA converges in 3–4 iterations. In the SSFM, on the other hand, the $\mathfrak{N}A_p$ term is computed four times (as long as the Runge–Kutta integration method is employed) to perform the integration in Δz.

The GPU elapsed time $T_{\text{total}}^{\text{GPU}}$ consists of the time required to perform computations on GPU (denoted by $T_{\text{comp}}^{\text{GPU}}$) plus the time for sending data to and receiving them from the GPU (denoted by $T_{\text{send}}^{\text{GPU}}$ and $T_{\text{recv}}^{\text{GPU}}$, respectively):

$$T_{\text{total}}^{\text{GPU}} = T_{\text{send}}^{\text{GPU}} + T_{\text{comp}}^{\text{GPU}} + T_{\text{recv}}^{\text{GPU}}. \tag{4}$$

Table 3 contains the code profiling results. The corresponding times are given for a single MPA iteration. For $P = 1$ and $P = 3$ modes, the overheads significantly exceed $T_{\text{comp}}^{\text{GPU}}$. As the number of modes increases, $T_{\text{comp}}^{\text{GPU}}$ increases faster than $T_{\text{send}}^{\text{GPU}}$ and $T_{\text{recv}}^{\text{GPU}}$. For 15 modes, $T_{\text{comp}}^{\text{GPU}}$ is larger than $T_{\text{send}}^{\text{GPU}} + T_{\text{recv}}^{\text{GPU}}$.

Apparently, as the time resolution increases, so does the computational load. In this case, the use of GPU becomes beneficial. Table 4 displays the results obtained for different values of N_t. While the computation time on both CPU and

Table 3. The computation time of the $\mathfrak{N}A$ term for a single MPA iteration, $N_t = 2^{12}$

Number of modes	Number of data points sent	Data size, MB		Time, ms		
		Send	Recv	Send	Computation of $\mathfrak{N}A_p$	Recv
1	00 122 880	1.875	1.25	0.70	0.01	0.35
3	00 614 400	9.375	7.50	4.43	0.09	1.50
6	11 966 080	30.000	26.25	8.27	0.87	5.00
10	14 915 200	75.000	68.75	18.00	30.00	15.00
15	10 333 800	159.375	150.40	38.02	97.10	36.00

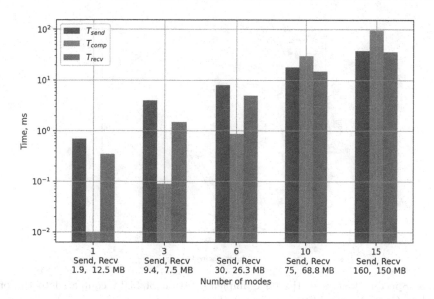

Fig. 4. GPU computation time of the $\mathfrak{N}A$ term versus the number of modes, with $N = 2^{12}$ points along the t axis

GPU increases with N_t, GPU outruns CPU already at six modes for $N_t = 2^{16}$. For lower numbers of modes, the CPU implementation is still advantageous (Fig. 4). The same conclusions are valid for the SSFM.

4.3 Single and Double Precisions

It is well known that, using single precision instead of double precision, one can save a significant amount of time on GPUs. However, the choice of single precision can affect the accuracy. For this reason, it is important to consider many aspects of floating-point behavior to achieve the highest performance with the precision required for a specific application [11]. In this section, we investigate the

Table 4. The computation time of a single MPA iteration on a 10-core CPU and GPU for N_t points along the t axis

Number of modes	Time, ms					
	$N_t = 2^{12}$		$N_t = 2^{14}$		$N_t = 2^{16}$	
	CPU	GPU	CPU	GPU	CPU	GPU
1	0.1	1.5	0.4	5.0	1.1	12.8
3	0.7	5.6	9.0	20.0	23.8	66.2
6	7.6	13.9	105.0	65.0	267.5	236.0
10	78.9	63.0	1115.0	258.0	3187.3	767.0
15	321.8	171.0	4522.0	745.0	13 335.0	1944.0

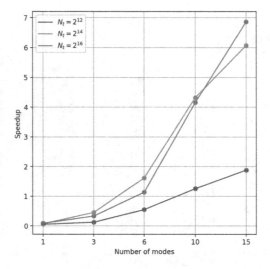

Fig. 5. Speedup factors of the GPU implementation of MPA compared to the one based on OpenMP, for different values of P and N_t

impact of the floating-point precision on the speed and accuracy of GMMNLSE solvers (Fig. 5).

We have both single- and double-precision versions of our C++ codes. The SSFM and MPA are executed for a fiber length of 1 m and a pulse power of 10 kW. The corresponding results are shown in Table 5. Although the results are somewhat heterogeneous, we can see that switching from double to single precision roughly provides a two-fold speedup both on CPU and GPU. The results of the single- and double-precision codes agree up to the fifth digit in all cases, except for a pulse power of 10 kW (a rather high value), where the relative difference is about 0.2%. This error is much less than the errors due to choosing a coarse integration step. Thus we conclude that the single-precision code can be employed in practice as it provides a relative speedup of about 1.5 compared to the double-precision code.

Table 5. Solution time for SSFM and MPA using double or single precision

Number of modes	Solution time, s							
	SSFM				MPA			
	CPU		CPU + GPU		CPU		CPU + GPU	
	double	single	double	single	double	single	double	single
1	3.6	1.6	6	5	0.8	0.4	1.4	1.0
3	24.0	13.0	22.0	14.0	5.0	3.0	5.0	4.0
6	122.0	60.0	71.0	41.0	20.0	16.0	26.0	12.0
10	912.0	391.0	203.0	129.0	86.0	76.0	68.0	45.0
15	3519.0	1481.0	542.0	352.0	275.0	250.0	150.0	102.0

4.4   Impact of the Integration Step Size

The accuracy of the SSFM and MPA is strongly affected by the integration step size (Δz and L, respectively). Essentially, the value of Δz is a trade-off between computational speed and accuracy. It is, therefore, crucial to estimate the maximal step value for the solver for which a stable solution can be obtained in the fastest manner. Modifying a rule of thumb from [13], we propose to relate Δz to the characteristic length L_C, defined as

$$L_C = \left(\frac{1}{L_\mathfrak{D}} + \frac{1}{L_\mathfrak{N}} \right)^{-1}. \tag{5}$$

Then the solver step is expressed as

$$\Delta z = \frac{L_C}{n}, \tag{6}$$

where n is the safety factor for the step size, i.e., the larger n is, the more accurate and time-consuming the solver is.

Table 6 provides the maximum relative error of the SSFM algorithm, the MPA, and the difference between both methods. The computations are done for several values of the pulse power and safety factor. The fiber length is set to 5 m. As expected, the solution error decreases as the safety factor increases. However, the accuracy of the solution still depends on the input pulse power, suggesting that the safety factor should also be adjusted to the energy (i.e., be a function of the pulse energy, as well as $L_\mathfrak{N}$ and $L_\mathfrak{D}$).

Table 6. The maximum relative error (in %) for different values of the safety coefficient n

Power, W	L_C, m	n	Δz, m	Max. relative error, %		
				SSFM	MPA	Difference between SSFM and MPA
10 000	0.1	100	10^{-3}	6.3	3.4	7.0
		1000	10^{-4}	$1.5 \cdot 10^{-2}$	$1.0 \cdot 10^{-2}$	4.0
		10 000	10^{-5}	$1.2 \cdot 10^{-4}$	$1.5 \cdot 10^{-3}$	4.0
100	5.0	100	$5 \cdot 10^{-2}$	0.5	0.1	$2.8 \cdot 10^{-1}$
		1000	$5 \cdot 10^{-3}$	$1.1 \cdot 10^{-1}$	$1.2 \cdot 10^{-1}$	$1.3 \cdot 10^{-1}$
		10 000	$5 \cdot 10^{-4}$	$2.0 \cdot 10^{-3}$	$1.2 \cdot 10^{-3}$	$1.2 \cdot 10^{-1}$
1	50	100	$6 \cdot 10^{-1}$	$6.0 \cdot 10^{-2}$	$6.0 \cdot 10^{-2}$	$1.1 \cdot 10^{-1}$
		1000	$5 \cdot 10^{-2}$	$1.5 \cdot 10^{-3}$	$4.0 \cdot 10^{-4}$	$3.0 \cdot 10^{-3}$
		10 000	$5 \cdot 10^{-4}$	$2.0 \cdot 10^{-4}$	$1.3 \cdot 10^{-4}$	$1.3 \cdot 10^{-3}$

4.5   Adaptive Step Size

As we have shown, choosing an appropriate value for the integration step size beforehand is not a straightforward procedure. An alternative approach is to tune the step size during integration. It is a common technique originally applied in ordinary differential equation solvers with adaptive steps. The idea behind this is that the integration is done with several values of the step. If the difference between solutions exceeds a given threshold, the step size is reduced according to a certain rule. On the contrary, if the difference is smaller than a threshold, the step is increased. The application of adaptive step algorithms to GMMNLSE solvers is considered in [3,8]. Note that these works rely on some assumptions and limitations regarding the width of the input pulse, the allowed range of Δz, and others. Following [6], we have implemented a Runge–Kutta solver of the fourth order for integrating the nonlinear term in Eq. 1. This approach does not require additional limitations with respect to the original solver.

We took the adaptivity criterion from [5] and implemented it in our C++ code. The magnitude by which the step has to be adjusted depends on the difference between $A_p(z_{k-1}, t)$ and $A_p(z_k, t)$, obtained by the Runge–Kutta integration method of the fourth order. The solution error at each step (for all modes and the whole field) is estimated by the formula

$$\varepsilon = \sum_{p=0}^{P} \sum_{i=0}^{N_t} \left(\frac{k_4}{a_{\text{tol}} + r_{\text{tol}} \cdot \max(A_p(t_i, z_k), A_p(t_i, z_{k-1}))} \right)^2, \tag{7}$$

where k_4 is the fourth-order derivative in the Runge–Kutta solver; a_{tol} and r_{tol} are, respectively, the absolute and relative error levels that should be set for the Runge–Kutta solver. The real and imaginary parts of ε are computed, and the greatest of them is taken. As our computations demonstrate, to obtain accurate

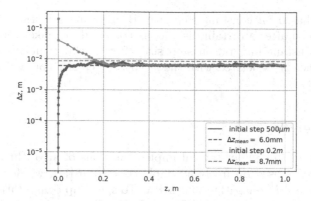

Fig. 6. Step-size evolution for initial step sizes of 500 μm and 0.2 m. The fiber length is 1 m; the pulse power is 1 kW.

results, the value of ϵ must be smaller than 0.5. First, we check how the adaptive algorithm behaves when the initial value of Δz is too small or too large. We consider a fiber length of 1 m and a pulse power of 1 kW. The step size can be either 500 μm or 0.2 m. Figure 6 shows that the algorithm adjusts the integration step size in both cases, bringing it to a constant level after traversing a certain distance. Fig. 7 describes how the adaptive step algorithm works with different values of r_{tol}. The values of Δz converge at higher values as the r_{tol} parameter increases. Thus we can influence the solution accuracy by setting the value of r_{tol} instead of Δz. Note that the adaptive step version of the solver is 20% slower

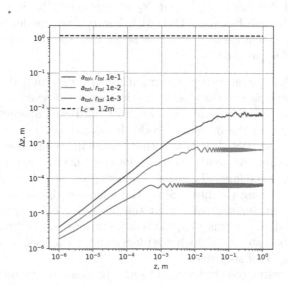

Fig. 7. Step-size evolution in a fiber of 1 m with an initial integration step size of 1 μm and a pulse power of 1 kW

than the one based on constant step size. Bearing in mind that the step size reaches a plateau after a certain distance is traversed, it makes sense to switch back to the constant integration step size after reaching the plateau. In this case, the overheads associated with the adaptive step size computation become negligible.

5   Conclusions

We considered in this paper several implementations of algorithms for solving the GMMNLSE. Based on freely available code from [12], we developed C++ versions of the SSFM algorithm and MPA. To speed up computations, we parallelized the code using the OpenMP and CUDA frameworks, which enabled us to run the code on both CPU and GPU. Several parallelization strategies were considered. Our main results can be summarized as follows:

1. The parallelization of the FFT parts in the SSFM makes sense for small numbers of modes ($P < 6$) and large numbers of time points ($N_t > 2^{14}$). In particular, the performance for $P = 3$ modes and $N_t = 2^{16}$ was enhanced by 50%.
2. Even single-threaded MPA is faster than the SSFM by 30% while providing almost the same level of accuracy.
3. The profiling showed that a significant amount of time is spent in the data transfer between host and device. As the temporal resolution of computations increases, so does the complexity of the algorithm, making GPU computations advantageous. The effect of using GPU increases with the number of modes and N_t. For $P \leq 3$ and $N_t < 2^{14}$, the GPU implementation is slower than the one based on OpenMP. For $P = 15$ modes and $N_t = 2^{16}$, the GPU implementation provided a seven-fold speedup compared to the OpenMP implementation.

We showed that the accuracy of computations is determined by the ratio of the integration step size to the characteristic length. However, this dependency can not be formulated as a simple rule. In this regard, we implemented an adaptive step algorithm in the developed code. It adjusts the integration step size during computations. We also showed that the adaptive strategy based on the Runge–Kutta method efficiently corrects the step size in cases when its initial value is too small or too large. The integration step size stabilizes after traversing a certain distance along the fiber. Since the adaptive algorithm leads to additional overheads, we suggest using it at the beginning of computations until a plateau is reached. Once this happens, computations may switch back to the constant integration step size. Such a strategy allows the user to avoid concerns related to the choice of step size.

Finally, we investigated the impact of single precision on computational speed and accuracy. With single precision instead of double precision in the SSFM and MPA, we achieved speedup factors of about 2 and 1.5, respectively, while the agreement between the results of both versions was up to the fifth digit. However, we noticed a difference of about 0.2% in the presence of strong nonlinearities (in our case, a pulse power of 10 kW).

References

1. Agrawal, G.P.: Fiber-Optic Communication Systems. Wiley, Hoboken (2021). https://doi.org/10.1002/9781119737391
2. Amdahl, G.M.: Validity of the single processor approach to achieving large scale computing capabilities. In: Proceedings of the April 18–20, 1967, Spring Joint Computer Conference on - AFIPS. ACM Press (1967). https://doi.org/10.1145/1465482.1465560
3. Farag, N.G.A., Eltanboly, A.H., EL-Azab, M.S., Obayya, S.S.A.: On the analytical and numerical solutions of the one-dimensional nonlinear Schrodinger equation. Math. Probl. Eng. **2021**, 1–15 (2021). https://doi.org/10.1155/2021/3094011
4. Frigo, M., Johnson, S.G.: The design and implementation of FFTW3. Proc. IEEE **93**(2), 216–231 (2005)
5. Hairer, E., Wanner, G.: Solving Ordinary Differential Equations II. Springer, Berlin Heidelberg (1991). https://doi.org/10.1007/978-3-662-09947-6
6. Heidt, A.M.: Efficient adaptive step size method for the simulation of supercontinuum generation in optical fibers. J. Lightwave Technol. **27**(18), 3984–3991 (2009). https://doi.org/10.1109/JLT.2009.2021538
7. Korotkevich, A.O., Lushnikov, P.M.: Proof-of-concept implementation of the massively parallel algorithm for simulation of dispersion-managed WDM optical fiber systems. Opt. Lett. **36**(10), 1851–1853 (2011). https://doi.org/10.1364/ol.36.001851
8. Liu, X.: Adaptive higher-order split-step Fourier algorithm for simulating lightwave propagation in optical fiber. Opt. Commun. **282**(7), 1435–1439 (2009). https://doi.org/10.1016/j.optcom.2008.12.051
9. Lushnikov, P.M.: Fully parallel algorithm for simulating dispersion-managed wavelength-division-multiplexed optical fiber systems. Opt. Lett. **27**(11), 939 (2002). https://doi.org/10.1364/ol.27.000939
10. Poletti, F., Horak, P.: Description of ultrashort pulse propagation in multimode optical fibers. J. Opt. Soc. Am. B **25**(10), 1645 (2008). https://doi.org/10.1364/josab.25.001645
11. Whitehead, N., Fit-Florea, A.: Precision and performance: floating point and IEEE 754 compliance for NVIDIA GPUs TB-06711-001_v11.8 (2022). https://docs.nvidia.com/cuda/pdf/Floating_Point_on_NVIDIA_GPU.pdf
12. Wright, L.G.: Gmmnlse-solver (2017). https://github.com/WiseLabAEP/GMMNLSE-Solver-FINAL. Accessed 08 Feb 2022
13. Wright, L.G., et al.: Multimode nonlinear fiber optics: massively parallel numerical solver, tutorial, and outlook. IEEE J. Sel. Top. Quantum Electron. **24**(3), 1–16 (2018). https://doi.org/10.1109/JSTQE.2017.2779749

On a Template Programming Approach for Shared Memory Parallel Architectures with Applications to the Fully Implicit Stokes Solver

N. M. Evstigneev$^{(\boxtimes)}$ (iD) and O. I. Ryabkov

Federal Research Center "Computer Science and Control" of the Russian Academy
of Sciences, Moscow, Russian Federation
evstigneevnm@yandex.ru

Abstract. In this paper, we consider a fully implicit Stokes solver implementation targeting both GPU and multithreaded CPU architectures. The solver is aimed at the semistructured mesh often emerging during permeability calculations in geology. The solver basically consists of four main parts: geometry and topology analysis, linear system construction, linear system solution, and postprocessing. A modified version of the AMGCL library developed by the authors in earlier research is used for the solution. Previous experiments showed that the GPU architecture can deliver extremely high performance for such types of problems, especially when the whole stack is implemented on the GPU. However, the GPU memory limitation significantly reduces the available mesh sizes. For some applications, the computation time is not as important as the mesh size. Therefore, it is convenient to have both GPU (for example, CUDA) and multithreaded CPU versions of the same code. The direct code port is time-consuming and error-prone. Several automatic approaches are available: OpenACC standard, DVM-system, SYCL, and others. Often, however, these approaches still demand careful programming if one wants to deliver maximum performance for a specific architecture. Some problems (such as the analysis of connected components, in our case) require totally different optimal algorithms for different architectures. Furthermore, sometimes native libraries deliver the best performance and are preferable for specific parts of the solution. For these reasons, we used another approach, based on C++ language abilities as template programming. The main two components of our approach are array classes and 'for each' algorithms. Arrays can be used on both CPU and CUDA architectures and internally substitute the memory layout that best fits the current architecture (as an 'array of structures' or 'structure of arrays'). 'For each' algorithms generate kernels or parallel cycles that implement parallel processing for indexing data structures. For other algorithms, we use the Thrust library. The internal AMGCL multiarchitecture approach is also employed. In

The reported study was funded by the Russian Science Foundation (project № 23-21-00107).

© The Author(s), under exclusive license to Springer Nature Switzerland AG 2023
L. Sokolinsky and M. Zymbler (Eds.): PCT 2023, CCIS 1868, pp. 152–166, 2023.
https://doi.org/10.1007/978-3-031-38864-4_11

this work, we demonstrate that this approach can deliver a performance that is very close to that of native-architecture programming models for general problems such as matrix assembly. At the same time, specific algorithms can be implemented for some fine-grained tasks as analysis of connected components.

Keywords: Template metaprogramming · GPU · CPU · CUDA · OpenMP · C++ · AMGCL · Stokes solver · Coupled linear systems · Fully implicit methods

1   Introduction

We start with a concrete problem and observe how our approach can be incorporated into its solution. We need to solve a Stokes-type coupled linear system. This results in a saddle-point finite dimensional linear problem discretized by means of a converging approximation as follows:

$$\mathcal{A}x = b \Leftrightarrow \begin{pmatrix} A & B^{\mathsf{T}} \\ B & 0 \end{pmatrix} \begin{pmatrix} u \\ p \end{pmatrix} = \begin{pmatrix} f \\ 0 \end{pmatrix}, \tag{1}$$

where A is the discrete Laplace operator, B is the discrete divergence operator, B^T is the discrete gradient operator, u is the velocity vector, p is the pressure vector, and f is a right-hand-side vector. The system can be solved using a Krylov-type linear solver (in our case, we apply the GMRES method) with a left or right preconditioner. The preconditioner for the coupled system is constructed in a BFBt [4] or block triangular form. An Algebraic Multigrid (AMG) method is applied at each stage of the selected preconditioners. Here we apply a heavily modified version of the AMGCL solver [1,2]. The original problem (1) is initially solved using a Graphics Processing Unit (GPU). It basically consists of four main parts: geometry and topology analysis of the computational domain, assembly of the linear system (1), linear system solution, and data postprocessing for storage and analysis. More details on the preconditioning strategies, discretization, and performance on GPUs of the developed solver are given in [6]; test data of AMG modifications are considered in [5, 10].

In this paper, we discuss the extension of the developed solver to CPU or CPU-GPU implementations for shared-memory computational architectures. Two main approaches to the problem exist.

The seemingly easier way one employs directive-based compilers to annotate parallel sections which are capable of extending these sections to CPUs, GPUs, or possibly other coprocessors. Examples of such standards are OpenACC (www.openacc.org), OpenHMPP (handwiki.org/wiki/OpenHMPP) [3], C-DVMH (http://dvm-system.org) [7], and others. These standards encapsulate the lower-level programming for parallel parts of the code on the compiler side and allow the user not to focus on the specific parallel design of the code. Basically, they provide a loose relationship between an application code and the use of a hardware accelerator, which is indeed an advantage. Moreover, such approaches as SAPFOR (from the authors of DVM) can be used to extend the project to distributed-memory systems. As it turns out, the extension of our Stokes solver project based on programming standards with compiler directives is quite restrictive. The complexity of the used methods in several parts and their interaction is primarily due to the low-level CUDA C++ kernels and template metaprogramming. Such an approach is determined by the desire to facilitate the utilization of GPU capabilities at maximum. Thus the original method is well optimized for the GPU architecture and uses various highly optimized kernels to analyze the computational domain (including Connected Component Labeling and topological analysis), assemble system (1) in the compressed row storage format right on a GPU, and solve it using the highly modified AMGCL solver [5] only on a GPU without any data movement from the accelerator to the host memory. With these methods already implemented, it makes no sense to rewrite the code in a higher-level approach with compiler directives that can degrade the achieved performance on a GPU accelerator.

The other approach makes use of embedded domain-specific languages that are based on modern C++ and can handle different accelerations, such as GPUs. These include SYCL (www.khronos.org/sycl/) [9], RaftLib (www.raftlib. io, Vulkan (https://vulkan.org/), and others. Within our paradigm, one would be most interested in using SYCL since it is a C++17 (so far) comparable language that can be used to redesign the CUDA kernels and extend the list of available accelerations. In our case, however, it is necessary to design different algorithms for different accelerators in this case. Such a code redesign is error-prone and time-consuming (under the assumption that we already have a designed near-optimal code based on CUDA C++).

As an alternative to these approaches, we use our own designed extensions of data structures and operations based on modern C++ with the use of template metaprogramming. The two main components of our approach are array classes and 'for each' algorithms. The use of a particular accelerating coprocessor can be encapsulated into these components. Currently, only the host CPU (OpenMP and serial) and CUDA C++ supporting devices are implemented. Arrays can be used for both CPU and CUDA architectures and internally substitute the memory layout that best fits the current architecture (as 'array of structures' or 'structure of arrays'). Moreover, 'for each' algorithms simply generate kernels or parallel cycles for looping over data in parallel. For other algorithms, we use the Thrust library. Our current library is called SCFD (an acronym for Scalable Computation Framework Details).

The structure of the paper is as follows. In Sect. 2, we describe the design and implementation of SCFD classes, including data structures, 'for each' operations, memory modules, and utilities. In Sect. 3, we demonstrate the performance of our template library on a simple example and compare the results with raw pointers on CPU and GPU. Next, we consider the performance of the Stokes solver ported from GPU-only code to Serial+OpenMP+GPU code. Also, we compare the results of several approaches, namely, OpenMP, GPU-only (while there is enough memory available on a device), and GPU-unified memory. In the last section, we present the conclusions drawn from our research.

2   The Implementation

The implementation details are provided with regard to the source code of the library. The interested reader is encouraged to consult the code along with the description. The code can be found in a GitHub repository given below.

As previously stated, our C++ library consists of several small parts (we call them *modules*). Each part is aimed to deliver a certain type of architecture abstraction. Currently, the library is header-only, so most of the time the headers provide both definition and declaration. In some cases, the implementation of the class or function is moved to a separate header having the "_impl" suffix in this case. For example, a class declared in the file "scfd/for_each/cuda.h" is defined in "scfd/for_each/cuda_impl.cuh". This is done to allow for the separation of architecture-specific parts of the code (CUDA kernels in the case above) into separate object files. Most of the time, the structure of folders replicates the namespace structure. For example, the class scfd::for_each::cuda is declared in the above-mentioned file "scfd/for_each/cuda.h".

The library parts correspond to different namespaces. Currently, the public repository contains the following parts:

- scfd::utils. It includes some basic utilities to simplify cross-architecture programming. For example, scalar_traits unifies calls to some of the math functions for different architectures and scalar types; device_tag.h contains a simple macro to unify the definitions of functions (it adds the __device__ tag for the CUDA case); constant_data helps in working with small data structures similar to CUDA constant memory. There are other macros and functions such as CUDA_SAFE_CALL, timer wraps, and so on.
- scfd::static_vec. It includes a class of vector templates of static size and basic vector operations which can be used both on CPUs and GPUs.
- scfd::static_mat. It includes a class of matrix templates of static size, as well as basic matrix and vector-matrix operations that can be used both on CPUs and GPUs.
  Note that static_vec and static_mat should not be considered kind of a basis for a linear-algebra library but rather useful small static arrays that can work on different architectures.
- scfd::geometry. A very limited set of geometry algorithms, such as simplex intersection.
- scfd::arrays. It includes classes of templates of multidimensional arrays suited for different architectures. They are described in Subsect. 2.1.
- scfd::for_each. It includes classes that enable the writing of universal code parts for parallel execution. They are described in Subsect. 2.2.
- scfd::memory. It includes a basic abstraction of memory allocation and copy operations mainly intended as a sublayer of array classes. It can be used as a standalone module. For details, see Subsect. 2.3.
- scfd::reduce. It is intended as an abstract reduction operation layer hiding the details of other libraries such as Thrust and CUB. The current public version, however, is limited.

One of the primary ideas is the orthogonality of the modules. There are, of course, some internal dependencies between modules. For example, all modules depend on `scfd::utils`. However, these dependencies were diminished as far as it was possible. Arrays can be useful in normal CUDA kernels or C++ cycles without `scfd::for_each` and, vice versa, `scfd::for_each` primitives will work with plain pointers if needed. SCFD is not a solid framework but rather a set of primitives and concepts helping to write and implement efficient parallel codes in a straightforward manner.

2.1   The Implementation of Data Structures

The concept `scfd::arrays` provides lightweight template classes for multidimensional arrays. Arrays in `scfd::arrays` should be considered more as "array pointers" or "array references" rather than solid array classes. Copy and assignment of these objects do not lead to data copy but rather to the creation of a new reference to the existing data through the new object instance. The "normal" data-structure behavior is the one inherent to STL or Thrust. However, the copy semantics of objects in Thrust makes them unsuitable for direct usage in CUDA kernels, so the Thrust approach is to use iterators. Even though iterators are a good choice for many algorithms, often (especially in scientific applications) their usage reduces the code readability. Simple access by index is more suitable in these cases. Multidimensional arrays are even more useful in other cases. These `scfd::arrays` can be passed directly to a CUDA kernel thanks to their "shallow" copy semantics and give access to data elements through one or several ordinal indexes.

The concept `tensor_base` class is an internal class that implements most parts of the multiarray functionality. This class is not intended for direct use in the code; `tensor_array_nd` is derived from `tensor_base` and gives public functionality. The template parameters of this class are as follows:

```
template<class T, ordinal_type ND, class Memory,
         template <ordinal_type... Dims> class Arranger,
         ordinal_type... TensorDims>
class tensor_array_nd
```

Here we have the following:

- `class T`, the element type of the array. Note that, currently, only POD data types (such as scalar types and simple structures) are supported.
- `ordinal_type ND`, the number of dimensions of a multidimensional array; `ordinal_type` stands for the internal SCFD type `scfd::arrays::ordinal_type`. This type defines all indexing inside arrays and, for the moment, is managed by the global macro `SCFD_ARRAYS_ORDINAL_TYPE`. The default `ordinal_type` is `int`.
- `class Memory`, a class that manages all memory operations (for now, these are allocation, free, and copy). This class defines whether we use the device memory, the unified memory, or the host memory.

- template <ordinal_type... Dims> class Arranger, a template parameter. It defines how multidimensional array elements are arranged in the linear memory. Usually, one uses one of the predefined Arranger classes from scfd::arrays; however, a custom Arranger can be written.
- ordinal_type... TensorDims, additional dimensions (called *tensor dimensions*). An empty list is allowed. Each value in TensorDims is either dyn_dim, which is a predefined constant, or a positive ordinal value. In the last case, the corresponding dimension is defined in the compile type and can not be changed during array allocation.

Note that the total number of tensor_array_nd dimensions equals ND + sizeof... (TensorDims). This array can be interpreted as an ND-dimensional array of tensors of rank (sizeof... (TensorDims)). Consider the following example (namespaces are omitted). The code

```
tensor_array_nd <float ,2, cuda_device ,
               first_index_fast_arranger ,3> cuda_array;
```

represents a two-dimensional CUDA device array of three-dimensional floating point vectors, and

```
tensor_array_nd <double ,3, host ,
               last_index_fast_arranger ,2,2> host_array;
```

is a two-dimensional host array of 2×2-matrices of char elements. Now we can access the elements of these arrays using operator():

```
float  x  =  cuda_array (i1 ,i2 ,0) ,
       y  =  cuda_array (i1 ,i2 ,1) ,
       z  =  cuda_array (i1 ,i2 ,2) ;
```

or

```
float  a11  =  host_array (i1 ,i2 ,i3 ,0 ,0) ,
       a12  =  host_array (i1 ,i2 ,i3 ,0 ,1) ,
       a21  =  host_array (i1 ,i2 ,i3 ,1 ,0) ,
       a22  =  host_array (i1 ,i2 ,i3 ,1 ,1) ;
```

Note that the CUDA array is not accessible from the host code, and vice versa. The element-wise copy (as the one implemented in thrust::device_vector) is not implemented here to avoid its use by inexperienced GPU users.

Let us explain last_index_fast_arranger and first_index_fast_ arranger in more detail. These are the Arranger template parameters listed above. The first arranger makes the last indexes (which correspond to "tensor dimensions" in our arrays) to be the fastest regarding memory layout, i.e., the *row-major order*, used in plain C-arrays. The second arranger corresponds to *col-major order*, used in Fortran arrays. It is known (see, for example, [8]) that the memory layout of data strongly influences the performance of CUDA devices owing to the specific cache organization of the GPU. Structure of Arrays

(SoA) is usually preferred. At the same time, Array of Structures (AoS) usually fits better for host CPU processing because of cache misses. In the examples above, we chose `first_index_fast_arranger` for the CUDA array and `last_index_fast_arranger` for the CPU array. This means that `cuda_array` is located in the device memory as three successive two-dimensional arrays, which corresponds to SoA, while `host_array` is a three-dimensional array of 2 × 2-matrices, which corresponds to AoS. Usually, this choice of the Arranger parameters is optimal. However, the optimal layout depends on the algorithm, the interpretation of the dimensions, the order of processing of the elements, the current hardware, and others. That is why the Arranger parameter can be set during `tensor_array_nd<>` instantiation.

We see that the list of `tensor_array_nd<>` template parameters is quite extensive. Considering the notes about the usually preferred Arranger type for different memory types, we added shortcut versions of the `tensor_array_nd<>` template with the default Arranger type deduced from the Memory parameter. For instance, the arrays from the example given above can be equivalently declared as

```
tensor1_array_nd <float ,2, cuda_device ,3> cuda_array;
```

and

```
tensor2_array_nd <double ,3, host ,2,2> host_array;
```

where the number after the word `tensor` corresponds to the tensor rank (the number of tensor dimensions). For tensors of rank 0 (i.e., scalars), the word `tensor` can be omitted:

```
array_nd <float ,2, cuda_device > cuda_array_2d;
```

is a two-dimensional CUDA device array. In the case of one-dimensional arrays, the suffix "`_nd`" can be omitted:

```
tensor2_array <double , host ,2,2> host_matrix_array;
```

is a one-dimensional array of 2 × 2-matrices; the `array` class stands for a one-dimensional array:

```
array <float , cuda_device > cuda_array_1d;
```

As we mentioned earlier, `scfd::arrays` uses "shallow" copy semantics. This leads to the question of whether these arrays satisfy RAII. Technically, the answer is yes. All data allocated with arrays will be freed as the array instances are destroyed, and a double-free situation will not happen. However, it is important to note that the `scfd::arrays` described above are not reference-counting. Instead, an array that allocates new memory by the `init` method gets the "owner" status and is responsible for freeing data. Neither of its copies has the "owner" status. This means that when an "owner" array is destroyed, all its copies are invalidated. This unsafe behavior is caused by the ability to pass `scfd::arrays` directly to the CUDA kernels. Reference-counting pointers do not make much sense when passed to device kernels since each thread would have its own copy of the pointer. The semantics of "shallow" copies is similar to the semantics of iterators, which are invalidated when the data structure is erased. This makes sense, considering that iterators are used in the Thrust library to access data from kernels. To make current `scfd::arrays` at least partially safer, we added move semantics that transfers the "ownership" during array move. To avoid any unsafe behavior (accidental loss of data due to the "owner" array destruction), one must use `scfd::arrays` in the host part of the program as members of non-copyable classes or classes with "deep" copy semantics. In the experimental private version of `scfd::arrays`, we implemented additional `shared_array` (reference-counting) and `unique_array` (move-only) classes. These classes can not be used directly in GPU kernels but have a special method `get()` to create a "shallow" "non-owning" `array`. They are to be released in the public repository as soon as all tests are completed.

2.2 The Implementation of 'For Each' Operations

The concept `scfd::for_each` delivers simple abstractions to execute a certain operation with each element from the sequence. The operation is performed on each element independently. In fact, `scfd::for_each` is very close to `std::for_each` from the modern C++ standard (main the difference is the support of CUDA device kernels); it is also close to the `thrust::for_each` algorithm. We can regard the differences as just cosmetic. First, `scfd::for_each` uses indexes instead of iterators, which, in our opinion, is a more convenient solution for scientific applications. Indexes can be shifted if needed, for example, in MPI-scattered arrays. Also, n-dimensional versions of `scfd::for_each` exist and they are useful for processing regular n-dimensional arrays, e.g., for structured grid indexing. In fact, we can consider `scfd::for_each` more as a minor abstraction layer for current and future parallel platforms.

All classes in `scfd::for_each` can be divided into two groups: "plain" `for_each` classes (work with one-dimensional indexes) and n-dimensional `for_each` classes (work with n-dimensional execution grids). All parameters of execution (as the CUDA block size) are supposed to be stored in the `for_each` class instance. Each class corresponds to a particular parallel platform or even a particular execution strategy within a given platform. Currently, the following are implemented:

- Serial CPU. A one-threaded CPU implementation that is useful for debugging. Classes: `serial_cpu` and `serial_cpu_nd`.
- Parallel CPU using OpenMP. Classes: `openmp` and `openmp_nd`.
- Parallel GPU using CUDA. Classes: `cuda` and `cuda_nd`.

One-dimensional `scfd::for_each` classes have the following public interface:

```
template < class Func >
void operator ()( Func f , T i1 , T i2) const ;
template < class Func >
void operator ()( Func f , T size ) const ;
void wait () const ;
```

We can see that this interface is a template itself because we need to pass an arbitrary operation functor; T is the ordinal type used. The first method performs f for all indices in the range $[i1, i2)$. The second method is a shortcut to the first and works in the range $[0, \text{size})$. The third method synchronizes the calling thread with the device that performs for_each (in the case of the last being asynchronous). It is obvious that the implementation of for_each is rather trivial. Here, n-dimensional scfd::for_each classes have basically the same interface but with n-dimensional ranges.

2.3   The Implementation of Memory Models and Utilities

In Sect. 2.1, we mentioned the template parameter Memory of scfd::arrays classes. For example, we used the cuda_device type for CUDA device arrays and the host type for host CPU arrays. These types are defined in the scfd::memory module. The general Memory class interface is as follows:

```
struct <current_memory_name>
{
    typedef      ...       host_memory_type;
    typedef      ...       pointer_type;
    typedef      ...       const_pointer_type;
    static const bool     is_host_visible = ...;
    static const bool     prefer_array_of_structs = ...;

    static void    malloc(pointer_type* p, size_t size);
    static void    free(pointer_type p);
    static void    copy_to_host(size_t size,
                                const_pointer_type src,
                                pointer_type dst);
    static void    copy_from_host(size_t size,
                                  const_pointer_type src,
                                  pointer_type dst);
};
```

where

- host_memory_type declares the Memory class that can be used to copy data from a device if current_memory cannot be accessed directly from a host. For example, for the cuda_device memory (which represents the CUDA device memory itself), host_memory_type is cuda_host memory (which represents the host CUDA pinned memory). If current_memory is directly accessible from a host, then host_memory_type coincides with current_memory.
- pointer_type and const_pointer_type are, for the moment, void* and const void*.
- is_host_visible specifies whether current_memory is directly accessible from a host.
- prefer_array_of_structs is used as a hint for the default array layout (see Sect. 2.1 about AoS and SoA layouts).

- `malloc` and `free` functions are wrappers to allocate and free `current_memory` (CudaMalloc is used for `cuda_device`, for example); `size` is given in bytes.
- `copy_to_host` and `copy_from_host` functions are wrappers that copy data between `current_memory` and `host_memory_type` if the memory is not accessible from a host; `size` is given in bytes.

Note that the Memory class is somewhat similar to the Allocator concept from Thrust or STL but with some additional abilities, such as copy-to-host functions. Currently, Memory is supposed to be a static class, so all methods are supposed to be static. The module `scfd::arrays` explicitly uses this feature. Additional parameters can be passed only through additional static fields or methods. However, we intend to extend this concept and provide a means to have some information inside the Memory class itself, similar to the Allocator concept.

3   Simple Application and Benchmarks

In this section, we describe the tests of the developed SCFD library on a simple yet illustrative example. All tests were conducted on the following hardware:

- Intel Xeon Gold 6248R CPU @ 3.00 GHz × 2 with 48 cores each and 1 TB of RAM;
- Intel Xeon E5-2697 v2 @ 3.00 GHz with 12 cores and 64 GB of RAM;
- Nvidia Tesla V100S GPU on PCIE with 32 GB;
- Nvidia GeForce RTX 3090 with 24 GB;
- Nvidia GeForce GTX TITAN X with 12 GB;
- Nvidia GeForce GTX TITAN Black with 6 GB.

The set of new and old hardware allowed us to compare the results on a wide range of computational architectures. The number of OpenMP threads was selected to maximize the efficiency by conducting multiple preliminary automatic tests.

Table 1. Results of cross product tests on GPUs, measured by the `ncu` utility in GFLOPS

GFLOPS	AoS	SoA	tensor
GTX Titan Black	66.89	30.54	66.60
GTX Titian X	126.69	90.21	126.72
RTX 3090	192.55	237.08	236.96
Tesla V100	246.20	221.40	246.72

The test problem is the cross product of two arrays of 3D floating-point vectors of size N, i.e., the cross product of vectors $\mathbf{u}, \mathbf{v} \in \mathbb{R}^{N \times 3}$, from which we obtain a vector $\mathbf{w} \in \mathbb{R}^{N \times 3}$ defined as $\mathbf{w}_j = \mathbf{u}_j \times \mathbf{v}_j$, $\forall j = 0, \ldots, N-1$. The size N is selected to ensure that it fills up 95% of the GPU memory; thus N ranges from $5 \cdot 10^7$ to $8 \cdot 10^8$. In particular, $N = 1 \cdot 10^8$ for the first CPU configuration, and $N = 1 \cdot 10^7$ for the second one. We observed no difference in the general behavior for single and double precision in all tests (except for absolute execution times). For this reason, only the double-precision results for floating-point vectors are given in the table. Each test was carried out 10 000 times. The main point of this example is to test our implementation of data structures, memory layout, and 'for each' operations with raw pointers and low-level kernels on GPUs and OpenMP optimized for loops on CPUs. We define a GPU layout of vectors as an SoA (see Sect. 2.1), i.e.,

$$\mathbf{u} := ((u_{0,0}, u_{1,0}, \ldots, u_{N-1,0})(u_{0,1}, u_{1,1}, \ldots, u_{N-1,1})(u_{0,2}, u_{1,2}, \ldots, u_{N-1,2}))^{\mathsf{T}}.$$

The CPU layout is defined as the AoS, i.e.,

$$\mathbf{u} := ((u_{0,0}, u_{0,1}, u_{0,2}), (u_{1,0}, u_{1,1}, u_{1,2}), \ldots, (u_{N-1,0}, u_{N-1,1}, u_{N-1,2}))^{\mathsf{T}}.$$

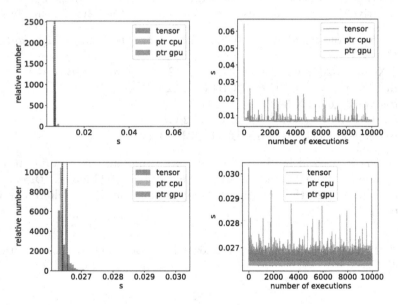

Fig. 1. Wall-clock time for the computation of the cross product on CPUs with OpenMP. Top: first CPU. Bottom: second CPU

We start by comparing the results of the CPU tests (see the graphs in Fig. 1). The most suitable CPU layout is more important for the older hardware than for the newer one. Optimally aligned vectors coincide with the raw pointer execution time, whereas misaligned data are executed slower, by 3% on the new CPU and by 12% on the old one. It is quite likely that the cause is the larger cache size.

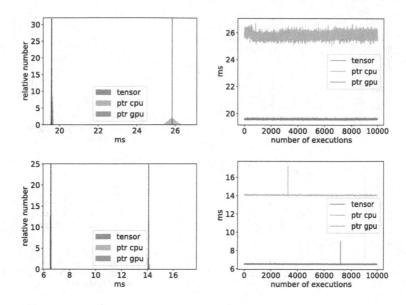

Fig. 2. Wall-clock time for the computation of the cross product on GPUs. Top: TITAN X. Bottom: TITAN Black

Results for older GPUs are provided in Fig. 2. We definitely observe a dependence on the layout of vectors, which gives a much clearer difference: a factor of 2.1 for TITAN X and 1.9 for TITAN Black. This behavior is expected and is in full compliance with the used hardware.

Results for newer GPUs are shown in Fig. 3. Interestingly enough, the layout affects the efficiency in a classical manner for Tesla V100 (increasing the performance by 20% under the SoA layout), while the effect is the opposite for GTX 3090. This is likely because the Ampere architecture is tuned for neural network training (including convolution networks), where the CPU-type data layout of AoS is common. In addition, the 40 MB level 2 cache is seven times as large as that for the Volta architecture (Tesla V100 card) and can suit and precache the stride of our CPU vector layout. Note that switching between memory Arrangers can be done in our implementation if hardware preferences are known with a simple template configuration, as it is demonstrated in Sect. 2.1. The numbers of floating-point operations per second for GPUs are given in Table 1. We can see the dependence of the SoA or AoS memory layout more closely.

4   Stokes Solver Performance

In this section, we consider tests on a rather sophisticated Stokes solver, discussed in the introduction. The sources of the tests are several real problems related to flows in porous media. Some of these problems are discussed in [6]. The redesign of the code from GPU-only to CPU/GPU code is done in a short time since

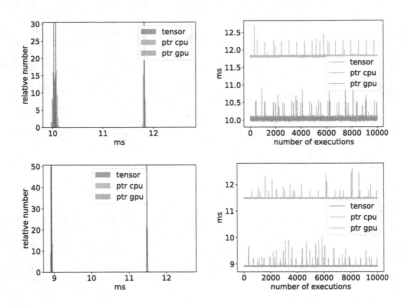

Fig. 3. Wall-clock time for the computation of the cross product on GPUs. Top: Tesla V100. Bottom: GTX 3090

the original GPU code uses the SCFD framework for data storage and memory operations. The replacement of low-level CUDA kernels with 'for each' kernels is performed straightforwardly. To consider an alternative approach, we also implemented for the solver the ability to handle CUDA unified memory arrays. This is done by applying the `cudaMallocMannaged` memory operation to our Memory class operation (`malloc`, see Sect. 2.3). Such a substitution of memory for the internal structure of the solver was made by just changing a configuration template parameter in the data-types header file. Unified memory was incorporated into the modified AMGCL library by using `thrust::universal_vector` arrays in most places via a layer of abstraction type. As a result, we have the additional ability to compare the performance of CUDA device memory with that of CUDA universal memory. The test results are given in Table 2 and Fig. 4. In the tests, we used the best hardware from the list given at the beginning of Sect. 3 (Tesla V100 GPU and Xeon Gold CPUs). The solver used single-precision floating-point arrays for both CPUs and GPUs. For each test case, its cubic size "`linear size`^{3}" and the total active number of unknowns are both given in Table 2. Note that the cubic size and the number of unknowns are different because of the porosity. Only active unknowns are used in the problem solution.

We see that the wall time depends linearly on the problem size (see Fig. 4, left) for the device and OpenMP variants of the solver, confirming the correctness of the implementation. We can also see that the original GPU implementation is about 12 times as fast as the OpenMP CPU variant, rendering the solution to a problem with 82 million unknowns in 20 s against 4 min for the OpenMP variant.

Table 2. Wall-clock time for the Stokes solver tests under different ported variants: omp is an OpenMP CPU multithreaded variant using 76 threads (best performance), unified is the CUDA-device variant with unified memory, device is the original CUDA code.

linear size	unknowns	time omp, s	time unified, s	time device, s	omp/unified	omp/gpu
200	7 538 792	19.74	4.76	3.17	4.15	6.23
300	16 846 460	43.20	9.59	5.40	4.51	8.00
400	38 746 275	93.39	16.91	9.95	5.52	9.39
500*	81 661 178*	226.00	36.41	19.29	6.21	11.72
450*	123 483 006*	381.00	365.00		1.04	
600	143 120 364	459.40	775.70		0.59	
700	214 362 520	781.70	1407.00		0.56	

*The number of unknowns and the domain size are different because of the porosity.

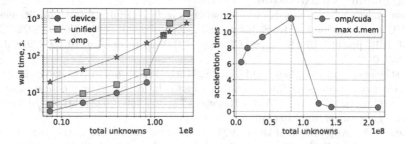

Fig. 4. Left: wall-clock time for the Stokes solver tests. Right: device/host acceleration for maximum device performance (device or unified memory). By **max d. mem**, we denote the maximum problem size that fits the device memory.

The unified memory implementation is less efficient than the device memory by a factor of two approximately. Once the unified managed memory starts using the host memory, the GPU performance drastically decreases (see Fig. 4, right). We can recommend the use of the OpenMP implementation, instead of the unified memory GPU variant, for large problems that do not fit into the GPU memory.

5 Conclusions

In this report, we considered a Template Programming Approach for shared-memory parallel architectures. The approach is implemented in the SCFD header-only library and allows simplifying the implementation of the parallel code and the process of porting the code from CPU to GPU-like coprocessors. The library is aimed to provide the maximum performance of parallel codes (with no penalty, unlike data structures using raw pointers). We tested it on various computational architectures with shared memory and demonstrated that a rather sophisticated solver can be ported to different parallel architectures in the minimum time. We encourage readers to try our library, which can be downloaded at https://github.com/oryabkov/SCFD-all.

References

1. Demidov, D.: AMGCL: an efficient, flexible, and extensible algebraic multigrid implementation. Lobachevskii J. Math. **40**(5), 535–546 (2019). https://doi.org/10.1134/S1995080219050056

2. Demidov, D.: AMGCL – a C++ library for efficient solution of large sparse linear systems. Softw. Impacts **6**, 100,037 (2020). https://doi.org/10.1016/j.simpa.2020.100037D

3. Dolbeau, R., Bihan, S., Bodin, F.: HMPP: a hybrid multi-core parallel programming environment. In: Workshop on General Purpose Processing on Graphics Processing Units (GPGPU 2007) (2007)

4. Elman, H., Howle, V., Shadid, J., Shuttleworth, R., Tuminaro, R.: A taxonomy and comparison of parallel block multi-level preconditioners for the incompressible navier-stokes equations. J. Comput. Phys. **227**(3), 1790–1808 (2008). https://doi.org/10.1016/j.jcp.2007.09.026

5. Evstigneev, N.M.: Analysis of block stokes-algebraic multigrid preconditioners on GPU implementations. In: Sokolinsky, L., Zymbler, M. (eds.) PCT 22022. CCIS, vol. 1618, pp. 116–130. Springer, Cham (2022). https://doi.org/10.1007/978-3-031-11623-0_9

6. Evstigneev, N.M., Ryabkov, O.I., Gerke, K.M.: Stationary stokes solver for single-phase flow in porous media: A blastingly fast solution based on algebraic multigrid method using GPU. Adv. Water Resour. **171**, 104,340 (2023). https://doi.org/10.1016/j.advwatres.2022.104340

7. Kataev, N.: Application of the LLVM compiler infrastructure to the program analysis in SAPFOR. In: Voevodin, V., Sobolev, S. (eds.) RuSCDays 2018. CCIS, vol. 965, pp. 487–499. Springer, Cham (2019). https://doi.org/10.1007/978-3-030-05807-4_41

8. Mei, G., Tian, H.: Impact of data layouts on the efficiency of GPU-accelerated IDW interpolation. SpringerPlus **5**(1) (2016). https://doi.org/10.1186/s40064-016-1731-6

9. Reinders, J., Ashbaugh, B., Brodman, J., Kinsner, M., Pennycook, J., Tian, X.: Data Parallel C++. Apress (2021). https://doi.org/10.1007/978-1-4842-5574-2

10. Ryabkov, O.I.: Implementation of the algebraic multigrid solver designed for graphics processing units based on the AMGCL framework. In: Sokolinsky, L., Zymbler, M. (eds.) PCT 2022. CCIS, vol. 1618, pp. 131–142. Springer, Cham (2022). https://doi.org/10.1007/978-3-031-11623-0_10

Parallel Computing in the Tikhonov Regularization Method for Solving the Inverse Problem of Chemical Kinetics

Konstantin Barkalov[1]([✉])[iD], Marina Usova[1][iD], Leniza Enikeeva[2]([✉])[iD], Dmitry Dubovtsev[3], and Irek Gubaydullin[2,3]

[1] Lobachevsky State University of Nizhny Novgorod, Nizhny Novgorod, Russian Federation
konstantin.barkalov@itmm.unn.ru

[2] Ufa State Petroleum Technological University, Ufa, Russian Federation
leniza.enikeeva@yandex.ru

[3] Institute of Petrochemistry and Catalysis, Subdivision of the Ufa Federal Research Center of the Russian Academy of Sciences, Ufa, Russian Federation

Abstract. We investigate the advantages and disadvantages of the refining processes employed in gasoline production. As a way of increasing the environmental friendliness of motor fuel, we suggest using alkylation to a greater extent during its blending and for improving its quality. The work describes the scheme of chemical transformations of the sulfuric acid alkylation process taking into account the target reactions and side effects. Based on the chemical nature of the studied reactions, the authors pose the inverse problem of chemical kinetics and consider the regularization method for its solution. The global optimization problem corresponding to the regularized inverse problem was solved using a parallel optimization algorithm. We provide the results of computational experiments on a supercomputer which show the adequacy of the obtained solution. The Tikhonov regularization method is an algorithm intended to find an approximate solution to incorrectly posed operator problems. Using this method, the authors solve the task of finding the reaction constants of sulfuric acid alkylation of isoalkanes by alkenes.

Keywords: Global optimization · Multiextremal functions · Parallel computing · Chemical kinetics · Inverse problems · Regularization

1 Introduction

To meet the environmental protection requirements, the standards of clean gasoline in the world are currently moving toward low contents of sulfur, olefins, and aromatic substances and high octane numbers. This means that the refining industry requires stricter fuel product standards and cleaner production processes. Gasoline is a result of the blending of products of several refining processes, such as catalytic reforming, isomerizate, catalytic cracking, and sulfuric

© The Author(s), under exclusive license to Springer Nature Switzerland AG 2023
L. Sokolinsky and M. Zymbler (Eds.): PCT 2023, CCIS 1868, pp. 167–181, 2023.
https://doi.org/10.1007/978-3-031-38864-4_12

acid alkylation. The use of each component is limited by certain factors, including sulfur content, saturated vapor pressure, the content of aromatic hydrocarbons, and the octane number of the final product [10].

The product of catalytic cracking is a catalyst obtained as a by-product of the cracking of vacuum gas oil (fraction 350–500°C). It contains aromatic hydrocarbons, olefins, and a small amount of hydrocarbons from the feedstock structure and is a source of sulfur in commercial gasoline.

An isomerizate of a high-octane component is obtained in the process of catalytic isomerization of light gasoline fractions (i.b.p-62°C). The octane number of the isomerizate reaches up to 92 points, depending on the research method. However, its excessive addition during blending leads to an increase in the pressure of saturated vapors in commercial gasoline and the formation of steam plugs in the power system during the hot season [10].

The source of aromatic contents in gasoline is a reformate obtained during catalytic reforming of heavy gasoline fractions (fraction 85 (105)–180°C). The involvement of lighter fractions in reforming feedstocks results in an increase in the proportion of benzene in the reformate.

Alkylated gasoline fully complies with the operational and environmental requirements of modern European, US, and Russian industrial standards for the production of fuels for automotive internal combustion engines and is an ideal and essential component of reformed environmentally friendly gasoline. The production rate of alkylate abroad exceeds 70 million tons a year; in the Russian Federation, it reached 2 million tons in 2019. Alkylate is obtained as a result of the alkylation of isoalkanes by alkenes in the presence of a catalyst. The most commonly used process catalyst in Russia is sulfuric acid. The advantages of alkylate include a high octane number (up to 90 points, depending on the research method), low saturated vapor pressure, low content of heteroatomic compounds, and good chemical stability. In addition, the sensitivity of alkylate does not exceed 5 points [2].

There are target and side reactions, which proceed by the carbonium-ion mechanism. The process is carried out in several stages:

1. The first stage is the addition of an acid proton to an olefin to produce a *tert*-butyl carbation:

$$CH_3-CH = CH_3-CH \quad + \quad H^+ \quad \longrightarrow \quad CH_3-CH^+ \quad | \quad CH_3-CH_2$$

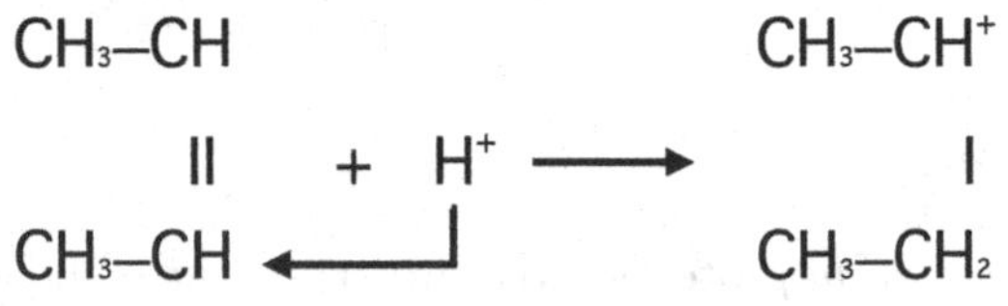

Fig. 1. The addition of an acid proton to an olefin to produce a *tert*-butyl carbation

2. In the second stage, the formed carbonium ion interacts with paraffin hydrocarbon. In this case, the hydrogen anion from the tertiary carbon atom of the isoparaffin hydrocarbon passes into the carbonium ion formed in the first stage of the reaction:

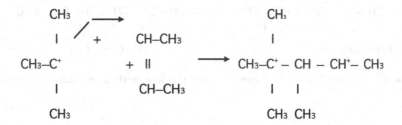

Fig. 2. The interaction of the formed carbonium ion with paraffin hydrocarbon

3. The third stage consists of the addition of a tertiary carbonium ion to the second olefin molecule to form carbonium:

$$
\begin{array}{ccc}
CH_3 & & CH_3 \\
| & \nearrow \quad + \quad CH\text{–}CH_3 & | \\
CH_3\text{–}C^+ & \quad + \quad || & \longrightarrow \quad CH_3\text{–}C^+ - CH - CH^+ - CH_3 \\
| & \quad CH\text{–}CH_3 & | \quad | \\
CH_3 & & CH_3 \ CH_3
\end{array}
$$

Fig. 3. The addition of a tertiary carbonium ion to the second olefin molecule

4. The fourth stage consists of the skeletal isomerization of the secondary carbonium ion:
5. The fifth stage is the interaction of the formed carbonium ions with an isoparaffin molecule by a tertiary carbon-hydrogen bond with the formation of target products and a carbonium ion from isoparaffin (Figs. 1, 2, 3, 4 and 5):

For ease of use when compiling the model, we offer below a scheme containing the reactions in the sulfuric acid alkylation process (Fig. 6).

It should be noted that the temperature range of the process is from 2°C to 15°C. Determining the optimal value for a given composition of feedstocks is one of the study objectives. The solution to the problem of constructing a model of the process of sulfuric acid alkylation of isobutane with butylenes is relevant in this regard [10].

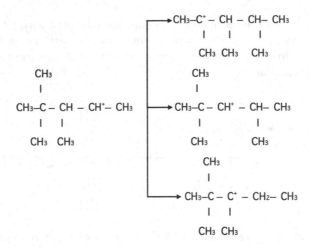

Fig. 4. The skeletal isomerization of the secondary carbonium ion

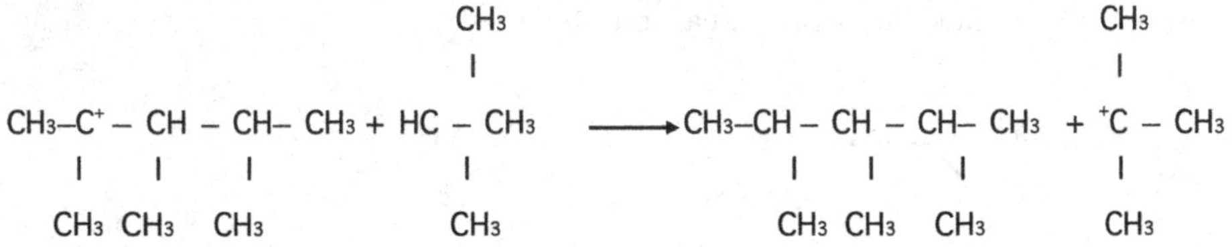

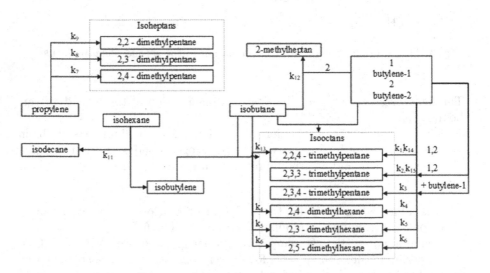

Fig. 5. The interaction of the formed carbonium ions with an isoparaffin molecule

Fig. 6. The scheme of reactions of the sulfuric acid alkylation process

Since the mathematical model of the chemical reaction is a system of differential equations, it is only possible to find the values of the constants in this system numerically (see, e.g., [5]). Note that the objective function in such problems is usually multiextremal, i.e., it has many local extrema apart from the global one.

Assuming some additional properties of the objective function, it is possible to construct efficient deterministic methods for finding a global solution. For example, we can assume that the ratio of the function increment to the corresponding argument increment can not exceed some threshold. In this case, the functions are called Lipschitzian, and the problem itself is a Lipschitz optimization problem. This paper continues a series of papers where the parallel methods of Lipschitz optimization proposed in [12] are investigated and modified in their application to solving inverse problems of chemical kinetics.

The main part of the paper is organized as follows. Section 2 describes the mathematical model of the chemical reaction under study. The formal statement of the Lipschitz global optimization problem and the general scheme of the search for algorithms are given in Sect. 3. In that section, we also present a scheme of the proposed asynchronous parallel algorithm for solving multiextremal problems. The results of the numerical solution of the inverse problem of chemical kinetics are discussed in Sect. 4.

2   The Problem Statement

To optimize the technological process, it is necessary to know the kinetic laws and mechanisms of chemical reactions. To determine them, we should evaluate the kinetic parameters of chemical reactions by solving the inverse problem of chemical kinetics [1]. In most cases, the equations of chemical kinetics are systems of ordinary nonlinear differential equations for the concentrations of substances x_i (1) with initial conditions (2):

$$\frac{dx_i}{dt} = \sum_{j=1}^{J} \nu_{ij}\omega_j, \quad i = 1,\ldots.I, \; \omega_j = k_j^0 \cdot \exp\left(-\frac{E_j}{RT}\right) \cdot \prod_{i=1}^{M} x_i^{|a_{ij}|}, \qquad (1)$$

$$t = 0, \; x_i(0) = x_i^0. \qquad (2)$$

Here $k_j^0 \cdot \exp\left(-\frac{E_j}{RT}\right)$ are the so-called rate constants of the reaction stages; I is the number of substances involved in the reaction; J is the number of reaction stages; ν_{ij} are stoichiometric coefficients; E_j are the activation energies of the reactions (cal/mol); R is the universal gas constant (cal/(mol · K)); T stands for the temperature (K); a_{ij} are the stoichiometric coefficients; k_j^0 are pre-exponential multipliers.

The inverse problem of chemical kinetics is a global optimization problem implying the need to determine the vector of reaction rate constants $(k_1, k_2, \ldots, k_J)$ at which the deviation of the calculated concentrations of the reaction components from the experimental ones is minimal. Thus, to determine the rate constants of the reaction, it is necessary to solve the inverse problem of chemical kinetics by repeatedly solving the direct problem, that is, by iterating over the rate constants of the stages (or a set of pre-exponents and activation energies) according to some algorithm. To solve the optimization problem, it is necessary to minimize the functional (3), which expresses the deviation of experimental data from the calculated values:

$$FF = \sum_{i=1}^{M} \sum_{j=1}^{N} |x_{ij}^{calc} - x_{ij}^{exp}|. \tag{3}$$

Here x_{ij}^{calc} are the calculated values, x_{ij}^{exp} are experimental data, M is the number of experimental points, and N is the number of substances involved in the reaction. To solve the instability issue in optimization problem (3), consider the minimization problem in the general form

$$f(z) \rightarrow \inf, \quad z \in D, \tag{4}$$

where D is some given set and $f: D \rightarrow R^1$ is a function (functional) defined on it.

In this inverse problem of chemical kinetics, a number of kinetic parameters act as a point z (as a rule, a vector of reaction rate constants), while the function f is the deviation of the calculated concentrations of the reaction components from empirical data (functional (3)). Problem (4) can be attributed to one of two classes of problems, which in the literature are called correctly posed and incorrectly posed minimization tasks, respectively. Inverse problems of chemical kinetics are *incorrectly posed problems* (or, in other words, *ill-posed problems*). According to Hadamard, a problem is considered to be *correctly posed* if: 1) its solution exists, 2) the solution is unique, and 3) the solution is stable to variations in the initial data. If at least one of the listed requirements does not hold, the task is considered incorrectly posed. The inverse problems of chemical kinetics encountered in practice usually have a solution, and condition 1 is, thus, fulfilled. Most often, however, conditions 2 and 3 do not hold [1]. To solve ill-posed problems approximately, we need special methods to construct a solution to problem (4). Such methods exist and are commonly called regularization methods. In this paper, we rely on a regularization method suggested by A. N. Tikhonov and called the *stabilization method*. Also, we use the classical machine-learning apparatus, i.e., normalization of features and scaling. The main task that we will consider is the minimization problem

$$f^0(z) \rightarrow \inf, \quad z \in D \subset Z, \tag{5}$$

in which we assume D to be a convex closed set in a Hilbert space Z. The function $f^0: D \rightarrow R^1$ is considered continuous and convex on D. Suppose that problem (5) has a solution, i.e., the set D^* is nonempty. Denote by z^0 the norm-minimal solution to the problem. Suppose that instead of an exact function f, we know its approximation f_δ, where $\delta \in [0, \delta_0], \delta_0 > 0$, is a sufficiently small number, and, moreover,

$$|f^\delta(z) - f^0(z)| \leq \delta(1 + ||z||^2), \quad \forall z \in D. \tag{6}$$

The main construction of the Tikhonov method is the smoothing function or Tikhonov function

$$T_\alpha^\delta(z) \equiv f^\delta(z) + \alpha\|z\|^2, \quad z \in D, \tag{7}$$

where $\alpha > 0$ is the regularization parameter; $\alpha\|z\|^2$ is called the stabilizing term. Consider the auxiliary minimization problem

$$T_\alpha^\delta(z) \to \inf, \quad z \in D. \tag{8}$$

Various numerical methods can be applied to approximate the solution of this problem. Suppose that, as a result of a finite number of iterations, we obtain a point $z_\alpha^{\delta,\epsilon}$ such that

$$T_\alpha^\delta(z) \equiv \min T_\alpha^\delta(z) \leq T_\alpha^\delta(z_\alpha^{\delta,\epsilon}) \leq T_\alpha^\delta + \epsilon, \tag{9}$$

where $\epsilon > 0$ is a number that characterizes the accuracy of the solution to minimization problem (8). In this case, minimization problem (8) for each fixed pair δ, α has, as a rule, a much larger "margin of stability" than the original problem (4) and, in most cases, is correctly posed.

3   The Parallel Global Optimization Algorithm

3.1   The Optimization Problem

As we mentioned above, the task of identifying the model parameter values can be considered a Lipschitz global optimization problem. From a formal point of view, this problem is a mathematical programming problem of the form

$$\varphi^* = \varphi(y^*) = \min\{\varphi(y) : y \in D\}, \tag{10}$$

$$D = \{y \in R^N : a_i \leq y_i \leq b_i, \ 1 \leq i \leq N\}, \tag{11}$$

where the vectors $a, b \in R^N$ correspond to the lower and upper bounds of the search region, and $\varphi(y)$ is the objective function, which satisfies the Lipschitz condition

$$|\varphi(y_1) - \varphi(y_2)| \leq L\|y_1 - y_2\|, \quad y_1, y_2 \in D. \tag{12}$$

We assume that the function $\varphi(y)$ is multiextremal and is given as a "black box" (i.e., as some subroutine with a vector of parameters as its input and the calculated value of the function as its output). Moreover, we suppose that each application of this procedure (hereinafter referred to as a *search trial*) is a time-consuming operation. This formulation of the problem is fully consistent with the inverse problem of chemical kinetics.

There are several algorithms that can be applied to solve Lipschitz optimization problems. These include, among others, the nonuniform covering method [3,4], and diagonal and simplicial partition methods [7,8]. In this paper, we rely on the global search algorithm proposed by Strongin [12]. Under this approach, the original multidimensional problem (10) is reduced to a one-dimensional optimization problem using Peano–Hilbert curves.

In fact, using a continuous one-to-one mapping (Peano curve) $y(x)$ of the segment $[0, 1]$ of the real axis onto the hyperinterval D in (11), we can reduce the original problem (10) to the one-dimensional problem

$$\varphi(y^*) = \varphi(y(x^*)) = \min\{\varphi(y(x)) : x \in [0, 1]\},$$

where the one-dimensional function $\varphi(y(x))$ satisfies the Hölder condition

$$|\varphi(y(x_1)) - \varphi(y(x_2))| \le H |x_1 - x_2|^{1/N}$$

with $H = 2L\sqrt{N + 3}$. The numerical construction of various approximations of such mappings is discussed in [11,12].

Thus, the search trial at some point $x' \in [0, 1]$ will involve, in the first place, the construction of the image $y' = y(x')$ and only then the computation of the function value $z' = \varphi(y')$.

3.2 Characteristic Algorithms

The global search algorithm we use belongs to the class of *characteristic algorithms*, and this greatly simplifies the process of its parallelization. Recall that a numerical optimization method belongs to the class of characteristic algorithms if the algorithmic scheme of this method can be described as follows.

At the first iteration, the trials are performed at the points $x^1 = 0$ and $x^2 = 1$. Then, each following $(k + 1)$-th, $k \ge 2$, iteration of the global search is executed as described below.

1. Renumber the points of the previous trials by increasing their x-coordinates (the new order is determined by the subscripts):

$$0 = x_0 < x_2 < \ldots < x_k = 1.$$

2. For every interval $(x_{i-1}, x_i), 1 \le i \le k$, we calculate a value $R(i)$ called the *interval characteristic*. In the general case, $R(i)$ can depend on the points x^i and the trial results $z^i = f(x^i)$, $1 \le i \le k$.
3. Find the interval (x_{t-1}, x_t) with the largest characteristic $R(t)$, i.e.,

$$R(t) = \max\{R(i) : 1 \le i \le k\}.$$

4. Examine the stop condition

$$\Delta_t \le \epsilon,$$

   where $\epsilon > 0$ is a given accuracy. If the stop condition is satisfied, then the global search should be terminated; otherwise, the calculations continue.
5. Select a point x^{k+1} of the current iteration within the interval (x_{t-1}, x_t) in accordance with some rule $S(t)$, i.e.,

$$x^{k+1} = S(t) \in (x_{t-1}, x_t).$$

6. Calculate the function value $z^{k+1} = f(x^{k+1})$.

7. Evaluate a global minimum estimate.
8. Increase the iteration number $k = k + 1$ and proceed to the next iteration.

As a possible interpretation of this scheme, we can consider the interval characteristic $R(i)$ as a measure of the global minimum being within the interval (x_{i-1}, x_i). To construct a concrete form of the interval characteristic, we can use a lower envelope (or minorant) of the function to be minimized or a mathematical expectation of the function values, etc. Most well-known global optimization methods can be formulated in accordance with this characteristic scheme, e.g.,

- uniform grid methods with a successively reduced step;
- random search (Monte Carlo) algorithms;
- the Piyavskii algorithm [9];
- one-step Bayesian algorithms proposed by Kushner and Žilinskas [13];
- information algorithms proposed by Strongin [12].

All these methods are based on different mathematical models but are presented in a general characteristic scheme.

It should also be noted that the length of the interval with the largest characteristic is examined at the stop condition. It is possible if the optimization method converges to the global minimum. The details of these methods are given in the cited sources. Here we highlight the main points.

For the Piyavskii method, the interval characteristic $R(i)$ is an estimate (with the inverse sign) of the minimum value of the objective function $f(x)$ in the interval (x_{i-1}, x_i). As a result, the point of a new trial is taken within the interval containing the estimate of the minimum value of $f(x)$ over the search domain.

The Kushner technique and the Žilinskas method are constructed in the framework of the approach when the objective function is regarded as a sample of some Wiener process. For the Kushner technique, the point x^{k+1} of the current iteration is the most probable point at which the function value $f(x^{k+1})$ is not greater than the value

$$z_k^* - \gamma(z_k^+ - z_k^*),$$

where z_k^+ and z_k^* are estimates of the function maximum and minimum values, respectively. For the Žilinskas method, x^{k+1} is the point where the maximum average improvement of the current estimate of the global extremum is expected.

The Strongin global search algorithm is constructed in the framework of the information approach to global optimization (see [12]). This method has an adaptive scheme to evaluate the numerical estimate of the unknown Lipschitz constant.

3.3   Parallel Algorithm with Asynchronous Trials

The global search algorithm (GSA) belongs to the class of characteristic algorithms; this fact suggests a possible way to parallelize it. As previously mentioned, the interval characteristic $R(i)$ can be regarded as some measure of finding the global minimum point in the given interval. Then, instead of a single best interval, several intervals with the highest characteristics can be chosen at once, and successive trials can be carried out in these intervals in parallel. Moreover, the scheme of characteristic algorithms also allows for asynchronous parallelization, which minimizes the downtime of processors when the trial complexity depends on a particular point in the search domain.

Let us now examine the parallel algorithm with asynchronous trials in more detail. It implements a parallel scheme of the "master/worker" type. The master process accumulates search information, evaluates on its basis the Lipschitz constant for the target function, determines new trial points, and sends them to the worker processes. Worker processes receive points from the master, carry out new trials at these points, and send the results to the master.

When describing the parallel algorithm, we assume that there are $p+1$ computational processes: one master and p worker processes.

At the beginning of the search, the master process (let it be process number 0) initiates p parallel trials at p different points of the search domain, two of which are boundary points and the rest are internal points, i.e., at the points $\{y(x^1), y(x^2), \ldots, y(x^p)\}$, where $x^1 = 0$, $x^p = 1$, $x^i \in (0, 1)$, $i = 2, \ldots, p-1$.

Suppose now that k trials have been performed (in particular, k can be 0), and the worker processes perform trials at points $\{y(x^{k+1}), y(x^{k+2}), \ldots, y(x^{k+p})\}$.

If a worker process completes the trial at some point (let it be the point $y(x^{k+1})$, corresponding to process number 1), then it sends the results of the trial to the master process. Note that, in this case, we have a set of inverse images of the trial points

$$S_k = \left\{ x^{k+1}, x^{k+2}, \ldots, x^{k+p} \right\},$$

where the trials have already started but are not completed yet.

After receiving the trial results at the point $y(x^{k+1})$ from the worker process, the master selects a new trial point x^{k+p+1} for it, according to the rules corresponding to the scheme of the characteristic algorithm.

1. Renumber the set of inverse images of the trial points

$$X_k = \left\{ x^1, x^2, \ldots, x^{k+p} \right\},$$

which contains all inverse images at which the trials have either been carried out or are being carried out, arranged in an ascending order (determined by the subscripts), i.e.,

$$0 = x_1 < x_2 < \ldots < x_{x+p} = 1.$$

2. Calculate the values

$$M_1 = \max \left\{ \frac{|z_i - z_{i-1}|}{(x_i - x_{i-1})^{1/N}} : x_{i-1} \notin S_k, x_i \notin S_k, 2 \leq i \leq k+p \right\},$$

$$M_2 = \max \left\{ \frac{|z_{i+1} - z_{i-1}|}{(x_{i+1} - x_{i-1})^{1/N}} : x_i \in S_k, 2 \leq i < k+p \right\},$$

$$M = \max\{M_1, M_2\},$$

where $z_i = \varphi(y(x_i))$ for all $x_i \notin S_k$. If M equals 0, then assume $M = 1$.

3. Assign to each interval (x_{i-1}, x_i), $x_{i-1} \notin S_k$, $x_i \notin S_k$, the characteristic $R(i)$, calculated by the formula

$$R(i) = rM\Delta_i + \frac{(z_i - z_{i-1})^2}{rM\Delta_i} - 2(z_i + z_{i-1}), \tag{13}$$

where $r > 1$ is a method parameter and $\Delta_i = (x_i - x_{i-1})^{1/N}$.

4. Find the interval $[x_{t-1}, x_t]$ to which the maximum characteristic corresponds, i.e.,

$$R(t) = \max\{R(i) : x_{i-1} \notin S_k, x_i \notin S_k, 2 \leq i \leq k+p\}.$$

5. Determine the inverse image $x^{k+p+1} \in (x_{t-1}, x_t)$ of the new trial point by the formula

$$x^{k+p+1} = \frac{x_t + x_{t-1}}{2} - \text{sign}(z_t - z_{t-1})\frac{1}{2r}\left[\frac{|z_t - z_{t-1}|}{M}\right]^N.$$

Immediately after calculating the next trial point $y^{k+p+1} = y(x^{k+p+1})$, the master process adds it to the set S_k and forwards it to the worker process, which initiates a trial at this point.

The master process completes the algorithm when one of two conditions holds: $\Delta_t < \epsilon$ or $k + p > K_{\max}$. The first one corresponds to stopping the algorithm by accuracy, and the second one, by the number of trials. The real number $0 < \epsilon < 1$ and the integer $K_{\max} > 0$ are algorithm parameters.

4   Numerical Experiments

To determine the constants of the process reactions, it is necessary to solve a system of differential equations that describes the change in the concentrations of the reaction components over time [2].

In preliminary experiments, we estimated the approximate time to calculate one objective function using the corresponding sequential algorithm. The computer architecture used for the experiments was based on Intel® Core™ i7-10750H processors at 2.60 GHz. The average computation time of the objective function was about 0.2 sec, which characterizes the problem as being computationally complex. Solving the problem with the sequential algorithm would require no less than 1 million trials, that is, at least 54 h (as an estimate). Therefore, only the parallel algorithm with a stopping criterion based on the number of trials $K_{\max} = 10^6$ was used for the calculations.

The numerical experiments were performed with the parallel asynchronous algorithm outlined in Sect. 3.3, running 160 processes: 159 processes calculated the values of the objective function (worker processes), and one master process controlled the algorithm. The experiments were conducted on the Lobachevsky supercomputer, installed at the University of Nizhni Novgorod. The asynchronous global optimization algorithm was implemented in C++ (with GCC 9.5.0 and Intel MPI). The computation of the objective function values was implemented in Python 3.9.

Table 1. Dependence of the function minimum value φ^* on the regularization parameter α

α	φ^*	Time (sec.)
0.0	0.573920	838.9
0.001	0.540750	853.9
0.002	0.547907	850.0
0.003	0.583529	831.5
0.004	0.579725	821.4
0.005	0.615638	815.4
0.006	0.612614	834.7
0.007	0.619546	807.3
0.008	0.604817	830.4
0.009	0.630010	814.4
0.01	0.632944	825.2
0.02	0.669092	155.8
0.03	0.681520	809.2
0.04	0.736035	816.4
0.05	0.729415	804.7
0.07	0.759134	803.6
0.06	0.723404	810.9
0.08	0.808238	811.8
0.09	0.837868	828.6
0.1	0.810454	806.2

The short time obtained when solving the problem by the parallel algorithm (approximately 14 min per problem) made it possible to investigate thoroughly the dependence of the solution on the regularization parameter α. Table 1 shows the minimum values of the objective function found for the corresponding value of the regularization parameter and the time for solving the problem (in seconds). The algorithm was run with the method parameter $r = 4.0$ from (13) and the accuracy $\epsilon = 10^{-4} \|b - a\|$. After a given number of iterations or after reaching the specified accuracy with the global search method, the solution was refined by the Hooke–Jeeves local method [6] with the accuracy $\epsilon = 10^{-4} \|b - a\|$.

A detailed study of the region of the regularization parameter values in a neighborhood of $\alpha = 0$ (from 0.1 to 0.01 with steps of 0.01 and from 0.01 to 0.001 with steps of 0.001) showed that the value of the minimum decreases as α decreases. The best solution, equal to 0.54075, was obtained with the regularization parameter $\alpha = 0.001$.

In the course of the research, we calculated the functional $f(z)$ without taking into account the addition of the regularization term (Fig. 7). Afterward, we carried out a similar calculation taking into account the regularization term. The results for $\alpha = 0.002$ were 0.527 without regularization and 0.547 with regularization.

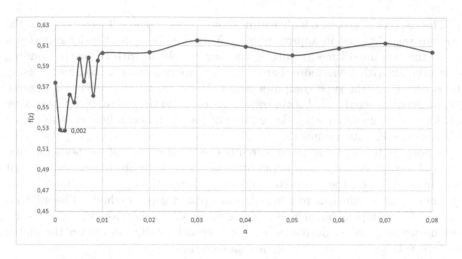

Fig. 7. The value of the functional $f(z)$ without taking into account the addition of the regularization term

The speedup of the parallel global optimization algorithm was estimated for the problem to which the best solution was found, i.e., the problem with regularization parameter $\alpha = 0.001$. Since solving the problem in serial mode would require about two days, the speedup was evaluated with respect to a parallel launch involving a smaller number of processes. Table 2 shows the running time and speedup of the parallel algorithm using 80 and 160 processes with respect to the running time on 40 processes.

Table 2. The speedup of the parallel global optimization algorithm

p	Time (sec.)	Speedup
40	2778.7	—
80	1495.5	1.9
160	853.9	3.3

5 Conclusions

We solved in this paper an incorrectly posed problem using the Tikhonov regularization method and found the reaction constants of the process of sulfuric acid alkylation of isoalkanes by alkenes. The optimization method allowed us to find an accurate description of the experimental data. The authors plan to use the Tikhonov regularization method in forthcoming research to build kinetic models of other chemical processes.

The parallel global search algorithm showed good results. The solution to the problem was obtained in approximately 15 min on the Lobachevsky supercomputer; the estimated time for solving the same problem with the corresponding sequential algorithm was more than 50 h. The experiments were conducted using 160 processes on the supercomputer nodes. However, an increase in the dimension of the considered global optimization problem (in the case of complex inverse problems of chemical kinetics, the number of parameters can be hundreds) leads to a decrease in search quality.

A possible topic for further research is the development of methods for analyzing the accumulated search information to identify groups of parameters that have little effect on the objective function. To find the optimal values of such parameters, it is sufficient to employ local optimization methods. The analysis can rely, for example, on machine-learning methods. In this case, the cost of solving the whole problem decreases, and it becomes feasible to obtain the global solution with good accuracy in an acceptable time.

Acknowledgments. This research was partially funded by projects № FSWR-2023-0034, № 075-02-2022-883 (development of the parallel global optimization algorithm), and № FMRS-2022-0078 (investigation of the chemical kinetics problem).

References

1. Adriazola, J.: On the role of tikhonov regularizations in standard optimization problems (2022). https://doi.org/10.21203/rs.3.rs-2376984/v1
2. Cao, P., Zheng, L., Sun, W., Zhao, L.: Multiscale modeling of isobutane alkylation with mixed c4 olefins using sulfuric acid as catalyst. Ind. Eng. Chem. Res. **58**(16), 6340–6349 (2019). https://doi.org/10.1021/acs.iecr.9b00874
3. Evtushenko, Y., Malkova, V., Stanevichyus, A.A.: Parallel global optimization of functions of several variables. Comput. Math. Math. Phys. **49**(2), 246–260 (2009). https://doi.org/10.1134/S0965542509020055
4. Evtushenko, Y., Posypkin, M.: A deterministic approach to global box-constrained optimization. Optim. Lett. **7**, 819–829 (2013). https://doi.org/10.1007/s11590-012-0452-1
5. Gubaydullin, I., Enikeeva, L., Barkalov, K., Lebedev, I.: Parallel global search algorithm for optimization of the kinetic parameters of chemical reactions. Commun. Comput. Inf. Sci. **1510**, 198–211 (2021)
6. Hooke, R., Jeeves, T.: "Direct search" solution of numerical and statistical problems. J. ACM **8**(2), 212–229 (1961). https://doi.org/10.1145/321062.321069
7. Paulavičius, R., Žilinskas, J., Grothey, A.: Investigation of selection strategies in branch and bound algorithm with simplicial partitions and combination of Lipschitz bounds. Optim. Lett. **4**(2), 173–183 (2010). https://doi.org/10.1007/s11590-009-0156-3
8. Paulavičius, R., Žilinskas, J., Grothey, A.: Parallel branch and bound for global optimization with combination of Lipschitz bounds. Optim. Method. Softw. **26**(3), 487–498 (2011). https://doi.org/10.1080/10556788.2010.551537
9. Piyavskii, S.: An algorithm for finding the absolute extremum of a function. Comp. Math. Math. Phys. **12**(4), 57–67 (1972)

10. Semenov, I., Shelkovnikov, A.: Modeling of the process of isoparaffin sulfuric alkylation. Modern Technol. Sci. Technol. Prog. 1, 72–73 (2021). https://doi.org/10.36629/2686-9896-2021-1-1-72-73
11. Sergeyev, Y.D., Strongin, R.G., Lera, D.: Introduction to Global Optimization Exploiting Space-filling Curves. Springer Briefs in Optimization, Springer, New York (2013). https://doi.org/10.1007/978-1-4614-8042-6
12. Strongin R.G., Sergeyev Y.D.: Global Optimization with Non-convex Constraints. Sequential and Parallel Algorithms. Kluwer Academic Publishers, Dordrecht (2000). https://doi.org/10.1007/978-1-4615-4677-1
13. Törn, A., Žilinskas, A. (eds.): Global Optimization. LNCS, vol. 350. Springer, Heidelberg (1989). https://doi.org/10.1007/3-540-50871-6

Parallel Implementation of the Time-Reversal Mirror Method for Retrieving the Position and Type of a Seismic Source from Observational Data

Anastasia Galaktionova[ID] and Galina Reshetova[✉][ID]

Institute of Computational Mathematics and Mathematical Geophysics,
Siberian Branch of the Russian Academy of Sciences, Novosibirsk, Russian Federation
kgv@nmsf.sscc.ru

Abstract. In this article, we present a parallel algorithm for determining the type of a seismic source from seismic observational data using the Time-Reversal Mirror (TRM) method. This problem has a wide range of applications, including virtual source modelling, non-destructive testing of materials and engineering structures, and earthquake source location.

Our proposed algorithm is motivated by the need to retrieve not only the location but also the type of the source. To achieve this, we use numerical simulations based on a three-dimensional model of a dynamic elasticity theory and a finite-difference scheme on staggered meshes.

To parallelize the algorithm, we use MPI functions and the domain decomposition approach. To improve the efficiency, we rely on techniques such as data exchange in the computational background and the non-blocking MPI functions. We present and discuss the results obtained from our numerical simulations, which demonstrate the possibility of determining the type of seismic source. The proposed algorithm can be used in a variety of scientific and engineering applications, particularly in earthquake source location and non-destructive testing.

Keywords: Wave propagation · Seismic source · Time-Reversal Mirror · Numerical solutions · Finite difference schemes · Parallel programming · MPI · Domain decomposition

1 Introduction and Motivation

The problem of reconstructing the type of a seismic source is of great importance when studying the properties of geological media and the processes of their corruption near zones of focal destruction. The development of observation networks and the accumulation of an increasing amount of survey data simultaneously with the development of new mathematical algorithms make it possible to use seismic data for source-type reconstruction.

© The Author(s), under exclusive license to Springer Nature Switzerland AG 2023
L. Sokolinsky and M. Zymbler (Eds.): PCT 2023, CCIS 1868, pp. 182–196, 2023.
https://doi.org/10.1007/978-3-031-38864-4_13

The sources of seismic waves can be artificial or natural depending on their origin. Earthquake sources of natural origin include those associated with faults or shear movements of surfaces inside the Earth, volcanic tremors, microseismic noise, and so on. Artificial sources are of technogenic origin (for example, above-ground and underground nuclear explosions, explosions in quarries and mines, and others). Seismic sources can serve for studying the internal structure of oil and mineral deposits, mapping underground faults, and other kinds of scientific research. The excitation of the source results in the generation of seismic waves, which then propagate in geological media, reflecting from and refracting at inhomogeneous inclusions, and can be recorded on the free surface by seismic receivers, such as geophones or hydrophones. The registered signals can be subjected to special processing and interpretation to study the internal structure and mechanisms of the motion of Earth's faults.

Several approaches have been proposed over the past decades to solve the problem of retrieving a seismic source. Among them, we distinguish the emission tomography in the reconstruction of the spatial distribution of sources of microseismic radiation in the Earth's crust [1], waveform inversion methods for earthquake sources [2,3], and others. The inversion method, first proposed in [2], is based on minimizing the misfit between observational data and synthetic data for a set of test sources using finite difference modeling in the time domain. Unfortunately, this method can not retrieve the source type (indeed, when solving a system of differential equations, it is necessary to determine the response of the source to the receiver for one of the preselected source types, i.e., a monopole, a horizontal or vertical dipole) [4].

To solve the problem of retrieving the type of a seismic source, we use the Time-Reversal Mirror (TRM) method. This approach has a wide range of applications, including nondestructive testing of materials in industrial engineering [5,6], simulation of virtual sources [7], and many others associated with geophysical problems [8–11]. The applicability of the TRM method for locating sources is not new and is described in the literature, for example, in the context of the location of acoustic emission sources in the core [12] and seismic sources [13]. Nevertheless, whether it is feasible to use this method to determine the source type is still an issue attracting huge interest.

The paper is organised as follows. Section 2 is devoted to the description of the seismic source type retrieval algorithm. Section 3 contains the mathematical statement of the problem and the boundary conditions, and Sect. 4 presents the finite difference scheme on the staggered grid derived by the finite volume technique applied to this mathematical statement. The numerical test is discussed in Sect. 5. The conclusion summarizes the study and points directions for further work.

2 Algorithm for Retrieving the Seismic Source Type

The problem of retrieving the position of a seismic source within a geological medium using only free-surface seismograms and the velocity and density parameters of the medium is of great interest for practical geophysical and seismological applications. Retrieving not only the position of the source but also its type is a more complex problem that requires more subtle approaches to its solution.

The algorithm for retrieving the source type relies on the Time-Reversal Mirror method (TRM), which is based on a consequence of the principle of time reversibility in media without attenuation. This principle consists in the possibility of using the "inverted" time signal registered in the receivers as a function of sources located at one point. In this case, the wave field must be concentrated in the source both in space and time and, consequently, generate an amplitude expansion at the source point. We investigate in this paper whether the resulting wave field contains information about the properties of the original source, in addition to its spatial location.

The algorithm for determining the source type consists of the two stages described below.

Step 1. We simulate the wave field of wave propagation from the source. To do this, we solve a system of differential equations from dynamic elasticity theory and record traces of the wave field components at each moment using a series of receivers. We assume that the seismic waves are produced by a certain type of subsurface source (different types in different experiments). The recorded seismograms are input data for the second stage.

Step 2. Assume that the location and type of the source are unknown. The seismograms recorded in the previous step are reversed in time. Afterward, each reversed trace appears as a function of the time of sources located on the free surface at the same points where the trace was recorded. The TRM process is carried out by solving the same system of differential equations with the same velocity and density parameters of the medium but with a new set of sources on the free surface.

Under such a procedure, the wave field must be concentrated in the source position at the time corresponding to the moment the wave arises. To see the spatial location of the source inside the computational domain, instead of visualizing the components of the wave field at some time t^m, we calculate the sum E_{sum} of the total energy E of the wave field for each grid point of the computational domain and all previous computational moments t^i, namely,

$$E_{\text{sum}}(x_i, y_j, z_k, t^m) = \sum_{t^i \leq t^m} E(x_i, y_j, z_k, t^i). \tag{1}$$

The total energy $E(x_i, y_j, z_k, t^i)$ of the wave field is calculated by the formula

$$\begin{aligned}
E(x_i, y_j, z_k, t^i) &= \tau_{xx}(x_i, y_j, z_k, t^i)\varepsilon_{xx}(x_i, y_j, z_k, t^i) \\
&+ \tau_{yy}(x_i, y_j, z_k, t^i)\varepsilon_{yy}(x_i, y_j, z_k, t^i) + \tau_{zz}(x_i, y_j, z_k, t^i)\varepsilon_{zz}(x_i, y_j, z_k, t^i) \\
&+ 2\tau_{xy}(x_i, y_j, z_k, t^i)\varepsilon_{xy}(x_i, y_j, z_k, t^i) + 2\tau_{xz}(x_i, y_j, z_k, t^i)\varepsilon_{xz}(x_i, y_j, z_k, t^i) \\
&+ 2\tau_{yz}(x_i, y_j, z_k, t^i)\varepsilon_{yz}(x_i, y_j, z_k, t^i), \tag{2}
\end{aligned}$$

where x_i, y_j, z_k are the spatial-grid points of the computational domain, t^i is the time in the finite-difference scheme, and τ and ε are the stress and strain components, respectively.

We assume that the nature of the distribution of the total energy E of the wave field may indicate the type of the source. To confirm this assumption, we analyze in the following sections the simulated data and compare the spatial distribution of the energy E_{sum} and the polar plot of the radiation patterns in the numerical solution of the direct dynamic seismic problem and those obtained in the simulation of the inverse problem by the TRM method.

3   The Mathematical Statement of the Problem

Consider an elastic medium with a subsurface source of seismic waves. The propagation of elastic waves in such a medium is described by the following system of partial differential equations, known as the first-order velocity-stress formulation:

$$\rho \frac{\partial v_x}{\partial t} = \left(\frac{\partial \tau_{xx}}{\partial x} + \frac{\partial \tau_{xy}}{\partial y} + \frac{\partial \tau_{xz}}{\partial z} \right),$$

$$\rho \frac{\partial v_y}{\partial t} = \left(\frac{\partial \tau_{xy}}{\partial x} + \frac{\partial \tau_{yy}}{\partial y} + \frac{\partial \tau_{yz}}{\partial z} \right),$$

$$\rho \frac{\partial v_z}{\partial t} = \left(\frac{\partial \tau_{xz}}{\partial x} + \frac{\partial \tau_{yz}}{\partial y} + \frac{\partial \tau_{zz}}{\partial z} \right),$$

$$\frac{\partial \tau_{xx}}{\partial t} = (\lambda + 2\mu) \frac{\partial v_x}{\partial x} + \lambda \left(\frac{\partial v_y}{\partial y} + \frac{\partial v_z}{\partial z} \right) + F_{xx},$$

$$\frac{\partial \tau_{yy}}{\partial t} = (\lambda + 2\mu) \frac{\partial v_y}{\partial y} + \lambda \left(\frac{\partial v_x}{\partial x} + \frac{\partial v_z}{\partial z} \right) + F_{yy}, \qquad (3)$$

$$\frac{\partial \tau_{zz}}{\partial t} = (\lambda + 2\mu) \frac{\partial v_z}{\partial z} + \lambda \left(\frac{\partial v_x}{\partial x} + \frac{\partial v_y}{\partial y} \right) + F_{zz},$$

$$\frac{\partial \tau_{xy}}{\partial t} = \mu \left(\frac{\partial v_x}{\partial y} + \frac{\partial v_y}{\partial x} \right) + F_{xy},$$

$$\frac{\partial \tau_{xz}}{\partial t} = \mu \left(\frac{\partial v_x}{\partial z} + \frac{\partial v_z}{\partial x} \right) + F_{xz},$$

$$\frac{\partial \tau_{yz}}{\partial t} = \mu \left(\frac{\partial v_y}{\partial z} + \frac{\partial v_z}{\partial y} \right) + F_{xz}.$$

Elastic waves in this system are described by the displacement velocities (v_x, v_y, v_z), and the stress tensor components $(\tau_{xx}, \tau_{yy}, \tau_{zz}, \tau_{xy}, \tau_{xz}, \tau_{yz})$ are given in a Cartesian coordinate system. The Lamé moduli λ and μ, and the density ρ characterize the elastic medium.

The functions $F_{xx}, F_{yy}, F_{zz}, F_{xy}, F_{xz}$, and F_{yz} on the right-hand side of Eqs. 3 determine a generalized moment-tensor source. Different sources can be set up by varying the values of these functions. In particular, in the case of

$F_{xx} = F_{yy} = F_{zz} = f(t) \cdot \delta(x - x_0, y - y_0, z - z_0)$, we obtain a source of the volumetric type. Here $f(t)$ defines the source signal wavelet in time (for example, the Ricker wavelet) and $\delta(x - x_0, y - y_0, z - z_0)$ is the Dirac delta function centered at the source point (x_0, y_0, z_0).

We apply the finite-difference method on staggered grids [14] to numerically simulate the process of seismic wave propagation by solving system (3).

On the free surface of the medium under consideration, we impose a condition that physically corresponds to the wave action on the Earth's surface. The condition is that the normal stresses $(\tau_{xx}, \tau_{yy}, \tau_{zz})$ and the shear stresses $(\tau_{xy}, \tau_{xz}, \tau_{yz})$ on the free surface are equal to zero. When sampling the medium, the normal stresses are localized in integer nodes, and the shear stresses in half-integer ones. Therefore the conditions upon the stresses will be formulated differently from the point of view of the computational scheme.

We assume in the numerical experiments that data are recorded in an unlimited space. To this end, all the boundaries of the computational domain, except for the free surface, are surrounded by a convolutional perfectly matched absorbing boundary layer (CPML) [15].

4   The Numerical Simulation

To numerically solve the problem under study, we use the explicit finite-difference staggered grid discretization of linear system 3. To this end, we construct a grid with integer nodes $t^n = n\Delta t$, $x_i = i\Delta x$, $y_j = j\Delta y$, $z_k = k\Delta z$ and half-integer nodes $t^{n+1/2} = (n + 1/2)\Delta t$, $x_{i+1/2} = (i + 1/2)\Delta x$, $y_{j+1/2} = (j + 1/2)\Delta y$, $z_{k+1/2} = (k + 1/2)\Delta z$, where Δt, Δx, Δy, and Δz denote the grid sampling intervals for the time and spatial variables (t, x, y, z) (Fig. 1).

The wave field components and medium parameters are defined at different times and space grid nodes. Assume that the medium parameters are constant within each grid cell $[x_{i-1/2}, x_{i+1/2}] \times [y_{j-1/2}, y_{j+1/2}] \times [z_{k-1/2}, z_{k+1/2}]$, and the possible discontinuities are aligned with the directions of the grid lines. Define the components of the displacement velocities as $(v_x)_{i+1/2,j,k}^{n-1/2}$, $(v_y)_{i,j+1/2,k}^{n-1/2}$, and $(v_z)_{i,j,k+1/2}^{n-1/2}$; the normal stress tensor components as $(\tau_{xx})_{i,j,k}^n$, $(\tau_{yy})_{i,j,k}^n$, and $(\tau_{zz})_{i,j,k}^n$; and the shear stress tensor components as $(\tau_{xy})_{i+1/2,j+1/2,k}^n$, $(\tau_{xz})_{i+1/2,j,k+1/2}^n$, and $(\tau_{yz})_{i,j+1/2,k+1/2}^n$.

Let $f_{i,j}^n = f(t^n, x_i, y_j, z_k)$ be a discrete function. We introduce the second-order centered finite-difference time operator

$$D_t[f]_{i,j,k}^n = \frac{(f)_{i,j,k}^{n+1/2} - (f)_{i,j,k}^{n-1/2}}{\Delta t}, \tag{4}$$

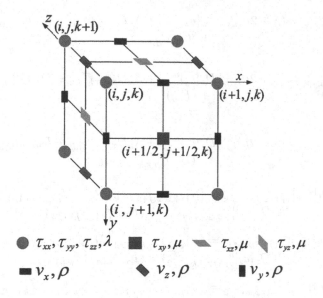

Fig. 1. Finite-difference staggered grid

and the second-order centered finite-difference spatial operators

$$D_x[f]_{i,j,k}^n = \frac{(f)_{i+1/2,j,k}^n - (f)_{i-1/2,j,k}^n}{\Delta x}, \tag{5}$$

$$D_y[f]_{i,j,k}^n = \frac{(f)_{i,j+1/2,k}^n - (f)_{i,j-1/2,k}^n}{\Delta y}, \tag{6}$$

$$D_z[f]_{i,j,k}^n = \frac{(f)_{i,j,k+1/2}^n - (f)_{i,j,k-1/2}^n}{\Delta y}. \tag{7}$$

The finite-difference scheme on the staggered grid is derived by the finite volume (balance law) technique [16] and is as follows:

$$D_t[v_x]_{i+1/2,j,k}^{n-1/2} = \langle 1/\rho_0 \rangle_{i+1/2,j,k} \left(D_x[\tau_{xx}]_{i+1/2,j,k}^{n-1/2} + D_y[\tau_{xy}]_{i,j+1/2,k}^{n-1/2} \right. \\ \left. + D_z[\tau_{xz}]_{i,j,k+1/2}^{n-1/2} \right) \tag{8a}$$

$$D_t[v_y]_{i,j+1/2,k}^{n-1/2} = \langle 1/\rho_0 \rangle_{i,j+1/2,k} \left(D_x[\tau_{xy}]_{i,j+1/2,k}^{n-1/2} + D_y[\tau_{yy}]_{i,j+1/2,k}^{n-1/2} \right. \\ \left. + D_z[\tau_{yz}]_{i,j+1/2,k}^{n-1/2} \right), \tag{8b}$$

$$D_t[v_z]_{i,j,k+1/2}^{n-1/2} = \langle 1/\rho_0 \rangle_{i,j,k+1/2} \left(D_x[\tau_{xz}]_{i,j,k+1/2}^{n-1/2} + D_y[\tau_{yz}]_{i,j,k+1/2}^{n-1/2} \right. \\ \left. + D_z[\tau_{zz}]_{i,j,k+1/2}^{n-1/2} \right), \tag{8c}$$

$$D_t[\tau_{xx}]^n_{i,j,k} = (\lambda + 2\mu)_{i,j,k} D_x[v_x]^n_{i,j,k} + \lambda(D_y[v_y]^n_{i,j,k} + D_z[v_z]^n_{i,j,k}) \\ + (F_{xx})^n_{i,j,k}$$ (8d)

$$D_t[\tau_{yy}]^n_{i,j,k} = (\lambda + 2\mu)_{i,j,k} D_y[v_y]^n_{i,j,k} + \lambda(D_x[v_x]^n_{i,j,k} + D_z[v_z]^n_{i,j,k}) \\ + (F_{yy})^n_{i,j,k}$$ (8e)

$$D_t[\tau_{zz}]^n_{i,j,k} = (\lambda + 2\mu)_{i,j,k} D_z[v_z]^n_{i,j,k} + \lambda(D_x[v_x]^n_{i,j,k} + D_y[v_y]^n_{i,j,k}) \\ + (F_{zz})^n_{i,j,k}$$ (8f)

$$D_t[\tau_{xy}]^n_{i+1/2,j+1/2,k} = \{\mu\}_{i+1/2,j+1/2,k}(D_y[v_x]^n_{i+1/2,j+1/2,k} \\ + D_x[v_y]^n_{i+1/2,j+1/2,k}) + (F_{xy})^n_{i+1/2,j+1/2,k}$$ (8g)

$$D_t[\tau_{xz}]^n_{i+1/2,j,k+1/2} = \{\mu\}_{i+1/2,j,k+1/2}(D_z[v_x]^n_{i+1/2,j,k+1/2} \\ + D_x[v_z]^n_{i+1/2,j,k+1/2}) + (F_{xz})^n_{i+1/2,j,k+1/2}$$ (8h)

$$D_t[\tau_{yz}]^n_{i,j+1/2,k+1/2} = \{\mu\}_{i,j+1/2,k+1/2}(D_z[v_y]^n_{i,j+1/2,k+1/2} \\ + D_y[v_z]^n_{i,j+1/2,k+1/2}) + (F_{yz})^n_{i,j,k}.$$ (8i)

Here the effective medium parameters in the half-integer nodes are defined through arithmetic averaging,

$$\langle f \rangle_{i+1/2,j,k} = (f_{i,j,k} + f_{i+1,j,k})/2,$$
$$\langle f \rangle_{i,j+1/2,k} = (f_{i,j,k} + f_{i,j+1,k})/2,$$
$$\langle f \rangle_{i,j,k+1/2} = (f_{i,j,k} + f_{i,j,k+1})/2,$$

or harmonic averaging [17],

$$\{f\}_{i+1/2,j+1/2,k} = \begin{cases} \left[\left(\frac{1}{f_{i,j,k}} + \frac{1}{f_{i+1,j,k}} + \frac{1}{f_{i,j+1,k}} + \frac{1}{f_{i+1,j+1,k}}\right)/4\right]^{-1} \\ \quad \text{if } f_{i+m,j+m} \neq 0, \ m = \overline{0,1}; \\ \\ 0 \quad \text{if } f_{i+m,j+m} = 0 \text{ for some } m = \overline{0,1}. \end{cases}$$ (9)

The scheme obtained here is an explicit finite-difference scheme of the second order in time and space for a homogeneous elastic medium. The stability conditions and dispersion properties can be found in [14].

5   The Numerical Test

For the calculation, we choose a cube domain of size 3020 m × 3020 m × 3020 m with a grid step of 20 m. The width of the perfectly matching layer is 400 m. In this domain, the medium is homogeneous, $v_p = 3000$ m/s, $v_s = v_p/\sqrt{3}$, and $\rho = 2000$ kg/m^3. The time step is $3 \cdot 10^{-3}$ s, and the registration time is 13.5 s.

The frequency of the source $f_0 = 5$ Hz. The point source is located in the center of the computational domain. The receivers are evenly spaced on the free surface with a step of 20 m. The values of the normal stress components $(\tau_{xx}, \tau_{yy}, \tau_{zz})$ at each instant are recorded by the receivers and then used as seismograms.

In the first stage, the total energy E_{sum} of the direct wave field (1) is calculated for different types of sources. In our case, we use sources directed in the yz plane at a fixed angle ($90°$, $30°$, $45°$, or $60°$) to the free surface plane. We are considering the three-dimensional case, so we use slices in the plane containing the source to display the result (Fig. 2). Since there are several such slices, it is sometimes useful to view them all to obtain more complete information.

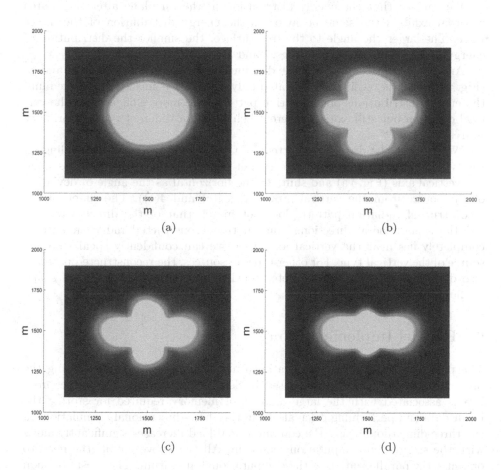

Fig. 2. Distribution of the total energy E_{sum} of the direct wave field in the plain xy (z fixed): (a) vertical source; (b) $30°$ source; (c) $45°$ source; (d) $60°$ source

Afterward, we forget about the simulation and assume that we only know the seismogram and the coordinates of the receivers. Now we follow the same procedure as before, with the only difference being that the sources are now the former receivers and the signals in the sources are the recorded and time-reversed seismogram traces. In the same manner, we calculate the total energy (Fig. 3).

We also take into account the radiation pattern. This flat picture is easier to perceive than the distribution of energy. To construct the diagram, we consider the energy value only at those points of the plane that are at a certain distance from the source. The obtained values are given in a polar coordinate system (Fig. 4).

We can see that the energy distribution in the xy plane after the source retrieval exhibits the same behavior as the energy distribution of the direct wave. The larger the angle to the free surface, the smaller the distribution of energy in one of the directions (Figs. 2 and 3).

Another is the situation with the distribution in the vertical planes xz and yz (Fig. 4). Since the receivers are located only on the free surface of the medium, the energy distributions and radiation patterns are more elongated in the vertical direction but still exhibit different behaviors for different types of primary sources.

We see that the directivity pattern of the direct wave varies depending on the type of source. The general direction of the vertical wave diagram lies along the vertical axis (Fig. 4 a) and shifts to the horizontal as the angle of deviation of the source from the vertical grows (Fig. 4(c) and 4(e)). The shape of the reconstructed radiation pattern does not match that of the direct wave but has the same general direction. Thus, if the reconstructed radiation pattern completely lies near the vertical axis, then we can confidently speak about a source of the vertical type. For other types of sources, the reconstructed patterns also differ, and the type can be determined by comparing the elongated shape of the radiation pattern.

6   Parallel Implementation

The parallelization of the computational algorithm was carried out using the properties of the algorithm proposed in Sect. 2. The complexity of the problem is associated with the large amount of memory required for storing the input data and performing calculations in the three-dimensional formulation. In the three-dimensional case, the computational load increases significantly along with the size of the computational domain. All the above entails the need to organize the parallelization of the computational algorithm. The most common and convenient approach to this relies upon the method of splitting the computational domain. The domain decomposition technique is a general name for methods dedicated to solving boundary value problems for differential equations by splitting them into smaller problems on subdomains of the original domain and organizing the data exchange between these subdomains.

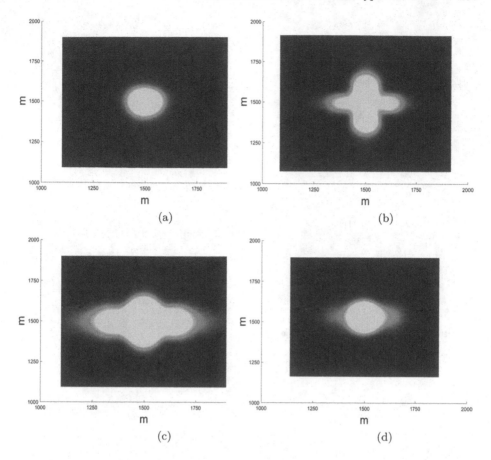

Fig. 3. Total energy E_{sum} distribution after TRM in the plain xy (z fixed): (a) vertical source; (b) 30° source; (c) 45° source; (d) 60° source

To organize the data exchange between neighboring processes, we use the so-called `itable` process numeration [18].

All computed parameters $(u_x, u_y, u_z, \tau_{xx}, \tau_{yy}, \tau_{zz}, \tau_{xy}, \tau_{xz}, \tau_{yz})$ in the simulation are distributed among several processes. The distribution of data among processes is shown in Fig. 5. The number in the matrix indicates the rank of the process to which the element belongs. Here we consider an example with eight processes.

We prepare a process grid matrix `itable` to quickly search for adjacent processes. In Fig. 6, NULL stands for `MPI_PROC_NULL` and means that if a message is sent to it, there will be no real data transfer. In the program, each process has its own (`myranki,myrankj,myrankk`) coordinates in the process grid. For example, the coordinates of process number 5 are $(2, 2, 1)$. Each process can find its neighbors by referring to `itable(myranki ± 1, myrankj ± 1, myrankk ± 1)`. Under this representation of data, sending and receiving operations are carried

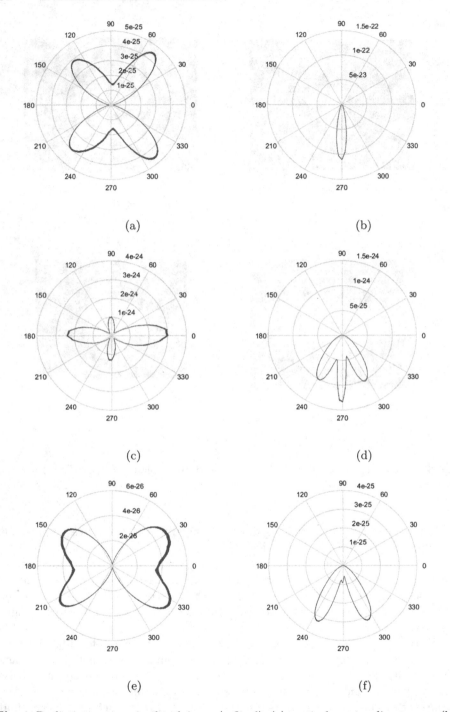

Fig. 4. Radiation pattern in the plain xz (y fixed): (a) vertical source, direct wave; (b) vertical source, after TRM; (c) 45° source, direct wave; (d) 45° source, after TRM; (e) 30° source, direct wave; (f) 30° source, after TRM

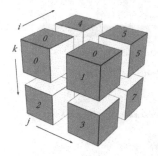

Fig. 5. An example of data distribution among eight processes

out uniformly. The arguments of called functions and the number of calls do not depend on the location of the data volume. If data are located on an edge, then sending or receiving from the corresponding direction will not be carried out since the argument will be `MPI_PROC_NULL`.

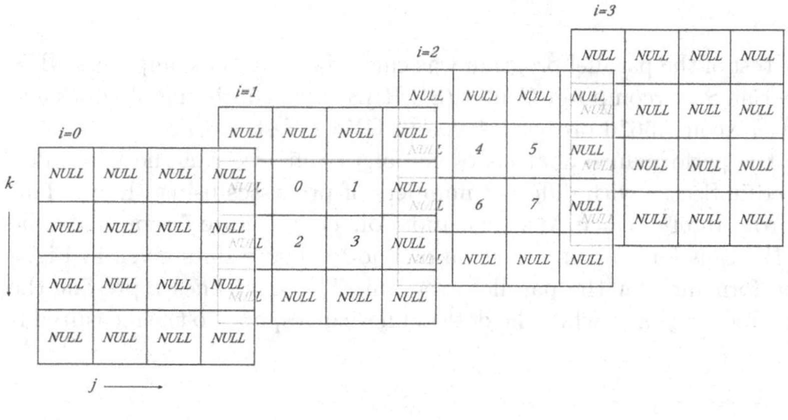

Fig. 6. An example of a grid of eight processes with two processes in each of the three dimensions

To speed up the parallel algorithm, we also apply several simple but efficient approaches. It is well known that the bottleneck in any parallel algorithm is the data exchange procedure between neighboring processes. We use nonblocking `Isend/Irecv` routines that allow us to send messages in the computational background without interrupting the calculations within subdomains [19]. In addition, computations in each subdomain start on its internal nodes, leaving the edge nodes, which require data from a neighboring process, unused. Computations within the subdomain take some time; during this time, the nonblocking MPI functions `Isend/Irecv` manage to deliver the necessary data. Thus this approach allows us to overlap the communication process.

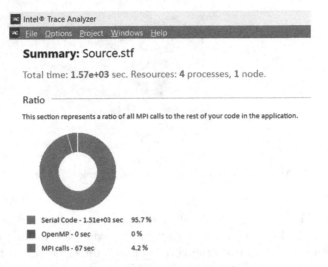

Fig. 7. An example of a ratio of all MPI calls for four processes on one node from Intel® Trace Analyzer and Collector

The test of the parallel program was carried out on the computers NKS-1P of the Siberian Supercomputer Center (SB RAS) [20], consisting of nodes equipped with Intel Xeon X5670 processors at 2.93 GHz (Westmere).

For the performance analysis of the algorithm, we ran the test calculation described in Sect. 5 with different numbers of processes using "Event Timeline" traces from Intel® Trace Analyzer and Collector. Figure 7 represents the ratio of all MPI calls for four processes on one node. The results given in Fig. 8 show good performance for the parallel program. The solid lines represent the ideal speedup and efficiency, while the dotted lines correspond to the measured results.

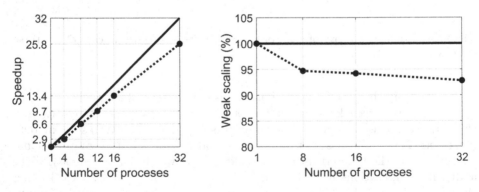

Fig. 8. Strong scaling speedup and weak scaling efficiency. Solid lines represent the ideal speedup and efficiency; dotted lines represent the measured speedup and efficiency.

7 Conclusions

We described an algorithm for retrieving the type of a seismic source from seismic observational data, based on the Time-Reversal Mirror method. The main advantage of this approach is that it makes it possible to determine not only the spatial location of the source but also its type, which was confirmed by numerical simulations.

The simulations were based on finite-difference schemes of the second order on staggered grids to approximate the three-dimensional model of a dynamic elasticity problem.

The parallelization technique was implemented through the functions of the MPI library and the domain decomposition approach. To organize data exchange between neighboring processes, we used the `itable` process numbering, which ensures easy and uniform communication between processes. To improve the efficiency, we relied on such techniques as data exchange in the computational background and the nonblocking MPI functions `Isend` and `Irecv`.

Acknowledgments. This work was financially supported by the Russian Science Foundation (grant № 22-21-00759, https://rscf.ru/en/project/22-21-00759/). The research was carried out on shared HPC facilities at the Siberian Supercomputer Center [20].

References

1. Maxwell, S.C., Urbancic, T.I.: The role of passive microseismic monitoring in the instrumented oil field. Geophysics **20**, 636–639 (2001)
2. Kim, K., Fee, D., Yokoo, A., Lees, J.M.: Acoustic source inversion to estimate volume flux from volcanic explosions. Geophys. Res. Lett. **42**(13), 5243–5249 (2015). https://doi.org/10.1002/2015GL064466
3. Bleibinhaus, F.: Full-waveform inversion of controlled-source seismic data. In: Beer, M., Kougioumtzoglou, I., Patelli, E., Au, I.K. (eds.) Encyclopedia of Earthquake Engineering, pp. 1–13. Springer, Berlin (2016). https://doi.org/10.1007/978-3-642-36197-5_376-1
4. Iezzi, A.M., Fee, D., Kim, K., Jolly, A.D., Matoza, R.S.: 3-D acoustic multipole waveform inversion at Yasur volcano, Vanuatu. J. Geophys. Res.: Solid Earth **124**(8), 8679–8703 (2019). https://doi.org/10.1029/2018JB017073
5. Fink, M., Wu, F., Cassereau, D., Mallart, R.: Imaging through inhomogeneous media using time reversal mirrors. Ultrason. Imaging **13**, 179–199 (1991)
6. Fink, M., Prada, C.: Acoustic time-reversal mirrors. Inv. Prob. **17**(1), R1–R38 (2001). https://doi.org/10.1088/0266-5611/17/1/201
7. Wapenaar, K., Thorbecke, J.: Review paper: virtual sources and their responses, part i: time-reversal acoustics and seismic interferometry. Geophys. Prospect. **65**(6), 1411–1429 (2017). https://doi.org/10.1111/1365-2478.12496
8. Larmat, C., Montagner, J.-P., Fink, M., Capdeville, Y., Tourin, A., Clevede, E.: Time-reversal imaging of seismic sources and application to the great Sumatra earthquake. Geophys. Res. Lett., **33**(19) (2006) https://doi.org/10.1029/2006GL026336

9. Larmat, C., Tromp, J., Liu, Q., Montagner, J.-P.: Time reversal location of glacial earthquakes. J. Geophys. Res. **113**(B9), B09314 (2008). https://doi.org/10.1029/2008JB005607
10. Montagner, J.-P., et al.: Time-reversal method and cross-correlation techniques by normal mode theory: a three-point problem. Geophys. J. Int. **191**(2), 637–652 (2012). https://doi.org/10.1111/j.1365-246X.2012.05619.x
11. Aslanov, T.G.: Definition of earthquake focus coordinates using a combined method. Herald of Dagestan State Technical University. Tech. Sci. **44**(2), 118–125 (2017). https://doi.org/10.21822/2073-6185-2017-44-2-118-125
12. Reshetova, G.V., Anchugov, A.V.: Digital core: simulation of acoustic emission in order to localize its sources by the method of wave field reversal in reverse time. Geol. Geophys. **62**(4), 597–609 (2021)
13. Givoli, D.: Time reversal as computational tool in acoustics and elastodynamics. J. Comput. Acoust. **22**(3), 1430001 (2014). https://doi.org/10.1142/S0218396X14300011
14. Virieux, J.: P-SV wave propagation in heterogeneous media: velocity-stress finite-difference method. Geophysics **51**, 889–901 (1986). https://doi.org/10.1190/1.1442147
15. Komatitsch, D., Martin, R.: An unsplit convolutional perfectly matched layer improved at grazing incidence for the seismic wave equation. Geophysics **725**, sm155-sm167 (2007). https://doi.org/10.1190/1.2757586
16. Samarskii, A.A.: The Theory of Difference Schemes. CRC Press, Boca Raton (2001)
17. Moczo, P., Kristek, J., Vavrycuk, V., Archuleta, R.J., Halada, L.: 3D heterogeneous staggered-grid finite-difference modeling of seismic motion with volume harmonic and arithmetic averaging of elastic moduli and densities. Bull. Seism. Soc. Am. **92**(8), 3042–3066 (2002). https://doi.org/10.1785/0120010167
18. Aoyama, Y., Nakano, J.: RS/6000 SP: Practical MPI Programming. IBM Redbooks (1999)
19. Reshetova, G., Cheverda, V., Koinov, V.: Comparative efficiency analysis of MPI blocking and non-blocking communications with Coarray Fortran. In: Voevodin, V., Sobolev, S. (eds.) RuSCDays 2021. CCIS, vol. 1510, pp. 322–336. Springer, Cham (2021). https://doi.org/10.1007/978-3-030-92864-3_25
20. Novosibirsk Supercomputer Center of SB RAS. http://www.sscc.icmmg.nsc.ru

Parallel Implementation of Fast Algorithms in the Vortex Particle Method

Alexandra Kolganova[✉] and Ilia Marchevsky[ORCID]

Bauman Moscow State Technical University, Moscow, Russian Federation
kolganchik@gmail.com

Abstract. The problem considered in this paper arises in the vortex particle method and is similar to the N-body problem, which is the problem of determining the velocities of all the particles taking into account their mutual interaction. The direct algorithm does not provide the performance required for actual problems. Based on the classical Barnes–Hut algorithm, we develop a hybrid algorithm that includes some ideas of the Fast Multipole Method. Our algorithm provides accuracy control and has quasilinear computational complexity. We construct the k-d tree by a nonrecursive parallel algorithm and store the tree nodes in a linear array. The developed algorithm is adapted for computing on GPUs with Nvidia CUDA technology; all subroutines are optimized for GPU architectures. The developed code provides higher performance than all known analogues. We conducted several numerical experiments with the algorithm on modern multicore CPUs and GPUs. When running on GPUs, the algorithm is able to process tens of millions of particles per second.

Keywords: N-body problem · Barnes–Hut method · Multipole expansion · OpenMP · Nvidia CUDA · Tree construction

1 Introduction

Vortex particle methods of computational hydrodynamics constitute a highly specialized class of numerical methods that allow modeling incompressible flows and computing flows around profiles [1, 2]. The main field of application of these methods is associated with problems of engineering analysis requiring the computation of nonstationary aerohydrodynamic loads acting on structural elements of technical systems in a liquid or gas flow (in the last case, the flow must be essentially subsonic to neglect the compressibility effect).

Vortex particle methods belong to the class of meshless Lagrangian methods. They are most appropriately used in modeling flows around moving or deformable surfaces, including the solution of coupled Fluid-Structure Interaction problems. Recently, the interest in Lagrangian methods has steadily increased due to many factors. Among these factors, we should note, in the context of our research, the rapid growth in the performance of graphics cards, whose architecture offers an opportunity for a highly efficient implementation of particle methods.

© The Author(s), under exclusive license to Springer Nature Switzerland AG 2023
L. Sokolinsky and M. Zymbler (Eds.): PCT 2023, CCIS 1868, pp. 197–211, 2023.
https://doi.org/10.1007/978-3-031-38864-4_14

When considering the latest publications, we note that the most widespread particle methods are SPH, MPM, and DEM, along with a large number of their modifications in which the computational variables are "physical", specifically, density/mass, velocity/momentum, energy/enthalpy, and so on. Moreover, a characteristic feature of these methods is that the influence of particles becomes apparent only at relatively small distances, usually comparable with the typical distance between separate particles.

Another feature of vortex particle methods is the use of vorticity as the primary computational variable (at the same time, knowing the vorticity distribution in an incompressible flow is sufficient to reconstruct other fields, such as the velocity and pressure; in the case of compressible flows, it is also necessary to consider in the flow domain the stream function or its analogue for three-dimensional flows). On the one hand, this approach makes it possible to operate with much smaller numbers of vortex particles (in contrast to the above-mentioned particle methods) since the vorticity, as a rule, is different from zero only in a neighborhood of streamlined surfaces and in the wakes behind them, whereas, in the rest of the flow domain, it is absent or exponentially small, i.e., the vorticity can be neglected there. On the other hand, it follows from the governing equations that it is possible to reconstruct the flow velocity at an arbitrary point only by taking into account the influence of the entire vorticity at this point, i.e., the influence of all vortex particles, and this influence decreases proportionally to the distance or the squared distance, i.e., rather slowly. Therefore, vortex particles are long-range interacting particles. The last fact is a significant impediment to vortex methods. In particular, the evolution of vorticity in the flow domain is modeled by the transfer of vortex particles; within the framework of the deterministic diffusion velocity model, the transfer velocity is the sum of the flow velocity and the diffusive velocity. We will not touch upon the calculation of the latter (the corresponding algorithms are well-known). The calculation of convective velocities requires considering the influence of all vortex particles, which makes the task similar to the N-body problem. Although the N-body problem is one of the classical problems of numerical mathematics and the methods to solve it are well-studied, vortex particle methods have very significant features that do not always allow for the direct application of existing algorithms. In this paper, we consider algorithms only for 2D flows, in which the influence function of a vortex particle differs from that of a three-dimensional gravitational problem.

In this work, we aim to develop an algorithm for the fast approximate calculation of the velocities generated by vortex particles in plane flows. This would make it possible to control the accuracy of the result and efficiently perform calculations on CPUs and GPUs.

The paper is organized as follows. In Sect. 2, we present the governing equations. Section 3 describes the results of applying a direct algorithm using OpenMP technology for shared memory and Nvidia CUDA for graphics accelerators. Section 4 contains a description of a tree-based fast algorithm and its CPU and GPU implementations. Conclusion summarizes the study and points directions for further work.

2   The Governing Equations

We consider a two-dimensional plane viscous incompressible flow around an air-foil with a surface line S that satisfies the continuity condition and the Navier–Stokes equation

$$\nabla \cdot \mathbf{V} = 0, \qquad \frac{\partial \mathbf{V}}{\partial t} + (\mathbf{V} \cdot \nabla)\mathbf{V} = -\frac{\nabla p}{\rho} + \nu \Delta \mathbf{V},$$

in which $\mathbf{V}$ is the velocity field, p is the pressure field, and ρ and ν are, respectively, the constant density and kinematic viscosity of the flow.

We supplement these equations with no-slip boundary conditions on the airfoil boundary and perturbation decay conditions at infinity, namely,

$$\mathbf{V} = \mathbf{0} \ \text{ for } \ \mathbf{r} \in S \qquad \text{and} \qquad \mathbf{V} \to \mathbf{V}_\infty, \ p \to p_\infty \ \text{ as } \ |\mathbf{r}| \to \infty.$$

We assume, for the sake of simplicity, that the airfoil is immovable. However, this assumption is not essential, and all the results can be easily transferred to the general case with an arbitrary motion of S.

If we regard the vorticity $\boldsymbol{\Omega} = \nabla \times \mathbf{V}$ as the primary computational variable and bear in mind that the vorticity vector in 2D flows has only one nonzero component, i.e., $\boldsymbol{\Omega} = \Omega \mathbf{k}$, then we can apply the curl operation to the Navier–Stokes equation and obtain the following scalar vorticity evolution equation (a detailed derivation thereof can be found in [3,4]):

$$\frac{\partial \Omega}{\partial t} + (\mathbf{V} \cdot \nabla)\Omega = \nu \Delta \Omega. \tag{1}$$

Since the vorticity distribution is represented as a set of vortex particles, we have

$$\Omega(\mathbf{r}) = \sum_{i=1}^{N} \Gamma_i \delta(\mathbf{r} - \mathbf{r}_i),$$

where $\mathbf{r}_i$ and Γ_i are, respectively, the position and the circulation of the i-th particle, and $\delta(\boldsymbol{\xi})$ is the 2D Dirac delta function. Thus Eq. (1) can be solved by transferring vortex particles with velocity $\mathbf{V} + \mathbf{W}$ without changing their circulations:

$$\frac{d\mathbf{r}_i}{dt} = \mathbf{V}(\mathbf{r}_i) + \mathbf{W}(\mathbf{r}_i), \qquad \frac{d\Gamma_i}{dt} = 0, \quad i = 1, \dots, N, \tag{2}$$

where $\mathbf{W}$ is the so-called diffusive velocity, which is proportional to the viscosity coefficient,

$$\mathbf{W} = -\nu \frac{\nabla \Omega}{\Omega}.$$

Note that new vortex particles are also generated in the neighborhood of the airfoil surface line; their circulations can be found by solving the corresponding integral Eq. [5,6]. Nevertheless, after being generated, new vortex particles also move in the flow domain according to Eq. (2).

The velocity field $\mathbf{V}$ can be reconstructed according to the Biot–Savart law by calculating the integral over the flow domain F:

$$\mathbf{V}(\mathbf{r}) = \mathbf{V}_\infty + \int \frac{\mathbf{k} \times (\mathbf{r} - \boldsymbol{\xi})}{2\pi |\mathbf{r} - \boldsymbol{\xi}|^2} \Omega(\boldsymbol{\xi}) \, dS_\xi,$$

or taking into account the vorticity representation through vortex particles:

$$\mathbf{V}(\mathbf{r}) = \mathbf{V}_\infty + \sum_{w=1}^{N} \frac{\Gamma_w}{2\pi} \frac{\mathbf{k} \times (\mathbf{r} - \mathbf{r}_w)}{|\mathbf{r} - \mathbf{r}_w|^2}.$$

This velocity field is unbounded in the vicinity of vortex particles. For this reason, in the simulations, a small smoothing radius ϵ is introduced (so that point vortices turn into circular Rankine vortices). Accordingly, the regularized velocity field becomes

$$\mathbf{V}(\mathbf{r}) = \mathbf{V}_\infty + \sum_{w=1}^{N} \frac{\Gamma_w}{2\pi} \frac{\mathbf{k} \times (\mathbf{r} - \mathbf{r}_w)}{\max\{|\mathbf{r} - \mathbf{r}_w|^2, \epsilon^2\}}. \tag{3}$$

(note that other types of smoothing can also be used [1]).

Thus, the computation of the velocities $\mathbf{V}_i = \mathbf{V}(\mathbf{r}_i)$ of all vortex particles requires $O(N^2)$ operations, or $5N^2$ if we accept that only multiplications and divisions are taken into account.

3   The Direct Algorithm

The implementation of the direct algorithm seems trivial but is acceptable only when the number of vortex particles does not exceed a few tens of thousands. Such an algorithm is implemented in the first version of the code VM2D [7,8] (freely available at https://github.com/vortexmethods/VM2D), in which only "direct" computational algorithms are used. The typical part of the subroutine that computes the convective velocities accounts for about 80–90% of the whole computational cost of the simulation. However, the direct algorithm for computing the convective velocities can be easily parallelized through known technologies.

3.1   OpenMP for Shared Memory and MPI for Cluster Systems

With OpenMP technology, it is possible to achieve an almost linear (ideal) speedup when the number of vortex particles becomes close to $N = 10^5$ or higher (Fig. 1)

The recommended number of vortex particles in real-life problems is of the order of 10^6. Bearing this in mind, we conducted several numerical experiments to estimate the time required by the direct algorithm to calculate the velocities of $N = 10^6$ and $N = 2 \cdot 10^6$ vortex particles (Table 1). We used two compilers in the

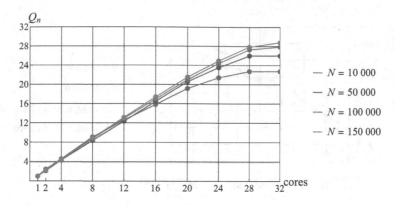

Fig. 1. The speedup of computations using OpenMP on a server with two 18-core Intel Xeon Gold 6254 processors

computations, namely, Intel C++ Compiler Classic 20.2 (on a workstation with two Intel Xeon 6254 processors and a personal computer with an 8-core Intel i9-9900 processor) and Intel oneAPI C++ Compiler 2023.0 (on a workstation with an 18-core Intel i9-10980XE processor).

Table 1. Time required to calculate convective velocities by the direct algorithm, for $N = 10^6$ and $N = 2 \cdot 10^6$ vortex particles, on various CPUs (using OpenMP)

	Intel i9-9900	Intel i9-10980XE	2 × Intel Xeon 6254
	8 cores	18 cores	32 cores
10^6 particles	296 s	153 s	151 s
$2 \cdot 10^6$ particles	1220 s	680 s	625 s

An additional speedup can be achieved on cluster systems by using MPI technology. Since the algorithm is extremely simple and "uniform", it is possible to provide an ideal balancing for arbitrary numbers of nodes. Figure 2 shows the graphs of speedup versus the number of nodes (28 cores each) for $N = 300\,000$ and $N = 600\,000$ vortex particles.

We can see that the graphs of the speedup versus the number of nodes for tasks with $300\,000$ and $600\,000$ vortex particles approximately correspond to those of Amdahl's law for 0.40 and 0.25% of the sequential code, respectively.

The velocities of vortex particles are calculated at every time step of the simulation of an unsteady flow; the number of such steps is usually of the order of tens or hundreds of thousands. We can thus conclude that the trivial approach achieves a reasonable performance (no more than 1 s per time step) only in problems with no more than half a million vortex particles provided that a huge computer cluster is used, having about 100 nodes with more than 2000 cores in total. It is obvious that such an approach is extremely inefficient.

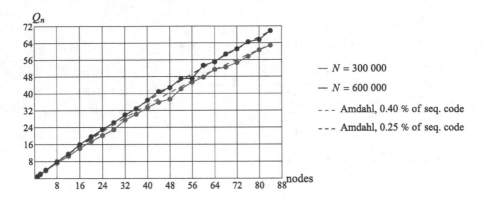

Fig. 2. Speedup of computations when using MPI on a cluster. Each node is equipped with two 14-core Intel Xeon E5-2690 v4 processors.

3.2   Nvidia CUDA for Graphics Accelerators

The direct algorithm for the computation of the velocities of vortex particles by formula (3) can be trivially implemented in the framework of Nvidia CUDA technology. The results obtained for some typical GPUs are shown in Table 2, for both single and double precision.

Table 2. Time required to calculate convective velocities by the direct algorithm, for $N = 10^6$ and $N = 2 \cdot 10^6$ vortex particles, on various GPUs (using Nvidia CUDA)

	GeForce		Titan V		Tesla V100		Tesla A100	
	2080 Ti, 68 sm		80 sm		80 sm		108 sm	
Particles	float	double	float	double	float	double	float	double
$N = 10^6$	2.0 s	64.8 s	2.1 s	4.8 s	3.2 s	4.7 s	2.5 s	3.8 s
$N = 2 \cdot 10^6$	7.8 s	262 s	11.2 s	19.1 s	12.8 s	18.6 s	10.2 s	14.9 s

Actually, the results are again almost the same: a performance of one time step per second can be achieved only for no more than half a million vortex particles (and single precision) but now on a single GPU instead of a large computer cluster.

Figure 3 shows the speedup in multi-GPU mode. Several MPI processes ran on a server with six Tesla A100 GPUs, each process on a separate GPU. The performance improved, but no more than 1 million vortices could be processed per second, even on such a powerful server.

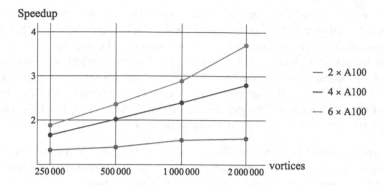

Fig. 3. Speedup of computations on several GPUs Tesla A100 for different numbers of vortices

4   Approximate Tree-Based Fast Algorithms

4.1   Tree-Based Fast Methods for the N-Body Problem

Biot–Savart law (more specifically, its discretized variant (3)) is indeed very similar to Newton's gravitational law. Therefore, all the approaches initially developed for the N-body problem can be adapted to vortex methods.

The simplest method (from the implementation point of view) is the Barnes–Hut (BH) algorithm [9], which has computational complexity $O(N \log N)$. However, a significant difference is associated with the fact that vortex particles in 2D problems can have both positive and negative circulations, while the masses of bodies are always positive. The corresponding adaptation of the classical BH algorithm was suggested in [10], but the resulting algorithm is not as efficient as the initial one.

The general idea of the Barnes–Hut method is to split the flow domain (the domain containing the vortex particles) hierarchically, that is, to build a k-d tree or a quadtree whose cells are regarded as clusters of vortex particles. Then, for each vortex particle, a tree traversal is executed: distantly placed cells (of small size compared to the distance to them) are regarded as one "summary" particle; tree leaves with a small relative distance are processed directly and point-to-point interactions are calculated.

Another method is the Fast Multipole Method (FMM) [11,12], which is based on similar ideas. In this case, however, only a quadtree is considered, and the influence is calculated not for individual particles but for the whole tree cells by constructing the so-called local expansions (which are power series in the distance from the tree cell). The influence of each cell is represented as a multipole expansion (power series in the distance from the influencing cell in negative degrees). The tree traversal is performed only once; particle interactions between neighboring cells are considered straightforwardly. Note that the numerical complexity of the FMM is only $O(N)$. Numerical experiments show that the classical BH has a higher computational cost than the FMM. However, we can not exert "smooth" control over the accuracy with the FMM: it works perfectly when the required accuracy is high (comparable with the machine accuracy), but it is hardly possible to save computation time by reducing the accuracy (as a matter of fact, machine precision is usually not required in vortex particle methods).

We can use these properties of two "basic" approaches for developing a hybrid modification, the BH/multipole algorithm, which can be regarded as an improved version of the BH method. The general algorithm is very similar to the classical variant of BH, but some specific features appear [13]:

- The tree traversal is performed down to some specified level (let us call the corresponding tree cells "lowest-level cells") but not down to separate particles, which correspond to the leaf cells in the whole tree.
- For each cell, not only the total mass (or circulation) is stored but also higher multipole moments, which are calculated directly for the leaf cells (for a cell containing a separate particle, only one monopole moment is nonzero and is equal to its circulation, while all higher-order moments are equal to zero) by summation of the moments of children cells after being shifted to the center of the parent cell.
- The influence is calculated for the lowest-level cells, in which a local (Taylor) expansion of the influencing function is constructed taking into account only those terms of the expansions of multipole terms having the proper order of magnitude. Thus we reduce the computation time by avoiding computing higher-order terms, which do not affect the accuracy.

Note that this approach turns out to be rather efficient in two-dimensional problems since all the operations with multipole terms and their local expansions can be expressed through simple multiplications of complex numbers.

4.2   CPU Implementation of the BH/Multipole Algorithm

The algorithm we briefly described above contains three user-defined parameters (Table 3) which influence the accuracy and numerical complexity of the algorithm. Signs "+" and "−" indicate whether the corresponding influence is essential or, respectively, can be neglected.

Table 3. Parameters of the hybrid BH/multipole algorithm and their influence

User-defined parameter	Influence	
	accuracy	complexity
Lowest level in the tree	−	+
Number of multipole terms	+	−
Proximity criterion	+	+

The optimal choice of these parameters requires a large number of numerical experiments. As a model problem, we considered the uniform distribution of vortex particles with random circulations $-0.01 \leq \Gamma_i \leq 0.01$ in a unit square. To estimate the accuracy, we calculated the mean relative error of the velocities of the particles and found the optimal parameters for $\delta V = 10^{-3}$, 10^{-5}, and 10^{-7}. These optimal parameters are used below in all computations.

The tree construction is a rather simple operation from a "logical" point of view, but its efficient implementation can be nontrivial. In the sequential code, it is enough, as a rule, to implement a recursive subroutine to construct the k-d tree; moreover, it can be constructed adaptively (Fig. 4) to exclude free space.

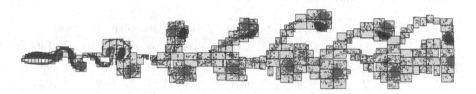

Fig. 4. Tree cells of the eighth level in the adaptive tree

At the same time, the efficient parallelization of the tree construction procedure, especially the adaptive variant, is a rather difficult task. Among the many approaches to solving it, we can point out the algorithm for the k-d tree construction suggested by T. Karras [14]. It is based on sorting 2D points according to the Morton order. Its main feature is associated with the nonrecursivity and the storage of all the tree nodes (both internal nodes and leaves) in a linear array. This algorithm is perfectly scalable since all internal nodes can be processed independently. The remaining part of the algorithm consists of two main operations:

- the upward tree traversal, during which the multipole moments of all the internal cells are calculated;
- the downward tree traversal, which is performed multiple times for the above-mentioned lowest-level cells, for which local expansions are constructed; the velocities of separate vortex particles, provided that they are placed in higher-level cells, are calculated through such expansions.

The results of numerical experiments with the OpenMP version of the algorithm (it is freely available at https://github.com/vortexmethods/fastm/BH) are shown in Table 4. Note that, here and further on, all simulations involve $N = 2 \cdot 10^6$ vortex particles.

The speedup and the parallelization efficiency with respect to the sequential code of the whole algorithm are given in Table 5. As we can see, the tree construction subroutine is less scalable than tree traversals.

In all considered cases, the time required for the computation of velocities of 2 million vortex particles is less than 1 s. The tree construction time depends only on the number of particles; with low accuracy, it is approximately 30% of the whole algorithm, whereas it is about 15% with high accuracy.

Table 4. The computation time of the BH/multipole algorithm (in milliseconds) on multicore CPUs with OpenMP

Accuracy	2 × Intel Xeon 6254 Gold (32 cores)			Intel i9-10980XE (18 cores)		
	Tree	Upward	Downward	Tree	Upward	Downward
10^{-3}	80	38	102	88	45	133
10^{-5}	72	63	171	82	67	217
10^{-7}	72	84	299	80	84	370

Table 5. Speedup and parallelization efficiency of the hybrid BH/multipole method on multicore CPUs with OpenMP

Accuracy	2 × Intel Xeon 6254 Gold (32 cores)				Intel i9-10980XE (18 cores)			
	Tree	Upward	Downward	Effic.	Tree	Upward	Downward	Effic.
10^{-3}	12.5	25.7	29.1	0.70	6.9	12.5	15.2	0.67
10^{-5}	14.4	27.2	28.5	0.78	7.4	12.7	14.9	0.71
10^{-7}	14.7	24.9	32.7	0.89	7.8	13.0	14.9	0.75

MPI parallelization can be employed for further speedup. However, in this case, node balancing becomes an essential task. For this reason, we limit ourselves to OpenMP.

Theoretical estimates obtained for the classical Barnes–Hut algorithm assert that the total numerical cost of the algorithm with the optimal parameters is $O(N \log N)$. The hybrid modification does not change this estimate, which is confirmed by the results of numerical experiments (Fig. 5). The computational time dependence on N is not "ideal" due to specific features of some operations, cache usage, and others.

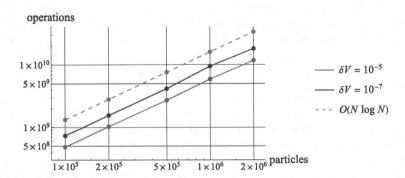

Fig. 5. The number of operations in the BH/multipole algorithm versus the number of vortex particles

Additionally, we provide a "summary" table containing the computation time for the developed BH/multipole algorithm with optimal parameters on three different CPUs (Table 6).

Table 6. The computation time of the BH/multipole algorithm on CPUs (in milliseconds) compared to that of the direct algorithm (in seconds)

Accuracy	2 × Xeon 6254 Gold	Intel i9-10980XE	Intel i9-9900
	32 cores	18 cores	8 cores
10^{-3}	220 ms	266	433
10^{-5}	306 ms	366	605
10^{-7}	455 ms	534	773
Direct	625 s	680 s	1220 s

4.3 GPU Implementation of the BH/Multipole Algorithm

First of all, let us mention an outstanding investigation conducted by a user of the popular internet resource Habr [15]. He considered several parallelization technologies, such as threads, OpenMP, OpenCL, and CUDA, and applied them to the direct algorithm and Barnes–Hut algorithm (in its classical variant). His conclusions are impressive; in the case of the direct algorithm, they are close to the results we presented above.

At the same time, the most widespread publication about the implementation of the Barnes–Hut algorithm on GPU with Nvidia CUDA is [16], written by Martin Burtscher and Keshav Pingali. They suggested and implemented an extremely efficient original algorithm and gave some advice on its optimization on different graphics cards. Note that the code available on Burtscher's web page works perfectly on rather slow graphics cards (with small numbers of streaming multiprocessors); on more powerful cards, such as Nvidia Titan V, Tesla V100, or Tesla A100, data races usually occur. However, some minor issues (mainly associated with the loss of `volatile` type qualifiers) can be fixed, and everything works as expected. This code works much faster compared to the most efficient algorithm from [15]. For this reason, we chose it as the basic code in the present research. Note also that many variations and modifications of this algorithm can be found on GitHub, including rather large projects (e.g., Galois, Patistar).

As the code is freely available, we modified it to implement the suggested hybrid BH/multipole algorithm. The resulting code can be found on GitHub (https://github.com/vortexmethods/fastm/BHcu).

The result is a GPU-adapted implementation of the BH/multipole algorithm with the following differences relative to the CPU code:

- a full quadtree is constructed instead of a k-d tree;
- a downward tree traversal is performed for the particles instead of the lowest-level cells, so local expansions are not constructed;

Moreover, the choice of optimal parameters for this algorithm differs from that for the CPU case since now we are dealing with a quadtree. Note also that now there are only two user-defined parameters: the number of multipole terms and the proximity criterion.

Table 7 contains the results of numerical experiments for the same model problem as in the previous section but solved now using the modified algorithm on GPUs [16].

Table 7. The computation time of the modified algorithm on GPUs (in milliseconds) compared to that of the direct algorithm (in seconds) for both single and double precisions

Accuracy	GeForce 2080 Ti		Titan V		Tesla V100	
	68 SM		80 SM		80 SM	
	double	float	double	float	double	float
10^{-3}	180	23	29	23	30	22
10^{-5}	332	37	49	35	59	34
10^{-7}	586	—	75	—	84	—
Direct	262 s	7.8 s	19.1 s	11.2 s	18.6 s	12.8 s

We can see that if the average accuracy is acceptable ($\delta V = 10^{-5}$), the computations can be performed with single precision, and for all considered graphics cards the speedup is of the order of 200–300 with respect to the direct algorithm.

The computations with double precision on the Nvidia Titan V and Tesla V100 cards are more time-consuming by a factor of 1.5. Note that these cards were initially developed for high-precision computations. In the case of GeForce 2080 Ti, we observe a nearly 10-fold decrease in performance for double precision. The accuracy $\delta V = 10^{-7}$ can be achieved only with double precision. The GPU code shows a performance that is nearly 10 times as high as that on multicore CPUs.

The modified algorithm initially suggested by Burtscher [13, 16] was merged with the k-d tree structure, constructed according to the Karras algorithm [14], which, as we suppose, is the most efficient for tree construction and its code is easily transferred to GPUs. Moreover, the CUDA Toolkit contains integer intrinsics, such as `__clz(int)`, which are particularly suitable for operations with Morton codes.

The resulting code requires less time for the tree construction and its downward traversal. However, the upward traversal becomes more complicated since it is additionally required to sort the internal nodes. A similar sorting operation is also performed for Morton codes of vortex particles; the `RadixSort` subroutine from the CUB library provides a means to do it on GPU with high efficiency. Also, some additional interface is added to ensure the compatibility of both data structures, and some minor changes are made in the remaining part of the code to take into account some required specific features. The obtained code can be found on GitHub (https://github.com/vortexmethods/fastm/BHgpu).

For comparison purposes, we present the results of the obtained algorithm with a k-d tree for intermediate and high accuracy levels (10^{-5} and 10^{-7}) with optimal parameters on three different GPUs (Table 8).

Table 8. The computation time of the code with k-d tree on GPUs (in milliseconds) for single and double precisions

Accuracy	GeForce 2080 Ti		Titan V		Tesla V100	
	68 SM		80 SM		80 SM	
	double	float	double	float	double	float
10^{-3}	154	21	27	20	30	19
10^{-5}	286	35	44	31	56	32
10^{-7}	496	—	67	—	77	—

As we can see by comparing this with Table 7, the tree structure exchange can reduce the whole time by 10%.

The attempts to provide additional speedup by using several GPUs installed on the same node produce the expected result only when the chosen parameters are nonoptimal, in which case the computation time is rather high. In the case of optimal parameters, it is possible to reduce the time for specific subroutines, but data exchange between devices requires nearly as much time as has been saved.

Note that the algorithm can be generalized to other operations related to vortex particle methods, such as integral equation solving, velocity computation at given points, and others.

5   Conclusions

We developed a code meant for the fast approximate solution of the N-body problem and adapted it for 2D vortex particle methods. The code is in general based on the classical Barnes–Hut algorithm but involves multipole expansions up to terms of higher orders. The developed algorithm is adapted for computing on GPUs with Nvidia CUDA technology. Considering the specific features of GPU architecture and thousands of simultaneously working CUDA cores, the GPU implementation of the algorithm is somewhat different and even easier: the clusterization of particles is not performed together with the construction of local expansions, and each CUDA core processes a single particle. The warp divergence problem is solved using the original algorithm [16] or by sorting the particles according to the Morton order in a k-d tree. As a result, closely placed particles have close indices in the global array stored in memory, and the tree traversal for them is similar.

We conducted several numerical experiments with this algorithm and can state that the algorithm described in this paper is able to process up to 30 million particles per second and has a quasilinear computational cost, namely, $O(N \log N)$. We plan to use it for developing an improved version of the VM2D code, which implements vortex particle methods for solving engineering problems.

References

1. Cottet, G.-H., Koumoutsakos, P.D.: Vortex Methods: Theory and Practice. Cambridge University Press, Cambridge (2000)
2. Branlard, E.: Wind Turbine Aerodynamics and Vorticity-Based Methods: Fundamentals and Recent Applications. Springer, Heidelberg (2017). https://doi.org/10.1007/978-3-319-55164-7
3. Dynnikova, G.Y.: The Lagrangian approach to solving the time-dependent Navier-Stokes equations. Doklady Phys. **49**(11), 648–652 (2004). https://doi.org/10.1134/1.1831530
4. Dynnikova, G.Y.: Vortex motion in two-dimensional viscous fluid flows. Fluid Dyn. **38**(5), 670–678 (2003). https://doi.org/10.1023/B:FLUI.0000007829.78673.01
5. Kuzmina, K.S., Marchevskii, I.K.: On the calculation of the vortex sheet and point vortices effects at approximate solution of the boundary integral equation in 2d vortex methods of computational hydrodynamics. Fluid Dyn. **54**(7), 991–1001 (2019). https://doi.org/10.1134/S0015462819070103
6. Marchevskii, I.K., Sokol, K.S., Izmailova, Yu.A.: T-schemes for mathematical modelling of vorticity generation on smooths airfoils in vortex particle methods. Herald Bauman Moscow State Tech. Univ. Ser.: Nat. Sci. **6**, 33–59 (2022). https://doi.org/10.18698/1812-3368-2022-6-33-59
7. Kuzmina, K.S., Marchevsky, I.K., Ryatina, E.P.: Open source code for 2D incompressible flow simulation by using meshless Lagrangian vortex methods. In: Proceedings of the 2017 Ivannikov ISPRAS Open Conference (ISPRAS), pp. 97–103, IEEE, Russia (2018). https://doi.org/10.1109/ISPRAS.2017.00023
8. Kuzmina, K., Marchevsky, I., Ryatina, E.: VM2D: open source code for 2D incompressible flow simulation by using vortex methods. Commun. Comput. Inf. Sci. **910**, 251–265 (2018). https://doi.org/10.1007/978-3-319-99673-8_18
9. Barnes, J., Hut, P.: A hierarchical $O(N \log N)$ force-calculation algorithm. Nature **324**(4), 446–449 (1986). https://doi.org/10.1038/324446a0
10. Dynnikova, G.Y.: Fast technique for solving the N-body problem in flow simulation by vortex methods. Comput. Math. Math. Phys. **49**, 1389–1396 (2009). https://doi.org/10.1134/S0965542509080090
11. Greengard, L.: The rapid evaluation of potential fields in particle systems. Ph.D. thesis. Yale University, USA (1988)
12. Greengard, L., Rokhlin, V.: A fast algorithm for particle simulations. J. Comput. Phys. **73**(2), 325–348 (1987). https://doi.org/10.1016/0021-9991(87)90140-9
13. Ryatina, E., Lagno, A.: The Barnes – Hut-type algorithm in 2D Lagrangian vortex particle methods. J. Phys.: Conf. Ser. **1715**(1), 012069. https://doi.org/10.1088/1742-6596/1715/1/012069

14. Karras, T.: Maximizing parallelism in the construction of BVHs, octrees, and k-d trees. In: Proceedings Fourth ACM SIGGRAPH / Eurographics conference on High-Performance Graphics, pp. 33–37. Eurographics Association, Paris (2012). https://doi.org/10.2312/EGGH/HPG12/033-037
15. N-body problem, or how to blow up a galaxy without leaving the kitchen (in Russian). https://habr.com/ru/post/437014/
16. Burtscher, M., Pingali, K.: Chapter 6 – An efficient CUDA implementation of the tree-based Barnes Hut n-body algorithm. In: GPU Computing Gems Emerald Edition. Applications of GPU Computing Series, pp. 75–92 (2011). https://doi.org/10.1016/B978-0-12-384988-5.00006-1

Supercomputer Simulation

Implementation of an Asymptotically Compact Algorithm for GPU Simulation of an Acoustic Equation

Andrey Zakirov[⊠][iD] and Anastasia Perepelkina[⊠][iD]

Keldysh Institute of Applied Mathematics, Moscow, Russian Federation
mogmi@narod.ru, zakirov@kintechlab.com

Abstract. In this paper, an acoustic equation is simulated with a numerical scheme involving a cross stencil. It is a memory-bound problem, and the performance depends greatly on data access patterns. In the compact update, all data are loaded and stored once per data update, in contrast to the usual update, where data accessed by stencil dependencies can be loaded several times. Also, we implement the asymptotically compact update in the TorreFold LRnLA algorithm on GPU. In the LRnLA algorithm, several time layers are grouped into one task that is asymptotically compact as a whole. Efficient memory transfers allow the processing of data in the CPU storage with the GPU power, so we demonstrate the efficiency through the solution of problems with more than 160 GB of data. Multi-GPU parallel scaling is also established. A performance of up to 50 billion LU/s (lattice updates per second) and 23 billion LU/s is obtained on RTX3090 for single and double precisions correspondingly.

Keywords: GPU · LRnLA · Stencil · Wave equation

1 Introduction

Computational physics is one of the main purposes of modern supercomputer programming and one of the heaviest tasks for it. A large part of simulation in physics is made with stencil codes. In a stencil scheme, be it finite-difference, finite-element, or even lattice Boltzmann [11], each node of a discrete mesh is updated through a function, the input data for which come from the data from the cells in the neighborhood. In cross stencils, the neighborhood is the von Neumann neighborhood. Physical problems are typically three-dimensional and require high resolution; thus, one update of the whole mesh requires a large amount of data to be saved and loaded. While the computational performance of modern processors increases, the gap between computing performance and memory bandwidth remains. For stencil problems that are memory-bound [13] and whose performance bottleneck is data throughput, special methods of memory-aware implementations are an interesting and relevant topic.

© The Author(s), under exclusive license to Springer Nature Switzerland AG 2023
L. Sokolinsky and M. Zymbler (Eds.): PCT 2023, CCIS 1868, pp. 215–230, 2023.
https://doi.org/10.1007/978-3-031-38864-4_15

At the same time, the computational performance itself can be increased with multilevel hybrid parallelism. One can take advantage of stencil locality both for localization in higher memory levels and for less communication in the parallel execution of tasks.

Even more computing efficiency can be obtained with loop transformation techniques, such as polygonal optimization [2], wavefront blocking [14], temporal blocking [1,15], and LRnLA algorithms [4]. With loop transformation, several layers in time can be grouped together, and data, loaded into faster memory levels, can be reused. With more locality of data access, more flexibility in constructing such methods is possible.

A cross stencil uses a center point and $2d$ neighbors in d-dimensional simulations. We propose to express the stencil update with even more locality by separating the contribution from the neighbors into parts.

This is inspired by the introduction of a compact update for LBM streaming patterns [20]. It was found that with the use of a unique feature of the LBM scheme, that is, in one substep (streaming), data is copied from the cell to its neighbors without modifications, the update can be expressed as follows: to fully update a group of 2^d cells, no more than 2^d cells should be loaded and no more than 2^d cells should be stored. This expression leads to an optimal operation-per-byte ratio for any kind of traversal, even before temporal blocking is used. The absence of halo dependencies makes both parallelism and temporal blocking convenient and efficient. It was later found that other fluid dynamics schemes, expressed through fluxes, can be reinterpreted as asymptotically compact [17,21]. Here we use the expression "compact update" to denote a task in which, on average, for one full stencil update, data from one cell has to be saved and loaded.

In this work, we construct an asymptotically compact update for the general expression of a stencil numerical scheme for use in conjunction with the LRnLA algorithm DiamondTorre (Sect. 2). Also, we implement the scheme as a code for CUDA GPU (Sect. 3) and benchmark the code's performance on equations of two types (Sect. 4).

2   The Algorithms

2.1   The Problem Statement

Let us start by expressing a stencil update in the form

$$f_{i,j,k}^{t+1} = f_{i,j,k}^t + \text{RHS}, \tag{1}$$

where $f_{i,j,k}^t$ is an unknown scalar or vector function defined on a grid. The grid is a collection of points $r_{i,j,k} = i\Delta x + j\Delta y + k\Delta z$, where i, j, and k are the integer coordinates of a mesh point, and Δx, Δy, and Δz are the mesh steps. Finally, RHS denotes a function that depends on the f^t values in the von Neumann neighborhood of the (i, j, k) node.

Let us define a finite difference scheme for an equation of the type

$$\frac{\partial^2 f}{\partial t^2} = V^2 \Delta f + G(f) = V^2 \left(\frac{\partial^2 f}{\partial x^2} + \frac{\partial^2 f}{\partial y^2} + \frac{\partial^2 f}{\partial z^2} \right) + G(f). \tag{2}$$

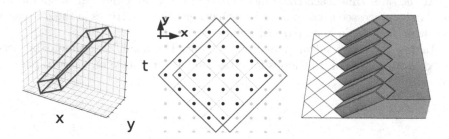

Fig. 1. DiamondTorre in x-y-t (left). DiamondTorre in x-y projection (center): points in the blue diamond are updated in one iteration, and points in the red diamond are updated in the next iteration. A row of asynchronous DiamondTorres (right). Such rows can tile the domain. (Color figure online)

With second-order finite difference discretization of the partial derivatives in space and time provided that mesh steps are equal, i.e., $\Delta x = \Delta y = \Delta z \equiv \Delta r$, we get

$$f_{x,y,z}^{t+1} = 2f_{x,y,z}^t - \left[f_{x,y,z}^{t-1} - \frac{\Delta t^2}{\Delta r^2} V^2 \sum_\clubsuit f^t - \Delta t^2 G(f_{x,y,z}^t) \right], \tag{3}$$

where the sum of values over the cross is defined as

$$\sum_\clubsuit f^t \equiv f_{x-1,y,z}^t + f_{x+1,y,z}^t + f_{x,y-1,z}^t + f_{x,y+1,z}^t + f_{x,y,z-1}^t + f_{x,y,z+1}^t - 6f_{x,y,z}^t.$$

2.2   LRnLA Algorithms

The LRnLA algorithm [4] DiamondTorre [5,19], used in the current code, is illustrated as a tower in x-y-t (Fig. 1). In the code, it is a loop with N_T iterations. At each iteration of the loop, data from the cells that fit into a diamond-shaped region in x-y is updated. This diamond is shifted by one cell (the stencil width) to the right along the x axis after each iteration.

The order of execution of DiamondTorres guarantees correct stencil dependencies. If the lower diamond base intersects the right boundary of the domain at its widest point, then the DiamondTorre has enough data to be fully processed. Thus, at the start, a row of DiamondTorres with the same y-coordinate is executed. The updates in these DiamondTorres are asynchronous, so each DiamondTorre can be assigned to a parallel thread. After this, the next row can be started (Fig. 1, right). Row by row, the whole simulation domain is tiled, and all cells are updated N_T times. DiamondTorre provides computation locality. Data in the DiamondTorre base persists in the thread registers, and only the stencil halo of each diamond is loaded on each step.

At the same time, each DiamondTorre contains a large number of operations and can be processed asynchronously with other DiamondTorres in the $y = \text{const}$ row, which results in good parallel ability.

Taking these two advantages into account, DiamondTorre should be preferred over traditional time loops for cross-stencil simulation on modern parallel processors.

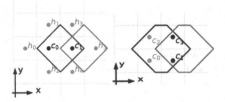

Fig. 2. Left: DiamondTorre update. The current iteration is outlined in blue, the next iteration is outlined in red. Right: DiamondTorre update. The current iteration is outlined in blue, the next iteration is outlined in red. (Color figure online)

2.3   Asymptotically Compact Update

The locality of the DiamondTorre can be expressed quantitatively with a measure as arithmetic intensity [13]. The number of operations in a DiamondTorre can be expressed as the number of updated nodes in a loop iteration multiplied by the number of iterations and by the number of floating-pointing operations per node update. The data required for the updates can be estimated as the projection of DiamondTorre onto x-y space. Additionally, data from the stencil halo of the updated nodes are read in the update.

To increase the locality, that is, the ratio of compute operations to data access operations, the amount of data read can be further decreased in a DiamondTorre by using the asymptotically compact update algorithm introduced in [21], constructed for flux-based schemes of computational fluid dynamics. Let us describe the construction of the asymptotically compact update for a general case of an explicit cross-stencil scheme in the form (2).

To distinguish it from classic DiamondTorre implementations, we introduce a new name, CompactTorre, to denote the asymptotically compact DiamondTorre.

Let us take a diamond base of minimum size. Note that the illustration is two-dimensional. In this projection, one cell corresponds to a row of N_z cells of the 3D simulation. Let us describe the usual (not compact) DiamondTorre using

Fig. 2 (left). To prepare for the iterations, load data for cells c_0, c_1 and h_0, h_1, h_2 into the registers. At each iteration,

1. load cells h_3, h_4, and h_5;
2. update cells c_0 and c_1;
3. save c_0 to the main memory storage;
4. shift data: $c_1 \rightarrow c_0$, $h_5 \rightarrow c_1$.

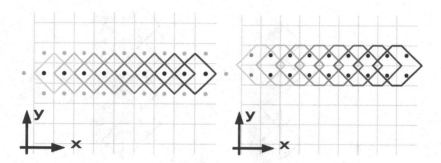

Fig. 3. Left: DiamondTorre with $N_T = 8$. Right: CompactTorre with $N_T = 8$. Orange cells are read, black cells are read and fully updated, and grey cells are read and partially updated (only RHS). (Color figure online)

There are N_T iterations. In the last iteration, save both c_0 and c_1 and do not perform the shift. This way, at each iteration, two values are updated, data of one cell are saved, and data of three cells are loaded. In total, $3(N_T + 1) + 2$ cells are accessed.

One iteration of the CompactTorre consists of the following steps:

1. load cells c_1 and c_3 (c_0 and c_2 are available from the previous iteration);
2. update the RHS of cells c_0 and c_2 by adding the contribution from c_0, c_1, c_2, and c_3;
3. update the RHS of cells c_1 and c_3 by adding the contribution from c_0, c_1, c_2, and c_3;
4. the RHS of cells c_1 and c_3 is finalized, so use it to update c_1 and c_3 values;
5. save c_0 and c_2 to the main memory storage;
6. perform the shift: $c_1 \rightarrow c_0$, $c_3 \rightarrow c_2$.

There are N_T iterations. So, no halo is used in the CompactTorre for the stencil dependencies. This is good for shared access in parallel execution of Torres and makes the implementation of data structure convenient. Two cells are updated at each iteration, two cells are loaded, and two cells are saved. In total, $2N_T$ cells are updated and $2N_T + 2$ cells are loaded in the course of one CompactTorre execution. Thus, if we take a large N_T, we can neglect the preparation stage and the final stage and obtain an optimal arithmetic intensity equal to 1. That is why the algorithm is *asymptotically compact*.

We see that even without the introduction of fluxes (as it was done in [21]) the asymptotically compact algorithm can be constructed. Another difference from [21] is that here the numerical scheme (3) contains three time layers. The implementation details concerning the values on which time layers are loaded and stored, as well as the proper treatment of the z axis, can be found in Sect. 3. The fact that CompactTorre requires less data per cell update than DiamondTorre is illustrated in Fig. 3.

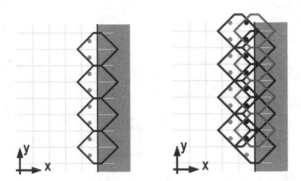

Fig. 4. The first and second rows of CompactTorre starting from the right boundary. The first row has one iteration and updates only the RHS; the second row is shifted and has two iterations. The second row has finalized the update of the rightmost cells.

Finally, let us confirm the correctness of the CompactTorre algorithm when the simulation domain is tiled with CompactTorres (Fig. 4). In the first row of CompactTorres, only the c_0 and c_2 cells are inside the domain. Their RHS are updated; this is the first and final iteration of this CompactTorres.

The second row is shifted by one cell in the x and y directions. In the ConeTorres of this row, c_1 and c_3 are the same cells that c_0 and c_2 were in the previous row, redistributed between neighboring CompactTorres Thus, only the remaining part of their RHS has to be computed. These CompactTorres have two iterations. In their last iteration, only the cells c_0 and c_2 are inside the domain.

The next row is shifted by one cell in the x and y directions once again. The whole domain is tiled with such rows. When the CompactTorre is not cut off by the boundary, it has N_T iterations. For the rows on the left boundary of the domain, only the top portion of ConeTorres is inside the domain.

3   The Implementation

The proposed algorithm is implemented in CUDA C++ for a multi-GPU workstation. As in the previous implementations of DiamondTorre [18,19] and CompactTorre [21], the code has the following features:

- The main data storage is in CPU RAM, and with CompactTorre locality properties the GPU-CPU data transfers are concealed.
- One CompactTorre is assigned to one CUDA block; cells along the z axis are distributed between CUDA threads.
- The CompactTorres are called row by row; a row may span several GPUs; all CompactTorres in a row can be processed in parallel.
- CompactTorre data are in the thread registers; save and load operations are performed between registers and the global memory.
- CUDA threads in a block communicate through the shared memory.

3.1   The Data Structure

The data structure is defined as shown in Listing 1.1.

Listing 1.1. Data Structures

```
struct Data{ ftype2 vals[Nx][Ny][Nz]; };// ftype2 is ftype[2];
struct Cell{ ftype val, rhs; };         // ftype is float or double
struct FArSh{
    struct CellLine{ ftype2 valsf[Ns][Nz]; }; // Ns=Nx+3
    CellLine cls[NFY]; };
```

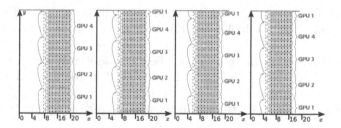

Fig. 5. Algorithm illustration for multi-GPU exchange

As in [17,21], there are three structures for data storage. The main data storage site is Data. It contains data values for the whole mesh and is located in slower memory: CPU RAM or SSD storage. For the data exchange between CompactTorre tasks, the FArSh data structure is defined in the GPU device memory. This data structure was introduced in [8]; it provides optimal data alignment for wavefront-type temporal blocking algorithms. CompactTorre reads data from FArSh and saves data to FArSh by overwriting the same data that were just read. FArSh is organized in CellLines. One line contains data for a sequence of cells that are read and overwritten by a CUDA thread during the algorithm execution. There is a separate FArSh on each GPU. The value NFY is equal to the number of cells in the y direction divided by the number of GPUs in use.

For each mesh point, Data contains a pair of values that correspond to the f value at two consecutive points in time. This is required since numerical scheme (3) includes three points in time. It turns out that it is enough to store only two values in the FArSh data as well. One of them corresponds to the middle layer f^t, and the other one stores either f^{t+1} or f^{t-1} since only one of these is required at any given time. The details are provided in Sect. 3.3.

3.2   Data Exchange

FArSh in the device memory is a cyclic structure. On the x axis, it contains cells from some i_{x0} to $i_{x0} + N_s$. After a row of CompactTorres is processed, data are overwritten; the rightmost data can be saved to the main storage. The new data for $i_{x0} - 1$ can be loaded in its place. The CompactTorres in a row have alternating positions on the y axis, and GPU-GPU exchanges take place; that is why FArSh is cyclic in y too. The periodic boundary is implemented in the y direction. Taking into account the CPU-GPU, GPU-GPU, and thread register-device memory data exchanges, the algorithm is as follows (Fig. 5)

1. Load $N_y \times N_z$ cells at i_{x0} from Data into a buffer, and then from the buffer into the FArSh of each device. These cells are written into the left side on the x axis (input), and with a shift in y equal to some iy_shift value.
2. Each GPU executes $NFY/2$ CompactTorres in a row in parallel CUDA blocks.
3. Copy data from the right side of FArSh (output) into the buffer and save $N_y \times N_z$ cells from the buffer into the main storage Data at coordinate $x = i_{x0} + N_T + 1$.
4. Copy a CellLine on the y-axis boundary of the FArSh device to the next device, i.e., from GPU 3 to GPU 4, from GPU 2 to GPU 3, and so on.
5. Shift in x: $i_{x0} - 1 \rightarrow i_{x0}$.
6. Shift the y coordinate for the FArSh storage: decrement iy_shift by one.
7. Repeat.

The buffer in steps 1 and 3 is required since the Data storage may be inaccessible from inside the GPU kernel, and the FArSh indexing is different from the Data indexing. It is efficient to use a GPU kernel for this copy.

3.3   The CompactTorre Kernel

Listing 1.2 provides the compact update, i.e., one iteration of the CompactTorre loop for the numerical scheme (3). Here, c[0], c[1], c[2], and c[3] correspond to the numbering in Fig. 2; vals_sh are stored in the shared memory. The shared memory is used to exchange data between CUDA threads that update the neighboring cells along the z axis.

At the start of the update, c[1] and c[3] contain f^t as val and partially computed RHS as rhs. At the end of the update, c[1] and c[3] contain f^{t+1} as val and f^t as rhs. Thus, the rhs field, instead of being reset to 0, is used to store information from another time layer. This allows to cut costs on memory storage as mentioned in Sect. 3.1. The periodic boundary is implemented in the z direction.

Listing 1.2. CompactTorre kernel

```
const ftype CFL= Vel*dt*dt/(dx*dx);
const ftype dt2=dt*dt;

inline __device__ void compact_step(Cell c[4], ftype* vals_sh){
  const int iz=threadIdx.x;
  c[0].rhs+= (-c[2].val-c[1].val)*CFL;
  c[2].rhs+= (-c[0].val-c[3].val)*CFL;
  const ftype c1Zm = vals_sh[(iz-1+Nz)%Nz    ],
              c1Zp = vals_sh[(iz+1)%Nz        ],
              c3Zm = vals_sh[(iz-1+Nz)%Nz+Nz],
              c3Zp = vals_sh[(iz+1)%Nz+Nz    ];
  ftype prev_val1=c[1].val, prev_val3=c[3].val;
  c[1].rhs+= (-c[0].val - c[3].val - c1Zp - c1Zm + 6*c[1].val)*CFL +
                                          dt2*Gfunc(c[1].val);
  c[3].rhs+= (-c[2].val - c[1].val - c3Zp - c3Zm + 6*c[3].val)*CFL +
                                          dt2*Gfunc(c[3].val);
  c[1].val = 2*c[1].val - c[1].rhs;
  c[3].val = 2*c[3].val - c[3].rhs;
  c[1].rhs = prev_val1;
  c[3].rhs = prev_val3;
}
```

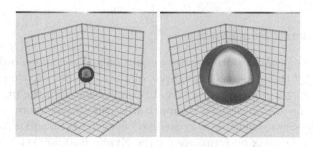

Fig. 6. Simulation results for the scalar wave equation. The color corresponds to the scalar value of f in the x-y-z domain at different instants.

4   The Benchmarks

In this section, we provide the simulation results of the implemented code and performance benchmarks.

4.1 Linear Scalar Wave Equation

To implement the scalar wave equation, we assume that $G(f) = 0$ in (2). We tested a sample problem with $N_x \times N_y \times N_z = 1024 \times 1024 \times 1024$ cells. The mesh and time step sizes are $\Delta r = 1$ and $\Delta t = 0.3$. The wave speed is equal to $V = 1$. The initial condition is $f = \exp(((x-x_0)^2 + (y-y_0)^2 + (z-z_0)^2)/5)$. The simulation result is shown in Fig. 6, where the color corresponds to the scalar value of f in the x-y-z domain at different instants.

4.2 The Sine-Gordon Equation

As a nonlinear example, we choose the 3D sine-Gordon equation [10]:

$$\frac{\partial^2 f}{\partial t^2} = \Delta f - \sin(f). \tag{4}$$

This equation describes coherent localized structures such as solitons. One of the solutions is a stationary or traveling breather (an oscillating soliton). Here we choose a stationary breather as a sample solution.

The analytical solution is taken as the initial condition [7] with $t = 0$:

$$f(x, y, z, t) = -4 \arctan \left(\frac{\sqrt{1-\omega^2}}{\omega} \sin(\omega t) \prod_{\xi=x,y,z} \operatorname{sech}\left(\xi\sqrt{1-\omega^2}\right) \right). \tag{5}$$

The ω parameter controls the size and oscillation frequency of the breather.

The simulation results are shown in Fig. 7. The size of the domain is $1024 \times 1024 \times 1024$ cells; the space and time steps are $\Delta r = 1 and \Delta t = 2\pi/640\omega$. The breather parameter is $\omega = 0.999$.

4.3 Performance Benchmarks

The performance peak for both the wave equation and the sine-Gordon equation is determined by the memory throughput of the GPU device, that is, the data exchange rate with the FArSh structure. In comparison with the previous implementations of the asymptotically compact algorithm, twice more data is stored per cell and, thus, twice more data exchanges between FArSh and Data take place. Let us estimate the peak performance for the Nvidia RTX3090 GPU with 24 GB of GPU memory and a maximum performance throughput equal to 850 GB/s. It follows from the asymptotically compact property (Sect. 2.3) that the complete data set from one cell should be loaded and saved per one cell update. The size of the data in one cell is sizeof(Cell) = $2 * $sizeof(float) = 8 bytes for single precision and 16 bytes for double precision. Thus, the performance peak can be estimated as $57 \cdot 10^9$ LU/s (lattice site updates per second) for single and $28.5 \cdot 10^9$ LU/s for double precision.

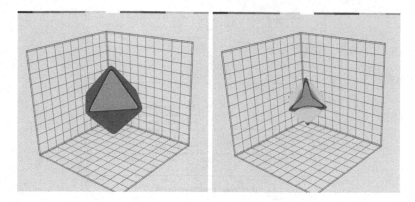

Fig. 7. Simulation results for the sine-Gordon equation. Color corresponds to the scalar value of f in the x-y-z domain at different time instants.

Performance Versus N_T. By N_T we denote the CompactTorre height parameter. As a rule, in LRnLA algorithms, the performance increases with N_T. Here, a higher N_T also leads to a better realization of the asymptotically compact property.

In the current implementation, however, the size of FArSh increases with N_T, and it is stored in the device memory. Thus, N_T is limited, but the limit is high enough for the performance to saturate for both single and double precisions.

We studied the performance dependence on N_T in a $4000 \times 2640 \times 1024$ domain (Fig. 8). The total memory is 80.6 GB for single precision and 161 GB for double precision. The data of the whole domain is stored in the Data structure in the CPU RAM.

In the case of single precision, the sine-Gordon equation and the linear wave equation are modeled with approximately equal performance. In the case of double precision though, the simulation requires twice as much data throughput, thus, the performance is approximately twice lower. The maximum N_T is lower, owing to the FArSh size limit. The performance for the sine-Gordon equation is even lower. A possible explanation is the computing cost of the double-precision special function evaluation. In that case, the problem is not memory-bound.

The highest recorded performance was 49.74 GLU/s for a single precision wave equation and 23.78 GLU/s for a double precision one.

Performance Versus N_z. By N_z we denote the number of nodes in the z-axis direction. At the same time, it is the number of parallel CUDA threads in a CUDA block. Thus the maximum value is 1024. Both Data size and FArSh size increase with N_z.

We studied the performance dependency on N_z under the same conditions as in the previous benchmark (Fig. 9. The performance increases with N_z since parallelism is increased. The performance saturates with relatively low N_z.

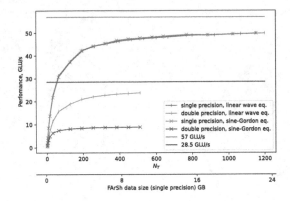

Fig. 8. Performance versus N_T

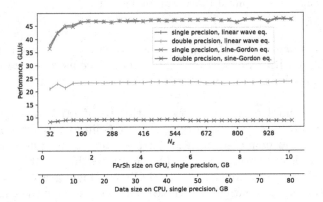

Fig. 9. Performance versus N_z

4.4   Parallel Scaling

We studied weak and strong parallel scaling in the multi-GPU setup with different parameters.

In the strong scaling, the domain size is fixed, and we study the performance against the number of GPUs in use (N_{GPU}) (Fig. 10). Overheads of data exchange between GPU increase together with N_{GPU}. With smaller tasks, overheads are more prominent, especially with a smaller size on the y axis since multi-GPU parallelism is applied in this direction. The use of single or double precision does not affect the scaling behavior.

In the weak scaling, the problem size in the y direction increases with N_{GPU} (Fig. 11). The scaling is close to linear when the data size is large enough (set 1: $2880 \times (1312 \cdot N_{\text{GPU}}) \times 1024$ mesh cells) and N_{GPU} is small. With higher N_{GPU}, overheads of data exchange become visible. For set 2 ($4000 \times (164 \cdot N_{GPUs}) \times 512$), the increase in performance is visible only up to $N_{\text{GPU}} = 4$.

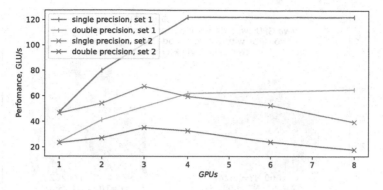

Fig. 10. Strong Scaling. Set 1: $4000 \times 2624 \times 1024$, $N_T = 500$. Set 2: $4000 \times 480 \times 1024$, $N_T = 500$

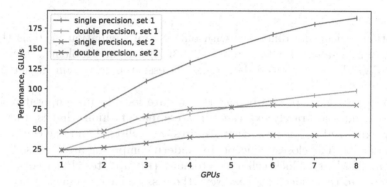

Fig. 11. Weak scaling. Set 1: $2880 \times (1312 \cdot N_{\mathrm{GPU}}) \times 1024$, $N_T = 500$. Set 2: $4000 \times (164 \cdot N_{\mathrm{GPU}}) \times 512$, $N_T = 800$

Figure 12 shows the effect of various connections between two GPUs. We compared the NVlink connection, a connection through the PCIe bridge inside one NUMA node, and a connection between different NUMA nodes.

5   Related Works

The most recent works in big data stencil simulation on GPU have been led by the authors of [6], where the updates of data that are stored in CPU RAM are referred to as 'out-of-core' simulations. Our research differs in that it is based on the theory of LRnLA algorithms. The decomposition of the task in space-time is different. LRnLA algorithms never include redundant halo computations. The decomposition is performed on the x, y, and t axes. The decomposition shape is diamond in x-y, not to be confused with Diamond temporal blocking [15], where the diamond shape is in x-t. The diamond shape follows the cross stencil area of influence, thus arithmetic intensity is increased.

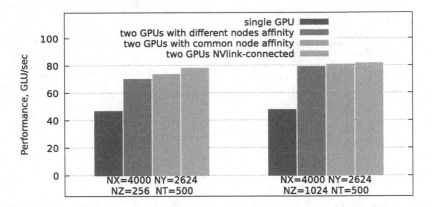

Fig. 12. Parallel efficiency with different connection types

Another conceptual difference with out-of-core simulation in [6] is the use of the wavefront-aligned data structure FArSh. Since the problems are memory-bound, aligned and coalesced data access is essential to obtain higher performance.

Finally, compact updates benefit the update locality in temporal blocking, yet stencil codes are rarely expressed in a compact fashion, that is, the stencil is rarely expressed in a manner that requires one cell load and one cell store per one cell update. The closest concepts in modern computing are the EsoTwist [3] update in LBM and block cellular automata [12] updates. Both concepts are very limited to their specific areas. Nevertheless, we have managed to construct a compact update in the general case of a stencil scheme.

6   Conclusions

The main contribution of this paper is the method of construction of asymptotically compact updates for cross-stencil schemes, which is not limited to flux schemes. The use of LRnLA algorithms in stencil computing leads to high locality and parallel ability of the code implementation of memory-bound stencil schemes, which is once again demonstrated by the performance of the code we have implemented. This is one of the rarest methods where data in CPU RAM can be updated in GPU without loss in performance, that is, CPU-GPU exchanges are concealed by the computations. Previously, the compact update was used in the LRnLA algorithms for fluid-dynamics codes, for the LBM method [20], and for cross-stencil methods written in fluxes [17, 21].

The introduction of compact updates greatly benefits the LRnLA method by eliminating spurious halo dependencies in the DiamondTorre. The optimal arithmetic intensity value of one cell update per one cell load and one cell store operations are coded in the update algorithm. It also leads to a convenient implementation of the FArSh data structure: neighboring asynchronous tasks never access the same CellLines. It opens new prospects for the development and use of LRnLA algorithms. The code development becomes easier with FArSh and compact updates, and the algorithms gain more parallelization options.

From now on, the use of the compact update is no longer limited to fluid dynamics. A similar method can be applied to popular schemes such as the FDTD method for fluid dynamics or the Levander scheme for seismic wave propagation. Here we used the fact that the RHS of the scheme is additive, still more complex functions can be inserted. The prerequisite is that the contribution of different cells can be applied one by one in any order.

It should be noted that the presented code has some deficiencies. The algorithm could be further decomposed on the z axis. By doing so, the number of cells would be no longer limited by the number of CUDA threads and FArSh data size. The data exchange for multi-GPU parallelism can be decreased in the same way. For this, one may use the CandyTorre [9] LRnLA algorithm.

Other optimizations may be applied to increase the performance. At the same time, we find the code implemented for this study to be relatively easy to work with. For this reason, we published it in the open repository [16]. The highest recorded performance is 49.74 GLU/s for a single precision wave equation, and 23.78 GLU/s for a double precision wave one.

Acknowledgment. The work was supported by the Russian Science Foundation (grant № 18-71-10004).

References

1. Endo, T.: Applying recursive temporal blocking for stencil computations to deeper memory hierarchy. In: 2018 IEEE 7th Non-Volatile Memory Systems and Applications Symposium (NVMSA), pp. 19–24. IEEE (2018)
2. Feautrier, P.: Some efficient solutions to the affine scheduling problem: part i. one-dimensional time. Int. J. Parallel Program. **21**(5), 313–348 (1992). https://doi.org/10.1007/BF01407835.
3. Geier, M., Schönherr, M.: Esoteric twist: an efficient in-place streaming algorithms for the lattice Boltzmann method on massively parallel hardware. Computation **5**(2), 19 (2017). https://doi.org/10.3390/computation5020019
4. Levchenko, V.D., Perepelkina, A.Y.: Locally recursive non-locally asynchronous algorithms for stencil computation. Lobachevskii J. Math. **39**(4), 552–561 (2018). https://doi.org/10.1134/S1995080218040108
5. Levchenko, V., Perepelkina, A., Zakirov, A.: DiamondTorre algorithm for high-performance wave modeling. Computation **4**(3), 29 (2016). https://doi.org/10.3390/computation4030029
6. Matsumura, K., Zohouri, H.R., Wahib, M., Endo, T., Matsuoka, S.: AN5D: automated stencil framework for high-degree temporal blocking on GPUs. In: Proceedings of the 18th ACM/IEEE International Symposium on Code Generation and Optimization, pp. 199–211 (2020)
7. Minzoni, A., Smyth, N.F., Worthy, A.L.: Evolution of two-dimensional standing and travelling breather solutions for the Sine-Gordon equation. Phys. D: Nonlinear Phenom. **189**(3–4), 167–187 (2004)

8. Perepelkina, A., Levchenko, V.D.: Functionally arranged data for algorithms with space-time wavefront. In: Sokolinsky, L., Zymbler, M. (eds.) PCT 2021. CCIS, vol. 1437, pp. 134–148. Springer, Cham (2021). https://doi.org/10.1007/978-3-030-81691-9_10

9. Perepelkina, A., Levchenko, V., Khilkov, S.: The DiamondCandy LRnLA algorithm: raising efficiency of the 3D cross-stencil schemes. J. Supercomput. **75**(12), 7778–7789 (2018). https://doi.org/10.1007/s11227-018-2461-z

10. Rigge, P.: Numerical solutions to the Sine-Gordon equation. arXiv preprint arXiv:1212.2716 (2012)

11. Succi, S.: The Lattice Boltzmann Equation: For Complex States of Flowing Matter. Oxford University Press, Oxford (2018)

12. Toffoli, T., Margolus, N.: Cellular Automata Machines: A New Environment for Modeling. MIT press, Cambridge (1987)

13. Williams, S., Waterman, A., Patterson, D.: Roofline: an insightful visual performance model for multicore architectures. Commun. ACM **52**(4), 65–76 (2009)

14. Wolfe, M.: Loops skewing: the wavefront method revisited. Int. J. Parallel Program. **15**(4), 279–293 (1986)

15. Wonnacott, D.G., Strout, M.M.: On the scalability of loop tiling techniques. IMPACT **2013**, 3 (2013)

16. Zakirov, A.: CompactWave repository. https://github.com/zakirovandrey/compactWave (2022)

17. Zakirov, A., Korneev, B., Perepelkina, A., Levchenko, V.: Compact LRnLA algorithms for flux-based numerical schemes. In: Sokolinsky, L., Zymbler, M. (eds.) PCT 2022. Communications in Computer and Information Science, vol. 1618, pp. 99–115. Springer, Cham (2022). https://doi.org/10.1007/978-3-031-11623-0_8

18. Zakirov, A., Levchenko, V., Ivanov, A., Perepelkina, A., Levchenko, T., Rok, V.: High-performance 3D modeling of a full-wave seismic field for seismic survey tasks. Geoinformatika **3**, 34–45 (2017)

19. Zakirov, A., Levchenko, V., Perepelkina, A., Zempo, Y.: High performance FDTD algorithm for GPGPU supercomputers. J. Phys.: Conf. Ser. **759**, 012100 (2016). https://doi.org/10.1088/1742-6596/759/1/012100

20. Zakirov, A., Perepelkina, A., Levchenko, V., Khilkov, S.: Streaming techniques: revealing the natural concurrency of the lattice Boltzmann method. J. Supercomput. **77**(10), 11911–11929 (2021). https://doi.org/10.1007/s11227-021-03762-z

21. Zakirov, A.V., Korneev, B.A., Perepelkina, A.Y.: Compact update algorithm for numerical schemes with cross stencil for data access locality. In: Proceedings of the 2022 6th High Performance Computing and Cluster Technologies Conference, pp. 51–58 (2022)

Quantum-Chemical Simulation
of High-Energy Azoxy Compounds

Vadim Volokhov[1] , Ivan Akostelov[2], Vladimir Parakhin[3] ,
Elena Amosova[1(✉)] , and David Lempert[1]

[1] Federal Research Center of Problems of Chemical Physics and Medicinal
Chemistry, Chernogolovka, Russian Federation
{vvm,aes,lempert}@icp.ac.ru
[2] Lomonosov Moscow State University, Moscow, Russian Federation
[3] N.D. Zelinsky Institute of Organic Chemistry, Moscow, Russian Federation
parakhin@ioc.ac.ru

Abstract. The paper presents a study of the thermochemical properties
of a series of substances containing an azoxy group associated with a
trinitromethyl group and a furazan ring and promising for the creation
of new high-energy density materials. The enthalpies of formation in
the gaseous phase have been obtained by quantum chemical calculations
using the Gaussian program package (G4MP2 and G4 methods). We
compare the methods of atomization and of homodesmotic reactions in
terms of accuracy, efficiency, and computational requirements. Also, we
suggest an extension of the method of homodesmotic reactions which
makes it possible to reduce the requirements for computing resources.
We analyze the dependence of the enthalpy of formation on the structure
of the compounds.

Keywords: Quantum-chemical calculations · Homodesmotic
reactions · Enthalpy of formation · High-enthalpy compounds

1 Introduction

The paper considers high-energy density materials (HEDMs) capable of storing and releasing large amounts of chemical energy under controlled conditions.
These compounds are widely used in military affairs, mineral exploration, mining, construction, metallurgy, and rocket and space technology. Compounds with
a high nitrogen content, which combine high energy intensity with resistance to
external influences, are promising as potential high-energy compounds.

The main parameter characterizing the prospects of a high-energy substance
is the enthalpy of formation $\Delta_f H°$ in the state of aggregation in which the substance under study will be used. Experimental calorimetric determination of the
enthalpy of formation of new substances faces some difficulties. Although modern
equipment makes it possible to measure with high accuracy the combustion of
the substance to water, nitrogen, and carbon dioxide, some nitrogen oxides can

© The Author(s), under exclusive license to Springer Nature Switzerland AG 2023
L. Sokolinsky and M. Zymbler (Eds.): PCT 2023, CCIS 1868, pp. 231–243, 2023.
https://doi.org/10.1007/978-3-031-38864-4_16

also be formed in the combustion process, and that, in turn, requires also their quantitative determination. The measurement error usually decreases with an increase in the mass of the test sample. However, when working with newly synthesized materials, one has to operate with a substance amount of no more than 100 mg. Trace impurities in such a small test sample introduce an unpredictable error in the measurement results.

It is very important to determine which compounds from the series under consideration have the best characteristics and are the most promising for practical synthesis and subsequent application. Predicting the enthalpy of formation of compounds that have not yet been synthesized helps to reduce the cost and speed up the process of creating new materials. Computational chemistry methods are widely used for such predictions. Existing quantitative structure-property relationship (QSPR) models [1–4] make it possible to reliably predict the enthalpy of formation only for certain well-studied classes of substances. When it comes to the prediction of the enthalpy of formation of compounds with high nitrogen content, quantum-chemical calculations based on *ab initio* approaches are more promising for this purpose. Such calculations require high-performance computing resources, and these requirements increase extremely rapidly as the complexity of the compound under study increases. The promising solution to this problem could be the approach considered in [5], in which quantum-chemical methods are used in combination with formal thermochemical reactions (a.k.a. homodesmotic reactions), composed in a special way to minimize possible errors.

Compounds containing an azoxy fragment are of great interest in the creation of new HEDMs. The highly polar $N{\rightarrow}O$ fragment makes it possible to achieve a high density of the resulting crystals and improve their detonation characteristics, while simultaneously reducing their sensitivity to external influences [6]. Several azoxy compounds described in [7] combine high enthalpy of formation, high density, and thermal stability. The introduction of a furazan fragment [8] made it possible to obtain a substance that surpasses traditional HEDMs (hexogen, octogen, CL-20) in specific impulse, which is an important characteristic of rocket fuels.

In this work, we calculate the enthalpy of formation in the gaseous phase of a series of structurally similar compounds (Table 1) containing an azoxy group bonded to a trinitromethyl group and a furazane ring. We use composite quantum-chemical methods G4 and G4MP2 and functional density theory (DFT) at the B3LYP level.

The paper is organized as follows. Section 2 describes the atomization reaction method for calculating the enthalpy of formation in the gaseous phase. Section 3 contains the description and main requirements of the method of homodesmotic reactions for calculating the enthalpy of formation in the gaseous phase. In Sect. 4, we discuss the results of our calculations. Section 5 contains information about computational details of our calculations. Conclusions summarize the study and point directions for further work.

Table 1. Compounds under study

№	Molecular formula	Structural formula
1	$C_2H_3N_5O_7$	$(O_2N)_3C$, $_+N=N$, $_-O$
2	$C_4H_3N_7O_8$	$(O_2N)_3C$, $_+N=N$, $_-O$ (furazan ring with CH_3)
3	$C_4H_3N_7O_9$	$(O_2N)_3C$, $_+N=N$, $_-O$ (furazan ring with $O-$)
4	$C_3H_2N_8O_8$	$(O_2N)_3C$, $_+N=N$, $_-O$ (furazan ring with NH_2)
5	$C_3N_{10}O_8$	$(O_2N)_3C$, $_+N=N$, $_-O$ (furazan ring with N_3)
6	$C_3N_8O_{10}$	$(O_2N)_3C$, $_+N=N$, $_-O$ (furazan ring with NO_2)
7	$C_4H_3N_9O_{10}$	$(O_2N)_3C$, $_+N=N$, $_-O$ (furazan ring with $N(O_2N)-$)
8	$C_5H_5N_{11}O_{12}$	$(O_2N)_3C$, $_+N=N$, $_-O$ (furazan ring with $N(O_2N)-CH_2-N(O_2N)-$)
9	$C_4N_{12}O_{15}$	$(O_2N)_3C$, $_+N=N$, $_-O$ (furazan ring with $N=N_+$, O_-, $C(NO_2)_3$)

2 Calculation of the Enthalpy of Formation in the Gaseous Phase by the Atomization Reaction Method

The atomization reaction method is based on the formation of a substance from individual atoms and attracts researchers with its simplicity and generality. Nevertheless, for its successful application, it is necessary to accurately take into account the electron correlation effect due to the significant change in the electronic structure that occurs during the transition from atoms to a molecule.

The G4 method described in [9] makes it possible to calculate the enthalpy of formation with an average deviation from the experimental data of 0.83 kcal/mol (on a sample of 454 substances). There is also a modification of the method, G4MP2 [10], which uses the theory of a lower order at one of the calculation stages; this can significantly reduce the calculation time, while only slightly reducing the accuracy (1.04 kcal/mol against 0.83 kcal/mol). In this work, we use both modifications of the G4 method.

3 Method of Homodesmotic Reactions

According to Hess's law, the enthalpy of a reaction does not depend on the specific way of its occurrence, so it is possible to use for calculations any thermodynamic reaction that connects reagents with products. By definition of the enthalpy of formation in the gas phase, the initial reagents should be simple substances (components of the target molecule) that are in stable standard states. The main advantage of using an arbitrary thermodynamic reaction is the possibility to choose one during which the electron environment of the atoms participating in the reactions changes minimally. Therefore, the required accuracy of calculations can be achieved without accurately taking into account the effects of electron correlation.

When a certain thermodynamic reaction is used, calculations require not only the values of the electron energy calculated by quantum chemical methods but also experimental enthalpies of formation of the reagents. If the necessary data on the reagents is not described in the literature, the enthalpy of formation can be calculated by the atomization reaction method. As compared to the calculation of the enthalpy of formation of the whole molecule under study, this approach makes it possible to reduce significantly the overall computational complexity of the problem since composite quantum chemical methods scale polynomially depending on the size of the system under calculation.

In this paper, homodesmotic reactions are reactions in which:

1) the following homodesmotic requirements for carbon atoms are met: the invariance of the number of carbon-carbon bonds between atoms of all degrees of hybridization $C_{sp^3}-C_{sp^3}$, $C_{sp^3}-C_{sp^2}$, $C_{sp^2}-C_{sp^2}$, $C_{sp^2}-C_{sp}$, $C_{sp}-C_{sp}$, $C_{sp^2}=C_{sp^2}$, $C_{sp^2}=C_{sp}$, $C_{sp}=C_{sp}$, $C_{sp}\equiv C_{sp}$, and the invariance of the number of carbon atoms of each degree of hybridization (sp^3, sp^2, sp) with 0, 1, 2, or 3 hydrogen atoms;

2) the number of O−C, O−N, O−O, N−C, and N−N bonds of all degrees of hybridization is preserved, and

3) the number of oxygen and nitrogen atoms of each degree of hybridization with 0, 1, 2, or 3 hydrogen atoms is preserved.

In this work, we used schemes of the homodesmotic reactions that meet the above requirements (see Table 2).

4   Results and Discussion

4.1   Enthalpy of Formation

For calculations, we used quantum-chemical methods within the Gaussian-09 program package. The optimized geometry, as well as electronic energies and zero-point energies, have been calculated by the composite quantum-chemical G4MP2 method.

Table 3 presents the electron energies and enthalpies of formation calculated by the atomization method of all reactants and products in accordance with the scheme of homodesmotic reactions (Table 2). Table 4 contains the enthalpies of formation obtained by the method of homodesmotic reactions using G4MP2 electronic energies and using DFT/B3LYP electronic energies in the 6-31G(2df,p) basis.

If we use G4MP2 electronic energies in the calculations, the enthalpy of formation of the substances under consideration, obtained by the method of homodesmotic reactions, matches up to two decimal places with that calculated by the atomization reaction method. The enthalpy of the reaction, which can be calculated by the method of homodesmotic reactions, is only one part of the equation for the enthalpy of formation, where the enthalpies of formation of the reagents make a significant contribution. Thus, when using the enthalpies of formation of reagents obtained by the atomization reaction method at a sufficiently high level of calculation, the enthalpies of formation of the substance obtained by the method of homodesmotic reactions differ only slightly from the enthalpies of formation obtained by the atomization method, as it can be seen in our calculation results.

If we use the DFT theory, the difference in the enthalpies of formation obtained using the method of homodesmotic reactions and the method of atomization is significant: the root mean square error (RMSE) is 3.94 kcal/mol, which significantly exceeds the value of 0.5 kcal/mol given in [5] for a test set of hydrocarbons only. The use of low-level theory methods for nitrogen- and oxygen-containing compounds requires adjustments. The enthalpies of the reaction in Table 4 are quite high, which indicates a significant difference in the electronic structure of the reagents and products. The error is systematic and may indicate that one of the reagents common to the most of homodesmotic reactions in the scheme is not sufficiently well chosen.

There are two common fragments for all molecules under consideration, namely, a furazane cycle and a trinitro-azoxy fragment. In this case, the largest

Table 2. Schemes of homodesmotic reactions for the compounds under study

relative deviation (5.3%) was obtained for substance 1; it does not contain a furazan ring but only a trinitro-azoxy fragment, which makes this fragment the most likely source of error. The problem redistribution of electron density can

Table 3. Electronic energy with thermal correction, CPU computation time, and enthalpy of formation by the atomization method for all reagents and products

№	G4MP2		DFT/B3LYP/6-31G(2df,p)		G4MP2
	H_{298}, *Hartree*	t, sec	H_{298}, *Hartree*	t, sec	$\Delta_f H^\circ_{(298(g))}$, kcal/mol
1	−877.012926	196801	−877.837966	37078	51.91
1-1	−782.500633	60798	−783.221605	19696	44.81
1-2	−264.114135	2685	−264.389484	1790	17.63
1-3	−169.590680	533	−169.757530	394	17.54
2	−1137.569669	564053	−1138.676128	27361	107.70
2-1	−302.143148	3261	−302.47059	1447	40.10
2-2	−430.149192	9945	−430.598307	3300	72.22
2-3	−207.620861	909	−207.840189	630	39.27
3	−1212.704727	861368	−1213.877501	67968	82.58
3-1	−192.822798	1010	−193.038338	623	−23.05
3-2	−117.683511	2444	−117.834064	1613	4.71
4	−1153.617485	484812	−1154.727716	84678	118.87
4-1	−133.731401	2646	−133.884435	1885	14.14
5	−1261.735381	1404714	−1262.960837	76533	203.50
5-1	−241.862692	1326	−242.13437	762	92.06
6	−1302.613288	1221768	−1303.860518	116456	135.21
6-1	−282.764932	1485	−283.050500	872	8.51
7	−1397.136810	2181467	−1398.485923	135874	135.26
7-1	−377.267136	8092	−377.663277	2857	21.93
8	−1695.955143	8507230	−1697.594818	294233	149.74
8-1	−676.084480	92916	−676.769862	28182	37.03
9	−1934.903865	21231201	−1936.734719	258679	192.56
TNAV	−915.043216	184095	−915.919989	40990	73.57

be caused by the introduction of a methyl radical thrice substituted by nitro groups to the nitrogen of the azoxy group. Furthermore, the formal preservation of the hybridization of the nitrogen atom as a result of the reaction (sp^2 in the N=O fragment of reagent **1-1** and sp^2 in the azoxy group of product **1**) is not enough to compensate for the error introduced by inaccurate consideration of electron correlation.

The fragment described could be a result of the formal interaction of reagents **1-1** and **1-2** (or **2-1**). To reduce the error, the new scheme of homodesmotic reactions has been introduced with the whole trinitroazoxy fragment within the trinitroazoxyvinyl (**TNAV**) molecule (Fig. 1) instead of two reagents, and the enthalpy of formation was recalculated for all molecules. The results of these calculations are shown in Table 5.

The RMSE of the enthalpy of formation when using the TNAV molecule in calculations has decreased to 1.57 kcal/mol, which can be considered quite

Table 4. Enthalpy of formation of the studied substances (kcal/mol) calculated by the method of homodesmotic reactions

№	G4MP2			DFT/B3LYP/6-31G(2df,p)		
	$\Delta_r H^\circ_{(298(g))}{}^a$	$\Delta_f H^\circ_{(298(g))}$	Calculation error[b]	$\Delta_r H^\circ_{(298(g))}{}^a$	$\Delta_f H^\circ_{(298(g))}$	Calculation error[b]
1	7.00	51.91	0.00	9.78	54.68	2.78
2	7.38	107.70	0.00	10.45	110.76	3.06
3	10.04	82.58	0.00	12.27	84.82	2.24
4	7.43	117.17	0.00	9.69	119.43	2.26
5	15.83	203.50	0.00	20.24	207.90	4.40
6	31.10	135.21	0.00	30.56	134.66	−0.54
7	17.73	135.26	0.00	22.64	140.16	4.91
8	17.10	149.74	0.00	21.19	153.81	4.08
9	29.59	192.56	0.00	36.81	199.78	7.22

[a] Enthalpy of the homodesmotic reaction
[b] Calculation error of the enthalpy of formation by homodesmotic reaction method in comparison to the enthalpy of formation by atomization method

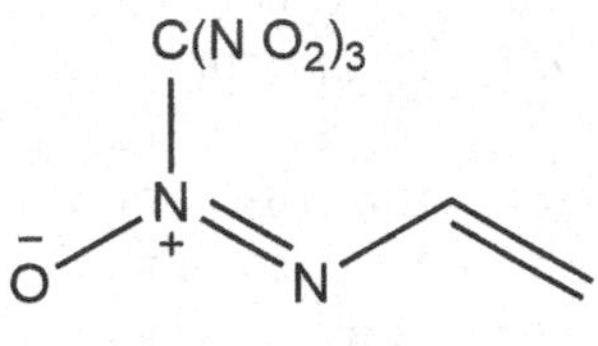

Fig. 1. Trinitroazoxyvinyl

Table 5. Enthalpy of formation of the studied substances (kcal/mol) calculated by the method of homodesmotic reactions

№	The reaction scheme	$\Delta_r H^\circ_{(298(g))}$	$\Delta_f H^\circ_{(298(g))}$	D^a
1	**TNAV + 1-3 → 1 + 2-3**	−0.40	51.44	−0.47
2	**TNAV + 2-2 → 2 + 2-3**	1.24	107.76	0.06
3	**TNAV + 2-2 + 3-1 → 3 + 2-3 + 3-2**	3.06	81.81	−0.77
4	**TNAV + 2-2 + 4-1 → 4 + 2-3 + 3-2**	0.48	116.43	−0.75
5	**TNAV + 2-2 + 5-1 → 5 + 2-3 + 3-2**	11.03	204.89	1.40
6	**TNAV + 2-2 + 6-1 → 6 + 2-3 + 3-2**	21.35	131.66	−3.55
7	**TNAV + 2-2 + 7-1 → 7 + 2-3 + 3-2**	13.43	137.16	1.90
8	**TNAV + 2-2 + 8-1 → 8 + 2-3 + 3-2**	11.98	150.81	1.08
9	2 **TNAV + 2-2 → 9 + 2-3 + 3-2**	18.39	193.77	1.21

[a] Deviation from the atomization enthalpy by G4MP2

acceptable. As it has been mentioned earlier, the G4MP2 method uses the theory of a lower order at one of the calculation stages which results in some calculation error. So it might be interesting to use enthalpies of formation of reagents calculated by the G4 method in the new schemes of homodesmotic reactions and compare the results with the enthalpies of formation calculated by the atomization reaction method using the G4 method. Unfortunately, the G4 method requires high computational costs, so it has been possible to use the atomization reaction method only for six substances out of nine. The calculation results and their comparison are shown in Table 6.

Table 6. Comparison of the enthalpy of formation calculated by the G4 method, the atomization method, and the method of homodesmotic reactions

№	G4	Homodesmotic	Deviation
1	45.13	46.88	−1.25
2	100.46	99.23	−1.23
3	74.80	73.38	−1.42
4	110.24	108.26	−1.98
5	195.36	195.82	0.46
6	123.75	123.30	−0.45
7	—	127.69	—
8	—	140.22	—
7	—	177.82	—

The RMSE in the calculation of the enthalpy of formation decreases to 1.25 kcal/mol. To reduce this error, a more detailed account of the correlation effect and a more thorough study of the criteria for homodesmotic reactions for nitrogen- and oxygen-containing compounds are required, which in turn requires a large amount of research work, but it is a promising prospect for further study since it can accelerate the development of new high-energy materials.

Table 7 shows the time costs for enthalpy calculations by various methods. The last column contains the cumulative time spent on the calculation of all reagents from the reaction schemes in Table 5.

The time for calculating the energy of the studied substances by the G4 method significantly exceeds the time required for calculations by other methods. The time for calculating the energy of the studied substances by the B3LYP method and of the reagents by the G4MP2 and G4 method in all cases (except the first one) turns out to be less than in the case of calculating the energy of the studied substances by the corresponding methods.

If we exclude the time costs for calculations of the energy of the reagents reused in many reactions (specifically: **TNAV**, **2-2**, **2-3**, and **3-2**, which in total account for 197 393 s for the G4MP2 method and 1 016 608 s for the G4 method), then the time costs for each compound will be greatly reduced (Fig. 2). Thus, in the case of studying a series of structurally similar molecules, we can reduce the use of computing resources by a factor of more than 20 as compared with the atomization method.

Table 7. CPU time to calculate the electronic energy of substances (sec)

№	Calculation of the whole compound			Calculation of reagents	
	G4	G4MP2	DFT/B3LYP	G4	G4MP2
1	878 680	196 800	37 078	984 271	185 537
2	6 725 371	564 052	27 361	1 014 478	194 949
3	12 861 161	861 368	67 968	1 021 810	198 404
4	9 580 979	484 812	84 678	1 019 361	200 039
5	26 897 475	1 404 714	76 533	1 027 069	198 720
6	27 745 456	1 221 768	116 456	1 024 584	198 878
7	—	2 181 467	135 874	1 039 338	205 484
8	—	8 507 230	294 233	1 214 287	290 309
9	—	21 231 201	258 679	1 016 608	197 393

4.2 Dependence of the Enthalpy on the Structure

To rationalize the design of new-generation substances, it is necessary to understand how structural features affect the observed physicochemical properties. Let us start the analysis with compound **1**, which contains only the trinitroazoxy fragment and may serve as a starting point for further comparison. The following regularities can be observed.

When the furazan fragment is added (compound **2**), the enthalpy of formation in the gaseous phase increases significantly (by 56 kcal/mol). The double bond between nitrogen and carbon, being the closest to the azoxy fragment, becomes stretched. It can be seen by comparison of the geometry of the furazan ring in the free form and in compound **2**. Coupling is observed between the azoxy group and the furazan ring. Bond stretching is caused by the strong negative inductive and mesomeric effect of the trinitroazoxy fragment, which destabilizes the furazan aromatic system.

The substitution of one methyl radical in the furazan ring for a methoxy group (compound **3**) leads to a decrease in the enthalpy of formation. This effect is quite expected—oxygen, owing to the mesomeric effect, stabilizes the previously destabilized aromatic system.

The introduction of nitrogen groups in compounds **4** and **6** leads to a slight increase in the enthalpy of formation. The amino group (compound **4**) partially stabilizes the ring in a similar way as the methoxy group.

The introduction of an azido group (compound **5**) significantly increases the enthalpy of formation; such an effect of a sharp ($\sim$ 80 kcal/mol) increase in the enthalpy of formation upon the introduction of an azido group into aliphatic compounds is described in [11]. However, it would not lead to an increase in the enthalpy of combustion since the environment of the atoms of the azido group undergoes only slight changes during combustion.

Small changes in the enthalpy of formation in compounds **7** and **8** are associated with the introduction of isolated systems R_2N-NO_2 into the molecule.

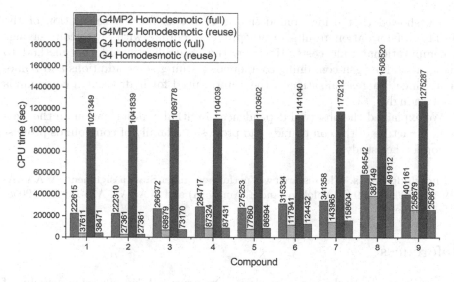

Fig. 2. Time costs for computing the enthalpy of formation by homodesmotic reactions without and with reuse of the molecule energies

When the second trinitroazoxy group is introduced into the furazan cycle, the enthalpy of formation drastically increases. The enthalpy of formation of compound **9** is higher by 32.95 kcal/mol than the expected sum of the enthalpies of formation of compound **1** and compound **2** (159.61 kcal/mol). This effect can be explained by an even greater destabilization of the furazan cycle.

Thus we can conclude that the most promising systems for further research are compounds with isolated R_2N-NO_2 systems and aromatic rings destabilized by strong acceptors.

5 Computational Details

Calculations were performed using the equipment of the Supercomputer Multiuser Center at Lomonosov Moscow State University [12, 13] (projects Enthalpy-2065 and Enthalpy-2219) and computational resources of FRC PCP MC RAS. Composite quantum-chemical methods G4 and G4MP2 and functional density theory (DFT) within the Gaussian program package were used for calculations. The parallelization within the Gaussian package is implemented by its own Linda software, which is not always quite efficient. When increasing the number of computing cores, the speedup effect is noticeable only up to eight cores and further it diminishes, thus making it rational to use eight cores per task in the calculations.

6 Conclusions

The enthalpy of formation in the gaseous phase of a series of previously undescribed azoxy compounds was calculated with high precision by composite G4 and G4MP2 methods within the Gaussian program package.

We showed that using homodesmotic reactions for the calculation of the enthalpy of formation results in acceptable accuracy with significant savings in computational time costs. However, the generalization of this method to nitrogen- and oxygen-containing compounds requires some additions and refinements since the generalization of the criteria used for hydrocarbon compounds is not enough.

We explained the observed dependence of enthalpy of formation on the electronic structure of the compounds and proposed a family of compounds promising for further study.

Acknowledgments. The research was performed under State assignments № AAAA-A19-119120690042-9 (V. Volokhov and E. Amosova) and № AAAA-A19-119101690058-9 (D. Lempert).

References

1. Redžepović I., Marković S., Furtula B.: On structural dependence of enthalpy of formation of catacondensed benzenoid hydrocarbons. MATCH Commun. Math. Comput. Chem. **82**, 663–678 (2019)
2. Gharagheizi, F.: Prediction of the standard enthalpy of formation of pure compounds using molecular structure. Aust. J. Chem. **62**(4), 376–381 (2009). https://doi.org/10.1071/CH08522
3. Vatani, A., Mehrpooya, M., Gharagheizi, F.: Prediction of standard enthalpy of formation by a QSPR model. Int. J. Mol. Sci. **8**(5), 407–432 (2007). https://doi.org/10.3390/i8050407
4. Teixeira, A.L., Leal, J.P., Falcao, A.O.: Random forests for feature selection in QSPR Models - an application for predicting standard enthalpy of formation of hydrocarbons. J. Cheminform **5**, 9 (2013). https://doi.org/10.1186/1758-2946-5-9
5. Wheeler, S.E.: Homodesmotic reactions for thermochemistry. WIREs Comput. Mol. Sci. **2**, 204–220 (2012). https://doi.org/10.1002/wcms.72
6. Yin, P., Zhang, Q., Shreeve, J.M.: Dancing with energetic nitrogen atoms: versatile N-functionalization strategies for N-heterocyclic frameworks in high energy density materials. Acc. Chem. Res. **49**(1), 4–16 (2016). https://doi.org/10.1021/acs.accounts.5b00477
7. Anikin, O.V., Leonov, N.E., Klenov, M.S., et al.: An energetic (nitro-NNO-azoxy)triazolo-1,2,4-triazine. Eur. J. Org. Chem. **26**, 4189–4195 (2019). https://doi.org/10.1002/ejoc.201900314
8. Leonov, N.E., Semenov, S.E., Klenov, M.S., et al.: Novel energetic aminofurazans with a nitro-NNO-azoxy group. Mend. Comm. **31**(6), 789–791 (2021). https://doi.org/10.1016/j.mencom.2021.11.006
9. Curtiss, L.A., Redfern, P.C., Raghavachari, K.: Gaussian-4 theory. J. Chem. Phys. **126**, 084108 (2007). https://doi.org/10.1063/1.2436888
10. Curtiss, L.A., Redfern, P.C., Raghavachari, K.: Gaussian-4 theory using reduced order perturbation theory. J. Chem. Phys. **127**, 124105 (2007). https://doi.org/10.1063/1.2770701
11. Zhou, J., Zhang, J., Wang, B.: Recent synthetic efforts towards high energy density materials: How to design high-performance energetic structures? FirePhysChem **2**(2), 83–139 (2022). https://doi.org/10.1016/j.fpc.2021.09.005

12. Voevodin, Vl.V., Antonov, A.S., Nikitenko, D.A., et al.: Supercomputer Lomonosov-2: largescale, deep monitoring and fine analytics for the user community. Supercomput. Front. Innov. **6**(2), 4–11 (2019). https://doi.org/10.14529/jsfi190201
13. Nikitenko, D.A., Voevodin, V.V., Zhumatiy, S.A.: Deep analysis of job state statistics on "Lomonosov-2" supercomputer. Supercomput. Front. Innov. **5**(2), 4–10(2019). https://doi.org/10.14529/jsfi180201

Parallel Algorithms for Simulation of the Suspension Transport in Coastal Systems Based on the Explicit-Implicit and Splitting Schemes

A. I. Sukhinov[1] , A. E. Chistyakov[1] , V. V. Sidoryakina[1(✉)] ,
I. Yu. Kuznetsova[2] , A. M. Atayan[1] , and M. V. Porksheyan[1]

[1] Don State Technical University, Rostov-on-Don, Russian Federation
cvv9@mail.ru
[2] Southern Federal University, Rostov-on-Don, Russian Federation
ikuznecova@sfedu.ru

Abstract. We consider two difference schemes that describe the convective-diffusion transfer and settling of multifractional suspensions in coastal systems. The first is based on an explicit-implicit scheme with reduced cost of arithmetic operations. This difference scheme uses an explicit approximation of the diffusion-convection operator (on the lower time layer) along the horizontal directions and an implicit approximation along the vertical direction. We determine the admissible values of the time step for this scheme from the conditions of monotonicity, solvability, and stability. We deem appropriate the use of this scheme, which naturally leads to a parallel algorithm, on grids having a relatively moderate number of nodes along each of the indicated horizontal directions, up to several hundred. The admissible value of the time step in this case is in the interval from 10^{-2} s to 1 s. The second is an additive scheme obtained by splitting the original spatial three-dimensional problem into a chain of two-dimensional ones in the horizontal directions and a one-dimensional problem in the vertical direction of the task. In this case, the allowable time step can be increased to several hundred seconds. We consider in detail the parallel implementation, based on the decomposition of the grid domain, of the set of two-dimensional diffusion-convection problems included in the chain. The speedup of the algorithm was estimated on the K60 computer cluster, installed at the Keldysh Institute of Applied Mathematics (Russian Academy of Sciences).

Keywords: Suspension diffusion-convection models · Explicit-implicit scheme · Splitting scheme · Parallel algorithms

The study was financially supported by the Russian Science Foundation (project № 22-11-00295, https://rscf.ru/project/22-11-00295/).

© The Author(s), under exclusive license to Springer Nature Switzerland AG 2023
L. Sokolinsky and M. Zymbler (Eds.): PCT 2023, CCIS 1868, pp. 244–258, 2023.
https://doi.org/10.1007/978-3-031-38864-4_17

1   Introduction

The transport of suspended matter is the most significant factor that affects the morpholithodynamic regime of coastal systems [1–4]. Under the influence of waves and currents, the mass of alluvial material begins to move while undergoing chemical and mechanical changes. The processes that arise in this case find their expression in both bottom and coastal formations that can reach significant scales in size [5,6]. To solve this problem, we need scientifically based mathematical models that remain reliable within a wide range of variation of the spatial and temporal scales.

To date, more than one hundred models of suspended matter transport have been created, and several hundred model computer programs are employed for the study of various types of water bodies with different spatiotemporal scales [7–9]. Each model, however, has its limitations. Models of suspended matter transport need further study.

In this paper, we consider parallel algorithms for the numerical simulation of spatial three-dimensional processes of transport of a multicomponent suspension based on schemes, namely, explicit-implicit and splitting schemes. In the explicit-implicit scheme, the approximation of the diffusion-convection operator along the horizontal coordinate directions is done on the lower layer, whereas the one-dimensional diffusion-convection-deposition operator along the vertical direction is applied on the upper time layer. In this case, the main computational costs are associated with the numerical solution by the tridiagonal matrix algorithm the set of independent three-point boundary value problems on the upper time layer [10,11]. The use of two-dimensional–one-dimensional additive schemes is based on the sequential solution on each time layer of a chain of two difference problems: two-dimensional convection-diffusion along the horizontal coordinate directions and one-dimensional convection-diffusion-deposition along the vertical coordinate direction [12,13]. We rely on implicit approximations for both problems; the initial-final solutions of these problems are connected within each time step. Under such a discretization method, the admissible time step can be hundreds or even thousands of seconds. We consider in detail the parallel implementation (based on the decomposition of the grid domain) of the set of two-dimensional diffusion-convection problems included in the chain. Also, we give the results of the corresponding numerical experiments.

2   Model of Multicomponent Suspension Transport

We use a rectangular Cartesian coordinate system $Oxyz$ in which the axes Ox and Oy lie on the surface of the undisturbed water surface and are directed to the north and east, respectively, while the axis Oz is directed downward.

Let $G \subset \mathbb{R}^3$ be the region where the process takes place. We assume that G is a parallelepiped: $G = \{0 < x < L_x,\ 0 < y < L_y,\ 0 < z \le L_z\}$. Moreover, we suppose that there are R types of suspension particles in the region G, and the concentration of particles of the r-th type at the point (x, y, z) at time t

is $c_r = c_r(x, y, z, t)$ (in units of mg/l), where t is the time variable (sec). The fraction number r is determined by the density and size of its particles (settling velocity of particles).

The system of equations describing the transfer of suspended particles can be written as follows [14–16]:

$$
\begin{cases}
\frac{\partial c_r}{\partial t} + \frac{\partial(uc_r)}{\partial x} + \frac{\partial(vc_r)}{\partial y} + \frac{\partial((w+w_{g,r})c_r)}{\partial z} \\
\quad = \frac{\partial}{\partial x}\left(\mu_{hr}\frac{\partial c_r}{\partial x}\right) + \frac{\partial}{\partial y}\left(\mu_{hr}\frac{\partial c_r}{\partial y}\right) + \frac{\partial}{\partial z}\left(\mu_{vr}\frac{\partial c_r}{\partial z}\right) + F_r, \quad r = 1,\ldots,R, \\
F_1 = (\alpha_2 c_2 - \beta_1 c_1) + \Phi_1(x, y, z, t), \\
\qquad\qquad \cdots\cdots\cdots\cdots\cdots\cdots\cdots\cdots\cdots\cdots \\
F_r = (\beta_{r-1}c_{r-1} - \alpha_r c_r) + (\alpha_{r+1}c_{r+1} - \beta_r c_r) + \Phi_r(x, y, z, t), \\
\qquad\qquad\qquad\qquad\qquad\qquad r = 2,\ldots,R-1, \\
\qquad\qquad \cdots\cdots\cdots\cdots\cdots\cdots\cdots\cdots\cdots\cdots \\
F_R = (\beta_{R-1}c_{R-1} - \alpha_R c_R) + \Phi_R(x, y, z, t).
\end{cases}
\tag{1}
$$

Here u, v, and w are the components of the fluid velocity vector $\mathbf{U}$, given in units of m/sec; $w_{g,r}$ is the settling velocity of particles of type r (m/sec); μ_{hr} and μ_{vr} are, respectively, the horizontal and vertical diffusion coefficients of particles of type r (m^2/sec); α_r and β_r are the transformation rates of particles of type r into particles of types $(r-1)$ and $(r+1)$, respectively, $\alpha_r \geq 0$, $\beta_r \geq 0$ (m/sec); Φ_r is the power of sources of particles of type r type, (kg/(m^{3}s)).

The terms on the left-hand side of the first equation in system (1) (except for the time derivative) describe the advective transport of particles: their motion under the action of fluid flow and gravity. The terms on the right side describe the diffusion of suspensions and their transformation from one type into another.

We assume that the settling velocity $w_{g,r}$ of particles in the aquatic environment is constant when the forces of gravity and resistance are equal, i.e., $w_{g,r} \equiv$ const.

We search for a solution to system (1) in some given region $Q_T = G \times (0 < t \leq T]$. The closure of Q_T is $\bar{Q}_T = \bar{G} \times [0 \leq t \leq T]$.

Taking into account the features of coastal systems, we assume that the coefficient μ_{hr} in a marine coastal system can be regarded as a constant ($\mu_{hr} =$ const), e10^3 m^2/s to 10^5 m^2/s. The coefficient μ_{vr} essentially depends on the spatial variables, primarily on the coordinate z, i.e., $\mu_{vr} = \mu_{vr}(x, y, z)$. The values of this coefficient are in the range from 10^{-1} m^2/s to $1\,$m^2/s.

We supplement Eq. (1) with initial conditions for $t = 0$:

$$
c_r(x, y, z, 0) = c_{r0}(x, y, z), \quad r = 1,\ldots,R, \quad (x, y, z) \in \bar{G},
\tag{2}
$$

and boundary conditions:
  – on the lateral surface of the parallelepiped G,

$$
c_r = \tilde{c}_r, \quad \tilde{c}_r = \text{const}, \quad r = 1,\ldots,R, \quad \text{if } (\mathbf{U}_G, \mathbf{n}) \leq 0,
\tag{3}
$$

$$
\frac{\partial c_r}{\partial \mathbf{n}} = 0, \quad r = 1,\ldots,R, \quad \text{if } (\mathbf{U}_G, \mathbf{n}) \geq 0,
\tag{4}
$$

where $\mathbf{n}$ is the outer normal vector to the boundary of the lateral surface of the region $\bar{G}$, $\mathbf{U}_G$ is the fluid velocity vector at the boundary of the lateral surface, and $\tilde{c}_r$ are known concentration values;

– on the lower face $\{0 \leq x \leq L_x,\, 0 \leq y \leq L_y,\, z = 0\}$ of the parallelepiped G (undisturbed free surface of the water body):

$$\frac{\partial c_r}{\partial z} = 0, \quad r = 1, \ldots, R; \tag{5}$$

– on the upper face $\{0 < x < L_x,\, 0 < y < L_y,\, z = L_z\}$ of the parallelepiped G (bottom surface):

$$\frac{\partial c_r}{\partial \mathbf{n}} = -\frac{w_{g,r}}{\mu_{vr}} c_r, \quad r = 1, \ldots, R. \tag{6}$$

The conditions for the well-posedness of problem (1)–(6) are studied in [16] under some smoothness conditions imposed upon the solution function, namely,

$$c_r(x, y, z, t) \in C^2(Q_T) \cap C(\overline{Q}_T), \quad \mathrm{grad}\, c_r \in C(\overline{Q}_T),$$

and the necessary smoothness of the domain boundary.

3   Construction of Schemes for the Suspension Transport Problem: Explicit-Implicit and Splitting Schemes

We now consider the explicit-implicit scheme. Let us rewrite the first equation in system (1) as

$$\frac{\partial c_r}{\partial t} = A c_r + f_r(x, y, z, t), \quad (x, y, z) \in G,\ 0 < t \leq T, \tag{7}$$

where $A c_r$ is an elliptic differential operator in space variables with lower derivatives for which the following representation holds:

$$A c_r = (A_{12} + A_3)\, c_r,$$

$$A_{12} c_r = -\frac{1}{2} \left(u \frac{\partial c_r}{\partial x} + v \frac{\partial c_r}{\partial y} + \frac{\partial (u c_r)}{\partial x} + \frac{\partial (v c_r)}{\partial y} \right)$$
$$+ \frac{\partial}{\partial x} \left(\mu_{hr} \frac{\partial c_r}{\partial x} \right) + \frac{\partial}{\partial y} \left(\mu_{hr} \frac{\partial c_r}{\partial y} \right),$$

$$A_3 c_r = -\frac{1}{2} \left((w + w_{g,r}) \frac{\partial c_r}{\partial z} + \frac{\partial}{\partial z} \left((w + w_{g,r})\, c_r \right) \right) + \frac{\partial}{\partial z} \left(\mu_{vr} \frac{\partial c_r}{\partial z} \right).$$

If the advective transport of suspended particles is described in the so-called symmetric form [17,18], the operator can be expressed as

$$\frac{1}{2} \left[u \frac{\partial c_r^n}{\partial x} + v \frac{\partial c_r^n}{\partial y} + (w + w_{g,r}) \frac{\partial c_r^n}{\partial z} + \frac{\partial (u c_r^n)}{\partial x} + \frac{\partial (v c_r^n)}{\partial y} + \frac{\partial ((w + w_{g,r}) c_r^n)}{\partial z} \right].$$

This expression allows constructing, as a result of discretization, a difference operator of advective transfer that has the property of skew symmetry.

Let us build a uniform grid ω_τ in the time interval $0 \leq t \leq T$:

$$\omega_\tau = \{t_n = n\tau, \ n = 0, 1, \ldots, N, \ N\tau = T\}$$

We construct in the region $\overline{G}$ a connected grid $\overline{\omega}_h$ expressed as the Cartesian product of three one-dimensional grids along the coordinate directions Ox, Oy, Oz:

$$\overline{\omega}_h = \overline{\omega}_x \times \overline{\omega}_y \times \overline{\omega}_z,$$
$$\overline{\omega}_x = \{x_i : x_i = ih_x, \ i = 0, 1, \ldots, N_x, \ N_x h_x \equiv L_x\},$$
$$\overline{\omega}_y = \{y_j : y_j = jh_x, \ j = 0, 1, \ldots, N_y, \ N_y h_y \equiv L_y\},$$
$$\overline{\omega}_z = \{z_k : z_k = kh_x, \ k = 0, 1, \ldots, N_z, \ N_z h_z \equiv L_z\}.$$

We denote the sets of the internal grid nodes of $\overline{\omega}_h$, $\overline{\omega}_x$, $\overline{\omega}_y$, and $\overline{\omega}_z$ by ω_h, ω_x, ω_y, and ω_z, respectively.

Next, we consider an explicit-implicit approximation. On the spatial-temporal grid $\omega_{\tau h} = \omega_\tau \times \omega_h$, we approximate problems (7) and (2)–(6) on grids with an assignment at nodes shifted by half the grid step speeds and along the corresponding coordinate direction.

After the discretization on the grid $\omega_{\tau h}$, we arrive at the system of three-point difference equations

$$\frac{\overline{c}_r^{n+1}}{\tau} + A_3 \overline{c}_r^{n+1} = \frac{\overline{c}_r^n}{\tau} - A_{12} \overline{c}_r^n + f_r, \quad n = 1, \ldots, N. \tag{8}$$

which can be implemented independently for a given value of the time layer and all grid nodes $\omega_x \times \omega_y$ by sequential tridiagonal matrix algorithm [19, 20].

Here and below, the dash over the function c_r^n means that it belongs to the class of grid functions, while the function c_r^n is considered a sufficiently smooth function of continuous variables.

To examine the restrictions imposed upon the constructed scheme (8) on the upper time layer of the grid $\omega_{\tau h}$, we consider the canonical form [17] of the grid equation, namely,

$$A(P)Y(P) = \sum_{\substack{Q_m \in \omega'(P) \\ m=1,2}} B(P, Q_m)Y(Q_m) + F(P), \quad P \in \omega_{\tau h},$$

$$P \equiv (x_i, y_j, z_k), \ Y(P) \equiv \overline{c}_r^n(x_i, y_j, z_k). \tag{9}$$

The values of the coefficients $A(P)$ and $B(P, Q_m)$, $m = 1, 2$, and the rightmost terms $F(P)$ are generated separately for the internal and boundary nodes. It should be noted that the values of the components $(u, v, w + w_{g,r})$ determined at half-integer grid nodes in the hydrodynamic block of the model are involved in the construction of all coefficients of grid Eq. (9).

Equation (10) should be supplemented with boundary conditions formulated for the grid function $Y(P)$, $P \in \overline{\omega}_h \backslash \omega_h$, and consistent with conditions (3)–(6).

Focusing on the difference scheme (10) for $\bar{c}_r^n$ and taking into account the relations for the internal nodes of the grid $\bar{\omega}_h$, we can write the following relations:

$$A\left(P\right) = \frac{1}{\tau} + \frac{1}{h_z^2}\left(\mu_{hr}\left(x_i, y_j, z_k + 0.5h_z\right) + \mu_{vr}\left(x_i, y_j, z_k - 0.5h_z\right)\right).$$

$$B\left(P, Q_1\right) = -\frac{w^{n+1}\left(x_i, y_j, z_k - 0.5h_z\right) + w_{g,r}}{2h_z} + \frac{\mu_{vr}\left(x_i, y_j, z_k - 0.5h_z\right)}{h_z^2}, \quad (10)$$

$$B\left(P, Q_2\right) = \frac{w^{n+1}\left(x_i, y_j, z_k + 0.5h_z\right) + w_{g,r}}{2h_z} + \frac{\mu_{vr}\left(x_i, y_j, z_k + 0.5h_z\right)}{h_z^2}.$$

We require that the coefficients $B\left(P, Q_1\right)$ and $B\left(P, Q_2\right)$ in (10) be positive with some "tolerance". Thus we obtain the following sufficient conditions for the positivity of the coefficients:

$$\frac{\left|w^n\left(x_i, y_j, z_k - 0.5h_z\right) + w_{g,r}\right| h_z}{\mu_{vr}\left(x_i, y_j, z_k - 0.5h_z\right)} \leq 1, \quad (11)$$

$$\frac{\left|w^n\left(x_i, y_j, z_k + 0.5h_z\right) + w_{g,r}\right| h_z}{\mu_{vr}\left(x_i, y_j, z_k + 0.5h_z\right)} \leq 1. \quad (12)$$

Conditions (11) and (12) imply a restriction upon the grid Péclet number, which ensures the correctness of the application of the tridiagonal matrix method [19], namely,

$$Pe_{hz}^{n+1}\left(x, y, z + 0.5h_z\right) \equiv \max_{(x,y,z)\in\omega_h} = \frac{\left|w_r'^{n+1}(x, y, z \pm 0.5h_z)\right| h_z}{\mu_{vr}(x, y, z \pm 0.5h_z)} \leq 1. \quad (13)$$

To study the stability and convergence of the difference scheme, we need to estimate the coefficient

$$D(P) \equiv A(P) - B(P, Q_1) - B(P, Q_2), \quad P \in \omega_h.$$

The estimate of the time step, which follows from the condition $D\left(P\right) > 0$ in the "worst" case, leads to the following inequality:

$$\tau \leq \frac{h_z}{\left|w^{n+1}(x_i, y_j, z_k - 0.5h_z) + w_{g,r}\right|}, \quad (x_i, y_j, z_k) \in \omega_h. \quad (14)$$

Inequality (14) expresses the Courant condition for the vertical component ($w + w_{g,r}$).

Let us estimate the admissible values of τ according to inequalities (13) and (14) as applied to coastal systems.

The characteristic values of the studied parameters are as follows:

$$h_z = (0.05\text{--}0.2) \text{ m},$$
$$\mu_{vr} = (0.1\text{--}1) \text{ m}^2/\text{s},$$
$$w + w_{g,r} = (10^{-4}\text{--}5 \cdot 10^{-3}) \text{ m/s}.$$

If we plug these values into (13), we see that it holds "with some tolerance". It is clear that these values of τ are just approximative. However, it is worth noting that in numerous computational experiments involving problems of suspension transport dynamics, we could corroborate the verisimilitude of the obtained estimates, including those for the time step τ.

Let us note some features of the discrete-model numerical implementation that stem from the explicit approximation of the operator of convective-diffusion transfer along the horizontal coordinate directions (that is, A_{12}), in particular, the stability conditions.

For the sake of simplicity, consider the scheme

$$\frac{\bar{c}_r^{n+1} - \bar{c}_r^n}{\tau} + A_{12}\bar{c}_r^n = 0. \tag{15}$$

From the sufficient condition for the stability of scheme (15), we obtain the following constraint on the time step:

$$\tau \leq \frac{1}{\|A_{12}\|}. \tag{16}$$

The estimates (14)–(16) of the admissible step τ have the form $0.1 \text{ sec} < \tau \leq 1 \text{ sec}$, which means that the model can be used for grids with "moderate" numbers of nodes in the horizontal directions (from 10^2 to 10^3 nodes) for simulated time intervals of several hours. We also consider an additive unconditionally stable splitting scheme, specifically, an implicit two-dimensional–one-dimensional splitting scheme that can be expressed as

$$\frac{\bar{c}_r^{n+1/2} - \bar{c}_r^n}{0.5\tau} = A_{12}\bar{c}_r^n + A_3\bar{c}_r^{n+1/2} + F_r^1, \quad n = 0, 1, \ldots, N-1,$$

$$\frac{\bar{c}_r^{n+1} - \bar{c}_r^{n+1/2}}{0.5\tau} = A_{12}\bar{c}_r^{n+1} + A_3\bar{c}_r^{n+1/2} + F_r^2, \quad n = 1, \ldots, N, \tag{17}$$

$$F_r \equiv F_r^1 + F_r^2.$$

Similarly to the previous one, we can obtain estimates of the admissible time step that can vary from several tens to several hundreds of seconds in coastal systems. This means that the constructed scheme can be applied to real-life problems.

4   Construction of Parallel Algorithms for Computing 2D Problems

We now consider the organization of parallel computing when solving the original problem based on scheme (17). The main computational costs are associated with the solution of two-dimensional grid problems of diffusion-convection

$$\bar{c}_r^{n+1} - 0.5\tau A_{12}\bar{c}_r^{n+1} = \bar{c}_r^{n+1/2} + 0.5\tau A_3\bar{c}_r^{n+1/2} + F_r^2, \quad n = 1, \ldots, N. \tag{18}$$

Let us write the iterative formula of the Seidel method for two-dimensional grid equations of diffusion-convection. To simplify the notations, we set

$$q_{i,j} \equiv q(x_i, y_j) \equiv \bar{c}_r^{n+1}(x_i, y_j, z_k) \tag{19}$$

for fixed values of r, n, $n+1$, and z_k.

If we introduce the iteration number s, then the iterative formula of the Seidel method for Eq. (18) bearing in mind the notation (19) can be written as

$$
\begin{aligned}
q_{i,j}^{s+1} + 0.5\tau &\left[\left(u(x_{i+1/2}, y_j)q_{i+1,j}^s - u(x_{i-1/2}, y_j)q_{i-1,j}^{s+1} \right) \frac{1}{2h_x} \right. \\
&+ \left(v(x_i, y_{j+1/2})q_{i,j+1}^s - v(x_i, y_{j-1/2})q_{i,j-1}^{s+1} \right) \frac{1}{2h_y} \\
&- \mu_h (q_{i+1,j}^s - 2q_{i,j}^{s+1} + q_{i-1,j}^{s+1}) \frac{1}{h_x^2} \\
&\left. - \mu_h (q_{i,j+1}^s - 2q_{i,j}^{s+1} + q_{i,j-1}^{s+1}) \frac{1}{h_y^2} \right] = \tilde{F}_{i,j}^2, \tag{20}
\end{aligned}
$$

where

$$
\begin{aligned}
u(x_{i\pm1/2}, y_j) &\equiv u^{n+1}(x_{i\pm1/2}, y_j, z_k), \\
v(x_i, y_{j\pm1/2}) &\equiv v^{n+1}(x_i, y_{j\pm1/2}, z_k), \\
\tilde{F}_{i,j}^2 &= F_r^2(x_i, y_j, z_k) + \bar{c}_r^{n+1/2}(x_i, y_j, z_k) \\
+0.5\tau[((w^{n+1/2} &+ w_{g,r})(x_i, y_j, z_{k+1/2})\bar{c}_r^{n+1/2}(x_i, y_j, z_{k+1}) \\
-(w^{n+1/2} &+ w_{g,r})(x_i, y_j, z_{k-1/2})c_r^{n+1/2}(x_i, y_j, z_{k-1}))\frac{1}{2h_z} \\
+\frac{1}{h_z}(\frac{1}{h_z}(\mu_v(x_i, y_j, & z_{k+1/2})\bar{c}_r^{n+1/2}(x_i, y_j, z_{k+1}) - \bar{c}_r^{n+1/2}(x_i, y_j, z_k)) \\
-\frac{1}{h_z}(\mu_v(x_i, y_j, & z_{k-1/2})\bar{c}_r^{n+1/2}(x_i, y_j, z_k) - \bar{c}_r^{n+1/2}(x_i, y_j, z_{k-1})))].
\end{aligned} \tag{21}
$$

For the sake of simplicity, we consider boundary conditions of the first kind for system (20), (21). After expressing $q_{i,j}^{s+1}$ from relation (20), we obtain the calculation formula of the Seidel method.

If the time step is correctly chosen according to the condition

$$
\tau \leq \frac{\min(h_x, h_y)}{\max\limits_{\omega_h}|u_{i\pm1/2,j,k}^{n+1}| + \max\limits_{\omega_h}|v_{i,j\pm1/2,k}^{n+1}|},
$$

then the Seidel method converges exponentially.

Let us consider the organization of calculations.

Decompose the two-dimensional computational domain on the grid $\omega_x \times \omega_y$ with respect to spatial variables x, y.

Denote by σ^l the subdomain number l, $0 \leq l \leq p-1$, where p is the number of subdomains into which the original domain has been decomposed.

At the internal nodes of the grid, the values of the grid concentrations $q_{i,j}$ are determined for $i \in \overline{1, N_x - 2}$ and $j \in \overline{1, N_y - 2}$. The calculated nodes of the region σ^l are the elements $q_{i,j}^l$ for $i \in \overline{1, N_x - 2}$ and $j \in \overline{1, N_2^s - 2}$. When splitting the original region, we pay attention to the fact that adjacent regions σ^l and σ^{l+1} intersect at two nodes in the direction perpendicular to the splitting lines, and equalities $u_{i,N_2^l-2}^l = u_{i,0}^{l+1}$, $u_{i,N_2^l-1}^l = u_{i,1}^{l+1}$ hold.

To represent a value q in the vector form, we associate a pair of indices i, j with the value m which describes the ordinal number of the element of the vector q, that is, $m = i + jN_x$, where $0 \leq m \leq n - 1$, and n is the length of vector $q = (q_0, q_1, \ldots, q_{n-1})^\top$.

We need to know two parameters for each subdomain σ^l, obtained by decomposition of the computational domain, namely, the initial index $j = N_1^l$ within the initial computational domain and the width of the N_2^l subdomain. The index number N_1^l, from which the corresponding fragment of the computational domain begins, can be calculated by the formula $N_1^s = \lfloor l(N_y - 2)/p \rfloor$, where $\lfloor x \rfloor$ is the floor function, which is defined as the greatest integer less than or equal to x. Below we will also need the ceiling function $\lceil x \rceil$, defined as the least integer greater than or equal to x. The width of the subregion σ^l along the axis Oy can be calculated by the formula $N_2^l = \lfloor (l + 1)(N_y - 2)/p \rfloor - N_1^l + 2$.

We will use the following parameters for assessing the complexity of the operations required to solve the systems: t_a denotes the time of execution of an arithmetic operation, t_{lat} is the time of organization of data transmission (latency), and t_x is the time needed for the transmission of a unit of data.

Figure 1 shows the graph of the dependence of the transfer time versus the volume of transmitted data between the nodes of the K60 computer system, installed at the Keldysh Institute of Applied Mathematics of the Russian Academy of Sciences (KIAM RAS). We see that the graph has a peak when the amount of transmitted data is approximately 512 floating-point numbers. Let us denote this value by $N_{\max} = 512$.

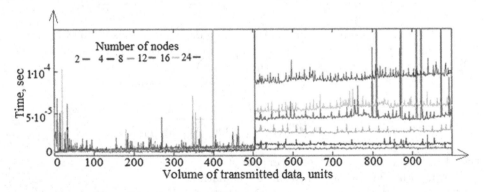

Fig. 1. The dependence of the data transmission time versus the volume of transmitted data for different numbers of computing nodes of the K60 computer system (KIAM RAS)

The calculation of data on a multiprocessor computer system can significantly reduce the computation time. Alas, we can not always expect high time efficiency from a computing system. In this case, it is correct to conduct a theoretical analysis of the computation time based on regression analysis.

Consider a multiple regression model. The vector t_{lat} is the total operating time of the computing system (in seconds), and vectors n and p are the explanatory factors, namely, the amount of transmitted data and the number of computing nodes used. The formula for the latency is as follows:

$$t_{\text{lat}}(p, n) = \begin{cases} 5.21 \times 10^{-6} + 1.53 \times 10^{-7}p \text{ if } n \leq 512, \\ 6.733 \times 10^{-6}p \text{ if } n > 512. \end{cases}$$

For the transmission time of a packet with a single element, we have $t_x = 3.3 \times 10^{-9}$ s.

The time spent on one iteration in the case of the sequential version of the algorithm is expressed as

$$t = 21t_a \left(N_x - 2\right)\left(N_y - 2\right).$$

When the parallel algorithm performs on a multiprocessor computer system, the calculation time is

$$t = 21t_a(N_x - 2) \max_l(N_2^l - 2) + 2(t_{\text{lat}}(p, N_x - 2) + (N_x - 2)t_x),$$

$$\left\lfloor \frac{N_y - 2}{p} \right\rfloor \leq \max_l(N_2^l - 2) \leq \left\lceil \frac{N_y - 2}{p} \right\rceil, \quad \max_l N_2^l \approx \frac{N_y - 2}{p}.$$

If the amount of transmitted data is greater than $N_x - 2 > N_{\max}$, then $k = \frac{N_x - 2}{N_{\max}}$ exchanges are performed, and the time spent by the parallel algorithm is

$$t = 21t_a \frac{(N_x - 2)(N_y - 2)}{p} + 2\left(t_{\text{lat}}\left(p, \left\lceil \frac{N_x - 2}{k} \right\rceil\right)k + (N_x - 2)t_x\right).$$

Thus the speedup of the parallel algorithm is expressed as

$$S_p = \frac{21pt_a(N_x - 2)(N_y - 2)}{21t_a(N_x - 2)(N_y - 2) + 2p\left(t_{\text{lat}}\left(p, \left\lceil \frac{N_x - 2}{k} \right\rceil\right)k + (N_x - 2)t_x\right)}.$$

Figure 2 shows the results of the parallel version of the algorithm for several numbers of processors with a variable decomposition of the computational domain. We see here two graphs: that of the speedup of the parallel version of the algorithm with splitting into two-dimensional explicit and one-dimensional implicit schemes based on MPI technology and that of the linear speedup versus the number of computers involved (taking into account various options for the decomposition of the computational domain). The maximum number of calculators used was 24, while the computational-grid size was $1000 \times 1000 \times 60$ nodes.

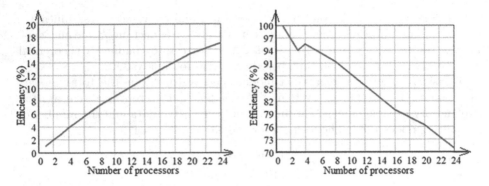

Fig. 2. The results of the parallel version of the algorithm for several numbers of processors with various decompositions of the computational domain

The efficiency of parallel programs on systems with distributed memory essentially depends on the communication environment. A reasonably complete communication environment is characterized by two parameters: the bandwidth, which determines the number of bytes transmitted per unit of time, and the latency. Communication operations are much slower than accessing local memory; therefore, the most efficient parallel programs are those with the minimum number of exchanges.

5   Numerical Experiments for the Simulation of Suspended Matter Transport

We consider the results of the software implementation of the mathematical model of suspended matter transport in a river mouth or estuary.

The input data for the water region and the suspended matter are the following: the length of the water body is 50 m; its width is 50 m; its depth is 2 m; the flow velocity is 0.2 m/s; the suspension sedimentation rate (according to Stokes) is 2.042 mm/s; the density of fresh water under normal conditions is 1000 kg kg/m^3; the suspended matter density is 2700 kg kg/m^3; the volume fraction of the suspended matter is 1/17.

The computational domain parameters are the following: the step along the horizontal spatial coordinates is 0.5 m; the step along the vertical spatial coordinate is 0.1 m; the calculation interval is 15 min; the time step is 0.25 s.

Figure 3 shows the geometry of the computational domain as a depth map.

Figures 4 and 5 depict the simulation results for the process of suspended matter transfer by mixing and flow of the water in the mouth of a river assuming a significant density gradient of the aquatic environment. The graph in Fig. 4 describes the average concentration versus depth. The graphs in Fig. 5 show the density in the section cut by the plane parallel to Oxz that passes through the center of the computational domain (at $y = 25$ m). In these figures, to the right

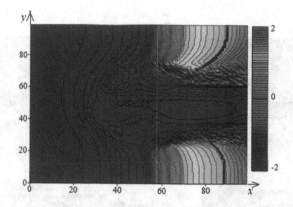

Fig. 3. Depth map of the computational domain

of the vertical cut, we can see the change in concentration of suspended matter in the stratified layers of the aquatic environment as the density changes with time.

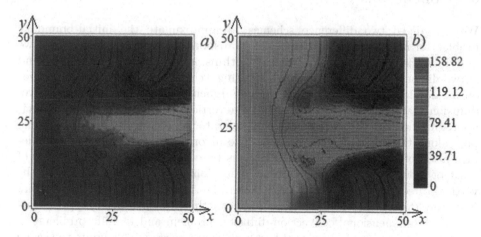

Fig. 4. The concentration of suspended matter in the aquatic environment: a) after 1 min of the estimated time; b) after 15 min of the estimated time

The developed software package can be used to calculate the transfer for both heavy particles and particles lighter than water.

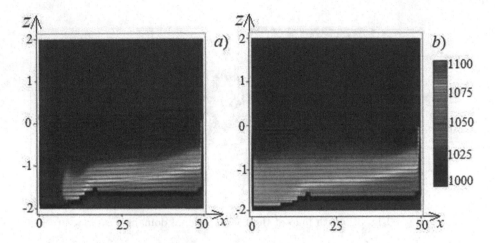

Fig. 5. The density field of the aquatic environment: a) after 1 min of the estimated time; b) after 15 min of the estimated time

6   Conclusions

We considered two difference schemes to approximate the initial-boundary problem of multicomponent suspension transport in coastal systems. Also, we described the corresponding parallel algorithms: an explicit-implicit scheme and a two-dimensional–one-dimensional splitting scheme. The first scheme relies on an implicit approximation for the one-dimensional operator of convective-diffusion transport and settling along the vertical coordinate and an explicit approximation for the two-dimensional operator of convective-diffusion transport along the horizontal coordinates. The algorithm for the numerical implementation of the explicit-implicit scheme is based on the sequential solution of a set of independent three-point (one-dimensional) difference problems in the vertical direction. This scheme leads to an algorithm with natural parallelism. However, the admissible time step—for both the explicit scheme approximating the two-dimensional convection-diffusion problem and real-life problems in coastal systems—is of the order of hundredths of a second. This limits the scope of the scheme for grids with "moderate" numbers of nodes in the horizontal directions for simulated time intervals of several tens of minutes.

Also, we considered another scheme, a two-dimensional–one-dimensional additive splitting scheme, which made it possible to replace the original problem with a chain of implicit two-dimensional horizontal and implicit vertical one-dimensional tasks. This allowed us to increase the admissible time step up to several hundred seconds and, at the same time, reduce interprocessor exchanges, which, for "classical" one-dimensional splitting schemes, become predominant compared to the execution time of computational operations (for example, in the numerical implementation of three-point difference equations by the sweep method on fractional time layers).

We also present the results of numerical experiments involving the constructed algorithms, implemented as a complex of parallel programs for the K60 computer system at the KIAM RAS. The experiments yielded acceptable values of speedup and efficiency (more than 70%) on a relatively moderate number of computers (up to 24). This supports the application of the constructed program package for the operational forecast of pollution in coastal systems.

References

1. Yan, H., et al.: Numerical investigation of particles' transport, deposition and resuspension under unsteady conditions in constructed stormwater ponds. Environ. Sci. Eur. **32**(1), 1–17 (2020). https://doi.org/10.1186/s12302-020-00349-y
2. Shams, M., Ahmadi, G., Smith, D.H.: Computational modeling of flow and sediment transport and deposition in meandering rivers. Adv. Water Resour. **25**(6), 689–699 (2002). https://doi.org/10.1016/S0309-1708(02)00034-9
3. Battisacco, E., Franca, M.J., Schleiss, A.J.: Sediment replenishment: influence of the geometrical configuration on the morphological evolution of channel-bed. Wat. Resour. Res. **52**(11), 8879–8894 (2016). https://doi.org/10.1002/2016WR019157
4. Liu, X., Qi, S., Huang, Y., Chen, Yu., Du, P.: Predictive modeling in sediment transportation across multiple spatial scales in the Jialing river Basin of China. Int. J. Sedim. Res. **30**(3), 250–255 (2015). https://doi.org/10.1016/j.ijsrc.2015.03.013
5. Cao, L., et al.: Factors controlling discharge-suspended sediment hysteresis in karst basins, southwest China: implications for sediment management. J. Hydrol. **594**, 125792 (2021). https://doi.org/10.1016/j.jhydrol.2020.125792
6. Serra, T., Soler, M., Barcelona, A., Colomer, J.: Suspended sediment transport and deposition in sediment-replenished artificial floods in Mediterranean rivers. J. Hydrol. **609**, 127756 (2022). https://doi.org/10.1016/j.jhydrol.2022.127756
7. Haddadchi, A., Hicks, M.: Interpreting event-based suspended sediment concentration and flow hysteresis patterns. J. Soils Sed. **21**(1), 592–612 (2020). https://doi.org/10.1007/s11368-020-02777-y
8. Jirka, G.H.: Large scale flow structures and mixing processes in shallow flows. J. Hydr. Res. **39**(6), 567–573 (2001). https://doi.org/10.1080/00221686.2001.9628285
9. Lin, B., Falconer, R.A.: Numerical modelling of three-dimensional suspended sediment for estuarine and coastal waters. J. Hydraul. Res. **34**(4), 435–456 (1996). https://doi.org/10.1080/00221689609498470
10. Murillo, J., Burguete, J., Brufau, P., García-Navarro, P.: Coupling between shallow water and solute flow equations: analysis and management of source terms in 2D. Int. J. Numer. Meth. Fluids **49**(3), 267–299 (2005). https://doi.org/10.1002/fld.992
11. Thomé, V., Vasudeva, Murthy, A. S.: An explicit-implicit splitting method for a convection-diffusion problem. Comput. Methods Appl. Math. **19**(2), 283–293 (2019). https://doi.org/10.1515/cmam-2018-0018
12. Ngondiep, E., Tedjani, A.H.: Unconditional stability and fourth-order convergence of a two-step time split explicit/implicit scheme for two-dimensional nonlinear unsteady convection diffusion-reaction equation with variable coefficients. Mathematics **8**, 1034 (2020). https://doi.org/10.21203/rs.3.rs-2380601/v1
13. Vabishchevich, P.N.: Additive Schemes (splitting Schemes) for Systems of Partial Derivative Equations. Numer. Methods Program. (Vychislitel'nye Metody i Programmirovanie), **11**, 1–6 (2009)

14. Sukhinov, A.I., Chistyakov, A.E., Protsenko, E.A., Sidoryakina, V.V., Protsenko, S.V.: Parallel algorithms for solving the problem of coastal bottom relief dynamics. Numer. Methods Program. **21**(3), 196–206 (2020)
15. Sidoryakina, V.V., Sukhinov, A.I.: Well-posedness analysis and numerical implementation of a linearized two-dimensional bottom sediment transport problem. Comput. Math. Math. Phys. **57**(6), 978–994 (2017). https://doi.org/10.1134/S0965542517060124
16. Sukhinov, A.I., Sukhinov, A.A., Sidoryakina, V.V.: Uniqueness of solving the problem of transport and sedimentation of multicomponent suspensions in coastal systems structures. In: IOP Conference Series: Journal of Physics: Conference Series, vol. 1479, no. 1, p. 012081 (2020)
17. Samarskii, A.A., Vabishchevich, P.N.: Numerical Methods for Solving Convection-Diffusion Problems. M.: Editorial (2004)
18. Vabishchevich, P.N.: Additive Operator-Difference Schemes (Splitting Schemes). De Gruyter, Berlin, Germany (2013)
19. Samarskii, A.A.: The Theory of Difference Schemes. Basel, Marcel Dekker Inc, New York (2001)
20. Samarskii, A.A., Gulin, A.V.: Numerical Methods in Mathematical Physics. Nauchnyimir, Moscow (2003)

Parallel Numerical Implementation of Three-Dimensional Mathematical Models of Hydrodynamics Taking into Account Vertical Turbulent Exchange

Elena A. Protsenko[1] , Alexander I. Sukhinov[2] ,
and Sofya V. Protsenko[1]([⊠])

[1] A. P. Chekhov Taganrog Institute (Branch of Rostov State University
of Economics), Taganrog, Russian Federation
{eapros,rab55555}@rambler.ru
[2] Don State Technical University, Rostov-on-Don, Russian Federation

Abstract. The article is devoted to the development, research, and parallel numerical implementation of three-dimensional mathematical models of hydrodynamics. The model is improved by adding a new method for computing the turbulent exchange coefficient in the vertical direction for shallow water bodies, refined as a result of a significant amount of expedition data records. The 3D mathematical model of wave processes is based on the Navier–Stokes equations of motion in regions with dynamically changing geometry of the computational domain. The three main indicators for evaluating computational efficiency are: speedup ratio, parallel efficiency and time saving ratio. The most important parameter is scalability, which is evaluated using the other three parameters as metrics. This study evaluates the comparative analysis of 28 threads compared to sequential computations with a single thread, which demonstrates the scalability of SWAN depending on the number of computational threads. Also, we consider the parallel implementation of three-dimensional mathematical models of hydrodynamics.

Keywords: 3D mathematical models of hydrodynamics · Turbulent exchange coefficient · Numerical simulation · Parallel numerical implementation

1 Introduction

In the modern world, there is a noticeable trend toward the integration of the mathematical apparatus with cutting-edge computing technologies to minimize time and computational costs when solving problems from various spheres associated with the human impact upon the environment, be it natural or

The study was financially supported by the Russian Science Foundation (Project № 23-21-00210, https://rscf.ru/project/23-21-00210/).

© The Author(s), under exclusive license to Springer Nature Switzerland AG 2023
L. Sokolinsky and M. Zymbler (Eds.): PCT 2023, CCIS 1868, pp. 259–268, 2023.
https://doi.org/10.1007/978-3-031-38864-4_18

technological. The key point in this process is the combination of this factor into a holistic computational process capable of large-scale physical modeling. The development of mathematical modeling methods currently requires a wide range of field experiments for verification. Yet, when modeling hydrodynamic processes, difficulties arise with the choice of the acceptable level of description for their dynamics and forecasts [1,2]. The solution to this issue can be the development and improvement of technologies for conducting model and field studies, taking into account the multiscale effect.

Major scientific schools around the world are currently engaged in the modeling of hydrodynamic wave processes. Many researchers have used numerical models based on CFD (Computational Fluid Dynamics) to study several types of nondestructive and destructive waves [3]. Below we dwell upon some advantages and disadvantages of modern wind-wave models.

Wind-wave models of the third generation, such as WAM, SWAN, and Wave-Watch, give realistic forecasts consistent with data obtained through analytical, numerical, and experimental approaches. Nevertheless, they also have several significant drawbacks. For instance, they require high-resolution bathymetry, and inaccurate bathymetry can lead to imprecise refraction calculations, whose results can extend to areas where refraction as such is insignificant.

SWAN (Simulation Waves Nearshore) is a hydrodynamic model designed to predict waves in coastal waters. Since the model takes into account the interaction of waves with water currents, the main SWAN equation is the balance equation of spectral action. It is formulated in Cartesian and spherical coordinates to account for small and large calculations. Computations with SWAN can range from complex cases requiring a complete, time-dependent, two-dimensional equation of conservation of the momentum of motion in spherical coordinates to simple one-dimensional cases requiring only a stationary, one-dimensional equation of conservation of energy. SWAN provides transmission through obstacles, such as breakwaters and rocks, and reflection from them. The spatial-filtered Navier–Stokes (SFNS) model is designed to simulate the interaction of waves with complex coastal structures [4].

The model of coastal spectral waves based on the equation of the balance of wave action with the effect of diffraction (WANTED) is employed to simulate changes in the dynamics of random waves in complex bathymetry. The simulated wave field without taking into account coastal currents differs from experimental data, whereas the results of the model taking into account currents clearly reproduce the amplification of the wave height in front of concave coastlines [5].

Due to the situation today in the world, foreign research may not be available to Russian scientists. This is why the development of their own approaches to modeling is becoming more and more urgent. Despite the significant amount of research devoted to modern approaches to turbulence modeling at various scales (LES, hybrid RANS/LES, DES, SAS), their transformation into a global and comprehensive structure is required. It is necessary to study not only their theoretical features but also the possibility of practical implementation [6].

We describe in this paper the study and parallel numerical implementation of a 3D hydrodynamic model aimed at predicting the development and ecological design of coastal systems taking into account the impact of mechanisms of multiscale turbulent mixing. This model provides reliable and timely forecasts.

The problems considered in this paper are characterized by incomplete data, hence the issue of calibration and verification of the corresponding mathematical models. Our solution to this relies on incorporating data from field studies.

The paper is organized as follows. The introduction describes the existing models of hydrodynamics and substantiates the relevance of the study. Section 2 is devoted to the spatially inhomogeneous 3D model of wave hydrodynamics. In Sect. 3 is devoted to the parameterization of the vertical turbulent exchange, we use in this research the LES approach. Section 4 contains parallel implementation of wind-wave models of the third generation. Section 5 contains parallel implementation of 3D model of wave hydrodynamics. Section 6 is devoted to the numerical implementation of 3D model of wave hydrodynamics and the prediction of the aquatic environment motion. Conclusion summarizes the study and points directions for further work.

2 Spatially Inhomogeneous 3D Model of Wave Hydrodynamics in a Shallow Water Body

The spatially inhomogeneous 3D model of wave hydrodynamics includes the following parts:

– the Navier–Stokes equations of motion,

$$u'_t + uu'_x + vu'_y + wu'_z = -\frac{1}{\rho}P'_x + (\mu u'_x)'_x + (\mu u'_y)'_y + (\nu u'_z)'_z,$$

$$v'_t + uv'_x + vv'_y + wv'_z = -\frac{1}{\rho}P'_y + (\mu v'_x)'_x + (\mu v'_y)'_y + (\nu v'_z)'_z, \qquad (1)$$

$$w'_t + uw'_x + vw'_y + ww'_z = -\frac{1}{\rho}P'_z + (\mu w'_x)'_x + (\mu w'_y)'_y + (\nu w'_z)'_z + g;$$

– and the continuity equation,

$$\rho'_t + (\rho u)'_x + (\rho v)'_y + (\rho w)'_z = 0, \qquad (2)$$

where $V = \{u, v, w\}$ is the velocity vector of the water current in a shallow water body; ρ is the aquatic environment density; P is the hydrodynamic pressure; g is the gravitational acceleration; μ and ν are the coefficients of turbulent exchange in the horizontal and vertical directions, respectively; n is the normal vector to the surface describing the computational domain boundary [10–12];

– and also the boundary conditions

$$\mathbf{V} = \mathbf{V}_0, \quad P'_n = 0,$$

$$\rho\mu\,(\mathbf{V}_\tau)'_n = -\boldsymbol{\tau}, \quad \mathbf{V}_n = 0, \quad P'_n = 0,$$

$$(\mathbf{V}_\tau)'_n = 0, \quad \mathbf{V}_n = 0, \quad P'_n = 0,$$

$$\rho\mu\,(\mathbf{V}_\tau)'_n = -\boldsymbol{\tau}, \quad w = -\omega - P'_t/(\rho g), \quad P'_n = 0,$$

$$\rho\mu\,(\mathbf{V}_\tau)'_n = -\boldsymbol{\tau}, \quad w = 0, \quad P'_n = 0,$$

where ω is the liquid evaporation intensity; $\mathbf{V}_n$, $\mathbf{V}_\tau$ are the normal and tangential components of the velocity vector; $\boldsymbol{\tau} = \{\tau_x, \tau_y, \tau_z\}$ is the tangential stress vector.

A raster model of the computational domain is built on the basis of observations at individual points in space. Operational territorial units (OUT) serve as a base for representing spatial information in a raster data model [8]. The territory of the objects is completely covered by a regular grid. Figure 1 shows a raster model of the computational domain. The data for the raster model were the measurements provided by the cadastral survey at points with known coordinates. We understand the contour of the image as a spatially extended gap, a drop in level, or an abrupt change in brightness values. Currently, there are many algorithms, and only some are widely used thanks to their versatility [9].

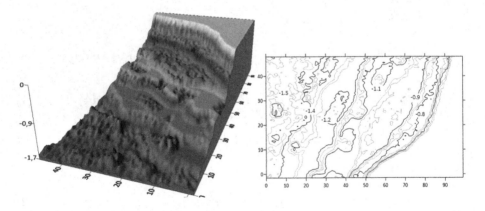

Fig. 1. The geometry of the calculated area

3   Parameterization of the Vertical Turbulent Exchange

We use in this research the LES approach, in which modern algebraic subgrid models are employed [8]. Also, the experimental evidence given here allows us to determine the vertical coefficient of turbulent exchange using parameterizations proposed by Belotserkovsky, Boussinesq, and Smagorinsky (Fig. 2).

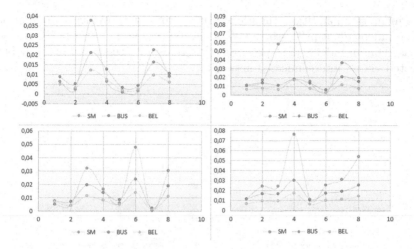

Fig. 2. Vertical turbulent exchange coefficient calculated based on various types of approximations for the parameterization of vertical turbulent mixing (horizontal values are given in m^2/s)

Based on the approaches described above to the computation of the coefficient of vertical turbulent exchange, we obtained distributions that are vertically inhomogeneous at all measurement points. The analysis showed that the parameterization results for all approaches were close in order of magnitude and also in the location of the peaks on the graphs. Based on the statistical analysis, we found that the coefficients obtained by Smagorinsky parameterization show the smallest standard deviation; moreover, under this parameterization, the hypothesis of the normality of the distribution is fulfilled in most cases.

4   Parallel Implementation of Wind-Wave Models of the Third Generation

For WAM, SWAN, and WaveWatch, the processes occurring in the aquatic environment are a black box. That is not the case for a three-dimensional model of hydrodynamics. We describe in this paper the study and parallel numerical implementation of a spatially inhomogeneous three-dimensional mathematical model aimed at predicting the development and ecological design of coastal systems taking into account the impact of mechanisms of multiscale turbulent mixing. It ensures the reliability and timeline of the corresponding forecasts [7].

The SWAN model is a third-generation wave prediction model developed at the Delft University of Technology. Since its initial release, this model has become a widely used and reliable tool for offshore and nearshore wave predictions. The parallel implementation of the SWAN software package is available in two versions (OpenMP and MPI). SWAN includes OpenMP compiler directives that tell the compiler how to generate multithreaded code on a computer with shared memory; in addition, the use of MPI technology provides communication between independent processors. SWAN can be run on a cluster of PC nodes as it is based on an independent processor that does not use shared memory but is connected via an interconnected network.

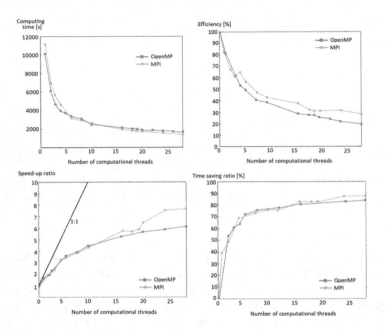

Fig. 3. The parallel computational efficiency of SWAN

All computations were performed on Intel Xeon E5-2670 computing nodes with a frequency of 2.3 GHz. Twenty-eight threads were employed. The main goal was to evaluate the scalability of the algorithm.

Figure 3 shows the scalability of SWAN, the MPI version is more efficient for all sizes of the computing area; this version is superior to the OMP version. Almost linear speedup is observed for small numbers of computational threads. The same results were obtained when using the time-saving factor. There is a clear and uniform alignment with numbers of flows exceeding approximately six.

5   Parallel Implementation of 3D Mathematical Models of Hydrodynamics

We carried out the parallel implementation of the algorithm based on the decomposition of the computational domain in two spatial directions using MPI. It allowed us to conduct a series of experiments on a multiprocessor computing system built on the basis of the OpenHPC open application stack and having 1440 processor cores at a frequency of 2.3 GHz and 10.24 TB of RAM.

The algorithm for distributing spatial propagation across individual processors provides load balance (for each time step) but does not guarantee that the communication is synchronized since not every computation on each processor requires the same effort. To avoid load imbalance, we employed nonblocking communication and added an array dimension, which provides an actively managed buffer space (Fig. 4).

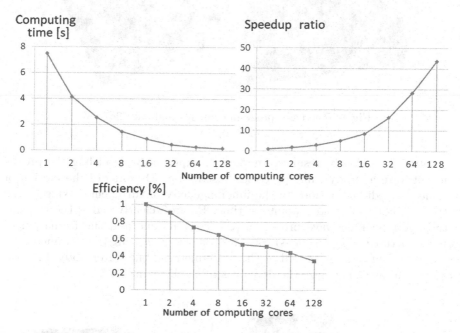

Fig. 4. The parallel computational efficiency of the 3D model of wave hydrodynamics

The following indicators were considered: speedup, parallel efficiency, and time savings on 128 nodes. The maximum speedup of 43.668 was attained on 128 processors. A drop in speedup was observed on 256 calculators. Figure 5 displays the indicators for evaluating the parallel computational efficiency of the 3D model of wave hydrodynamics depending on the number of processors. Thus the parallel implementation of the ATM algorithm can be efficiently used to solve problems of hydrodynamics on large numbers of nodes.

6   Results of the Numerical Experiments

The developed software package was used for the numerical implementation of the considered three-dimensional model of wave hydrodynamics and the prediction of the aquatic environment motion.

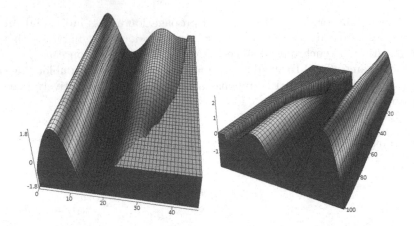

Fig. 5. The basic program elements and data flow

Figure 5 presents the results of numerical experiments modeling the propagation of wave hydrodynamic processes based on a 3D model of the motion of an aqueous medium considering the inhomogeneity of turbulent mixing in the vertical direction at various points in time. Figure 5 clearly shows the changes in the hydrodynamic wave process in the coastal zone and the formation of vortex structures. The developed software tools allow setting the parameters of the source of vibrations, as well as the bathymetry of the water body. Figure 6 provides a means to analyze the dynamics of the bottom relief.

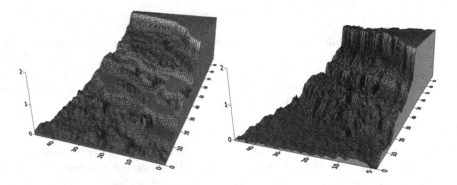

Fig. 6. Three-dimensional model of the aqueous medium motion

To verify the adequacy of the three-dimensional model, the computational results were compared with numerical and experimental data known to the authors of this study. We noted a good agreement with the results obtained on the main stages of propagation and collapse of the surface wave.

7   Conclusions

The paper presents the results of the mathematical modeling of three-dimensional wave processes in shallow water bodies taking into account the features of turbulent exchange. The optimal parameterization of the vertical turbulent exchange coefficient for the LES approach was used in the model. The initial modeling conditions were set based on the processing of remote sensing data converted into a raster model.

The main three indicators for evaluating the computational efficiency were speedup, time savings, and efficiency coefficients. The scalability was evaluated using the other three parameters as metrics. We carried out the parallel implementation of the 3D mathematical model of hydrodynamics. It can be efficiently used to solve problems of hydrodynamics on large numbers of calculators.

Also, we evaluated the performance on a single node against sequential computations using a single thread. This demonstrated the scalability of SWAN with respect to the number of computational threads. We found a clear and uniform alignment with numbers of flows exceeding approximately six.

References

1. Gushchin, V.A., Sukhinov, A.I., Nikitina, A.V., Chistyakov, A.E., Semenyakina, A.A.: A model of transport and transformation of biogenic elements in the coastal system and its numerical implementation. Comput. Math. Math. Phys. **58**(8), 1316–1333 (2018). https://doi.org/10.1134/S0965542518080092
2. Gushchin, V.A., Kostomarov, A.V., Matyushin, P.V., Pavlyukova, E.R.: Direct numerical simulation of the transitional separated fluid flows around a sphere and a circular cylinder. J. Wind Eng. Ind. Aerodyn. **90**(4–5), 341–358 (2002). https://doi.org/10.1016/S0167-6105(01)00196-9
3. Sukhinov, A.I., Chistyakov, A.E., Shishenya, A.V., Timofeeva, E.F.: Predictive modeling of coastal hydrophysical processes in multiple-processor systems based on explicit schemes. Math. Models Comput. Simul. **10**(5), 648–658 (2018). https://doi.org/10.1134/S2070048218050125
4. Protsenko, S., Sukhinova, T.: Mathematical modeling of wave processes and transport of bottom materials in coastal water areas taking into account coastal structures. In: MATEC Web of Conferences, vol. 132, p. 04002 (2017)
5. Alekseenko, E., Roux, B., et al.: Coastal hydrodynamics in a windy lagoon. Nonlinear Processes Geophys. **20**(2), 189–198 (2013). https://doi.org/10.1016/j.compfluid.2013.02.003
6. Alekseenko, E., Roux, B., et al.: Nonlinear hydrodynamics in a mediterranean lagoon. Comput. Math. Math. Phys. **57**(6), 978–994 (2017). https://doi.org/10.5194/npg-20-189-2013
7. Favorskaya, A.V., Petrov, I.B.: Numerical modeling of dynamic wave effects in rock masses. Dokl. Math. **95**(3), 287–290 (2017). https://doi.org/10.1134/S1064562417030139
8. Belotserkovskii, O.M., Gushchin, V.A., Shchennikov, V.V.: Decomposition method applied to the solution of problems of viscous incompressible fluid dynamics. Comput. Math. Math. Phys. **15**, 197–207 (1975)

9. Kvasov, I.E., Leviant, V.B., Petrov, I.B.: Numerical study of wave propagation in porous media with the use of the grid-characteristic method. Comput. Math. Math. Phys. **56**(9), 1620–1630 (2016). https://doi.org/10.1134/S0965542516090116

10. Sukhinov, A.I., Khachunts, D.S., Chistyakov, A.E.: A mathematical model of pollutant propagation in near-ground atmospheric layer of a coastal region and its software implementation. Comput. Math. Math. Phys. **55**(7), 1216–1231 (2015). https://doi.org/10.1134/S096554251507012X

11. Chetverushkin, B.N., Shilnikov, E.V.: Software package for 3D viscous gas flow simulation on multiprocessor computer systems. Comput. Math. Math. Phys. **48**(2), 295–305 (2008). https://doi.org/10.1007/s11470-008-2012-4

12. Davydov, A.A., Chetverushkin, B.N., Shil'nikov, E.V.: Simulating flows of incompressible and weakly compressible fluids on multicore hybrid computer systems. Comput. Math. Math. Phys. **50**(12), 2157–2165 (2010). https://doi.org/10.1134/S096554251012016X

13. Sukhinov, A.I., Nikitina, A.V., Semenyakina, A.A., Chistyakov, A.E.: Complex of models, explicit regularized schemes of high-order of accuracy and applications for predictive modeling of after-math of emergency oil spill. In: CEUR Workshop Proceedings, vol. 1576, pp. 308–319 (2016)

Comparison of Two Methods for Modeling the Dynamics of Gas Flows in a Protoplanetary Disk

Vitaliy Grigoryev$^{(\boxtimes)}$ (iD) and Tatiana Demidova (iD)

Crimean Astrophysical Observatory RAS, Crimea, Russian Federation
vitaliygrigoryev@crao.ru, proxima1@list.ru

Abstract. During the birth of a planetary system from a protoplanetary disk surrounding a young star, events such as collisions of formed dense gas and dust clumps, or the fall of such clumps of matter onto the disk from outside can occur in the disk itself. As a result of such events, a local increase in the density of matter is formed in the disk, which has a different velocity relative to the star than the surrounding matter. In this paper, we describe the numeric simulation of the evolution of a protoplanetary disk with the described heterogeneity, using for this two different approaches: the finite-volume method (PLUTO package) and the SPH method (Gadget-2 package). The computations were carried out in parallel mode. Based on the results obtained, we estimate the efficiency of parallelization at different stages of clump decay.

Keywords: T Tauri stars · Protoplanetary disks · Gas dynamics · Godunov methods · SPH

1 Introduction

T Tauri stars are classified as a separate class of variable stars [25] since they all have similar observational features. In addition to irregular brightness changes, emission lines are observed in the spectrum, and the stars are associated with dark gas and dust clouds. These features are related to the fact that these young stars are surrounded by gas-dust protoplanetary disks. It is assumed that most stars of less than 2 solar masses ($M_\odot$) pass through the T Tauri stage. A detailed description of this class of stars is given in the reviews [5,18,33]. The particular interest in this class of stars is associated with the fact that the Sun, at an early stage of its evolution, was a T Tauri type star, from the protoplanetary disk of which the Solar System was formed.

Studies of protoplanetary disks play an important role in the development of the theory of the formation of planetary systems. The substance of the protoplanetary disk at the beginning of its evolution contains mainly a gas component with a small admixture of dust ($\sim 1\%$). The dust and gas component of the protoplanetary disk acts as a building material for the planets, their satellites, and small bodies.

© The Author(s), under exclusive license to Springer Nature Switzerland AG 2023
L. Sokolinsky and M. Zymbler (Eds.): PCT 2023, CCIS 1868, pp. 269–284, 2023.
https://doi.org/10.1007/978-3-031-38864-4_19

Direct observations of protoplanetary disks have shown the presence of inhomogeneities on their surfaces, which are vortex-like structures, tightly wound spirals, two-armed spirals, and ring-like structures [6,21,22,32]. The discovery of asymmetries in protoplanetary disks has stimulated the development of a large number of models. In particular, their presence is associated with the motion of the unresolved planet [11–13,23,34,40], as well as the development of various kinds of instabilities [1,2,4,15,24,31,39,42] or global vertical magnetic fields [38].

However, there is a simpler mechanism for the formation of these types of structures associated with the rotation of the disk. For the first time, the assumption about the decay of a clump of matter in the gaseous rotating medium of a protoplanetary disk was proposed in [9], where it was assumed that a large amount of fine dust is released during a catastrophic asteroid collision. In addition, it was shown in [30] that a significant amount of fine dust can be ejected into the disk in the event of tidal disruption of the planet. However, in order to observe these processes, the mass of fine dust must be at least half the mass of the Moon.

In [10], the mechanism of cloudy accretion [19] was considered as a source of a massive clump of matter. The authors of the paper assumed that clumps of matter could fall onto the disk from the remnants of a protostellar cloud and studied the disintegration process of such a gas clump in the substance of a rotating disk. Calculations have shown that this mechanism makes it possible to explain all the observed features in the images of the protoplanetary disk within the framework of one model. In different phases of evolution, the clump is stretched into a vortex-like structure, which then twists into a spiral. Then, depending on the energy regime, a ring or a two-armed spiral is formed.

The fall of matter clumps onto a protoplanetary disk is a natural consequence of the formation of disks from a protostellar cloud. In [3,41], another mechanism for the formation of clumps wandering in space and capable of falling onto protoplanetary disks is described. The calculations of the authors showed that massive disks, as a result of gravitational instability, can throw out clumps of matter of a considerable mass. The invasion of such clumps into the protoplanetary disk significantly affects the dynamics of matter in the disk and can lead to the formation of new planets, as well as catastrophic events of destruction and ejection of planets from the system. However, the simulation of this process has currently been performed by only one method [10]. To verify the results, calculations by other methods are required.

The aim of this paper is to compare two approaches (implemented in two different packages) of hydrodynamical calculations. We solve the problem of the clump dissociation in the protoplanetary disk by two methods: the finite-volume (Godunov) scheme (PLUTO package [27]) and smoothed-particle hydrodynamics (SPH, Gadget-2 package [36,37]). The computation resolution was chosen similarly in both methods: 0.9×10^6 cells and 1×10^6 SPH particles. Both schemes can be used in parallel, which significantly speeds up the calculations and analysis of simulation results.

To start, we describe the mathematical model of the protoplanetary disk with the clump (equations, initial and boundary conditions) and give some essential commentaries on implementing this model in the packages. Then we describe the results of the simulations and compare them. Subsequently, we measure the efficiency of parallel computations in both packages and analyze the differences in simulation results and in efficiency measurements.

2   Model and Methods

The paper considers a model of a young solar-type star surrounded by an extended gaseous disk. At the initial moment, we placed a density perturbation in the disk; the value of the perturbation significantly exceeded the local value in the disk.

2.1   Basic Equations

We solved equations of nonstationary gas dynamics using two packages: PLUTO[1] [27] and Gadget-2[2] [36,37]. The packages were specially modified to calculate the hydrodynamics of protoplanetary disks[3] [8].

We calculated the time evolution of the density ρ, the velocity $\mathbf{v}$, and the pressure p by solving the equations of gas dynamics. To this end, we wrote the mass conservation equation as

$$\frac{\partial \rho}{\partial t} + \nabla \cdot (\rho \mathbf{v}) = 0, \tag{1}$$

and the Navier–Stokes equation

$$\frac{\partial(\rho \mathbf{v})}{\partial t} + \nabla \cdot \left(\rho \mathbf{v} \cdot \mathbf{v} - p\hat{I}\right)^T = -\rho \nabla \Phi + \nabla \cdot \Pi(\nu), \tag{2}$$

where $\hat{I}$ is the identity matrix, $\Phi = -GM_*/R$ is the gravitational potential on the star (G is the gravitational constant, M_* is the stellar mass, and R is the distance to the star), and $\Pi(\nu)$ is the viscous-stress tensor.

We used PLUTO to solve the energy conservation equation

$$\frac{\partial(\varepsilon_t + \rho\Phi)}{\partial t} + \nabla \cdot [(\varepsilon_t + p + \rho\Phi)\,\mathbf{v}] = \nabla \cdot (\mathbf{v} \cdot \Pi(\nu)). \tag{3}$$

Here the total energy density $\varepsilon_t = \rho\epsilon + \rho\mathbf{v}^2/2$ depends on the specific internal energy ϵ. We employed the ideal-gas approximation $p = \rho\epsilon(\gamma - 1)$ with $\gamma = 5/3$ for PLUTO and 7/5 for Gadget-2. As calculations confirmed, the best qualitative agreement of the density distribution is achieved with this choice of the parameter γ.

---

[1] http://plutocode.ph.unito.it/.
[2] https://wwwmpa.mpa-garching.mpg.de/gadget/.
[3] https://github.com/Proxima84/DUSTGADGET.

The entropy equation

$$\frac{\partial S}{\partial t} = \frac{1}{2}\frac{\gamma - 1}{\rho^{\gamma - 1}}\nabla \cdot (\mathbf{v} \cdot \Pi(\nu)),\tag{4}$$

where $S = p/\rho^\gamma$ is the entropy, was solved with Gadget-2.

The viscous stress tensor is defined as

$$\Pi(\nu) = \nu_1 \left[\nabla\mathbf{v} + (\nabla\mathbf{v})^T\right] + \left(\nu_2 - \frac{2}{3}\nu_1\right)(\nabla \cdot \mathbf{v})\hat{I},\tag{5}$$

where ν_1 is the kinematic viscosity coefficient, ν_2 is the second viscosity (equal to 0); ν_1 is defined differently in PLUTO and Gadget-2.

We neglected any radiation and cooling effects on the gas. In the outer regions of protoplanetary disks (1 au and farther), the gas and dust temperatures are lower than 300 K, which means that the blackbody radiation is insufficient for the energy balance during the time considered. Also, we do not take into account the effects associated with thermal conductivity.

PLUTO. We solved Eqs. (1)–(3) in conservative form by the Godunov approach using the PLUTO package [27]. The domain was given in 3D spherical coordinates (R, θ, φ). The grid contains $195 \times 18 \times 256$ cells in the domain $[0.4; 47.94] \times [77.34°; 102.66°] \times [0; 2\pi]$. We chose an R-grid defined with a logarithmic distribution of the cell sizes and a uniform grid along θ and φ, so each cell was a cube: $\Delta R \approx R\Delta\theta = R\Delta\varphi$.

We use the HLLC solver for the Riemann problem. Time integration is carried out with the second-order TVD Runge–Kutta method. A piecewise TVD linear reconstruction is applied to primitive variables.

The viscosity coefficient ν_1 is implemented with standard α-parametrisation of [35]:

$$\nu_1 = \alpha\frac{\rho c_s^2}{\Omega}; \qquad \alpha = 0.03.\tag{6}$$

Here c_s is the local speed of sound, and Ω is the Keplerian frequency (see Eq. (9)). The parabolic viscosity term was integrated with an explicit multistage timestepping scheme based on Legendre polynomials.

Gadget-2. This package solves Eqs. (1), (2), and (4) using the smoothedparticle hydrodynamics method [17,26] with variable smoothing length. The method introduces an interpolation kernel $W(\mathbf{r}, h)$ that determines the influence of a neighboring particle on the physical value of the considered particle depending on the distance $\mathbf{r}$ between them. In the paper, a kernel in the form of a cubic spline was used, by analogy with [28]. The h parameter is the smoothing length. It determines the radius of the sphere, particles trapped inside which affect the value of the physical quantity in the center of the sphere. The smoothing length is determined by the required number of particles N located in the sphere of radius h. We set the value $N = 30 \pm 2$.

Dissipative processes in the disk are described using the concept of numerical viscosity, which is related to kinematic viscosity (6). The standard form for representing the numerical viscosity in SPH was taken from [29].

We used the Leapfrog integrator to solve the equations of gas dynamics. The integrator ensures the preservation of the physical invariants of the system in the absence of dissipation and gives a fourth-order accuracy $O(\Delta t^4)$. Also, we used a variable integration time step limited by the Courant–Friedrichs–Lewy criterion, described in [20].

The calculations were performed in a Cartesian coordinate system with the origin at the star center. The calculations involved 10^6 SPH particles, initially distributed in the domain according to the given density distribution (see Subsect. 2.2).

Dimensionalization. Equations (1), (2), (3), and (4) were solved in a dimensionless form. The units of dimensionalization were chosen identically in PLUTO and in Gadget-2. They are listed in Table 1.

Table 1. Units of dimensionalization ($M_\odot = 2 \times 10^{33}$ g is the solar mass, 1 au = 1.5×10^{13} cm (au—astronomical unit))

Parameter	Notation	Value	CGS Units	Commentary
Unit of mass	M_0	5.06×10^{31}	g	$M_\odot/(4\pi^2)$
Unit of length	L_0	1.50×10^{13}	cm	1 au
Unit of time	t_0	3.15×10^7	s	1 year
Unit of density	ρ_0	1.51×10^{-8}	g cm^{-3}	M_0/L_0^3
Unit of velocity	v_0	4.75×10^5	cm s^{-1}	$2\pi L_0/t_0$

2.2 Initial Conditions

The Disk. The initial density distribution ρ on the unperturbed disk is defined by the following formulas (see [10] for details):

$$\rho(r, z) = \frac{\Sigma_0}{\sqrt{2\pi}H(r)} \frac{r_{in}}{r} e^{-\frac{z^2}{2H^2(r)}}, \qquad \Sigma_0 = \frac{M_{disk}}{2\pi r_{in}(r_{out} - r_{in})}. \tag{7}$$

Here $r = R\sin(\theta)$ is the cylindrical radius (R is the spherical radius), $z = R\cos(\theta)$ is the height above the equatorial plane, $H(r)$ is the characteristic half thickness of the disk at radius r, r_{in} is the disk inner radius, Σ_0 is the average surface density of the disk, M_{disk} is the total mass of the protoplanetary disk, and r_{out} is the disk outer radius.

The half thickness of the disk depends on the absolute temperature T_{mid} in the equatorial plane:

$$H(r) = \sqrt{\frac{k_B T_{\text{mid}}(r) r^3}{GM_* \mu m_H}}; \qquad T_{\text{mid}}(r) = \sqrt[4]{\frac{\Gamma}{4}} \sqrt{\frac{R_*}{r}} T_*, \qquad (8)$$

where k_B is the Boltzmann constant; G is the gravitational constant; M_*, R_*, and T_* are the mass, radius, and surface temperature of the star, respectively; $\mu = 2.35$ is the mean molecular weight; m_H is the proton mass, and $\Gamma = 0.05$ [7,14,16].

The initial velocity distribution of the unperturbed disk is defined in a Keplerian approximation:

$$\mathbf{v} = (v_R, v_\theta, v_\varphi) = (0, 0, -\Omega r); \qquad \Omega = \sqrt{\frac{GM_*}{r^3}}. \qquad (9)$$

The Clump. We place the clump at the distance r_{clump} with azimuth position $\varphi = 90°$. The density of the clump is defined as $\rho_{\text{clump}} = 10.0\rho$, and its velocity $\mathbf{v}_{\text{clump}} = L\mathbf{v}$ when $r \in [r_{\text{clump}} - \Delta r_{\text{clump}}; r_{\text{clump}} + \Delta r_{\text{clump}}]$ and $\varphi \in [75°; 105°]$, $0 < L < 1$. In fact, the edges of the grid cells do not match the exact values of the borders of the clump defined here, therefore the real borders of the clump were used to simulate the clump in PLUTO and Gadget-2.

The density distribution in the vicinity of the clump location is shown in Fig. 1.

Input Parameters. The model parameters used are listed in Table 2.

Table 2. Parameters of the disk and the clump ($M_\odot = 2 \times 10^{33}$ g is the solar mass, $R_\odot = 7 \times 10^5$ km is the solar radius, 1 au = 1.5×10^{13} cm (au—astronomical unit))

Parameter	Value	Units
M_*	1	$M_\odot$
R_*	2	$R_\odot$
T_*	10000	K
M_{disk}	0.01	$M_\odot$
r_{in}	1	R_*
r_{out}	100	au
r_{clump}	10	au
Δr_{clump}	0.5	au
L	0.8	

The parameters of the clump give a total mass of about 2×10^{30} g, which is equivalent to Jupiter's mass.

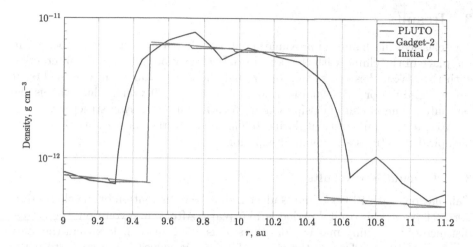

Fig. 1. The initial density distribution in the vicinity of the clump in the equatorial plane ($\theta = 0°$) along $\varphi = 90°$. The red line is the distribution in PLUTO cells; the blue line is the SPH-interpolated density calculated by Gadget-2; the green lines are the initial density according to the formulas. The interpolation of SPH was carried out in ParaView with constant smoothing length $h = 0.1$ au and divided by the Shepard summation.

2.3 Boundary Conditions

PLUTO. On the leftmost boundary on R (with index "b"), we assume an analog of sink cell (see below): the density and pressure in ghost cells are set to a fictitious zero (10^{-12}, that is, the smallest value in code units), the velocity components are extrapolated in a sub-Keplerian approximation from the nearest computational cells (values without index):

$$p_b = 10^{-12} p_0; \qquad \rho_b = 10^{-12} \rho_0; \qquad \mathbf{v}_b = \mathbf{v}\sqrt{\frac{r}{r_b}}, \tag{10}$$

with the constraint $v_{Rb} \leq 0$. Here p_0 is the code unit of pressure, defined through the corresponding values from Table 1.

On the rightmost boundary on R, we set an outflow boundary condition by applying the Keplerian approximation $v_\varphi = -\Omega r$ in the ghost cells (see (9)).

Also, we set a periodic boundary condition on φ. An outflow (zero-gradient for all values) condition was used on the θ direction.

Gadget-2. The sink cell was implemented to model the inner region of the disk: all SPH particles approaching closer than 0.4 au to the star were removed from calculations. Also, all particles beyond 100 au were considered to have left the system and they were also removed from calculations.

3 Results

The classical mechanics approximation shows that a material point located in the place of the clump with the same initial velocity but without the interaction with the disk makes one revolution around the model star in an elliptical orbit with a semi-major axis equal to 7.36 au in a time $\lesssim 20$ years. Thus, this is the estimated time of clump dissipation or spreading into the ring structure.

We ran the computations during $100t_0$. We expected the formation of unstable spiral structures and clump dissipation.

3.1 Calculation Results

Calculations with PLUTO and Gadget-2 show the dissipation of the clump during ~ 24 years. One orbital period is 18.5 years. After one revolution, the largest distance of the clump matter from the star is ~ 7.2 au (it is less than the start position of 10 au). During the first 11.5 years, it moves like a separate dense body, then it starts interacting with the regions of the disk of the same density.

Figure 2 depicts the density distributions in the equatorial plane obtained with both packages at the computation moment $20.0t_0$ (20 years). Note that the clump is stretched into a spiral with morphologically similar two-arm structures in both PLUTO and Gadget-2 simulations.

Also, the influence of clump matter in inner regions of the disk (<3 au) is clearly seen: a complex spiral structure surrounds the inner border in the case of PLUTO; in the case of Gadget-2, a spiral structure can also be discerned, although it is smoother.

To control the convergence of the results, calculations were also performed on a high-resolution grid ($390 \times 36 \times 512$) in PLUTO and with 2×10^6 particles in Gadget-2. The calculation results at $20.0t_0$ are shown in Fig. 3. We can see that the spiralization in inner regions is less pronounced, but two-armed spirals in outer regions are the same. Also, the position of the clump remnants is approximately the same, as well as the orbital period ($\sim 18.8t_0$) and the time of dissipation ($\sim 25t_0$).

The density distributions in the equatorial plane at computation time $82t_0$ are shown in Fig. 4. PLUTO calculations show complex spirals (it is very likely that they are the result of the development of the so-called *Vertical Shear Instability*, but this issue should be investigated in more detail at a later time). Gadget-2 calculations present much smoother spiral structures, qualitatively similar to those shown in PLUTO's results. However, the region close to the star ($R < 2.5$ au) seems to contain a rarefied matter. Thus, the difference in the definition of the boundary condition near the star in the methods under consideration probably has an effect.

3.2 Parallelization

Computations were performed on a system equipped with a 12th Gen Intel® Core™ i9-12900K $\times$ 16 processor (16 cores, 24 threads) and 32 GB RAM. The processor has eight Performance-cores (with Intel® Hyper-Threading Technology

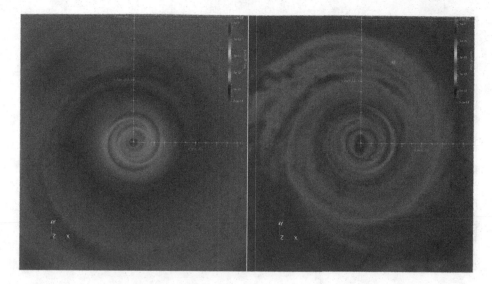

Fig. 2. The logarithm of the density distribution (in g cm^{-3}) in the equatorial plane after $20t_0$ of calculations, visualized with ParaView (on the left, PLUTO simulation; on the right, Gadget-2 simulation). The star is shown as a yellow sphere, not to scale. Distances along the axes are given in astronomical units. The rotation is clockwise.

and up to 5.20 GHz frequency) and eight Efficient-cores (no Hyper-Threading, up to 3.90 GHz frequency)[4]. The distribution of MPI threads among cores during runs was automatically determined.

In short, Godunov schemes assume the solution of a Riemann problem on each border between two cells. As a result of such a solution, we obtain the signal velocity with which perturbation propagates along the cell. The greater the value of that velocity and the smaller the size of the cell, the smaller the global integration time step. Gadget-2 code uses an individual time step for each particle, which is chosen taking into account the acceleration of the particle. In this case, the minimum time step is set as a problem parameter, based on which the size of the inner disk boundary is determined. The individual integration step for each particle is synchronized with the total running time of the system. This approach makes it possible to noticeably speed up the calculations. This explains PLUTO's longer computation time in Fig. 5, as compared with that of Gadget-2.

Gas relaxation occurs during the calculations, therefore we can expect a reduction in the calculation time of every integration step. Figure 5 confirms this assumption. Furthermore, the total count of particles in Gadget-2 decreases with time: some particles move further than 100 au, and those approaching closer than 0.4 au to the star are removed from the domain, which has a positive effect on the speed of calculations (but a negative effect on the resolution).

---

[4] https://www.intel.co.uk/content...

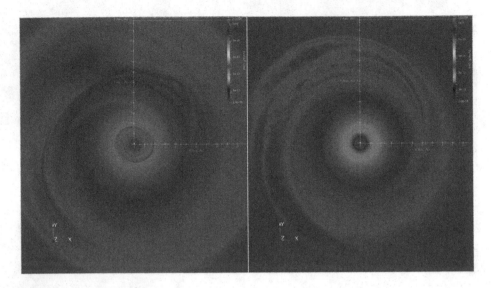

Fig. 3. The same as in Fig. 2 but on a high-resolution grid (390 × 36 × 512) in PLUTO and with 2×10^6 particles in Gadget-2

Parallel calculations in PLUTO are carried out by splitting the computational domain into disjoint boxes (of equal size if possible) surrounded with ghost cells that provide data exchange or realize border conditions. Thus, while the total volume of ghost layers is much less than the total volume of the computational zones, the speedup is linear (or sublinear), as can be seen in Fig. 6 up to six MPI threads for $81.0t_0$–$82.0t_0$. In the case of the run from $0.0t_0$ to $1.0t_0$, the change in the growth rate can be explained by the use of one or two Efficient-cores (slow ones) instead of Perfomance-cores (fast ones). The peak at 22 threads with speedup 8.36 in the case of PLUTO is explained by the dissimilarity of boxes in threads: one thread can get a 98 × 18 × 24 box (with a nonsmooth distribution of parameters of the gas close to the star), while another one gets a 97 × 18 × 23 one (with a smooth distribution of parameters far away of the star). If the slow core gets the smaller box, we achieve a balancing effect.

In Gadget-2, the computational domain is filled with the Peano–Hilbert curve, so that three-dimensional space is described by a one-dimensional curve. Then the curve is cut into segments of the same length; the number of these segments is equal to the number of MPI threads. An important feature of the Peano–Hilbert curve is that points that are close along the curve are also close in 3D space. In addition, this approach allows one to establish a one-to-one correspondence between the segments of the Peano–Hilbert curve and the hierarchical octree that is used to find neighbors in the SPH method. In addition, the tree contains information about pseudoparticles that are not computed in the local thread. This information is used to evaluate the need to exchange data between threads.

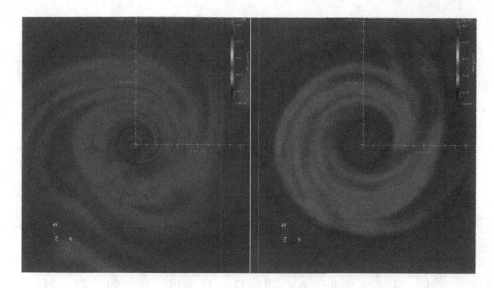

Fig. 4. The same as in Fig. 2 but for $82t_0$

Parallel calculations in Gadget-2 are organized in such a way that the best performance is achieved when the number of MPI threads is a power of 2. The principal model of communication in force calculations follows the hypercube strategy. If the number of processors is a power of 2, say 2^p, then a full cycle of all-to-all communications can be realized in $2^p - 1$ cycles, where there are $2^p - 1$ disjoint pairs of processors that exchange messages in each cycle. If the number of processors is not a power of 2, this scheme can still be used, but processors must be embedded in a hypercube circuit corresponding to the next higher power of 2. As a result, some processors will be unpaired in the communication subfraction cycle, which somewhat reduces the overall efficiency. That is why we see the minima of the estimated time in Fig. 5 near the number of MPI threads that is a power of two, namely, 4, 8, and 16.

The lower values of speedup in the case of $81.0t_0$–$82.0t_0$ are explained by the lower calculation time on one MPI thread.

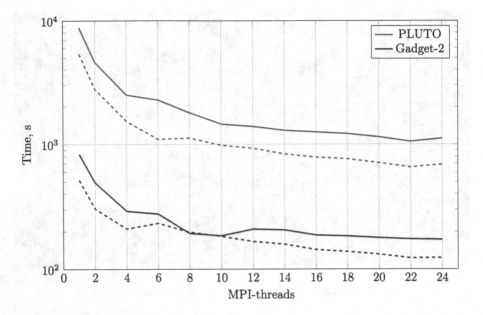

Fig. 5. The estimated time from $0.0t_0$ to $1.0t_0$ (solid graphs) and from $81.0t_0$ to $82.0t_0$ (dashed graphs) versus the count of MPI threads, with PLUTO (red graphs) and Gadget-2 (blue graphs) (Color figure online)

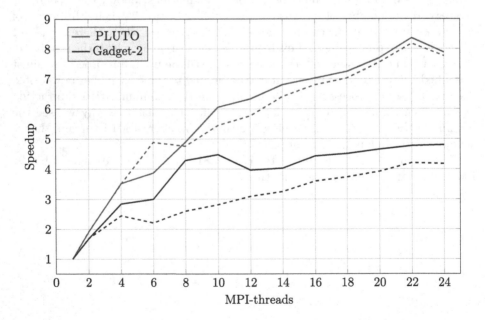

Fig. 6. The computation speedup from $0.0t_0$ to $1.0t_0$ (solid graphs) and from $81.0t_0$ to $82.0t_0$ (dashed graphs) versus the number of MPI threads, with PLUTO (red graphs) and Gadget-2 (blue graphs) (Color figure online)

4   Conclusions

The simulation of the interaction of the clump with the protoplanetary disk was done in two ideologically different ways: by the finite-volume method in the PLUTO package, and by the SPH method in the Gadget-2 package. Both packages showed qualitatively similar results of clump dissociation in the protoplanetary disk near T Tau-like stars after about one period of rotation. This produces complex spiral structures after interaction and global relaxation.

The differences in detail can be explained by the use of different viscosity models and the lowest R-boundary conditions. In fact, the relaxation occurs in the disk, so different waves could appear at the first moments of calculations.

Moreover, the impact of vertical borders (θ direction) in PLUTO is sufficient: we can not model the disk "swelling" if it takes place when the θ-borders are close to the equatorial plane. Nonetheless, wide borders on θ cause calculation problems: because of the exponential density distribution in the z direction, very small density values in the cells are expected. However, the exact model of the corona of the disk is a separate problem. Since the disk is modeled by particles in SPH, the disk is also limited in the z direction, usually particles cannot be located at heights greater than $3H(r)$ (8).

Also, we measured the efficiency of parallelization. The maximum speedup for PLUTO was 8.36 with 22 MPI threads; for Gadget-2, the maximum speedup was 4.8 with 24 MPI threads. For both packages, the speedup varied in the course of computations. Thus, computations with PLUTO were slower than with Gadget-2 for small numbers of MPI threads, yet data exchange between MPI threads in the case of PLUTO was less intense than in Gadget-2.

Acknowledgments. The computations were performed on equipment provided by the Russian Science Foundation (grant № 19-72-10063).

References

1. Bai, X.N., Stone, J.M.: Magnetic flux concentration and zonal flows in magnetorotational instability turbulence. ApJ **796**(1), 31 (2014). https://doi.org/10.1088/0004-637X/796/1/31
2. Banzatti, A., Pinilla, P., Ricci, L., Pontoppidan, K.M., Birnstiel, T., Ciesla, F.: Direct imaging of the water snow line at the time of planet formation using two ALMA continuum bands. ApJL **815**(1), L15 (2015). https://doi.org/10.1088/2041-8205/815/1/L15
3. Basu, S., Vorobyov, E.I.: A hybrid scenario for the formation of brown dwarfs and very low mass stars. ApJ **750**(1), 30 (2012). https://doi.org/10.1088/0004-637X/750/1/30
4. Birnstiel, T., Andrews, S.M., Pinilla, P., Kama, M.: Dust evolution can produce scattered light gaps in protoplanetary disks. ApJL **813**(1), L14 (2015). https://doi.org/10.1088/2041-8205/813/1/L14

5. Bouvier, J., Alencar, S.H.P., Harries, T.J., Johns-Krull, C.M., Romanova, M.M.: Magnetospheric accretion in classical T Tauri stars. In: Reipurth, B., Jewitt, D., Keil, K. (eds.) Protostars and Planets V, p. 479 (2007). https://doi.org/10.48550/arXiv.astro-ph/0603498

6. Cazzoletti, P., et al.: Evidence for a massive dust-trapping vortex connected to spirals. Multi-wavelength analysis of the HD 135344B protoplanetary disk. Astron. Astrophys. **619**, A161 (2018). https://doi.org/10.1051/0004-6361/201834006

7. Chiang, E.I., Goldreich, P.: Spectral energy distributions of T Tauri stars with passive circumstellar disks. Astrophys. J. **490**, 368–376 (1997). https://doi.org/10.1086/304869

8. Demidova, T.V.: Modelling the gas dynamics of protoplanetary disks by the SPH method. Astrophysics **59**(4), 449–460 (2016). https://doi.org/10.1007/s10511-016-9448-3

9. Demidova, T.V., Grinin, V.P.: Catastrophic events in protoplanetary disks and their observational manifestations. ApJL **887**(1), L15 (2019). https://doi.org/10.3847/2041-8213/ab59e0

10. Demidova, T.V., Grinin, V.P.: Clumpy accretion in pre-main-sequence stars as a source of perturbations in circumstellar disks. Astrophys. J. **930**(2), 111 (2022). https://doi.org/10.3847/1538-4357/ac53a6

11. Demidova, T.V., Shevchenko, I.I.: Three-lane and multilane signatures of planets in planetesimal discs. MNRAS **463**(1), L22–L25 (2016). https://doi.org/10.1093/mnrasl/slw150

12. Dong, R., Li, S., Chiang, E., Li, H.: Multiple disk gaps and rings generated by a single super-earth. II. Spacings, depths, and number of gaps, with application to real systems. ApJ **866**(2), 110 (2018). https://doi.org/10.3847/1538-4357/aadadd

13. Dong, R., Zhu, Z., Whitney, B.: Observational signatures of planets in protoplanetary disks I. Gaps opened by single and multiple young planets in disks. ApJ **809**(1), 93 (2015). https://doi.org/10.1088/0004-637X/809/1/93

14. Dullemond, C.P., Dominik, C.: The effect of dust settling on the appearance of protoplanetary disks. Astron. Astrophys. **421**, 1075–1086 (2004). https://doi.org/10.1051/0004-6361:20040284

15. Dullemond, C.P., Penzlin, A.B.T.: Dust-driven viscous ring-instability in protoplanetary disks. Astron. Astrophys. **609**, A50 (2018). https://doi.org/10.1051/0004-6361/201731878

16. Dutrey, A., Guilloteau, S., Simon, M.: Images of the GG Tauri rotating ring. Astron. Astrophys. **286**, 149–159 (1994)

17. Gingold, R.A., Monaghan, J.J.: Smoothed particle hydrodynamics: theory and application to non-spherical stars. MNRAS **181**, 375–389 (1977). https://doi.org/10.1093/mnras/181.3.375

18. Hartmann, L., Herczeg, G., Calvet, N.: Accretion onto pre-main-sequence stars. ARA&A **54**, 135–180 (2016). https://doi.org/10.1146/annurev-astro-081915-023347

19. Hartmann, L., Kenyon, S.J.: The FU Orionis phenomenon. ARA&A **34**, 207–240 (1996). https://doi.org/10.1146/annurev.astro.34.1.207

20. Hernquist, L., Katz, N.: TREESPH: a unification of SPH with the hierarchical tree method. ApJS **70**, 419 (1989). https://doi.org/10.1086/191344

21. Huang, J., et al.: The disk substructures at high angular resolution project (DSHARP). II. Characteristics of annular substructures. ApJL **869**(2), L42 (2018). https://doi.org/10.3847/2041-8213/aaf740

22. Huang, J., et al.: The disk substructures at high angular resolution project (DSHARP). III. Spiral structures in the millimeter continuum of the Elias 27, IM Lup, and WaOph 6 Disks. Astrophys. J. Lett. **869**(2), L43 (2018). https://doi.org/10.3847/2041-8213/aaf7a0

23. Jin, S., Li, S., Isella, A., Li, H., Ji, J.: Modeling dust emission of HL tau disk based on planet-disk interactions. ApJ **818**(1), 76 (2016). https://doi.org/10.3847/0004-637X/818/1/76

24. Johansen, A., Youdin, A., Klahr, H.: Zonal flows and long-lived axisymmetric pressure bumps in magnetorotational turbulence. ApJ **697**(2), 1269–1289 (2009). https://doi.org/10.1088/0004-637X/697/2/1269

25. Joy, A.H.: T Tauri variable stars. ApJ **102**, 168 (1945). https://doi.org/10.1086/144749

26. Lucy, L.B.: A numerical approach to the testing of the fission hypothesis. AJ **82**, 1013–1024 (1977). https://doi.org/10.1086/112164

27. Mignone, A., et al.: PLUTO: a numerical code for computational astrophysics. ApJS **170**(1), 228–242 (2007). https://doi.org/10.1086/513316

28. Monaghan, J.J.: Extrapolating B. Splines for interpolation. J. Comput. Phys. **60**(2), 253–262 (1985). https://doi.org/10.1016/0021-9991(85)90006-3

29. Monaghan, J.J.: Smoothed particle hydrodynamics. ARA&A **30**, 543–574 (1992). https://doi.org/10.1146/annurev.aa.30.090192.002551

30. Nayakshin, S., et al.: TW Hya: an old protoplanetary disc revived by its planet. MNRAS **495**(1), 285–304 (2020). https://doi.org/10.1093/mnras/staa1132

31. Okuzumi, S., Momose, M., Sirono, S.i., Kobayashi, H., Tanaka, H.: Sintering-induced dust ring formation in protoplanetary disks: application to the HL tau disk. ApJ **821**(2), 82 (2016). https://doi.org/10.3847/0004-637X/821/2/82

32. Pérez, L.M., et al.: The disk substructures at high angular resolution project (DSHARP). X. Multiple rings, a misaligned inner disk, and a bright arc in the disk around the T Tauri star HD 143006. Astrophys. J. Lett. **869**(2), L50 (2018). https://doi.org/10.3847/2041-8213/aaf745

33. Petrov, P.P.: T Tauri stars. Astrophysics **46**(4), 506–529 (2003). https://doi.org/10.1023/B:ASYS.0000003267.35552.f7

34. Ruge, J.P., Wolf, S., Uribe, A.L., Klahr, H.H.: Tracing large-scale structures in circumstellar disks with ALMA. A&A **549**, A97 (2013). https://doi.org/10.1051/0004-6361/201220390

35. Shakura, N.I., Sunyaev, R.A.: Black holes in binary systems. Observational appearance. A&A **24**, 337–355 (1973)

36. Springel, V.: The cosmological simulation code GADGET-2. MNRAS **364**(4), 1105–1134 (2005). https://doi.org/10.1111/j.1365-2966.2005.09655.x

37. Springel, V., Yoshida, N., White, S.D.M.: GADGET: a code for collisionless and gasdynamical cosmological simulations. New Astron. **6**(2), 79–117 (2001). https://doi.org/10.1016/S1384-1076(01)00042-2

38. Suriano, S.S., Li, Z.Y., Krasnopolsky, R., Shang, H.: The formation of rings and gaps in magnetically coupled disc-wind systems: ambipolar diffusion and reconnection. MNRAS **477**(1), 1239–1257 (2018). https://doi.org/10.1093/mnras/sty717

39. Takahashi, S.Z., Inutsuka, S.J.: Two-component secular gravitational instability in a protoplanetary disk: a possible mechanism for creating ring-like structures. ApJ **794**(1), 55 (2014). https://doi.org/10.1088/0004-637X/794/1/55

40. van der Marel, N., van Dishoeck, E.F., Bruderer, S., Pérez, L., Isella, A.: Gas density drops inside dust cavities of transitional disks around young stars observed with ALMA. A&A **579**, A106 (2015). https://doi.org/10.1051/0004-6361/201525658

41. Vorobyov, E.I., Steinrueck, M.E., Elbakyan, V., Guedel, M.: Formation of freely floating sub-stellar objects via close encounters. A&A **608**, A107 (2017). https://doi.org/10.1051/0004-6361/201731565
42. Zhang, K., Blake, G.A., Bergin, E.A.: Evidence of fast pebble growth near condensation fronts in the HL tau protoplanetary disk. ApJL **806**(1), L7 (2015). https://doi.org/10.1088/2041-8205/806/1/L7

Computer Modeling of Metal Nanoclusters and Substrate Interaction at Mesoscopic Level

Nikita Tarasov[1]([⊠])(iD), Viktoriia Podryga[1,2]([⊠])(iD), Sergey Polyakov[1]([⊠])(iD), and Vladimir Usachev[1,2]([⊠])(iD)

[1] Keldysh Institute of Applied Mathematics of the Russian Academy of Sciences, Moscow, Russian Federation
{nikita_tarasov,polyakov}@imamod.ru, pvictoria@list.ru
[2] Moscow Automobile and Road Construction, State Technical University (MADI), Moscow, Russian Federation
v.usachev99@list.ru

Abstract. The paper is devoted to the development and computer implementation of a numerical method for modeling the interaction of metal nanoclusters with a substrate at the mesoscopic level. This research as a whole is relevant in connection with the development of nanotechnologies for obtaining extremely thin metal coatings by various spraying methods. From a practical point of view, its relevance is determined by the lack of adequate mathematical models at the mesoscopic level to describe processes in the submicron size range. This work presents the mathematical model of a metallic medium consisting of spherical nanoclusters and a parallel numerical algorithm for its implementation. The model includes Maxwell's equations of electrodynamics to describe the evolution of the electromagnetic field, as well as the averaged equations of Newtonian dynamics to describe the motion of individual nanoclusters and the electron gas surrounding them. The numerical algorithm is based on the method of grids and the integration of the equations of motion of the particles. The algorithm is parallelized with respect to both space and particles. We devised a set of parallel programs and carried out preliminary model calculations. Nickel is used as the material for the nanoclusters and the substrate. The conducted numerical experiments show the efficiency of the proposed computer model.

Keywords: Mathematical modeling in spraying problems · Mesoscale approach · Maxwell's equations · Electrodynamics of smoothed particles · Parallel algorithms

1 Introduction

We consider the problem of computer modeling the process of spraying [1–12] nanoparticles on substrates. The relevance of the problem is associated with the

© The Author(s), under exclusive license to Springer Nature Switzerland AG 2023
L. Sokolinsky and M. Zymbler (Eds.): PCT 2023, CCIS 1868, pp. 285–298, 2023.
https://doi.org/10.1007/978-3-031-38864-4_20

development of new technologies for manufacturing ultrathin coatings in microelectronics, medical equipment, and other industries. Among spraying technologies, supersonic cold gas dynamic spraying [1–3], plasma spraying [4–7], and magnetron spraying [8–12] are the most frequently requested for practical purposes. One of the major concerns presented by these technologies is the nonlinearity and the spatiotemporal instability of spraying processes when manufacturing coatings with a thickness of about 100 nm or less. To deal with these issues, a detailed multiscale analysis of sorption processes is required, namely, one taking into account the relief and surface structure. A complete picture of the interaction of sprayed nanoparticles with the surface of a particular material or composite can be obtained through atomistic models supplemented with quantum effects. However, such an analysis encounters two fundamental difficulties: first, the lack of reliable data on the interaction potentials over a wide range of thermodynamic parameters for the atoms and molecules of the substances composing the nanoparticles and the substrate, and second, the ultra-high computational capacity required by direct atomic-molecular quantum modeling. At present, the way out of this situation is the use of highly simplified interaction models (including those that do not consider the quantum mechanical properties of substances) and averaging over small scales.

We suggest in this paper an approach based on an average over atomic scales. In the literature, it is sometimes called the *mesoscopic approach* [13]. Within the framework of this approach, we operate not with individual atoms and molecules but with their larger agglomerations, i.e., nanoclusters or nanoparticles of sizes in the range of 1–100 nm. This approach is used by many researchers (see, for example, [14, 15]). In the case under consideration, we assume that the interaction of nanoparticles with the substrate occurs at a temperature near the melting point of the materials that compose these objects. Therefore the approximation of a quasiliquid medium is valid. This approximation consists of weakly bound (by an electromagnetic field) nanoparticles having the shape of spheroids (hereinafter referred to as nanospheroids). The evolution of a system of nanospheroids under the conditions of the spraying problem is the subject of our research.

Let us refine the physical formulation of the spraying problem, limiting ourselves to metal systems and the analysis of the nanoparticle-substrate contact zone, in which the significance of computing the state of the environment surrounding the particle (e.g., a gas, plasma, or vacuum) is inferior in importance to the study of the interaction of individual nanoclusters with the substrate. In this case, the average velocities and temperature of nanoclusters, the temperature and pressure of the medium (in the case of a gas or plasma), and the temperature of the substrate are, indeed, taken into account. The mesoscopic level of detail we have chosen assumes that we consider the structure of nanoclusters and that of the substrate from a unified standpoint. Within this framework, all metal objects (the nanoparticles and the substrate) are considered systems formed by separate positively charged nanospheroids with sizes of about 10 nm, surrounded by an electron gas of negatively charged particles (electron clouds). Such a description corresponds to a quasineutral low-temperature metallic plasma [16].

To describe the considered metallic mesomedium, we will use the equations of Newtonian dynamics written for individual positively and negatively charged nanospheroids. In this case, we will take into account the action exerted on them by the Lorentz force and pressure forces from the environment. When describing individual nanospheroids, we assume that they have a single center of mass (moving with a certain translational velocity), a nonzero effective radius, a temperature (a measure of their kinetic energy), and a charge (a product of a certain number of electrons). As the model of an individual nanospheroid, we use a Gaussian profile with a given effective radius. We represent the sprayed particles and the substrate material as ensembles of nanospheroids whose configurations are set at the initial moment and then evolve in accordance with the equations of motion. In the future, we plan to consider also the processes of recharge of nanospheroids (the complete annihilation is possible for electron clouds) and the formation of neutral nanospheroids based on positively charged single crystals (in the case of a complete filling of their outer shells with electrons).

The motivation for the proposed model of sprayed particles and a substrate is the following. As a result of the interaction with the substrate, the incident particle may reflect from it, stick to it, or embed in it. In all three cases, the shape of the particle can significantly deviate from the original. Coalescing or splitting of particles, chipping of the substrate, and healing of cracks and discontinuities in it may also occur. All these phenomena can be successfully tracked down by changing the geometric configuration of the whole system of nanospheroids.

As a result, the implementation of the model of a metallic mesoenvironment consists in applying the smoothed particle method [17] in the contact zone of the spraying installation. The electrodynamics of the mesomedium is described by Maxwell's equations [18], split into quasistatic and dynamic parts. The motion of individual metal particles and the evolution of the substrate are described by the equations of dynamics for the general system of nanospheroids. Calculations are made from the system's initial state until it reaches some quasiequilibrium, determined by a given criterion. The overall goal of the proposed computational experiment is to determine the conditions for the so-called "soft" gluing (the adiabatic fusion of the nanocluster and substrate surfaces) of sprayed particles to the substrate surface.

For the numerical implementation of the electrodynamic part of the model, we employed the finite volume method [19] on Cartesian grids and the finite-difference time-domain (FDTD) method [20]. To implement the equations of dynamics of the nanospheroids, we resorted to a time-symmetric finite-difference scheme [21]. The general algorithm is based on the method of splitting by physical processes and involves the alternation of mesh and mesh-free calculations. Particular attention is paid to the implementation of the parallel version of the algorithm, for which we applied both the domain decomposition method [22, 23] and load-balancing algorithms [24, 25].

The approbation of the developed computer model was carried out on the problem of the interaction of nickel nanoclusters with a substrate of the same material. As part of this study, we conducted an analysis of the efficiency of the parallel implementation for several spatial configurations of the whole system of nanospheroids. In the numerical experiments, we showed that the spatial division of the region when solving the equations of electrodynamics can be geometrically homogeneous and does not consider the location of the particles. The distribution of the particles among the calculators is best done independently in accordance with their total number.

Regarding the physical adequacy of the numerical experiments, we noted that if the materials of the nanoclusters and the substrate have the same hardness and the translational velocity of the nanoclusters is sufficiently high, then the substrate material, instead of soft gluing, is destroyed starting from its rear surface.

The paper is organized as follows. Section 2 describes the problem of the interaction of nanoclusters with a substrate. Section 3 presents the mathematical models for the analysis of the problem, including Maxwell's equations and Newtonian dynamics. Section 4 is devoted to the general computational algorithm based on the FDTD method and the symmetric scheme for ordinary differential equations. Section 5 discusses the features of the parallel implementation of the developed algorithm. Section 6 presents the speedup and efficiency of the parallel implementation and discusses the results of the computational experiments series. Conclusion summarizes the study.

2   The Problem Formulation

Let us consider the problem of the interaction of metal nanoclusters with a substrate surface made of the same material. When testing the proposed meso-model, we assume that the medium exerts a weak influence on the nanoclusters and the substrate, which happens, for example, under technical vacuum conditions. In this situation, a description of the medium evolution is not required. At the initial moment, a certain number of nanoclusters, their location relative to the substrate, their translational velocities, their temperature, and that of the substrate are specified.

Figure 1 shows the model geometry of the problem under consideration. We do not take into account edge effects in the calculations. To do this, we select a fragment of the substrate with specific dimensions L_x and L_y and a volume of height L_V located above it. The total height L_z consists of the height L_V of the volume and the thickness L_S of the substrate. Next, we consider N_K nanoclusters placed randomly in the volume above the substrate. To simplify the problem, we assume that the clusters have a cubic shape with edge length l_K. The initial orientation of the clusters is set in such a way that their local coordinate system coincides with that of the substrate. According to the approach adopted above, each nanocluster consists of a system of nanospheroids of the same size with an effective radius R_K (see Fig. 2). In general, the radii of nanospheroids differ: positively charged nanospheroids (ionic-type nanospheroids) have a smaller radius

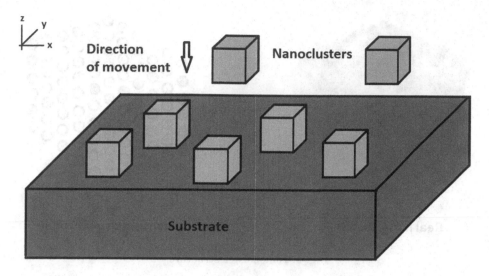

Fig. 1. Model geometry of the problem

than neutral (neutral-type nanospheroids) and negatively charged ones (electron clouds). Since the nanoclusters and the substrate are of the same material, the difference in the radii of the nanospheroids can be neglected in a first approximation. At the initial moment, the electron shells of nanospheroids form a common ordered structure that ensures the neutrality of the entire particle configuration.

3   Basic Equations

We describe the evolution of the electromagnetic field under the conditions of mesomedium dynamics using the system of Maxwell's equations [18] written in dimensionless variables:

$$\operatorname{div} \mathbf{B} = 0, \quad \operatorname{div}(\varepsilon_a \mathbf{E}) = \rho; \tag{1}$$

$$\frac{\partial \mathbf{B}}{\partial t} = -\operatorname{rot} \mathbf{E}, \quad \frac{\partial}{\partial t}(\varepsilon_a \mathbf{E}) = \operatorname{rot}\left(\frac{1}{\mu_a} \mathbf{B}\right) - \mathbf{j}. \tag{2}$$

Here $\mathbf{B}$ is the magnetic induction vector, $\mathbf{E}$ is the electric field strength vector, $\rho = \rho_e + \rho_i$ is the volume charge density divided into positively and negatively charged components, $\mathbf{j}$ is the current density vector created by the system of particles, and ε_a and μ_a are the absolute dielectric and magnetic permeabilities of the medium.

Equations (1) and (2) are considered in the entire computational domain and are supplemented with the necessary boundary and initial conditions. In particular, we assume that there is no magnetic field at the initial moment, and the electric field is induced only by a stationary system of charges and is equal to

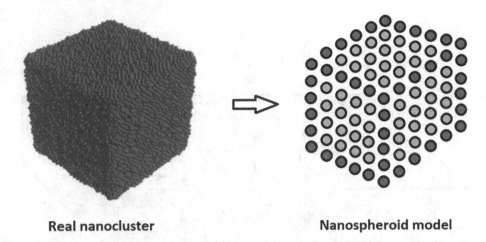

Real nanocluster   **Nanospheroid model**

Fig. 2. Nanocluster structure

zero at the boundaries. To ensure this condition, we setting up the translational velocities of nanoclusters as follows:

$$v_K = v_{\max}\left(1 - \exp(t - t/\tau_\nu)\right). \tag{3}$$

Equation (3) implies the existence of a small time interval τ_v in which the modulus of nanoclusters velocity v_K attains its maximum value.

As noted above, the nanoclusters and the substrate consist of a set of positively and negatively charged nanospheroids with different effective radii. The radii of positively charged nanospheroids correspond to the sizes of the corresponding single crystals, taking into account the number of their constituent atoms. The radii of negatively charged nanospheroids correspond to the electron cloud model. To simplify the subsequent numerical analysis, we leave out the binding of electron clouds with positively charged nanospheroids to form neutral nanospheroids. Also, we do not consider the process of ionization of neutral nanospheroids. Under these conditions, we describe the motion of nanospheroids and their field interaction with each other by means of the following system of equations of Newtonian dynamics, in which the Lorentz force is taken into account:

$$\begin{cases} \dfrac{d\mathbf{r}_{\alpha,k}}{dt} = \mathbf{v}_{\alpha,k}, \quad \dfrac{d\mathbf{p}_{\alpha,k}}{dt} = q_{\alpha,k}\left(\mathbf{E} + [\mathbf{v}_{\alpha,k} \times \mathbf{B}]\right), \\[2mm] \mathbf{p}_{\alpha,k} = m_{\alpha,k}\mathbf{v}_{\alpha,k}, \quad k = 1,\ldots,N_\alpha, \quad \alpha = +, -; \\[2mm] \rho_\alpha = \displaystyle\sum_{k=1}^{N_\alpha} q_{\alpha,k}\delta(\mathbf{r} - \mathbf{r}_{\alpha,k}), \quad \mathbf{j}_\alpha = \displaystyle\sum_{k=1}^{N_e} q_{\alpha,k}\delta(\mathbf{r} - \mathbf{r}_{\alpha,k})\mathbf{v}_{\alpha,k}. \end{cases} \tag{4}$$

Here $m_{\alpha,k}$, $q_{\alpha,k}$, $\mathbf{r}_{\alpha,k}$, $\mathbf{v}_{\alpha,k}$, $\mathbf{p}_{\alpha,k}$, and N_α are the masses, charges, radius vectors, velocity vectors, momentum vectors, numbers of nanospheroids of species α; $\delta(\mathbf{r} - \mathbf{r}_{\alpha,\mathbf{k}})$ is the modified Dirac delta function describing the charge density of the k-th nanospheroid of species α; ρ_α and $\mathbf{j}_\alpha$ are the partial densities of charge and current, respectively.

As the particle model, we employ the Gaussian profile

$$\delta(\mathbf{r} - \mathbf{r}_{\alpha,k}) \approx C_k(t) \exp\left[-|\mathbf{r} - \mathbf{r}_{\alpha,k}|^2 / R_{\alpha,k}^2\right], \tag{5}$$

which ensures the normalization condition for the δ-function at each moment through the parameter $C_k(t)$. Here $R_{\alpha,k} \equiv R_K$ are the effective particle radii. The mass $m_{\alpha,k} \equiv m_\alpha$ and the charge $q_{\alpha,k} \equiv q_\alpha$ have units of electron mass and charge, respectively, and depend on the actual number of ions and electrons that make up the nanospheroid. To simplify the analysis, we assume that each nanospheroid contains N_a atoms with nuclear charge Z_a each. Thus the total number of electrons in a neutral spheroid is $N_e^0 = N_a Z_a$. A significant part of electrons in metals is located in the conduction band on the nanospheroid surface. We assume that this number is of the order of $N_e = \left(\sqrt[3]{3N_e^0}\right)^2$ (in agreement with the ratio of the volume of the ball to the surface area of the sphere that limits the ball). Thus $q_+ = +N_e$, $q_- = -N_e$, $m_+ = N_a m_a / m_e$, and $m_- = N_e$.

4   The Numerical Algorithm

For the numerical study of the above-described mathematical model, we designed a general integration method of Eqs. (1), (2) and (4) based on splitting by physical processes and alternating mesh and mesh-free computations. We used structured Cartesian grids in this research. We solved both the two-dimensional and three-dimensional formulations of the problem.

Maxwell's equations of electrodynamics were solved by the finite volume method [19, 21]. Within the framework of this approach, we used the splitting scheme described below. The electric field was represented as the sum of two terms responsible for wave processes and processes associated with the evolution of the system of particles:

$$\mathbf{E} = \mathbf{E}^{(w)} + \mathbf{E}^{(p)} \tag{6}$$

For these terms, Eqs. (1)–(2) imply the following system of equations:

$$\mathrm{div}\left(\varepsilon_a \mathbf{E}^{(w)}\right) = 0, \quad \mathrm{div}\left(\varepsilon_a \mathbf{E}^{(p)}\right) = \rho, \tag{7}$$

$$\frac{\partial}{\partial t}\left(\varepsilon_a \mathbf{E}^{(w)}\right) = \mathrm{rot}\left(\frac{1}{\mu_a}\mathbf{B}\right) - \mathbf{j} - \frac{\partial}{\partial t}\left(\varepsilon_a \mathbf{E}^{(p)}\right). \tag{8}$$

With such a splitting, it turns out that it is possible to solve the second equation in (7) by introducing a quasistatic potential φ that satisfies the Poisson equation (see [18]), namely,

$$\mathrm{div}\left(\varepsilon_a \nabla \varphi\right) = -\rho. \tag{9}$$

The wave part of the electric field $\mathbf{E}^{(w)}$ and the magnetic induction vector $\mathbf{B}$ were calculated from Eqs. (8) and (2) using the explicit FDTD algorithm [20], which ensures the fulfillment of Eqs. (1) and (7) for these vectors when using staggered Cartesian grids.

The integration of equations of motion (4) of the nanospheroids was based on a well-known second-order symmetric scheme for ordinary differential equations considered in [21].

Let us formulate the general numerical algorithm used for solving the problem.

At the initial stage of a calculation, the geometry of the computational domain, including the free space containing the nanoclusters and the substrate, is set. Then we construct a uniform Cartesian grid that does not necessarily include the boundary points of nanoclusters and the substrate. Thus a complete system of nanospheroids is generated. At the same time, we verify that the initial coordinates of the nanospheroids ensure the electrical neutrality of the final mesomedium. Then the general time loop starts, within which the corresponding systems of Maxwell's Eqs. (1)–(2) and (8)–(9), as well as the equations of dynamics of the particle (4), are solved.

Let us clarify the details of the algorithm.

Firstly, when integrating Maxwell's equations, the spatial step h (which is chosen to be the same in all directions) and the time step τ determine the basic calculation accuracy, which is of the order of $O(h^2 + \tau^2)$. In this case, the spatial step must be consistent with the size of the nanoclusters (i.e., it must be of the order of their size or less). The time step is determined by the conditions of spatial and temporal stability, that is, the Courant condition and the stability condition imposed upon the right-side terms in Eqs. (2) and (8).

Secondly, when integrating Eq. (4), it may be necessary to reduce also the time step to meet the stability conditions. In this case, Eqs. (4) are solved n times with a smaller step $\tau_n = \tau/n$.

Thirdly, the final accuracy of calculations also depends on the parameters of the nanospheroids. Here we need to bear in mind that the effective radius of the nanospheroids R_K should not be much larger than the grid step h. In preliminary calculations, we set $R_K = n \cdot h$, where $n = 1, \ldots, 5$. In the end, we settled $R_K = 2 h$. The values of the δ-function were truncated at a precision level of 10^{-15}.

5   The Parallel Implementation

We adapted the numerical algorithm to calculations on computing clusters with shared memory, using for this the OpenMP standard. The program code was written in C++. The parallelization methodology is based on two main methods: the decomposition of the computational domain into compact domains [22, 23] and the load balancing of computers [24, 25].

To solve Maxwell's equations by an explicit scheme, we decomposed the computational domain. To do this, the entire domain was divided into regions so that a topological structure similar to a Cartesian computational grid was mapped onto the computational space. In fact, a two-dimensional (three-dimensional) lattice of calculators was constructed. In the three-dimensional case, the lattice satisfies the following conditions:

$$p = p_1 \cdot p_2 \cdot p_3, \quad \frac{p_1}{p_2} \approx \frac{N_1}{N_2}, \quad \frac{p_1}{p_3} \approx \frac{N_1}{N_3}, \quad \frac{p_2}{p_3} \approx \frac{N_2}{N_3}, \tag{10}$$

where p is the total number of parallel processes, while p_j and N_j are, respectively, the number of calculators and the grid size along the coordinate x_j, $j = 1, 2, 3$.

The use of shared memory when solving the problem as a whole turned out to be efficient in terms of the implementation of the second part of the calculations, related to the motion of particles. However, storing the vectors $\mathbf{E}^{(w)}$, $\mathbf{E}^{(P)}$, and $\mathbf{B}$ and assembling the vector $\mathbf{j}$ and the scalar function ρ at the integration step require that their data be converted into four-dimensional arrays (three spatial dimensions and one streaming) and a mechanism be implemented for allocating memory by each parallel thread independently from the others.

To compute the dynamics of nanospheroids, we resorted to the load balancing of the computers. To this end, the entire system of nanospheroids was initially divided into ensembles of approximately the same volume. We relied on dynamic balancing since subsequent versions of the code will include processes associated with the formation of neutral spheroids and their splitting into positively and negatively charged fragments. This involves the analysis of the computation time of the integration step of Eqs. (4) and the redistribution of the nanospheroids among parallel threads. In this case, a diffusion version of the algorithm is used when the number of nanospheroids in each flow changes gradually.

The final load-balancing algorithm contains the following steps:

1. Solve Eqs. (4) by p threads.
2. Determine the time t_k ($k = 0, \ldots, p - 1$) that it took the k-th thread to complete Step 1.
3. Compute the average execution time t_s of Step 1 and the relative time dispersion σ:

$$t_s = \frac{1}{p} \sum_{k=0}^{p-1} t_k, \quad \sigma = \max_k |(t_k - t_s)/t_s| \cdot 100\%. \tag{11}$$

4. Redistribute the nanospheroids by threads according to the formulas

$$N_k = N_k + \gamma N \cdot \frac{q_k}{Q}, \quad q_k = \frac{N_k}{t_k}, \quad k = 0, \ldots, p - 2;$$

$$N_{p-1} = N - \sum_{k=0}^{p-2} N_k, \quad N = N_+ + N_-, \quad Q = \sum_{k=0}^{p-2} q_k, \quad \gamma \sim 0.05, \tag{12}$$

if the dispersion σ exceeds 3–5%. Here N_k is the number of particles processed by the k-th parallel thread.

6   Results of the Computational Experiments

Let us analyze the data of preliminary numerical experiments. To do this, we considered the process of spraying individual nickel clusters on a nickel plate fixed from below with a steel frame. For testing purposes, we limited ourselves to one cubic nanocluster with edge size l_x. We assumed that the substrate is a nickel layer with a thickness three times that of the nanocluster and transverse dimensions (x, y) five times those of it. The geometry of the problem is shown in a central projection $(y = 0.5l_x)$ in Fig. 3.

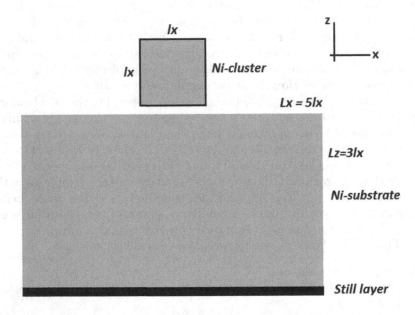

Fig. 3. Central projection of the computational domain

Nickel has a face-centered crystal lattice. Under normal conditions (temperature 273.15 K, pressure 1 atm), the length of the lattice edge (elementary cell edge) is $a \approx 0.35314$ nm [26]. If we consider a nickel nanocluster with 24 unit cells in each direction, then its linear size is 8.475 nm. The lattice of this cluster contains 58 825 atoms. With the given above dimensions of the substrate $(5l_x \times 5l_x \times 3l_x)$, it contains 4 210 873 atoms.

Direct modeling of the total system of atoms by the method of molecular dynamics [27] takes a significant amount of time even on a mid-range supercomputer. If we apply our new mesomodel, then the nanocluster can be replaced by a system of much smaller nanospheroids. In our calculations, we considered nanospheroids of various linear sizes: $3a$ (1.06 nm), $4a$ (1.41 nm), and $5a$ (1.77 nm). The corresponding numbers of positively charged nanospheroids in the nanocluster are 817, 161, and 89. In these cases, the numbers of positive nanospheroids in the substrate were 24 482, 11 537, and 6324, respectively.

According to the above estimate, the numbers of negative nanospheroids were 87, 30, and 5 in the nanocluster and 838, 508, and 340 in the substrate. Regarding the physical adequacy of the calculations, the first option turned out to be more suitable; from the point of view of the minimum of computation, the last one was the best. When analyzing larger systems, the geometric parameters of the model can vary over a wider range.

To assess the efficiency of the parallel version of the numerical algorithm, we chose the first option from the set of parameters. In this case, the total number of nanospheroids in the computation was equal to 25 386. The experiment consisted in computing the quasiequilibrium of the system of nanospheroids, which was attained in 20 000 time steps. Table 1 contains data concerning the computation time, speedup, and efficiency of parallelization depending on the number of parallel threads. The calculations were carried out on a node of the K60 GPU computer cluster installed at the Supercomputer Multiuser Center of the Keldysh Institute of Applied Mathematics (KIAM) of the Russian Academy of Sciences. The node features two Intel Xeon Gold 6142 v4 processors, with 16 cores each.

Table 1. Time, speedup, and efficiency of computations for the selected system of nanospheroids

Number of threads	1	2	4	8	16	32
Time, s	35 388	17 927	9274	4824	2694	1566
Speedup	1.0	1.974	3.816	7.336	13.136	22.592
Efficiency, %	100.0	98.7	95.4	91.7	82.1	70.6

An analysis of obtained data in terms of computation time, speedup, and efficiency showed that the developed parallel toolkit provides high efficiency in solving the considered class of problems. In the future, it is advisable to expand the capabilities of the developed model to computer clusters with distributed memory.

The analysis of the numerical results from the point of view of physical correctness confirmed the qualitative agreement between the calculated data and theoretical concepts. The numerical experiments showed, in particular, that if the materials of the nanoclusters and the substrate have the same hardness and the nanoclusters move with a supersonic translational velocity, then the substrate material is destroyed starting from its rear surface. This effect is known in the theory of strength of materials [28].

Regarding the limits of applicability of the nanospheroid model, it is worth noting the following.

First, when the temperature of a metallic solid body approaches the melting point as a result of adiabatic heating, large grains of the material gradually split up into small ones due to the weakening and breaking of molecular bonds in the so-called contact centers of the surfaces of neighboring grains. This process occurs together with the smoothing of the grain surface and the formation of micro- and nanospheres, from which individual atoms are later separated. For each specific material, it is possible to estimate the approximate value of the temperature deviation from the melting temperature, at which the grain structure is close to a system of nanospheroids. Specifically for nickel, the melting temperature of the bulk material is 1728 K [29]. Above this temperature, nickel is completely in the liquid phase. We are interested in the state of the softened solid phase. The temperature of this phase can be substantially lower than the melting point. In particular, the beginning of the structural rearrangement of solid metallic materials is associated with the Curie point, which is 627 K for nickel [29].

Second, the range of temperatures and pressures within which the representation of nanospheroids is valid can be determined more accurately by analyzing the phase diagrams and the dependence of various material properties on the cluster size. Specifically, there is evidence that the grain structure of the metal is determined either by the environment in which the natural material was formed or by the technology of its production. High-pressure electrolytic vapor deposition produces a mostly fine-grained metal structure. The subgrain size of nickel obtained by this method ranges from 40 to 60 nm [30,31]. If a nickel nanopowder is produced with particles in this size range, then their melting temperature drops to approximately 800 K [32–34]. Thus it can be noted that, depending on the method of obtaining the substrate and nanopowder particles, there is a rather wide range of temperatures and sizes of nanoparticles in which the model of nanospheroids is equally applicable both to individual nanoclusters and to the surface they form.

The accuracy of direct computations in the framework of the combination of the grid approach and the particle method is determined by matching the size of the grid cells and the number of particles per cell (in the region of nanoclusters and in the region of the substrate). In the numerical experiments, we used a ratio of about 10 to 1 or even more. When this is violated, the numerical solutions of Maxwell's equations become less smooth, leading to a loss in the accuracy of the general solution (the "electromagnetic field–particles" system becomes rigid). Too large a ratio improves the accuracy up to a point but increases the computational cost. In this case, the approximation accuracy in the macroscopic equations remains fixed.

7   Conclusions

We considered the problem of modeling the interaction of metal nanoclusters with a substrate. The problem is relevant for obtaining thin metal coatings in the context of various spraying technologies. We suggest a new mathematical model of a metallic medium with a mesoscopic resolution level. The model is based on the representation of nanoparticles and the substrate by a system of nanospheroids and includes Maxwell's equations of electrodynamics and the equations of Newtonian dynamics averaged over nanoscales taking into account the Lorentz force. The numerical algorithm is based on mesh and particle methods. The algorithm is parallelized with respect to both space and particles. The preliminary model computations confirmed the efficiency and adequacy of the proposed computer model.

Acknowledgments. The research was supported by the Russian Science Foundation (project № 21-71-20054). The numerical experiments were performed on the hybrid supercomputer K60 installed in the Supercomputer Centre of Collective Usage of KIAM RAS.

References

1. Papyrin, A., Kosarev, V., Klinkov, S., Alkhimov, A., Fomin, V.: Cold Spray Technology. Elsevier Science, Amsterdam (2007)
2. Poza, P., Garrido-Maneiro, M.A.: Cold-sprayed coatings: microstructure, mechanical properties, and wear behaviour. Prog. Mater. Sci. **123**, 100839 (2022). https://doi.org/10.1016/j.pmatsci.2021.100839
3. Vaz, R.F., Garfias, A., Albaladejo, V., Sanchez, J., Cano, I.G.: A review of advances in cold spray additive manufacturing. Coatings **13**(2), 267 (2023). https://doi.org/10.3390/coatings13020267
4. Danilin, B.S.: Application of Low-Temperature Plasma to the Deposition of Thin Films. Energoatomizdat, Moscow (1989). (in Russian)
5. Suryanarayanan, R.: Plasma Spraying: Theory and Applications. World Scientific Pub Co Inc., Singapore (1993)
6. Heimann, R.B.: Plasma Spray Coating: Principles and Applications, 2nd ed. Wiley-VCH, Weinheim (2008)
7. Nikiforov, A., Chen, Z.: Atmospheric Pressure Plasma - From Diagnostics to Applications. IntechOpen, London, UK (2019). https://doi.org/10.5772/intechopen.75279
8. Danilin, B.S., Syrchin, V.K.: Magnetron Sputtering Systems. Radio i svyaz' Publ., Moscow (1982). (in Russian)
9. Ivanovsky, G.F., Petrov, V.I.: Ion-Plasma Processing of Materials. Radio i svyaz' Publ., Moscow (1986). (in Russian)
10. Behrisch, R., Eckstein, W.: Sputtering by Particle Bombardment: Experiments and Computer Calculations from Threshold to MeV Energies. Springer, Berlin (2007). https://doi.org/10.1007/978-3-540-44502-9
11. Kuzmichev, A.I.: Magnetron Sputtering Systems, Vol. 1: Introduction to the Physics and Technology of Magnetron Sputtering. Avers, Kiev (2008). (in Russian)
12. Wang, F., Wu., J.: Modern Ion Plating Technology. Fundamentals and Applications. Elsevier, Amsterdam (2022)
13. Kos, Ž, Aplinc, J., Mur, U., Ravnik, M.: Mesoscopic approach to nematic fluids. In: Toschi, F., Sega, M. (eds.) Flowing Matter. SBM, pp. 51–93. Springer, Cham (2019). https://doi.org/10.1007/978-3-030-23370-9_3
14. Ziman, J.M.: Electrons in metals: a short guide to the Fermi surface. Contemp. Phys. **4**(2), 81–99 (1962). https://doi.org/10.1080/00107516208205311
15. Klimov, V.V.: Nanoplasmonics. Physmatlit, Moscow (2009). (in Russian)
16. Krall, N.A., Trivelpiece, A.W.: Principles of Plasma Physics. McGraw-Hill Book Company, New York (1973)
17. Monaghan, J.J.: Hydrodynamics and its diverse applications. Annu. Rev. Fluid Mech. **44**, 323–346 (2012). https://doi.org/10.1146/annurev-fluid-120710-101220

18. Landau, L.D., Lifshitz, E.M.: Course of Theoretical. Physics. Vol. 8: Electrodynamics of Continuous Media, 2nd ed. Pergamon Press, Oxford (1984)
19. Eymard, R., Gallouet, T.R., Herbin. R.: The finite volume method. In: Ciarlet, P.G., Lions, J.L. (eds.) Handbook of Numerical Analysis, vol. 7, pp. 713–1020. Elsevier, Amsterdam, North Holland (2000). https://doi.org/10.1016/S1570-8659(00)07005-8
20. Taflove, A., Hagness, S.C.: Computational Electrodynamics. The Finite-Difference Time-Domain Method, 3rd ed. Artech House, Boston (2005)
21. Samarskii, A.A.: The Theory of Difference Schemes, 1st ed. CRC Press, Boca Raton (2001)
22. Smith, B.F.: Domain decomposition methods for partial differential equations. In: Keyes, D.E., Sameh, A., Venkatakrishnan, V. (eds.) Parallel Numerical Algorithms. ICASE/LaRC Interdisciplinary Series in Science and Engineering, vol. 4, pp. 225–243. Springer, Dordrecht (1997). https://doi.org/10.1007/978-94-011-5412-3_8
23. Dolean, V., Jolivet, P., Nataf, F.: An Introduction to Domain Decomposition Methods: Algorithms, Theory and Parallel Implementation. SIAM, Philadelphia (2015)
24. Alakeel, A.: A guide to dynamic load balancing in distributed computer systems. Int. J. Comput. Sci. Netw. Secur. (IJCSNS) 10(6), 153–160 (2010)
25. Sanders, P., Mehlhorn, K., Dietzfelbinger, M., Dementiev, R.: Sequential and Parallel Algorithms and Data Structures: The Basic Toolbox. Springer-Verlag, Cham (2019). https://doi.org/10.1007/978-3-030-25209-0
26. Podryga, V.O., Polyakov, S.V., Puzyrkov, D.V.: Supercomputer molecular modeling of thermodynamic equilibrium in gas-metal microsystems. Num. Meth. Prog. 16(1), 123–138 (2015). (in Russian)
27. Rapaport, D.C.: The Art of Molecular Dynamics Simulation. Cambridge University Press, Cambridge (2004)
28. Ogorodnikov, V.A., Pushkov, V.A., Tyupanova, O.A.: Fundamentals of Physics of Strength and Fracture Mechanics: A Textbook. RFNC-VNIIEF, Sarov (2007). (in Russian)
29. Ripan, R., Chetyanu, I.: Inorganic Chemistry. Vol. 2: Chemistry of Metals. Mir, Moscow (1972). (in Russian)
30. Kovenskii, I.M., Povetkin, V.V.: Metal Science of Coatings. SP Intermet Inzhiniring, Moscow (1999). (in Russian)
31. Berezin, N.B., Berezina, T.N., Mezhevich, Zh.V., Sagdeev, K.A.: Structure and solderability of nickel-phosphorus coverings. Bull. Kazan Technol. Univ. 17(5), 243–245 (2014). (in Russian)
32. Tyagunov, G.V., et al.: About nickel and chrome and their alloys. Int. J. Appl. Fundam. Res. 8, 56–62 (2022). (in Russian)
33. Yuan, Z., Cheng, Z.: Properties of nickel in micro- and nanostructures. Int. Stud. Sci. Bull. 3, 68 (2017). (in Russian)
34. Liu, W., Yan, S.: Investigation of nickel properties in macro and nanostructures. Int. Stud. Sci. Bull. 1, 106 (2019). (in Russian)

Supercomputer Simulation of Plasma Flow in the Diamagnetic Mode of Open Magnetic Systems

A. Efimova$^{(\boxtimes)}$, M. Boronina , K. Vshivkov , and G. Dudnikova

Institute of Computational Mathematics and Mathematical Geophysics SB RAS,
prospect Ak. Lavrentjeva, 6, Novosibirsk 630090, Russia
anna.an.efimova@gmail.com, {boronina,kovsh}@ssd.sscc.ru

Abstract. A new 2D numerical model of the diamagnetic regime of an open plasma confinement trap is presented. A hybrid numerical model based on the kinetic approximation for the ion components of the plasma and the injected beam and the hydrodynamic approximation for electrons (PIC-MHD) is considered. The particle-in-cell method is used to solve the Vlasov kinetic equation. A new algorithm for solving the equations of motion of charged particles in the electromagnetic fields is used. This algorithm takes into account the condition of immutability of the electromagnetic fields at each time step. The parallel computing algorithm is based on decomposition with respect to space and particles. The basic principles of diamagnetic plasma confinement were verified, and various options for beam injection were considered. The calculation parameters were chosen close to the parameters of the experiments at the CAT facility (BINP SB RAS).

Keywords: Numerical methods · Hybrid model · PIC-method · Boris method · Gas-dynamic trap · High performance computing

1 Introduction

Currently, one of the most popular methods used in computational plasma physics is the particle-in-cell (PIC) method [1–3]. The software systems used to simulate processes in plasma are of great commercial value in the development of technological plasma systems. One of the publicly available commercial systems for numerical simulation is the COMSOL MULTIPHYSICS [4] package, the latest version of which includes a module for modeling plasma dynamics in a hydrodynamic approximation. To study the interaction of hot plasma with the surface, the codes (Monte Carlo) EIRENE [5] and DEGAS2 [6] have been developed. There are a number of 2- and 3-dimensional electromagnetic kinetic PIC codes (KARAT, VORPAL, OOPIC, etc.), which are used, in particular, to solve problems of the interaction of a laser pulse or an electron beam with a plasma. But the wider use of the PIC method, especially when solving three-dimensional problems of modeling plasma flows with very different spatial and

© The Author(s), under exclusive license to Springer Nature Switzerland AG 2023
L. Sokolinsky and M. Zymbler (Eds.): PCT 2023, CCIS 1868, pp. 299–310, 2023.
https://doi.org/10.1007/978-3-031-38864-4_21

temporal scales, are hindered by high requirements for memory and computer speed. This is due to the significant difference in time and space scales for the ionic and electronic components of the plasma. To overcome this shortcoming, the model ratio of the ion mass to the electron mass [7,8] is often used. Another way is to use hybrid models, in which for one of the plasma components the kinetic approximation and the PIC method are used, and for the other one, the hydrodynamic approximation, and the corresponding equations are solved by finite difference methods [9,10]. Despite the obvious advantages of hybrid models, they need to be improved. In particular, the problem of using the hybrid model in vacuum regions bordering on plasma ones has not been solved. In work [11] it is shown that the hybrid model is unstable, and only the use of numerical methods makes it possible to make it correct. Therefore, when solving specific problems, it becomes necessary to develop new approaches that take into account all the features of the simulated phenomenon. The shortcomings of various modifications of the particle method lead to the need to improve the method in one way or another and adapt it to the solution of new problems. It should be noted that work on improving the particle method continues at the present time, but theoretical studies of the particle method are mainly carried out abroad. So in the work of T. Umeda [12], an improved Boris algorithm for calculating particle velocities is proposed. The article by F. Li [13] describes a modification of the particle method that suppresses the countable Cherenkov instability. New, essentially parallel algorithms [14] are also being developed.

This paper presents numerical simulation of injection of charged particle beams into an open magnetic trap. The results of computational experiments are obtained using two-dimensional parallel code. The created two-dimensional axially symmetric numerical model relies on the solution of the Vlasov kinetic equation for the ion components of injected beam and background plasma by the particle-in-cell (PIC) method. For the electron component of the plasma, the magnetic hydrodynamics (MHD) approximation is used. The MHD equations for the electrons and Maxwell's equations are solved with the application of finite-difference schemes of second-order accuracy. In the system of Maxwell's equations for a self-consistent electromagnetic field, the bias current is not taken into account, the plasma quasi-neutrality condition is used, and the transfer coefficient due to the finite conductivity of the plasma is considered as constant. The model includes the possibility of continuous off-axis injection of two ion beams at an arbitrary angle to the magnetic field. We used a new scheme for calculating the trajectories of motion of charged particles, based on the analytical solution to the momentum equation [15]. It is taken into account the condition of immutability of the electromagnetic fields at each time step.

On the basis of computational experiments, the spatial and temporal characteristics of the arising cavities of the magnetic field and background plasma are investigated. With the created model, the concept of the diamagnetic regime of plasma confinement in open magnetic traps, as applied to the laboratory experiments on the CAT installation at the Budker Institute of Nuclear Physics SB RAS, is clarified and investigated [16].

The paper is organized as follows. Section 1 represents the introduction to the numerical simulation of the diamagnetic mode in open traps. In Sect. 2 the problem statement is presented. Section 3 is devoted to the parallel algorithm description. The description of the numerical experiments and their results are presented in Sect. 4. Section 5 gives a brief summary of the study.

2 Problem Statement

Let us consider formulation of the problem of creating the diamagnetic regime in an open magnetic trap at injection of charged particle beams. At the initial moment, the hydrogen background plasma of the density $n_0 = const$ is inside the cylindrical chamber of the radius R_0 and length L. The vacuum magnetic field $\mathbf{B} = (B_r, 0, B_z)$ is created by two coaxial coils with the same radii and currents on the boundary $r = R_0$. Two proton beams are introduced with a constant velocity $\mathbf{v} = V_0$ at the point with the coordinates $R = R_1$, $z = L/2$. The beams are injected at the angle $\pm\theta$ relative to the magnetic field and have the temperature T_i. The stationary electron and ion components of the background plasma are assumed to be cold: $T_e = 0$ and $T_i = 0$. The hybrid numerical model of the problem under consideration is based on a system of the Vlasov equations for the ion components of the plasma and the injected beam, magnetic hydrodynamics equations for the magnetized electron component of the plasma, and Maxwell's equations [3,17]:

$$\frac{\partial f_i}{\partial t} + \mathbf{v}\frac{\partial f_i}{\partial \mathbf{r}} + \frac{\mathbf{F}_i}{m_i}\frac{\partial f_i}{\partial \mathbf{v}} = 0,$$

$$\mathbf{F}_i = e\left(\mathbf{E} + \frac{1}{c}\mathbf{v} \times \mathbf{B}\right) + \mathbf{R}_i,$$

$$m_e\frac{d\mathbf{v}_e}{dt} = -e\left(\mathbf{E} + \frac{1}{c}\mathbf{v}_e \times \mathbf{B}\right) - \frac{\nabla p_e}{n_e} + \mathbf{R}_e = 0,$$

$$n_e\left(\frac{\partial T_e}{\partial t} + (\mathbf{v}_e \cdot \nabla)T_e\right) + (\gamma - 1)p_e\nabla \cdot \mathbf{v}_e = (\gamma - 1)Q_e,$$

$$\nabla \times \mathbf{B} = \frac{4\pi}{c}\mathbf{j},$$

$$\nabla \cdot \mathbf{B} = 0.$$

Here f_i is the ion distribution function, $\mathbf{B}$ and $\mathbf{E}$ are the magnetic and electric fields, $\mathbf{v}_e$ is the electron velocity, $v_i = \int f_i(\mathbf{r}, \mathbf{v}, t)\,\mathbf{v}\,d\mathbf{v}/n_i$ is the average ion velocity, p_e and T_e are the electron pressure and temperature, and m_i is the proton mass. The force $\mathbf{R}_i = -\mathbf{R}_e$ takes into account the momentum exchange between the electron and ion components of the plasma and beam; $\mathbf{R}_e = m_e(\mathbf{v}_i - \mathbf{v}_e)/\tau$, where τ is the characteristic time of ion-electron collision and m_e is the mass of the electron. As for the dissipation mechanisms, the plasma conductivity $\sigma = \tau n_e e^2 / m_e$ is taken into account. The heat generated by the electrons $Q_e = \mathbf{j}^2 / \sigma$, and the current $\mathbf{j} = n_e(\mathbf{v}_i - \mathbf{v}_e)$. Here it is assumed that the collision frequency is defined by the anomalous scattering processes on the fluctuations of electromagnetic fields and does not depend on the plasma and magnetic field parameters $(\tau = const)$. In the calculations, the adiabatic exponent $\gamma = 5/3$.

The model uses the condition of plasma quasi-neutrality, i.e., equality of the densities of the electron and ion components of the plasma, $n_e = n_i = n$ (the scales under consideration are larger than the Debye radius). In addition, only low-frequency processes are considered and bias currents are not taken into account. The electric field is determined from the motion equation of electrons under the assumption of $m_e = 0$. In this approximation, the dispersion effects associated with the electron component of the plasma, which determine the structure of magnetosonic waves propagating across the magnetic field, are ignored. The algorithm of the problem solution takes into account the large difference in the magnitude of the magnetic field of the trap, the injection of particles with non-linear density distribution in a cylindrical coordinate system, and the escape of particles through the trap mirrors. The electron component of the plasma and the magnetic field are calculated with the application of finite-difference schemes on staggered grids [1–3]. When the Vlasov equations are solved by the PIC method, transitions to Cartesian coordinates and back to cylindrical coordinates are carried out [2]. The volume of each cell of the grid is proportional to the distance to the axis of the cylinder; the mass and charge of the model particles also depend on their position relative to the Z-axis. The characteristic spatial size and time interval of the problem under consideration are $\lambda = c/\omega_{pi}$ and $T = 1/\omega_{iH}$, where $\omega_{pi} = \left(4\pi n_e e^2 / m_i\right)^{1/2}$ is the ion plasma frequency and $\omega_{iH} = eB_0 / (m_i c)$ is the ion cyclotron frequency. The step of the uniform spatial grid used in solving the problem is $0.05\,\lambda < h < 0.1\,\lambda$, and the time step is $10^{-6}T < \Delta t < 10^{-5}T$.

The kinetic equation for the ion component is solved by the particle-in-cell method, in which the ion component of the background plasma and injected beams is replaced by a set of model particles. The equations of motion for model particles with the index j correspond to the characteristics of the kinetic Vlasov equation:

$$\frac{d\mathbf{r}_j}{dt} = \mathbf{v}_j,$$

$$\frac{d\mathbf{v}_j}{dt} = \frac{q_j}{m_j}\left(\mathbf{E} + \frac{1}{c}\mathbf{v}_j \times \mathbf{B}\right) + \frac{1}{m_j}R_j.$$

The equations of ion motion are solved with the use of the new VD1 scheme, presented in [15], which enables exact solution to the non-relativistic motion equations of ions of background plasma and injected beams.

3   Parallel Algorithm

Parallelization of the algorithm and creation of a parallel numerical code is a prerequisite for speeding up the calculations, increasing the number of model particles and reducing the spatial step. The parallel computing algorithm created and implemented in our parallel code is based on the decomposition of both the spatial grid (in the longitudinal direction) and the particle grid [18]. Each subdomain is assigned to a group of processor cores; the particles of the subdomain are distributed among the cores of the group. At the initial stage, the background particles and the particles of the injected beams are distributed evenly between the cores of their group.

The calculation of the velocities and coordinates is one of two time-consuming procedures of the algorithm and takes $\sim 60\%$ of total time. In order to use auto-vectorization of the loop through the particle index the particles must be sorted by cell index. This also helps to avoid data dependencies and speed-up the second time-consuming procedure of the charge and current densities determination, which takes $\sim 35\%$ of total time. When some particles leave their subdomain their data are forwarded to one of the cores of the neighboring group, and since the time step smallness is the distinctive characteristic of the hybrid model, the number of particles is small ($J_{out} \ll 1\%$) and overheads are low. After receiving data from the neighboring group cores and boundary conditions applying the data are inserted into the empty places in the corresponding particle cell array if it is possible or added in to the end of the array. The result is arrays of the particles sorted by cell index on every time step.

Successive data distribution also ensures balanced loading of processor cores in the group. The algorithm calculates the average number p_i of the particles in a core assigned to subdomain i, on the basis of p_i increases the number of cores in group for the dense regions to even up p_i, and then redistributes the particles within their new group. It requires sending data of "superfluous" particles to fill the "empty" cores up to p_i particles and the further sorting of the particles among the cells in each core. Figure 1 represents two examples of particle distribution in the domain and the corresponding core distribution among groups. The rebalance leads to high overheads in the worst case affecting all cores, thus we apply the algorithm every T_1 ($\sim 10^5$ time steps).

On every time step the master cores of each group are responsible for the broadcasting, gathering grid information within the group and space grid computations. First the master cores distribute the data for electromagnetic fields in the group, and after performing of particle related procedures each core gathers 2D arrays of the mean charge and mean current densities. Then the master cores of the groups calculate the new currents, electric field, magnetic field and temperature with taking into account the exchanges of the adjacent boundary grid data between the master cores of the neighboring groups. Below the algorithm is presented.

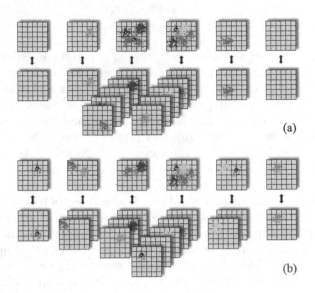

Fig. 1. The load balancing: distribution of the cores and the particles at different time steps.

```
Setinitialconditions;
for i = 1, 2, ..., N_external do
    Rebalance;
    for j = 1, 2, ..., N_internal do
        if core contains injection point then injection;
        if core = master then Fields BCAST from masters to slaves;
        Newparticlecoordinates;
        Boundaryconditionsforparticles;
        Particleexchangeswithneighbors;
        Particlesortingamongcellsinonecore;
        Meanchargedensities;
        Meancurrentdensities;
        Reducemeandensitiesfromslavestomasters;
        if core = master then
            Meandensitiesexchangewithneighbors;
            Boundaryconditions;
            Currents;
            Currentexchangewithneighbors;
            Electricfield;
            Electricfieldexchangewithneighbors;
            Magneticfield;
            Magneticfieldexchangewithneighbors;
            Temperature;
            Temperatureexchangewithneighbors.
```

The authors code is written on Fortran 95 using MPI and compiled using AVX2 optimization. The code allowed to reduce the calculation time by ten folds compared with the monoprocessor algorithm due to the big number of cores in regions with high density. Figure 2 demonstrates the computation times (a), speed-up (b) and efficiency (c) of the code for different number of cores np for the computational grid 40×120 and 10^4 particles entering the trap during $t = T$. The small number of cores doesn't allow performing the computations, thus we calculate the speed-up and the efficiency with initial number of cores 30, and it corresponds to linear decomposition ($n_g = 30$, $np = 30$). The speed-up was calculated as $S(np) = Time_{30}/Time_{np}$, the efficiency $Eff(np) = S(np) * 30/np$, where $Time_i$ is computation time using i cores. The blue color denotes computations until the moment $t = 5$, the red color denotes the computations until $t = 40$.

One may observe the super-linear speed-up, which corresponds to the "addition" of cores in the groups of high-density subdomains around the injection point [19]. However, on the early stages ($t = 5$) the speed-up and efficiency is low for big np : the scanty particles are concentrated near the injection point and the communication overheads inside groups with high number of cores increase the computations times. For the later stages ($t = 40$) the algorithm yields high efficiency.

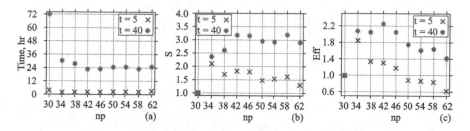

Fig. 2. Dependence of the computation times (a), speedup (b) and efficiency (c) on the number of cores np for $t = 5$ and $t = 40$.

The computation times non-linearly depend on the number cores np, because these np cores may be distributed among different numbers of groups n_g. Higher n_g leads to the thinner subdomains and smaller number of particles in the subdomains. Thus usually configurations with np/n_g between 2 and 4 are used. The spatial grid size N_z defines the maximal number of groups, which can not exceed $N_z/4$ (2 nodes + 2 ghost nodes of the subdomain in Z-direction). On practice, big number of cores ($np > 300$) is not used: the subdomain size remain the same with proportional increasing of N_z and N_g, but the time step due to the severe stability condition yields high number of time steps and consequent increase of computation time. The requirement for the computations is to be performed in few days, and the grid can not be increased significantly.

4   Results of Numerical Simulation

Let us consider some results of the numerical simulation of the interaction of ion beams with plasma in an open magnetic trap with the radius $R_0 = 15\,\text{cm}$ and the length $L = 60\,\text{cm}$. In the center of the system $(R = 0\,\text{cm},\ z = 30\,\text{cm})$, the magnetic field strength is $B_0 = 20\,\text{kGs}$, and the mirror ratio on the axis is 2.0. The density of the cold $(T_e = 0)$ background plasma is $n_0 = 10^{14}\,\text{cm}^{-3}$. Two ion beams are injected to the magnetic field of the trap from the point with the coordinates $R_1 = 0.5\,\text{cm},\ z = 30\,\text{cm}$ at the angle $\theta = \pm60°$. The temperature and velocity of the continuously injected ion beams are $T_i = 10\,\text{eV}$, and $V_0 = 4.4{\cdot}10^7\,\text{cm/s}$. The applied characteristics of the background plasma and injected beams correspond to the data of laboratory experiments [16]. Figures 3 and 4 show maps of magnetic field lines (a) and spatial distributions of ions of injected beams (b) at the time moments $t = 5\cdot10^{-7}\,\text{s}$ and $t = 5\cdot10^{-6}\,\text{s}$.

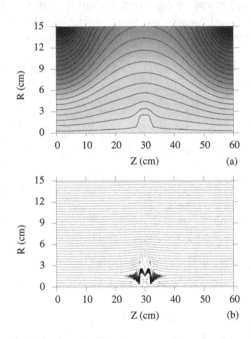

Fig. 3. Map of the magnetic field lines of the magnetic trap (a) and distribution of the ions of injected beam (black) and the background plasma (b), $t = 5\cdot10^{-7}\,\text{s}$.

From the graphs, it can be seen that continuous injection of beams results in displacement of the magnetic field and formation of magnetic cavity (magnetic bubble), in which the magnetic field pressure reaches only several percent of the initial one (Fig. 3). The spatial distributions of the ions of the injected beams and background plasma ions demonstrate the evolution of the structure of the continuously injected beams and the displacement of background plasma ions from the magnetic cavity region.

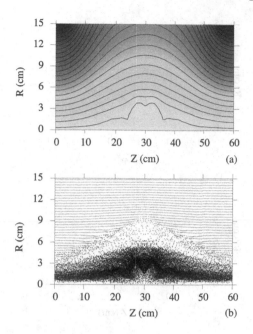

Fig. 4. Map of the magnetic field lines of the magnetic trap (a) and distribution of the ions of injected beam (black) and the background plasma (b), $t = 5 \cdot 10^{-6}$ s.

The isoline maps of the magnetic field pressure and plasma pressure of the injected beams (see Fig. 5) show the accumulation and capture of the plasma in the magnetic cavity region. The quasi-stationary diamagnetic regime is formed by the time $t = 4 \cdot 10^{-6}$ s, from which the transverse size of the magnetic cavity slightly changes.

The presented results of calculations performed on the basis of the created parallel code demonstrate the possibility of forming a quasi-stationary diamagnetic configuration of an open trap in the mode with continuous off-axis injection of ion beams as applied to the conditions of laboratory experiments on the CAT installation (BINP SB RAS). The calculation grid is 100×300 in size; the time step $\Delta t = 4 \cdot 10^{-6}$ T; the number of background particles $J_b = 1.2 \cdot 10^5$, 10^4 model particles are introduced per time unit $t = T$. For these parameters, the operating time was 26 h up to the time $t = 40$ T and 74 h up to $t = 80$ T. The calculations were carried out with 72 cores of Intel Xeon Phi 7290 processors of the Siberian Supercomputer Center, ICM&MG SB RAS, Novosibirsk.

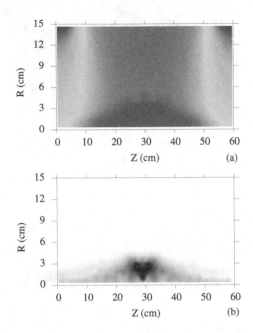

Fig. 5. Magnetic field pressure isolines (a) and plasma pressure isolines of the injected proton beams (b) at $t = 5 \cdot 10^{-6}$ s.

5   Conclusion

The article presents a hybrid (PIC-MHD) numerical model, based on which the problem of forming the diamagnetic plasma confinement regime in an open magnetic system with beam injection at an angle to the magnetic field is solved. The motion equations of the ions of the background plasma and injected beams were solved with the application of VD1 scheme, which takes into account the condition of constant values of the Lorentz force at each time step. The parallel computing algorithm created and implemented in our parallel code is based on decomposition with respect to the space and the particles. The algorithm made it possible to reduce the calculation time by ten folds compared with the monoprocessor algorithm. A series of computational experiments has shown that the continuous injection of beams is accompanied by displacement of the magnetic field and formation of a diamagnetic cavity, in which the magnetic field pressure reaches several percent of the pressure of the initial magnetic field. The results confirm the possibility of retaining high-temperature plasma in the diamagnetic regime of open magnetic traps as applied to the conditions of laboratory experiments at the BINP SB RAS. The created model adequately describes non-stationary non-linear processes in the system under consideration and can be used for further research on heating and plasma retention in the diamagnetic regime of linear magnetic traps.

This work was done within the framework of the Russian Science Foundation project (19-71-20026) by using the resources of the Siberian Supercomputer Center for Collective Use ICM&MG SB RAS.

References

1. Berezin, Y.A., Vshivkov, V.A.: Particle-in-cell method in rarefied plasma dynamics. Nauka, Novosibirsk, Russia (1980)
2. Birdsall, C.K., Langdon, A.B.: Plasma Physics and Numerical Simulation. Energoatomizdat, Moscow, Russia (1989)
3. Berezin, Y.A., Dudnikova, G.I., Liseikina, T.V., Fedoruk, M.P.: Fedoruk, M.P.: Modeling of nonstationary plasma processes. Novosibirsk State University, Institute of Computational Technologies SB RAS, Novosibirsk, Russia (2018)
4. Dickinson, E., Ekström, H., Fontes, H.: COMSOL multiphysics: finite element software for electrochemical analysis. A mini-review. J. Electrochem. Commun. **40**, 71–74 (2014). https://doi.org/10.1016/j.elecom.2013.12.020
5. Feng, Y., et al.: Recent improvements in the EMC3-Eirene code. J. Contrib. Plasma Phys. **54**(4–6), 426–431 (2014). https://doi.org/10.1002/ctpp.201410092
6. Cao, B., Stotler, D.P., Zweben, S.J., Bell, M., Diallo, A., Leblanc B.: Comparison of gas puff imaging data in NSTX with DEGAS 2 simulations. J. Fusion Sci. Technol. **64**(1), 29–38 (2013). https://doi.org/10.13182/FST13-A17044
7. Stroman, T., Pohl, M., Niemiec, J.: Kinetic simulations of turbulent magnetic-field growth by streaming cosmic rays. J. Astrophys. **706**, 38–44 (2009). https://doi.org/10.1088/0004-637X/706/1/38
8. Dieckmann, M.E., Murphy, G.C., Meli, A., Drury, L.O.C.: Particle-in-cell simulation of a mildly relativistic collision of an electron-ion plasma carrying a quasi-parallel magnetic field. Electron acceleration and magnetic field amplification at supernova shocks. J. Astron. Astrophys. **509**, A89 (2010). https://doi.org/10.1051/0004-6361/200912643
9. Caprioli, D.: Hybrid simulations of particle acceleration at shocks. J. Nuclear Phys. B (Proc. Suppl.) **256–257**, 48–55 (2014). https://doi.org/10.1016/j.nuclphysbps.2014.10.005
10. Weidl, M.S., Winske, D., Jenko, F., Niemann, C.: Hybrid simulations of a parallel collisionless shock in the large plasma device. J. Phys. Plasmas **23**(12), 122102 (2016). https://doi.org/10.1063/1.4971231
11. Vshivkova, L.V., Dudnikova., G.I.: Dispersion analysis of the hybrid plasma model. J. Bull. Nov. Comp. Center Num. Anal. **16**, 101–106 (2013)
12. Umeda, T.: A three-step Boris integrator for Lorentz force equation of charged particles. J. Comput. Phys. Commun. **228**, 1–4 (2018). https://doi.org/10.1016/j.cpc.2018.03.019
13. Li, F., et al.: Controlling the numerical Cerenkov instability in PIC simulations using a customized finite difference Maxwell solver and a local FFT based current correction. J. Comput. Phys. Commun. **214**, 6–17 (2017). https://doi.org/10.1016/j.cpc.2017.01.001
14. Khaziev, R., Curreli, D.: hPIC: a scalable electrostatic particle-in-cell for plasma-material interactions. J. Comput. Phys. Commun. **229**, 87–98 (2018). https://doi.org/10.1016/j.cpc.2018.03.028
15. Voropaeva, E., Vshivkov, K., Vshivkova, L., Dudnikova, G., Efimova, A.: New motion algorithm in the particle-in-cell method. J. Phys. **2028**(1), 012011 (2021). https://doi.org/10.1088/1742-6596/2028/1/012011

16. Beklemishev, A.D.: Diamagnetic, bubble equilibria in linear traps. J. Phys. Plasmas **23**, 082506 (2016). https://doi.org/10.1063/1.4

17. Boronina, M.A., Dudnikova, G.I., Efimova, A.A., Genrikh, E.A., Vshivkov, V.A., Chernoshtanov, I.S.: Numerical study of diamagnetic regime in open magnetic trap. J. Phys. Conf. Ser. **1640**(1), 012021 (2020). https://doi.org/10.1088/1742-6596/1640/1/012021

18. Chernykh, I., et al.: High-performance simulation of high-beta plasmas using PIC method. J. Commun. Comput. Inf. Sci. **1331**, 207–215 (2020)

19. Boronina, M.A., Chernykh, I.G., Genrikh, E.A., Vshivkov, V.A.: Parallel realization of the hybrid model code for numerical simulation of plasma dynamics. J. Phys. Conf. Ser. **1336** (2019). https://doi.org/10.1088/1742-6596/1336/1/012017

Computer Simulation of the Three-Dimensional Synthesis of Phase Images of Nanometer Scale Objects

Gennady Levin[1], Gennady Vishnyakov[1], and Yaroslaw Ilyushin[2,3](✉)

[1] The All-Russian Research Institute for Optical and Physical Measurements, 46 Ozernaya st., Moscow 119361, Russian Federation
vniiofi@vniiofi.ru
[2] Moscow State University, Physical Faculty GSP-2, Moscow 119992, Russian Federation
ilyushin@phys.msu.ru
[3] Kotel'nikov Institute of Radio Engineering and Electronics, Russian Academy of Sciences, Moscow 125009, Russian Federation
ire@cplire.ru

Abstract. The article is devoted to the analysis and further improvement of the well-known Transfocal Scanning Optical Microscopy (TSOM) method, previously proposed by other authors. We analyze this approach step by step and simulate it thoroughly. Our simulation includes a rigorous numerical solution of the Maxwell equations for the electromagnetic field of light in an optical microscope using the Finite Difference in Time Domain (FDTD) method and the synthesis of a TSOM image in strict accordance with the original author's instructions.

After that, we propose an approach to the synthetic formation of three-dimensional phase images of nanometer scale objects with wave field back projection. We also carefully simulate is step by step, similarly to the previous one. Then we compare both the method newly proposed by us and the old one, using several benchmark test objects. We demonstrate the advantages of synthetic phase images over amplitude image synthesis. Finally, we show how the synthetic phase images can be used in pattern recognition algorithms for applied defectoscopic purposes.

Keywords: Optical microscopy · Nanotechnology · Pattern recognition · Detection algorithms

1 Introduction

Precise measurements of the geometric parameters of microscale and nanoscale objects, the control of manufacturing tolerances, and the detection of small displacements of microscale parts in various technological processes are priority

The research is carried out using the equipment of the shared research facilities of HPC computing resources at Lomonosov Moscow State University [1].

© The Author(s), under exclusive license to Springer Nature Switzerland AG 2023
L. Sokolinsky and M. Zymbler (Eds.): PCT 2023, CCIS 1868, pp. 311–322, 2023.
https://doi.org/10.1007/978-3-031-38864-4_22

tasks of modern optical microscopy. In particular, the optical quality control of photolithographic matrices and printed circuit boards (PCB) are among the most important of them [2–5]. In some cases, the deviations of the positions under control from their prescribed values are on the order of nanometers. This is well exceeded by both the classical Rayleigh diffraction limit [6] and pixel resolution of the matrix photodetectors [7] in the object space. All these reasons create a need for new image processing techniques aimed at extracting valuable information from optical microscopy images. One of the new directions in modern microscopy is related to the techniques for the measurement of the dimensions of the simplest microscale objects from their wave diffraction patterns, the so-called optical diffractometry [8,9]. However, these techniques require the numerical solution of both direct and inverse optical problems of wave diffraction on the object under investigation. A simpler approach to the problem of detection of nanoscale defects in the industrial production of optical images has been developed by the National Institute of Standards and Technology (NIST), USA [10–12]. This technique is essentially based on the recognition of nanometer scale deviations of the objects from the reference on three-dimensional diffraction patterns specially formed in the image space of the conventional optical microscope. It is worth noting that the superresolution in the classical sense of the term, i.e., the formation of an image overcoming the Rayleigh resolution limit, is not the goal of this approach. Nevertheless, it has been shown in these and other papers [4,13–15] that the nanoscale deviations of the geometrical parameters from the prescribed values produce characteristic signatures in the wave diffraction patterns that appear to be detectable.

The technique suggested by the authors is called TSOM (Transfocal Scanning Optical Microscopy). The method is basically based on the registration of a series of two-dimensional images in transverse coordinates while the focus of the microscope moves along its optical axis. Afterward, that stack of two-dimensional images is sliced normally to the images' planes. Thus a two-dimensional image (TSOM-image in the author's terminology) is formed [10,16].

It turned out that such representation of microscopic measurement data is very suitable for comparative analysis of objects with very similar geometrical parameters, e.g., objects differing by several nanometers. The comparison of such TSOM images to the set of benchmark images allows the detection of these deviations from the prescribed geometry.

The TSOM image is in fact a distribution of the optical intensity (the square of the electromagnetic field amplitude), obtained by scanning the object with a microscope that is gradually refocused. To improve its information capacity, the resolution and scanning range are required. As a consequence, the amount of time needed for the whole TSOM image registration grows up. One more disadvantage of the TSOM technique is the neglect of the phase of the optical field. This, we think, restricts its capabilities for discrimination of small changes in the object under investigation.

However, the practice of interferometric optical microscopy shows that the phase of the wave field is one of its most informative characteristics. Let us call the two-dimensional distribution of the optical wave path difference, which can be retrieved immediately from the interference patterns, the phase image of the object. The analysis of such phase images significantly exceeds the accuracy of several very different measurement techniques based on the analysis of amplitude images of immediate interference patterns. Thus, in the paper [17], the authors suggest a method of analysis of the phase images obtained from the Linnick interference microscope. It was shown there that this method can detect nanometric movements of the objects without data inversion or superresolution procedures, both theoretically and in real experiments.

The present paper aims to investigate the application of three-dimensional phase diffraction images of nanometric objects for industrial detection of manufacturing defects. Also, we suggest the registration of the amplitude and phase of the field for a unique position of the microscope focal plane. Other field distributions in other planes are computed numerically using the wave propagation laws in free space instead of physically changing the focal plane position of the microscope lens. Also, we present numerical results that simulate the formation of the diffraction pattern as well as its amplitude and phase. Moreover, we study and compare the detection of deviation of the objects from each other using phase images and other techniques.

The paper is organized as follows. In the Sect. 1, a brief bibliographic review is given and the motivation and objectives of the paper are formulated. The Sect. 2 is devoted to a detailed description of the image synthesis algorithms, investigated in this paper. In the Sect. 3, we give necessary information on the method of numerical electrodynamics (FDTD), which we use in this study. A special Subsect. 3.1 is devoted to the analysis of the efficiency of the parallelization of the numerical algorithm in the computer code implemented by us. Section 4 contains analysis and discussion of the numerical results obtained in this study. Conclusion (the Sect. 5) summarizes the study and points directions for further work.

2   Algorithms for Image Synthesis

Consider the problem of the formation of some object images in the Linnick interference microscope. Numerical techniques for the computer simulation of such microscopic images have been discussed in detail (see, for example, [17,18]).

Let $E_z(x, y, \phi)$ be the distribution of the complex wave field amplitude in the focal plane of the microscope [17], where x and z are the coordinates in the image plane, y is the position of the focal plane of the microscopic lens, and ϕ is the incidence angle of the coherent plane wave that illuminates the object, with respect to the y axis (the optical axis of the microscope; see Fig. 1). Following [10–12,16], we restrict our considerations to objects infinitely long in the z direction. In this case, the field does not depend on the z coordinate. For the simulation, the amplitude and phase distributions in the (x, y) plane are independently calculated for a number of incidence directions ϕ_i. According to [16], the most informative range of focal positions of the microscope is a certain

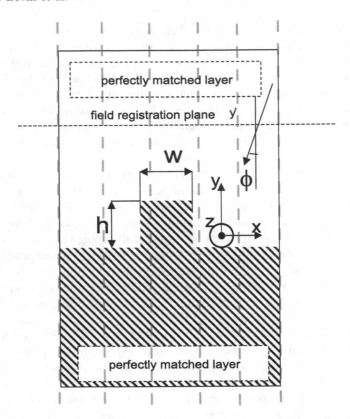

Fig. 1. Computational domain geometry

range of several wavelengths above and beneath the object plane. We also assume that the object is illuminated by a collimated wave incident in the direction ϕ_i within the range of incidence angles determined by the optical system of the particular microscope used. The TSOM image [10, 16] is the distribution of the radiation intensity

$$\sum_i |E_z(x, y, \phi_i)|^2, \tag{1}$$

where N is the number of partial incidence directions ϕ_i. Thus the TSOM image is the field intensity averaged over the whole range of partial incidence directions allowed by the microscope optical system. In the present paper, we suggest using phase images instead of TSOM images. According to the general idea of the proposed approach, it can be expressed by the formula

$$\sum_i \arg(E_z(x, y, \phi_i)), \tag{2}$$

where $\arg(\cdot)$ denotes the argument of the complex value, e.g., the complex amplitude of the partial wave field $E_z(x, z, \phi_i)$ or the phase of this partial field. We call this phase distribution the FAMOR image, and the technique of its formation—the backward propagation phase microscopy.

In contrast to the TSOM method, we suggest computing all the partial fields that constitute the phase synthetic image (2), from a single amplitude and phase distribution registered in an arbitrary plane of the image space close to the plane of best image focusing in an interferometric or holographic microscope. Modern techniques of digital interferometric or holographic microscopy allow retrieving and digitizing the complex amplitude of the wave field from interferometric images in an arbitrary plane at any distance y from the best-focusing plane, above or below it. To this end, we use back-propagation algorithms.

Thus, the following operations are necessary for the synthetic formation of the amplitude or phase image:

1. Illuminate the object with a plane monochromatic wave incident in the direction ϕ_i to the normal of the object plane.
2. Register the interference image of the object in the plane optically conjugated to the object plane, for each incidence angle ϕ_i from a certain set of them.
3. Retrieve the amplitude and phase of the field from an interference image in the plane $y = 0$ (the zero plane) using the Fourier transform procedure or by phase steps.
4. Compute the amplitude and phase in other planes $y = const$ for values of y lying in some range of several wavelengths above and below the zero plane, using for this some backpropagation procedure.
5. Average the phase or amplitude (TSOM) over the whole range of incidence angles ϕ_i.
6. Localize separate objects in these synthetic amplitude (TSOM) or phase images.
7. Compute the differences between pairs of amplitude (TSOM) or phase images to detect deviations in the geometric parameters of the objects from each other.

As a result of amplitude (TSOM) or phase image-processing procedures, we obtain the distributions of the informative parameters of the wave field (phase and amplitude) in a three-dimensional domain in the space of the object images. The analysis of these distributions allows comparing the imaged objects to each other. Nanometer-scale objects, not observable with traditional optical microscopes due to the classical Rayleigh diffraction resolution limit [6], can be detected in amplitude (TSOM) or phase images.

To investigate the discriminational capabilities of these two three-dimensional imaging methods, we simulated all the stages of the formation and processing of the interferometric microscopic images by numerically solving the Maxwell equations for the vectorial electromagnetic field with respect to its polarization and scattering on the object. We modeled the registration of the image using the numerical approximation of a specially modernized Linnick interferometric microscope, which is capable of registering the interferometric image with a high degree of accuracy.

3   Numerical Simulations of the Optical Wave Scattering on an Object

In this study, we use the Finite-Difference in Time Domain (FDTD) numerical technique for the calculation of the electromagnetic scattering of an optical wave on an object. Proposed in 1966 [19], the method has become one of the basic numerical techniques in electrodynamics and is widely used for simulations in optical [17,18] and radiophysical [20,21] applications.

The numerical simulation of the electromagnetic wave scattering on an object of constant cross-section profile and infinitely long in the z direction has been performed by the FDTD method for an s-polarized incident wave [22] with an electric wave field parallel to the z axis, i.e., $\mathbf{E} = (0, 0, E_z)$. The magnetic permeability of the object was assumed to be 1, owing to the optical frequencies of the field under consideration.

The Maxwell equations for the electric and magnetic vector components relevant to the considered problem (H_x, H_y, E_z) [23],

$$\frac{\partial H_x}{\partial t} = -\frac{\partial E_z}{\partial y}, \tag{3a}$$

$$\frac{\partial H_y}{\partial t} = \frac{\partial E_z}{\partial x}, \tag{3b}$$

$$\frac{\partial E_z}{\partial t} = \frac{1}{\varepsilon} \left(\frac{\partial H_y}{\partial x} - \frac{\partial H_x}{\partial y} - \sigma E_z \right), \tag{3c}$$

are approximated by finite differences with the standard leap-frog scheme of the FDTD technique [19,23]:

$$H_x^{n+1/2}(i, j+1/2) = H_x^{n-1/2}(i, j+1/2) + \frac{\delta t}{\delta y} \left[E_z^n(i,j) - E_z^n(i,j+1) \right], \quad (4a)$$

$$H_y^{n+1/2}(i+1/2, j) = H_x^{n-1/2}(i+1/2, j) + \frac{\delta t}{\delta y} \left[E_z^n(i+1,j) - E_z^n(i,j) \right], \quad (4b)$$

$$E_z^{n+1}(i,j) = E_z^n(i,j) + \frac{\delta t}{\varepsilon(i,j)\delta y} \left[H_y^{n+1/2}(i+1/2, j) - H_y^{n+1/2}(i-1/2, j) \right] \tag{4c}$$

$$+ \frac{\delta t}{\varepsilon(i,j)\delta y} \left[H_x^{n+1/2}(i, j-1/2) - H_x^{n+1/2}(i, j+1/2) \right].$$

At the side walls of the solution domain, we impose a periodic wave boundary condition corresponding to the wave incidence angle ϕ. The front and back edges of the domain, which are parallel to the underlying surface of the object, are implemented with the so-called perfectly matched layers (PML) [24], ensuring the complete absorption of all the incident electromagnetic power with no reflection, regardless of the incidence angle. The scattered field is registered at some plane y' that is parallel to the object surface and then propagated back to the microscope focal plane y employing a specially implemented numerical procedure [18],

$$E_z(x,y,\phi) = \frac{1}{2\pi} \int\limits_{-\Xi_x}^{\Xi_x} d\kappa_x \int dx' \exp(i\sqrt{k^2 - \kappa_x^2}(y-y')+i\kappa_x(x-x')) \, E_z(x',y',\phi),$$

(5)

where $k = 2\pi/\lambda$ is the wave number of the illuminating wave and Ξ_x is the maximal transverse wave number that can be registered with the microscope thanks to its resolution capability. We assume that the microscope has an ideal lens whose resolution fits the classical Rayleigh diffraction limit.

3.1 Parallelization of Computations and Developing Codes

Since the iterations of the discretized Maxwell Eq. (4) are independent, FDTD calculations are essentially parallel and are easily implemented by OMP or MPI computing standards. For relatively small domains, which fit into the shared memory of a single computer, cyclic iterations over all the nodes of a one-, two-, or three-dimensional finite-difference grid (Fig. 1) are immediately parallelized with the `#pragma omp parallel for` directive. Larger domains requiring the distributed memory of several computer nodes can be divided into several smaller subdomains as shown by the vertical dashed lines in Fig. 1. Then electric (4c) and magnetic (4a, 4b) rotor Maxwell equations are iterated independently in each subdomain, and after each iteration cycle, the processes exchange their new boundary values with their neighboring processes, which are responsible for the adjacent subdomains. This data exchange can be implemented by the Message Passing Interface (MPI).

Practically, most simulations in this study were performed on the Tshebysheff and Lomonosov-1 parallel clusters at SRCC MSU computing facilities. Typically, one computer node (two CPUs, i.e., 8–12 processing cores) was used for every simulation with code using the Open MP standard. The parallelization efficiency in this case practically reaches its theoretical limit (the speedup is proportional to the number of cores).

For the MPI codes, the efficiency analysis is not as simple as for the Open MP ones. However, the volume of data passed from one process to the neighboring one is $N \propto L/h$, where L is the length of the border and h is the cell size. On the other hand, the computational load at each step of the FDTD scheme is proportional to S/h^2, where S is the area of the partial subdomain allocated to the given process (see Fig. 1). Thus, the fraction of computing time used for data exchange vanishes with the cell size as $(L/h)/(S/h^2) \propto h$. This means that for large domains the parallelization efficiency of MPI codes can also approach its theoretical values.

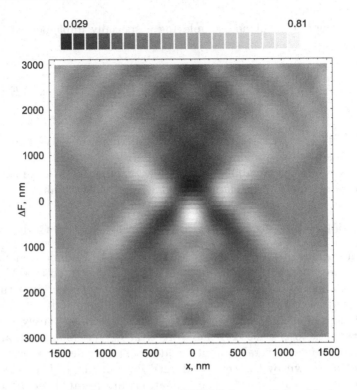

Fig. 2. Amplitude synthetic (TSOM) image of the object

4   Simulation Results

The profile of a rectangular shape on the flat underlying surface, infinitely long in the z direction, is used as the test object in the numerical simulation. The values of its height and width ($h = 105$ nm and $w = 38$ nm, respectively) were chosen following [25], as well as the illuminating wavelength $\lambda = 546nm$ and the material of the object (Si, dielectric permittivity $\epsilon = 5$ [26]). The cell size of the numerical grid in the FDTD scheme was chosen equal in both directions x, y and small enough (1 nm) to explore the effects of the nanometric variations of the object size, shape, and position. For the domain size of 3000×3000 nm (see Figs. 2, 3, 4 and 5), this yields a grid size of 3000×3000 cells, correspondingly.

The set of illumination directions of object I spans the range $(-12°, +12°)$ with $1°$ step. Thus the effective numerical aperture of the illumination for this range of illumination directions is approximately $NA = \sin(12°) \approx 0.2$. Since the object does not vary in the z direction, only (x, y) cross sections of the field are computed and analyzed. The amplitude (TSOM) and phase (FAMOR) images of the object are shown in Figs. 2 and 3. Obviously, the phase (FAMOR) image has a simpler structure with a single maximum, corresponding to the object location.

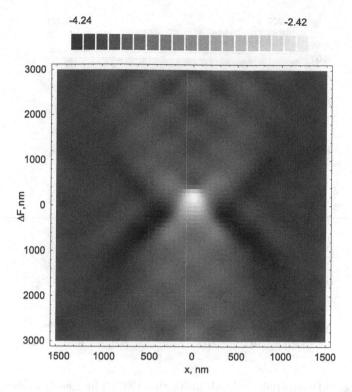

Fig. 3. Phase synthetic image of the object

Figures 4 and 5 show the difference images (difference between a pair of images of two objects). The phase difference image also has a much simpler structure than the amplitude (TSOM) one.

The two objects have different widths and heights ($h_1 = 105$ nm and $w_1 = 38$ nm; $h_2 = 95$ nm, $w_2 = 42$ nm) but equal cross-section areas ($h_1 \times w_1 = h_2 \times w_2 = 3990$ nm^2). The phase difference image is much simpler and more interpretable, as well as more sensitive to the variations of the geometry of the objects, even when the cross-section area remains constant.

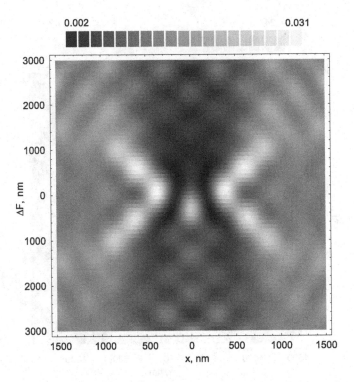

Fig. 4. Differential amplitude synthetic (TSOM) image of the object

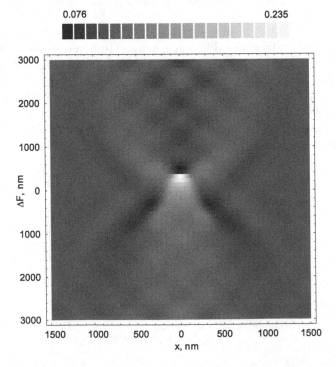

Fig. 5. Differential phase synthetic image of the object

5   Conclusions

The theoretical investigation and numerical simulations of both techniques used in synthetic image formation (amplitude or phase) for application to industrial nanotechnology diagnostics show that making use of the wave field phase as its informative characteristic is strongly preferable. We studied the potential capabilities of the method used with real optical instruments having limited physical parameters. The simulation results show the possibility of detection of local defects in the nanometer scale samples on the three-dimensional phase images. These results also clearly demonstrate the advantages of phase image synthesis over its amplitude counterpart (TSOM).

We designed and investigated a new alternative processing technique appropriate for optical microscopic images. The technique is essentially based on the processing of the phase of the optical wave registered by the interference microscope. We performed numerical studies and comparative tests with the alternative technique based on the wave amplitude. We established the advantages of the phase approach for industrial diagnostic purposes.

References

1. Sadovnichy, V., Tikhonravov, A., Voevodin, V., Opanasenko, V.: "Lomonosov": Supercomputing at moscow state university. In: Contemporary High Performance Computing: From Petascale toward Exascale. Chapman & Hall/CRC Computational Science, Boca Raton, United States, Boca Raton, United States, pp. 283–307 (2013)
2. Alford, W.J., VanderNeut, R.D., Zaleckas, V.J.: Laser scanning microscopy. Proc. IEEE **70**(6), 641–651 (1982)
3. Wang, W., Chen, S., Chen, L., Chang, W.: A machine vision based automatic optical inspection system for measuring drilling quality of printed circuit boards. IEEE Access **5**, 10817–10833 (2017)
4. Rau, H., Wu, C.H.: Automatic optical inspection for detecting defects on printed circuit board inner layers. Int. J. Adv. Manuf. Technol. **25**, 940–946 (2005)
5. Kaur, B., Kaur, G., Kaur, A.: Detection and classification of printed circuit boards defects. Open Trans. Inf. Proc. **2014**, 8–16 (2014)
6. Born, M., Wolf, E.: Principles of Optics. Pergamon Press, Oxford (1975)
7. Levin, G.G., Minaev, V.L., Ilyushin, Y.A., Oshlakov, V.G.: Calibration of matrix photodetectors and precision positioning of objects according to raster images. Meas. Tech. **60**(6), 571–577 (2017)
8. Buhr, E., Michaelis, W., Diener, A., Mirandé, W.: Multi-wavelength VIS/UV optical diffractometer for high-accuracy calibration of Nano-scale pitch standards. Meas. Sci. Technol. **18**(3), 667–674 (2007)
9. Silver, R.M., Attota, R., Marx, E.: Model-based analysis of the limits of optical metrology with experimental comparisons. In: Bosse, H., Bodermann, B., Silver, R.M. (eds.) Modeling Aspects in Optical Metrology, vol. 6617, pp. 266–278. SPIE, International Society for Optics and Photonics (2007)
10. Attota, R., Germer, T.A., Silver, R.M.: Through-focus scanning-optical-microscope imaging method for nanoscale dimensional analysis. Opt. Lett. **33**(17), 1990–1992 (2008)

11. Attota, R.K., Weck, P., Kramar, J.A., Bunday, B., Vartanian, V.: Feasibility study on 3-D shape analysis of high-aspect-ratio features using through-focus scanning optical microscopy. Opt. Express **24**(15), 16574–16585 (2016)
12. Attota, R.: Noise analysis for through-focus scanning optical microscopy. Opt. Lett. **41**(4), 745–748 (2016)
13. Ryabko, M., Koptyaev, S., Shcherbakov, A., Lantsov, A., Oh, S.: Method for optical inspection of nanoscale objects based upon analysis of their defocused images and features of its practical implementation. Opt. Express **21**(21), 24483–24489 (2013)
14. Ryabko, M., et al.: Through-focus scanning optical microscopy (TSOM) considering optical aberrations: practical implementation. Opt. Express **23**(25), 32215–32221 (2015)
15. Peng, R., Jiang, J., Hao, J., Qu, Y.: Lateral movement and angular illuminating non-uniformity corrected TSOM image using Fourier transform. Opt. Express **28**(5), 6294–6305 (2020)
16. Attota, R., Silver, R.: Nanometrology using a through-focus scanning optical microscopy method. Meas. Sci. Technol. **22**(2), 024002 (2010)
17. Levin, G.G., Ilyushin, Y.A., Minaev, V.L., Moiseev, N.N.: Measurement of nanomovements of an object from the optical phase image. Meas. Tech. **53**(7), 782–788 (2010). https://doi.org/10.1007/s11018-010-9577-8
18. Levin, G.G., Ilyushin, Y.A., Zolotarevskii, Y.S., Kononogov, S.A.: Nanometrology: Simulation of scattering processes of optical radiation by nanodimensional structures. Meas. Tech. **52**(12), 1289–1293 (2009)
19. Yee, K.: Numerical solution of initial boundary value problems involving Maxwell's equations in isotropic media. IEEE Trans. Antennas Propag. **14**, 302–307 (1966)
20. Ilyushin, Y.A., Padokhin, A.M.: Reflectometric altimetry of the sea level using the GPS satellite signals: errors caused by sea surface waves. In: 2019 Russian Open Conference on Radio Wave Propagation (RWP), vol. 1, pp. 309–312 (2019)
21. Ilyushin, Y.A., Padokhin, A.M., Smolov, V.E.: Global navigational satellite system phase altimetry of the sea level: systematic bias effect caused by sea surface waves. In: 2019 PhotonIcs & Electromagnetics Research Symposium - Spring (PIERS-Spring), pp. 1618–1627 (2019)
22. Totzeck, M., Tiziani, H.: Interference microscopy of sub-λ structures: a rigorous computation method and measurements. Optics Commun. **136**(1), 61–74 (1997)
23. Taflove, A., Brodwin, M.E.: Numerical solution of steady-state electromagnetic scattering problems using the time-dependent Maxwell's equations. IEEE Trans. Microw. Theory Tech. **23**(8), 623–630 (1975)
24. Berenger, J.P.: A perfectly matched layer for the absorption of electromagnetic waves. J. Comput. Phys. **114**(2), 185–200 (1994)
25. Levin, G.G., Vishnyakov, G.N., Ilyushin, Y.A.: Synthesis of three-dimensional phase images of nanoobjects: numerical simulation. Optics Spectrosc. (English translation of Optika i Spektroskopiya), **115**(6), 938–946 (2013)
26. Philipp, H.R., Taft, E.A.: Optical constants of silicon in the region 1 to 10 eV. Phys. Rev. **120**, 37–38 (1960)

A Parallel Algorithm for a Two-Phase Gas-Solid-Particle Model with Chemical Reactions and Laser Radiation

Elizaveta Peskova[✉]

National Research Mordovia State University, 68 Bolshevistskaya str.,
Saransk 430005, Russian Federation
e.e.peskova@math.mrsu.ru

Abstract. The article is devoted to the development of a parallel computational algorithm for the model of a two-phase chemically active medium with laser radiation. The model consists of a system of low-Mach-number approximations of Navier–Stokes equations for multicomponent reacting mixtures, supplemented by equations of chemical kinetics, an equation for the radiation intensity, and equations for the solid phase. The solid phase is described in terms of particle concentrations. We describe them employing systems of convection-diffusion-reaction equations supplemented with thermal terms from laser radiation and reaction terms for compounds on the surface. The general solution algorithm is based on the splitting scheme for physical processes: chemical reactions, convection-diffusion, and stationary process for pressure correction. We use the WENO scheme to construct the computational algorithm for approximating the convective terms in the Navier–Stokes equations. Moreover, we use the RADAU5 plug-in module to calculate the equations of chemical kinetics and the equations for the radiation intensity and the temperature of the solid phase. The time derivatives are approximated explicitly. This approach guarantees the efficiency of using the suggested difference scheme for parallel implementation. The parallel algorithm is based on the principles of geometric parallelism; the MPI standard is used for interprocessor interaction. To obtain information about the efficiency of the parallel algorithm, we performed calculations on a sequence of shredding grids with different numbers of computing nodes. We applied the parallel code to compute the flow of a two-phase gas-solid medium with chemical reactions of light hydrocarbons in the gas phase and on the particle surface under the influence of laser radiation.

Keywords: Two-phase media · Navier–Stokes equations ·
Computational fluid dynamics · Radical chain reactions · Parallel
algorithms

The reported study was funded by the Russian Science Foundation (project № 23-21-00202).

ⓒ The Author(s), under exclusive license to Springer Nature Switzerland AG 2023
L. Sokolinsky and M. Zymbler (Eds.): PCT 2023, CCIS 1868, pp. 323–335, 2023.
https://doi.org/10.1007/978-3-031-38864-4_23

1   Introduction

Improving the efficiency of hydrocarbon processing under catalysts and external energy supply is a nontrivial and urgent task of the modern chemical industry. One of the perspective areas is laser catalysis which offers the advantage of controlled exposure of laser radiation to a gas and/or a solid dispersed substance. A test workbench is available at the Institute of Catalysis (Siberian branch of the Russian Academy of Sciences) for the study of photochemical and thermal effects of infrared laser radiation on a two-phase gas-dust medium of mixtures of light hydrocarbons and catalytically active nanoparticles [1]. The comprehensive study of the laser radiation effect on a two-phase medium requires that the physicochemical processes occurring in such media be calculated and also experimentally investigated. The importance of computational experiments resides in the possibility to research in detail the influence of the material and size of gas-dust particles, the composition of the gas mixture, the temperature of the reactor walls and that of the starting materials, the power of the laser radiation on the conversion of raw materials, and the yield of useful products.

In the present article, we present the results obtained with the software tools we created to model the dynamics of multicomponent gases and solid ultradisperse particles, taking into account heterogeneous reactions and the absorption of laser radiation by the gas components and particles. We previously created a numerical model to study the two-phase flow of gas and particles in a one-dimensional formulation with hydrocarbon conversion brutto reactions, heat exchange between particles and gas, and heating of particles by laser radiation [2]. Currently, it is necessary to expand the model by replacing the brutto reactions with a more accurate kinetic scheme of radical chain reactions in gas and on the surface of particles affected by laser radiation. This modification, using an extended scheme of chemical reactions, will allow for the simulation of a multitemperature medium of a reacting gas with ultra- and highly dispersed particles, which is studied in experiments.

However, it becomes clear that regular calculations of the problem require unacceptably large amounts of computer time, already at the stage of inclusion of the simplest radical chain kinetic scheme reactions described by a stiff system of up to a dozen of ODEs. The modification of the model using an extended kinetic model of heterogeneous and homogeneous reactions with dozens of ODEs determines the urgency of the task of parallelization of the calculations. We plan to modify in the future the algorithm and the program and extend them to 3D grids, introducing higher-order approximation schemes that require large computational resources. In the meantime, We have decided to use a parallel algorithm based on the principles of geometric parallelism. The nontriviality of the task of creating a parallel code with geometric parallelism stems from the presence of radiation transfer and the ellipticity of the gas-dynamics part of the equations, which, in turn, is due to the subsonic flow of the gas-dust medium [3]. The speed of such a flow is primarily influenced by the thermal effects of chemical reactions, the absorption of laser radiation, and the heat exchange between gas and particles. Laser exposure to a gaseous medium often causes a nontrivial response of the medium. It leads to the emergence of nonlinear multiscale effects described by stiff systems. The use of parallel technologies for modeling laser radiation processes is an efficient method that allows avoiding the computational difficulties associated with such tasks [4]

The purpose of this research is to extend the model developed previously to account for complex kinetic schemes, modify the numerical algorithm to use the WENO scheme for the reconstruction of polynomials, accomplish the parallel implementation of calculations using the MPI technology, and study the efficiency of the parallelization on model problems.

The paper is organized as follows. Section 1 is devoted to the literature review and topicality. In Sect. 2, we introduce the one-dimensional model of the subsonic flow of gas and fine particles with laser radiation and intense heat exchange between gas and particles. Section 3 contains description of the parallel algorithm for studied model. Section 4 presents the result of the numerical experiment. Conclusion summarizes the study and points directions for further work.

2   The Mathematical Model

Let us consider a one-dimensional model of the subsonic flow of gas and fine particles with laser radiation and intense heat exchange between gas and particles [2,5,6]:

$$\frac{\partial U}{\partial t} + \frac{\partial F(U)}{\partial x} - \frac{\partial H(U)}{\partial x} = W. \tag{1}$$

Here U is the vector of conservative variables, $F(U)$ is the vector of convective flows, $H(U)$ is the vector of diffusion flows, and W is the vector of source terms:

$$U = \begin{pmatrix} \rho_g Y_m \\ \rho_i \\ \left(\rho_g + \sum_i \rho_i\right)u \\ \rho_g h_g + \sum_i \rho_i h_i \end{pmatrix}, \quad F(U) = \begin{pmatrix} \rho_g u Y_m \\ \rho_i u \\ \left(\rho_g + \sum_i \rho_i\right)u^2 + p_d \\ \left(\rho_g h_g + \sum_i \rho_i h_i\right)u \end{pmatrix}, \quad H(U) = \begin{pmatrix} J_m \\ 0 \\ 0 \\ q \end{pmatrix},$$

$$W = \begin{pmatrix} R_m \\ 0 \\ 0 \\ \left(n_g\alpha + \sum_i n_i\alpha_i\right)F - \sum_i 4\pi s_i^2 n_i \sigma(T_i^4 - T_g^4) \end{pmatrix}.$$

The system of Eq. (1) includes M equations for the transfer of the gas mixture components, N equations for the dust fractions transfer, the motion equation of the mixture of gas and particles, and the enthalpy equation for the gas and particles. Moreover, the system is supplemented by the ideal gas law, the equation for the radiation intensity, and the temperature equation for the particles [7,8]:

$$p_{\mathrm{g}} = \rho_{\mathrm{g}} R T_{\mathrm{g}} \sum_m \frac{Y_m}{M_{\mathrm{w}m}}, \tag{2}$$

$$\frac{\partial F}{\partial x} + \left(n_{\mathrm{g}}\alpha + \sum_{i=1}^{N} n_i\alpha_i \right) F = 0, \tag{3}$$

$$\frac{dm_i C_{DV} T_i}{dt} = \pi s_i^2 F - 4\pi s_i^2 \sigma \left(T_i^4 - T_{\mathrm{g}}^4 \right) - a\pi \frac{s_i^2}{2} p_{\mathrm{g}} c_t \frac{\gamma+1}{\gamma-1} \left(\frac{T_i}{T_{\mathrm{g}}} - 1 \right) - QR. \tag{4}$$

Here ρ_{g} is the gas mixture density, Y_m is the mass fraction of the m-th gas component, M is the number of components in the gas mixture, J_m is the diffusion flow of the m-th gas component, R_m is the rate of formation or flow of the m-th component, u is the gas and particle flow velocity, ρ_i is the density of particles of fraction i, N is the number of particle fractions, p_d is the dynamic pressure component, h_{g} is the gas enthalpy, h_i is the enthalpy of particles of fraction i, q is the heat flux, n_{g} is the concentration of absorbed gas molecules per unit volume, n_i are the concentrations of dust fraction particles, F is the radiation intensity, α, α_i are absorption coefficients, T_{g} is the gas temperature, T_i are the dust fraction particle temperatures, s_i is the radius of particles of fraction i, σ is the Stefan–Boltzmann constant, $M_{\mathrm{w}m}$ is the molecular weight of the m-th component of the mixture, R is the universal gas constant, C_{DV} is the heat capacity of the particle substance at constant volume, c_t is the average thermal velocity of gas molecules, a is the coefficient of accommodation, γ is the adiabatic index of the gas mixture, Q is the reaction thermal effect, and R is the number of transformations per unit of time.

System (1) must be supplemented with initial and boundary conditions. The fulfillment of these conditions is determined by the specific task being solved. The conditions on the flow in and the flow out are required for the calculation of a one-dimensional model. The composition of the gas mixture by Y_m, ρ_i, the temperatures $T_{\mathrm{g,in}}$ and $T_{i,\mathrm{in}}$ of gas and dust, the velocity u_{in}, and the radiation intensity F_{in} are given at the input. The output pressure is set to p_{out}.

3   The Parallel Algorithm

3.1   Decomposition of the Computational Domain

A structured grid of segments is used in this study to extend the mathematical model to account for radical kinetic schemes. We construct a partition of the region into Δ_j, $j = 1, \ldots, n_{\mathrm{cells}}$, where n_{cells} is the number of cells. We set the values of gas-dynamics parameters, concentrations of mixture components, and particles in each grid cell.

We divide the computational domain into disjoint subdomains, and the initial problem is given as a set of boundary value problems in these subdomains to organize parallel computations. The boundary conditions from the initial problem are set at the subdomain boundaries that coincide with the boundaries of the initial computational domain. The internal boundaries contain information obtained as a result of data exchange with neighboring subdomains.

3.2 The Numerical Scheme for the Solution of the Problem in a Subdomain

To construct the computational algorithm, we resort to a splitting scheme by physical processes. The use of a splitting scheme by physical processes for system (1)–(4) determines the efficiency of its implementation on parallel computing systems and allows carrying out computations with a significantly larger time step in comparison with the direct solution of the complete system.

The numerical scheme can be divided into the set of blocks described below.

B1: According to the splitting method, we distinguish a system of equations containing only source terms from the mass transfer equations:

$$\begin{cases} \dfrac{\partial \rho Y_1}{\partial t} = R_1, \\ \dfrac{\partial \rho Y_2}{\partial t} = R_2, \\ \dots\dots\dots \\ \dfrac{\partial \rho Y_m}{\partial t} = R_m. \end{cases} \tag{5}$$

We use the RADAU5 plug-in [9] to solve the resulting system.

B2: The solution of Eq. (3) for the radiation transfer using the RADAU5 plug-in module [9].

B3: The solution of the system of Eq. (1), leaving aside the source term R_m and the dynamic pressure component p_d, to find the gas density ρ_g, the particle density ρ_i, the concentrations Y_m of mixture components, the total enthalpy of the gas and particles, and the preliminary velocity vector u (since the pressure contribution is not taken into account when solving the system). According to the finite volume method, we obtain the scheme

$$\frac{U_j^{n+1} - U_j^n}{\Delta t} + \frac{\widetilde{F}_{j+1/2} - \widetilde{F}_{j-1/2}}{h} - \frac{\widetilde{H}_{j+1/2} - \widetilde{H}_{j-1/2}}{h} - W_j = 0. \tag{6}$$

Here U_j^{n+1} is the desired vector of conservative variables. Convective flows $\widetilde{F}_{j+1/2} = \widetilde{F}(U_{j+1/2}^r, U_{j+1/2}^l)$ are calculated according to the Rusanov–Lax–Friedrichs scheme [10,11]; $U_{j+1/2}^r$ and $U_{j+1/2}^l$ are the values of the vector U of variables to the right and the left of the boundary between cells j and $j+1$. We use a WENO scheme of the 5-th order of accuracy to find these values [12]. More exactly, we introduce a vector of variables $f = f(U) = (\rho Y_i, \rho_i, u, h_g, h_i)$ using the WENO algorithm, calculate it by interpolation on six grid cells, and then recalculate the value of the desired vectors, namely, $U^r_{j+1/2} = U(f^r_{j+1/2})$ and $U^l_{j+1/2} = U(f^l_{j+1/2})$.

Diffusion and heat flows at the boundaries between the cells $\tilde{H}_{j+1/2}$ are calculated according to a scheme with central differences.

B4: The solution of Eq. (4) for the particle temperature using the RADAU5 plug-in module [9].

B5: The computation of the gas temperature using the known values of the total enthalpy of the mixture and the particle temperature.

B6: The computation of the dynamic pressure component p_d and the velocity u:

$$\Delta p_d^{n+1} = \frac{\rho_g^n + \sum_i \rho_i^n}{\Delta t} (\nabla \cdot u^* - S), \tag{7}$$

$$u^{n+1} = u^* - \frac{\Delta t}{\rho_g^n + \sum_i \rho_i^n} \nabla p_d^{n+1}. \tag{8}$$

The velocity u^* calculated in the **B3** block does not take into account the contribution of the dynamic pressure component p_d^{n+1}. In Eq. (7), $S = \nabla \cdot u^{n+1}$ is the correction for the divergent restriction of the velocity vector. We obtain it by converting the continuity equation into a nondivergent form, the equation for the temperature of the gas mixture, and the equation of state for the gas mixture (2). The correction S is calculated from the values at the next time step found in the previous stages of the numerical scheme [6]:

$$S \equiv \nabla \cdot u = \frac{1}{\rho_g C_p T_g} \left(-\sum_{i=1}^{N} \rho_i \frac{C_p(T_g - T_i)}{\zeta_i} + n_g \alpha F \right) \tag{9}$$

$$+ \frac{1}{\rho_g C_p T_g} \left(\nabla \cdot \lambda \nabla T_g + \sum_m \rho_g D_{m,\text{mix}} \nabla Y_m \nabla h_m \right)$$

$$+ \frac{1}{\rho_g} \sum_m \frac{M_w}{M_{wm}} (\nabla \cdot \rho D_{m,\text{mix}} \nabla Y_m) + \frac{1}{\rho_g} \sum_m \left(\frac{M_w}{M_{wm}} - \frac{h_m}{C_p T_g} \right) R_m,$$

where $C_p(T_g)$ is the heat capacity of the gas mixture at constant pressure, ζ_i is the thermal relaxation time of the particle in the medium, $\lambda(T_g)$ is the thermal conductivity of the gas mixture, $D_{m,\text{mix}}$ is the average diffusion coefficient of the m-th component of the gas mixture, $h_m(T_g)$ is the enthalpy of the m-th component, and M_w is the average molecular weight of the gas mixture.

We use the Jacobi iterative method to solve the elliptic Eq. (7).

3.3   The Scheme of the Parallel Program

The parallel program is based on the MPI (Message Passing Interface) technology for distributed memory systems. We use the MPICH library to implement the interprocessor exchange mechanisms and the software package operation.

The program consists of several main modules, and each runs on a selected number of processors:

1. The parallel computing initialization module.
   The decomposition of the computational domain, the calculation of the grid parameters, and the determination of the types of boundary cells (internal subdomain or boundary) are in this module.
2. The module for generating the initial data.
   The module reads from the initial data files, allocates the memory, and fills the arrays of primitive and conservative variables.
3. The module for computing the boundary conditions.
4. The module for doing the B1 block calculation of chemical-kinetics equations.
5. The module for doing the B2 block calculation of the radiation intensity.
   The distinguishing feature of parallel calculations in this block is the change in the radiation intensity for the space variable. Therefore, the variable F is exchanged using the functions MPI_Send() and MPI_Recv() in this block.
6. The module for doing the B3 block calculation of gas-dynamics characteristics and concentrations at the next time step.
   The three fictitious cells on the borders are allocated for each subdomain at the first stage since the numerical algorithm uses a WENO scheme of the fifth order of accuracy.
7. The module for doing the B4 block calculation of the particle temperature.
8. The module for doing the B5 block calculation of the gas temperature.
9. The module for interprocessor data exchange of the density, concentrations, enthalpy, and preliminary velocity vector.
   The exchange at this stage is enforced by the need to calculate the dynamic pressure component based on data on the next time layer. The paired blocking functions MPI_Send() and MPI_Recv() are used to perform the exchange. Their choice is determined by the fact that the exchange occurs only between two processors.
10. The module for doing the B6 block calculation of the dynamic pressure component and flow velocity.
    It is necessary to determine the maximum pressure change at each iteration since the dynamic pressure component is computed by solving an elliptic equation with a given value for stopping the iterations. The function MPI_Allreduce() is used to perform this task. The paired blocking functions MPI_Send() and MPI_Recv() are used at each iteration to perform the exchange of the dynamic component.
11. The module for interprocessor data exchange of the pressure and flow velocity dynamic component.
12. The data saving module.

3.4 Efficiency Analysis of the Parallel Algorithm

The parallel version of the algorithm was programmed in C++. We studied the algorithm performance by applying it to the task described in Sect. 4. The time required to perform a certain number of time steps was measured for different numbers of processors and computational cells. The experiments were carried out on a workstation featuring 32 computing nodes at the National Research Mordovia State University. Table 1 contains the performance results obtained during the experiments.

Table 1. Results of computational experiments

n_{cells}	n_{proc}	Time, sec	Speedup, %	Efficiency, %
6400	1	10.34	1	1
	4	12.8	3.69	0.92
	16	1.0	10.34	0.64
	32	0.81	12.76	0.4
102 400	1	162.35	1	1
	4	41.5	3.91	0.98
	16	13.3	12.21	0.76
	32	8.58	18.92	0.59
1 638 400	1	2604.16	1	1
	4	664.1	3.92	0.99
	16	180.2	14.45	0.90
	32	92.5	28.15	0.88

The data presented in Table 1 demonstrates a decrease in algorithm efficiency for any number of cells when the number of computing nodes increases. Most probable, this is due to an increase in the number of interprocessor exchanges. The drop in efficiency can also be associated with the integration of the chemical-kinetics system at each time step in each cell. The integration step is adaptive since the characteristic times of chemical transformations are significantly less than the gas-dynamics time step in the RADAU5 module. Laser radiation is absorbed in regions with high concentrations of solid particles and contributes to a local increase in gas temperature, which has a direct effect on the integration step. "Colder" subdomains require fewer substeps than "hotter" ones. The static nature of the distribution of grid cells across processes in this case does not allow balancing the load on processes. Using the OpenMP technology inside cluster nodes can partially solve this problem.

Figures 1 and 2 show the graphs of the speedup and efficiency of the program versus the size of the grid. We can see from the graphs that the speedup approaches the number of computing nodes, and the efficiency reaches its maximum values when the size of the computational grid increases.

The obtained result demonstrates the high efficiency of the parallel algorithm in comparison with the sequential one for grids of large size. This gives a reason to assume that the efficiency will remain when moving from a one-dimensional problem to a multidimensional one.

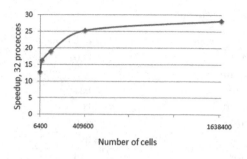

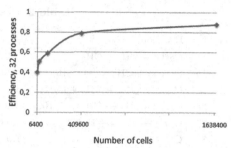

Fig. 1. Graph of the speedup versus the number of computational cells

Fig. 2. Graph of the efficiency versus the number of computational cells

4 The Numerical Experiments

The numerical simulation of a two-phase gas and dust flow with laser radiation and chemical reactions was carried out taking $\Omega = [0, 0.5 \text{ m}]$ as the integration region. Solid particles from one fraction form a clump in the center of the region with a maximum at coordinate 0.25 m at the initial moment (Fig. 3). The values of gas-dynamics parameters, gas concentrations and dust components, radiation intensity, and other parameters are given below:

$$u_{in} = 0.05 \text{ m/sec}, \ p = 101\,325 \text{ Pa}, \ T_{in,g} = 1073 \text{ K}, \ T_{in,i} = 1073 \text{ K},$$

$$F_{in} = 1.6 \cdot 10^{11} \text{ W/m}^2, \ Y_{in,CH_4} = 1, \ Y_m = 0, \ m = 2, ..., M,$$

$$s_i = 5 \cdot 10^{-9} \text{ m}, \ n_{i,max} = 10^{16} \text{ m}^{-3}.$$

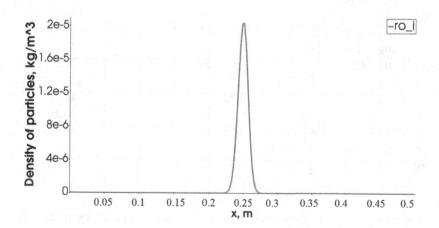

Fig. 3. Distribution of the density of particles, $t = 0$ sec

The two-temperature kinetic scheme (Table 2) is adopted to describe the scheme of chemical transformations; it includes $M = 16$, a component of the mixture, and one fraction of dust [13].

Table 2. Reaction scheme

№		Reaction	A_i, sec^{-1} or m$^3 \cdot$ mole$^{-1} \cdot$ sec^{-1}	E_i, kJ $\cdot$ mole^{-1}
1	1f	$C_2H_6 \rightarrow CH_3 + CH_3$	$2.4 \cdot 10^{16}$	366.0
	1b	$CH_3(s) + CH_3(s) \rightarrow C_2H_6$	$14.04 \cdot 10^7$	5.9
2	2f	$CH_3 + C_2H_6 \rightarrow CH_4 + C_2H_5$	$3.26 \cdot 10^6$	50.24
	2b	$CH_4 + C_2H_5 \rightarrow CH_3 + C_2H_6$	$21.08 \cdot 10^6$	90.0
3	3f	$C_2H_5 \rightarrow C_2H_4 + H$	$2.0 \cdot 10^{13}$	166.0
	3b	$C_2H_4 + H \rightarrow C_2H_5$	$1.0 \cdot 10^7$	6.3
4	4f	$H + C_2H_6 \rightarrow H_2 + C_2H_5$	$1.0 \cdot 10^8$	40.16
	4b	$H_2 + C_2H_5 \rightarrow H + C_2H_6$	$3.98 \cdot 10^7$	96.45
5	5f	$CH_3 + C_2H_4 \rightarrow C_3H_7$	$3.3 \cdot 10^5$	32.26
	5b	$C_3H_7 \rightarrow CH_3 + C_2H_4$	$3.0 \cdot 10^{14}$	139.0
6	6f	$C_2H_5 + C_2H_5 \rightarrow C_2H_4 + C_2H_6$	$1.65 \cdot 10^5$	3.34
7	7f	$C_3H_7 + C_2H_4 \rightarrow C_2H_5 + C_3H_6$	$2.65 \cdot 10^4$	27.6
8	8f	$CH_3 + C_2H_4 \rightarrow CH_4 + C_2H_3$	$4.16 \cdot 10^6$	46.56
	8b	$CH_4 + C_2H_3 \rightarrow CH_3 + C_2H_4$	$8.9 \cdot 10^4$	25.94
9	9f	$CH_3 + C_2H_3 \rightarrow CH_4 + C_2H_2$	$9.03 \cdot 10^6$	3.2
10	10f	$C_2H_3 + H \rightarrow C_2H_2 + H_2$	$1.2 \cdot 10^7$	0.0
11	11f	$CH_4 + H \rightarrow CH_3 + H_2$	$7.59 \cdot 10^7$	49.89
	11b	$CH_3 + H_2 \rightarrow CH_4 + H$	$3.3 \cdot 10^6$	51.05
12	12f	$CH_3 + CH_3 \rightarrow C_2H_5 + H$	$8.0 \cdot 10^8$	111.0
	12b	$C_2H_5 + H \rightarrow CH_3 + CH_3$	$1.08 \cdot 10^8$	3.64
13	13f	$C_2H_4 + H \rightarrow C_2H_3 + H_2$	$5.42 \cdot 10^8$	62.36
	13b	$C_2H_3 + H_2 \rightarrow C_2H_4 + H$	$9.7 \cdot 10^4$	34.75
14	14f	$CH_4 \rightarrow CH_3(s) + H$		100.0
	14b	$CH_3 + H \rightarrow CH_4$	$1.9 \cdot 10^8$	1.15
15	15f	$C_2H_3 \rightarrow C_2H_2 + H$	$6.93 \cdot 10^{12}$	186.0
	15b	$C_2H_2 + H \rightarrow C_2H_3$	$54.98 \cdot 10^5$	10.6
16	16f	$C_2H_2 + CH_3 \rightarrow C_3H_4 + H$	$33.72 \cdot 10^4$	32.03
	16b	$C_3H_4 + H \rightarrow C_2H_2 + CH_3$	$49.98 \cdot 10^6$	16.74
17	17f	$C_3H_4 + H \rightarrow C_3H_3 + H_2$	$7.23 \cdot 10^7$	18.87
18	18f	$C_3H_4 + C_3H_3 \rightarrow C_6H_6 + H$	$6.99 \cdot 10^5$	50.21
19	19f	$C_6H_6 + CH_3 \rightarrow CH_4 + C_6H_5$	$26.2 \cdot 10^6$	80.9
	19b	$CH_4 + C_6H_5 \rightarrow C_6H_6 + CH_3$	$19.99 \cdot 10^5$	36.0
20	20f	$C_3H_3 + C_3H_3 \rightarrow C_6H_6$	$8.85 \cdot 10^7$	48.0

Reactions 1b and 14f in the given scheme proceed on particles at the temperature of the solid phase consisting of one particle fraction; the remaining stages proceed in the gas phase. The reactions rates in the gas phase are determined from the formula

$$w_r = k_r \cdot \prod_c Y_m,$$

$$k_r = A_r \cdot e^{-E_r/RT_g},$$

where r is the number of the reaction in the gas phase, and m is the number of the gas component entering the r-th reaction.

The rate of reaction $1b$ can be determined from the formula

$$w_{1b} = k_{1b} \cdot [CH_3(s)] \cdot [CH_3(s)],$$

$$k_{1b} = A_{1b} \cdot e^{-E_{1b}/RT_i}.$$

The rate of reaction $14f$ is

$$w_{14f} = k_{14f} \cdot [CH_4],$$

$$k_{14f} = \alpha_1 \pi s_i^2 n_i \sqrt{\frac{8k_B T_g}{\pi m_{CH_4}}} \cdot e^{-E_{14f}/RT_i},$$

where $\alpha_1 = 1$ is a constant.

Figures 4, 5, 6 and 7 display the modeling results on a grid with a step of $2.5 \cdot 10^{-3}$. The time integration step is $1.0 \cdot 10^{-5}$. The computations extended up to the time $T = 1$ s.

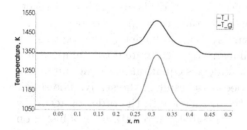

Fig. 4. Temperature   **Fig. 5.** Velocity

For the given values of the problem parameters, Fig. 4 shows that the input radiation heats the particles above the gas temperature by about 200 K, considering the losses due to endothermic reactions on the particle surface. The maximum temperature in the particle clump reaches 1500 K. The heat exchange of particles with gas and chemical reactions causes the gas in the clump to heat up to 1280 K, which leads to an increase in gas pressure. The clump of particles begins to spread out asymmetrically against the velocity of the gas and along the direction of its movement. The gas velocity takes on an S-shape (see Fig. 5). Methane is converted (Fig. 6) into a clump of particles with the release of hydrogen (Fig. 7).

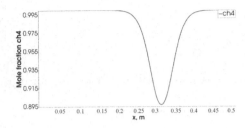 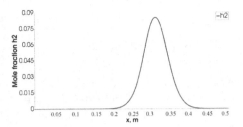

Fig. 6. Mole fraction of CH$_4$ **Fig. 7.** Mole fraction of H$_2$

The results of the numerical simulation correspond to experimental data. Chemical reactions occur near the particles, and then the reaction products are transferred to adjacent areas since laser radiation contributes to the active generation of radicals on the surface of solid reaction particles due to a significant increase in the system's internal energy. The decomposition reaction of methane does not occur at the specified gas temperatures in the absence of particles, which confirms the thesis about the need to introduce gas-dust particles into the reactor and the influence of laser radiation on them.

5   Conclusions

We considered a one-dimensional mathematical model of the dynamics of a reacting gas and ultradisperse particles with laser radiation and a radical kinetic mechanism. The model includes a subsonic system of Navier–Stokes equations, an equation for radiation transfer, an equation for determining the temperature of particles, and a stiff system of chemical kinetics equations. For the numerical solution, we used a parallel solver developed as a result of the study. The solver implements the finite volume method with an increase in the order of accuracy by the WENO scheme. The organization of parallel computations was based on MPI technology. The computations were carried out on a workstation at the National Research Mordovia State University and showed good scalability for the program. We considered a model problem, which demonstrated the adequacy of the results of computational experiments and the possibility of application of the parallel solver to experimental tasks. We plan to modify the algorithm to 3D grids. Also, we plan to use the suggested approach to the parallel solution of problems of two-phase reacting media to adapt the algorithm to 3D grids. The use of parallel technologies combined with the explicitly iterative Chebyshev scheme is also seen as a promising direction of research [14].

Acknowledgments. The author thanks V. N. Snytnikov and E. A. Lashina for the helpful discussions and comments.

References

1. Snytnikov, V.N., Masyuk, N.S., Markelova, T.V., Parmon, V.N.: A laser catalysis apparatus. Instrum. Exp. Tech. **62**(3), 474–482 (2021)
2. Snytnikov, V.N., Peskova, E.E., Stoyanovskaya, O.P.: Mathematical model of a two-temperature medium of gas-solid nanoparticles with laser methane pyrolysis. Matem. Mod. **35**(4), 24–50 (2023)
3. Peskova, E.E.: Numerical modeling of subsonic axisymmetric reacting gas flows. J. Phys. Conf. Ser. **2057**, 012071 (2021). https://doi.org/10.1088/1742-6596/2057/1/012071
4. Shlenov, S., Smirnov, A., Bezborodov, A.: Parallel algorithm for filamentation of high-power super-sport laser pulses. In: Proceedings of the International Conference on Parallel and Distributed Processing Techniques and Applications, Conference on Real-Time Computing Systems and Applications, vol. 1, pp. 286–291 (2006)
5. Day, M.S., Bell, J.B.: Numerical simulation of laminar reacting flows with complex chemistry. Combust. Theory Model. **4**(4), 535–556 (2000). https://doi.org/10.1088/1364-7830/4/4/309
6. Gubaydullin, I.M., Zhalnin, R.V., Masyagin, V.F., Peskova, E.E., Tishkin, V.F.: Simulation of propane pyrolysis in a flow-through chemical reactor under constant external heating. Math. Models Comput. Simul. **13**(3), 437–444 (2021)
7. Snytnikov, V.L.N., Snytnikov, V.N., Masyuk, N.S., Markelova, T.V.: The absorption of CO2 laser radiation by ethylene in mixtures with methane. J. Quant. Spectrosc. Radiat. Transfer **253**(107119), 1–6 (2020)
8. Gurentsov, E., Eremin, A.V., Falchenko, M: Modelling of heat transfer processes of laser heated nanoparticles with gas environment. Physical-Chemical Kinetics in Gas Dynamics 11 (2011)
9. Hairer, E., Wanner, G.: Solving Ordinary Differential Equations: Stiff and Differential-Algebraic Problems, 2nd edition. In: Springer Series in Computational Mathematics, vol. 14 (1996). https://doi.org/10.1007/978-3-642-05221-7
10. Rusanov, V.V.: The calculation of the interaction of non-stationary shock waves and obstacles. USSR Comput. Math. Math. Phys. **1**(2), 304–320 (1962)
11. Lax, P.D.: Weak solutions of nonlinear hyperbolic equations and their numerical computation. Commun. Pure Appl. Math. **7**(1), 159–193 (1954)
12. Shu, C.W.: Essentially non-oscillatory and weighted essentially non-oscillatory schemes for hyperbolic conservation laws. In: ICASE Report pp. 97–65 (1997)
13. Lashina, E.A., Peskova, E.E., Snytnikov, V.N.: Mathematical modeling of non-stationary temperature conversion of methane-ethane mixtures in a wide temperature range. Chemistry for Sustainable Development 3 (2023). In print
14. Zhukov, V.T., Feodoritova, O.B., Novikova, N.D., Duben, A.P.: Explicit-iterative scheme for the time integration of a system of navier-stokes equations. Matem. Mod. **32**(4), 57–74 (2020)

MPI-Based Computational Algorithm for Modeling a Cylindrical Catalyst Grain During Oxidative Regeneration

Olga S. Yazovtseva[1]([✉]), Irek M. Gubaydullin[2], Elizaveta E. Peskova[1]([✉]),
Arina A. Usmanova[2]([✉]), and Andrey N. Zagoruiko[3]

[1] National Research Mordovia State University, Saransk, Russian Federation
kurinaos@gmail.com
[2] Institute of Petrochemistry and Catalysis of the Russian Academy of Sciences,
Ufa, Russian Federation
[3] Boreskov Institute of Catalysis, Siberian Branch of the Russian Academy
of Sciences, Novosibirsk, Russian Federation
zagor@catalysis.ru

Abstract. The article is devoted to the development of an efficient parallel algorithm for the numerical simulation of a cylindrical catalyst grain during the process of burning coke residua off the catalyst. The three-dimensional problem is reduced to a task in an axisymmetric formulation. The mathematical model of the process consists of a system of nonlinear parabolic partial differential equations and takes into account the mass transfer (diffusion and Stefan flow), the heat transfer, and chemical reactions. Reaction's effect is included as a source term in the parabolic equations. The effective thermophysical characteristics are interpolated by time-dependent polynomials in conformity with reference data. The simulated processes occur with different characteristic times, hence the high degree of stiffness in the studied system. The model's difference analog is given in a dimensionless form. We use an approach based on splitting by physical processes. Also, we isolate the solution of the chemical kinetics equations into a separate block. The chemical kinetics equations are stiff and require specialized solution methods. In the present research, we choose the Radau IIA method for this. For the equations of mass transfer and heat transfer, we use the integro-interpolation method. The numerical algorithm is implemented in C++ using MPI technology. The two-dimensional computational domain is divided into equal spatial cells. Each processor stores the data for computing the rates of chemical reactions and effective thermophysical characteristics. It should be noted that only boundary conditions are involved in the interprocessor exchange, which significantly reduces the program runtime. We investigate the efficiency of the developed parallel algorithm on the example of the process of oxidative regeneration of a cylindrical catalyst grain. We provide the corresponding results on the speedup of computations on several processors with different numbers of cells, as well as the graphs of substance concentrations and the temperature of the catalyst grain under various process conditions.

© The Author(s), under exclusive license to Springer Nature Switzerland AG 2023
L. Sokolinsky and M. Zymbler (Eds.): PCT 2023, CCIS 1868, pp. 336–350, 2023.
https://doi.org/10.1007/978-3-031-38864-4_24

Keywords: Oxidative regeneration · Nonlinear model · Chemical kinetics · MPI technology · Numerical methods

1   Introduction

At present, the oil and gas industry is based on the processing of hydrocarbons. Petroleum refining processes are impossible without the use of catalysts. During chemical reactions, the catalyst gets covered with coke residua. The composition of residua depends on many factors: the type of catalyst, the type of feedstock, the reaction conditions, and others. At the same time, researchers identify some general characteristics of coke: it mainly consists of carbon and hydrogen [1–3].

Coke residua must be removed from the surface of catalyst grains and pores if one wants to continue using the catalyst. Oxidative regeneration, that is, burning the accumulated coke off using an oxygen-containing mixture, is one of the most accessible methods for this. The combustion of coke leads to the overheating of the catalyst grain, which can cause irreversible damage. The empirical selection of technological parameters requires a large number of expensive laboratory experiments. Mathematical modeling is by far a more efficient method for predicting the course of the oxidative regeneration process [2,4,5].

The development of mathematical models for catalytic processes is a nontrivial task requiring both an extensive experimental base and efficient methods for solving the resulting problems. For correct modeling, it is necessary to take into account the heat and mass transfer and chemical transformations. As is known, the combination of such heterogeneous processes with a considerable difference in their characteristic times leads to stiff systems and, accordingly, to a significant increase in the computational complexity of the algorithms for the system solution [6].

One of the approaches to reduce the computation time is the use of parallel technologies.

The article [7] presents a parallel algorithm for the canonical substrate-enzyme model with explicit phase separation; the model includes kinetic equations and diffusion. The research authors offer an analysis of the parallel algorithm speedup and conclude that it is efficient in such tasks.

The use of parallelization to speed up the calculation of kinetic parameters in various problem classes is described in [8]. As noted in the paper, a high degree of stiffness requires a special approach. Also, the distribution of the computational load among threads makes it possible to carry out the calculations in a reasonable time.

The development of software for some kinetic problems is covered in [9]. The software includes parallel task management and parallel algorithms for solving algebraic and differential equations on computer clusters. The efficiency of such a construction is analyzed.

An example of parallel numerical algorithms' implementation using MPI technology as applied to problems of mathematical physics is presented in [10]. An analysis of the computation time shows a significant speedup compared to the program's parallel version.

The present paper is the continuation of the research described in [1,2,4,5, 11–13]. The numerical algorithm is developed for a cylindrical grain model during oxidative regeneration. It is implemented in C++ using MPI technology. We analyze the efficiency of the algorithm and compare it with a sequential version of the problem solution. We also give the patterns of distribution over the catalyst grain for substances involved in the chemical reaction, provide the dynamics of the coke mass fraction, and analyze the catalyst grain temperature during the process of burning the coke residua off. For data analysis and visualization, we used the ParaView package.

Oxidative regeneration is a complex nonstationary process. Coke burning occurs at quite high temperatures. The accompanying chemical reactions are exothermic, hence the heating of the catalyst grain. In the process of burning coke, the surface of the reaction area changes.

The book [2] suggests a mathematical model of various regimes of oxidative regeneration. The authors note that oxidative regeneration, like any other catalytic process, should be studied in a stepwise manner. The model consists of three stages: the kinetic model, the grain model, and the catalyst-layer model. The model of oxidative regeneration exhibits a high degree of stiffness since it takes into account chemical transformations, heat transfer, and diffusion. This results in algorithms with high computational complexity. A current topic is the development of numerical algorithms that make it possible to conduct computational experiments with such models in a reasonable time.

Our research aims to develop an efficient parallel algorithm for the numerical simulation of a cylindrical catalyst grain during the process of oxidative regeneration taking into account how the effective heat capacity and the effective thermal conductivity depend on the temperature.

The paper is organized as follows. Section 1 is devoted to introduction and literature review. In Sect. 2, we present mathematical model of oxidative regeneration of a cylindrical catalyst grain. Section 3 contains the numerical algorithm for the model in the Sect. 2. Section 4 is devoted to the parallel solution algorithm. Section 5 is for the numerical results. Conclusion summarizes the study and points directions for further work.

2   Modeling the Processes in a Catalyst Grain

The first stage of the modeling process is the kinetic model. A proven kinetic model of oxidative regeneration is given in [1], namely,

$$2\Theta_C + O_2 \longrightarrow 2\Theta_{CO}, \quad W_1 = k_1(T)\,\Theta_3^2\,y_1;$$
$$\Theta_{CO} + O_2 \longrightarrow \Theta_{CO} + CO_2, \quad W_2 = k_2(T)\,\Theta_2\,y_1;$$
$$\Theta_{CO} \longrightarrow \Theta_C + CO, \quad W_3 = k_3(T)\,\Theta_2;$$
$$\Theta_{CH_2} + O_2 \longrightarrow \Theta_{CO} + H_2O, \quad W_4 = k_4(T)\,\Theta_1\,y_1; \tag{1}$$
$$\Theta_{CO} + \Theta_{CO} \longrightarrow 2\Theta_C + CO_2, \quad W_5 = k_5(T)\,\Theta_2^2;$$
$$\Theta_{CH_2} \rightleftarrows \Theta_C + Z_{H_2}, \quad W_6 = k_6(T)\,\frac{\rho_C}{R_C}(\Theta_1^* - z_1);$$
$$\Theta_{CO} \rightleftarrows \Theta_C + Z_O, \quad W_7 = k_7(T)\,\frac{\rho_C}{R_C}(\Theta_2^* - z_2).$$

Here W_i, $i = \overline{1,7}$, are the rates of the stages of chemical reaction (W_r, $r = \overline{1,5}$, have units of mole/(l·sec²), while W_6 and W_7 have units of g/(m²·sec)); $k_j(T)$, $j = \overline{1,7}$, are the reaction rate constants of the stages (the units of k_j correspond to ω_j); Θ_l, $l = \overline{1,3}$, are the degrees of the buildup of carbon complexes on the coke surface (Θ_1 is the hydrogen-carbon complex, Θ_2 is the oxygen-carbon complex, and Θ_3 is the free carbon surface); y_1 is the concentration of oxygen in the gas phase in mole fractions; z_1 and z_2 are the concentrations of hydrogen and oxygen in the coke layer in mass fractions; $\Theta_1^* = \dfrac{\Theta_1}{6}$ and $\Theta_2^* = \dfrac{4\Theta_2}{3}$ are the amounts of hydrogen and oxygen adsorbed by coke in relation to the current state of the coke deposit surface; ρ_C and R_C are the density (g/m³) and the average radius (m) of the granules of coke. Moreover,

$$\Theta_1 + \Theta_2 + \Theta_3 = 0.$$

The system of differential equations corresponding to the chemical transformations has the following form [2]:

$$\begin{cases} \dfrac{dq_c}{dt} = -M_C S_k(W_2 + W_3 + W_5), \\[2mm] \dfrac{d(z_1\,q_C)}{dt} = S_k W_6, \\[2mm] \dfrac{d(z_2\,q_C)}{dt} = S_k W_7, \end{cases} \tag{2}$$

where M_C is the molar mass of coke (g/mole) and S_k is the specific surface area of coke granules, that is, the reaction surface area (m²/g).

Also, we have the following differential equations based on the law of conservation of mass to determine the proportions of hydrogen-carbon and oxygen-carbon complexes [11,13]:

$$\begin{cases} \dfrac{d\theta_1}{dt} = -\dfrac{\gamma_k S_k}{c_0} W_4 - S_k W_6, \\[2mm] \dfrac{d\theta_2}{dt} = \dfrac{\gamma_k S_k}{c_0}(2W_1 - W_3 + W_4 - 2W_5) - S_k W_7, \end{cases} \tag{3}$$

where γ_k is the catalyst bulk density (g/m³) and c_0 is the molar density of the reaction mixture (mole/m³).

The second stage of the modeling process is the catalyst grain model. Obviously, the development of any mathematical model requires some assumptions. In this study, we make the following assumptions: the catalyst grain is cylindrical, the coke buildup has a hemispherical shape, and the coke is evenly distributed in the grain. Under these assumptions, we can go from Cartesian coordinates in three-dimensional space to cylindrical coordinates. By doing so, we significantly reduce the problem solution time. Thus the problem is formulated in an axisymmetric form.

The heat balance equation for a catalyst grain includes the heat transfer along the cylinder radius and the axis of the catalyst grain, as well as the heat release during the chemical reactions:

$$\frac{\partial c^* T_z}{\partial t} = \frac{1}{r}\frac{\partial}{\partial r}\left(r\frac{\partial \lambda^* T_z}{\partial r}\right) + \frac{\partial^2 \lambda^* T_z}{\partial z^2} + \gamma_k S_k \sum_{j=1}^{5} Q_j W_j, \qquad (4)$$

where T_z is the catalyst grain temperature (K), t is the time (sec), r is the catalyst grain radius (m), z is the axis of the cylindrical grain of the catalyst (m), c^* is the effective heat capacity coefficient of the catalyst (J/m^3/K), λ^* is the effective thermal conductivity of the catalyst (W/m/K), γ_k is the catalyst bulk density (g/m^3), and Q_j, $j = \overline{1,5}$, is the thermal effect of the j-th reaction stage.

Polynomial dependencies for effective thermophysical characteristics are obtained from reference data:

$$c^*(T_z) = (1 - \varepsilon)(\rho_k(A_k T_z^2 + B_k T_z + C_k)(1 - q_c) +$$
$$+ (A_C T_z^2 + B_C T_z + C_C)q_c), \qquad (5)$$
$$\lambda^*(T_z) = (1 - \varepsilon)(A_L T_z^2 + B_L T_z + C_L), \qquad (6)$$

where ρ_k is the density of the catalyst material; A_k, B_k, C_k and A_C, B_C, C_C are the coefficients of the polynomials describing the temperature dependence of the specific heats of the catalyst material and the coke, respectively; ε is the catalyst grain porosity; and A_L, B_L, and C_L are the coefficients of the polynomial describing the temperature dependence of the thermal conductivity of the catalyst material.

The material balance equation for the catalyst grain takes into account the chemical transformations, the diffusion, and the Stefan flow resulting from the change in the reaction volume:

$$\varepsilon\frac{\partial y_i}{\partial t} = \frac{1}{r}\frac{\partial}{\partial r}\left(r\frac{\partial D^* y_i}{\partial r} - r\mu y_i\right) + \frac{\partial}{\partial z}\left(\frac{\partial D^* y_i}{\partial z} - \mu y_i\right) + \frac{\gamma_k S_k}{c_0}\sum_{j=1}^{7}\nu_{ij} W_j, \qquad (7)$$

where y_i, $i = \overline{1,4}$ are the concentrations of substances in the grain pores in mole fractions; D^* is the effective diffusion coefficient (m^2/sec); μ is the Stefan flow velocity (m/sec); c_0 is the gas molar density (mole/m^3); and ν_{ij}, $i = \overline{1,4}$, $j = \overline{1,7}$, are the stoichiometric coefficients of the substances.

Several methods (see [14] and [15]) can be applied to calculate the value of the effective diffusion coefficient. The small size of the catalyst pores (4 to 5 nm) [2] makes it possible to compute the effective diffusion coefficient by the following formula, based on the Knudsen diffusion coefficient (see [16] and [17]):

$$D^* = \frac{2r_p \varepsilon}{3\delta} \sqrt{\frac{8RT_z}{\pi M}}, \tag{8}$$

where r_p is the pore radius (m), $\delta \approx 2$ is the tortuosity coefficient of the pores, R is the universal gas constant (J/K/mole), and M is the molar mass of the reaction mixture (g/mole).

The Stefan flow velocity is a quantity that changes over time. It is computed from the condition that its value is zero at the boundary:

$$\frac{1}{r}\frac{\partial}{\partial r}(r\mu) + \frac{\partial \mu}{\partial z} = \frac{\gamma_k S_k}{c_0}(W_1 + W_3 + W_5). \tag{9}$$

The balance equations are supplemented with the following initial and boundary conditions:

$$t = 0: \ q_c(0) = q_C^0, \ z_1(0) = z_1^0, \ z_2(0) = 0, \ \theta_1(0) = \theta_1^0, \ \theta_2(0) = 0,$$

$$T_z(0) = T(0), \ y_1(0) = y_1^0, \ y_i(0) = 0, i = \overline{2,4}, \ \mu = 0, \tag{10}$$

$$r = 0, \ z = 0: \ \frac{\partial y_i}{\partial r} = \frac{\partial y_i}{\partial z} = 0, \ \frac{\partial T_z}{\partial r} = \frac{\partial \Theta}{\partial z} = 0; \tag{11}$$

$$r = R_z: \ \lambda^* \frac{\partial T_z}{\partial r} = \alpha\left(T(0) - T_z\right), \ \frac{\partial y_i}{\partial r} = 0, i = \overline{1,4},$$

$$z = L: \ \lambda^* \frac{\partial T_z}{\partial z} = \alpha\left(T(0) - T_z\right), \ \frac{\partial y_i}{\partial z} = 0, i = \overline{1,4}.$$

Conditions (11) follow from the fact that the composition of coke residua, the temperature of the catalyst grain, and the temperature of the reaction mixture are known at the initial moment, and heat exchange between the catalyst grain and the reaction mixture surrounding it through the cylindrical wall and cylinder ends.

Equations (4) and (7) are of the diffusion type and can be integrated quite easily without regard to the chemical nature of the problem. However, the addition of source terms creates a significant difference in the characteristic times of the processes, which inevitably increases the degree of stiffness of the system. The stiffness analysis shows that the difference between the eigenvalues of the Jacobi matrix for the grain model can reach fifteen orders of magnitude. This is because fast chemical reactions occur against the background of a slow diffusion process.

We write the catalyst grain model in a dimensionless form (for convenience) as

$$
\begin{cases}
\dfrac{\partial y_i}{\partial \tau} = \dfrac{1}{\varphi \varepsilon_k} \dfrac{1}{\rho} \dfrac{\partial}{\partial \rho} \left(\rho \dfrac{\partial y_i}{\partial \rho} - \rho \hat{\mu} y_i \right) + \dfrac{R_z}{\varphi \varepsilon_k L^2} \dfrac{\partial}{\partial l} \left(R_z \dfrac{\partial y_i}{\partial l} - L \hat{\mu} y_i \right) + \\
\qquad\qquad\qquad\qquad\qquad\qquad\qquad\qquad + \dfrac{\hat{S}}{\varepsilon_k} \sum\limits_{j=1}^{5} \nu_{ij} \omega_j, \\[2mm]
\dfrac{\partial \Theta}{\partial \tau} = \dfrac{\lambda^* \tau_k}{c^* R_z^2} \dfrac{1}{\rho} \dfrac{\partial}{\partial \rho} \left(\rho \dfrac{\partial \Theta}{\partial \rho} \right) + \dfrac{\lambda^* \tau_k}{c^* L^2} \dfrac{\partial \Theta}{\partial l} + \dfrac{\hat{S} c_0}{T_{op} c^*} \sum\limits_{j=1}^{5} Q_j \omega_j, \\[2mm]
\dfrac{1}{\rho} \dfrac{\partial}{\partial \rho} (\rho \hat{\mu}) + \dfrac{R}{L} \dfrac{\partial \hat{\mu}}{\partial l} = \varphi \hat{S}(-\omega_1 + \omega_3 + \omega_5), \\[2mm]
\dfrac{\partial q_c}{\partial \tau} = -\dfrac{M_C c_0}{\gamma_k} \hat{S}(\omega_2 + \omega_3 + \omega_5), \\[2mm]
\dfrac{\partial z_1}{\partial \tau} = \dfrac{c_0}{\gamma_k q_c} \hat{S}(\omega_6 + z_1 M_C(\omega_2 + \omega_3 + \omega_5)), \\[2mm]
\dfrac{\partial z_2}{\partial \tau} = \dfrac{c_0}{\gamma_k q_c} \hat{S}(\omega_7 + z_2 M_C(\omega_2 + \omega_3 + \omega_5)), \\[2mm]
\dfrac{\partial \theta_1}{\partial \tau} = -\hat{S} \left(\omega_4 + \dfrac{c_0}{\gamma_k} \omega_6 \right), \\[2mm]
\dfrac{\partial \theta_2}{\partial \tau} = \hat{S} \left(2\omega_1 - \omega_3 + \omega_4 - 2\omega_5 - \dfrac{c_0}{\gamma_k} \omega_7 \right),
\end{cases}
\tag{12}
$$

with the following dimensionless initial and boundary conditions:

$$
\tau = 0: \quad q_c(0) = q_C^0, \ z_1(0) = z_1^0, \ z_2(0) = 0, \ \theta_1(0) = \theta_1^0, \ \theta_2(0) = 0,
$$

$$
\Theta(0) = \dfrac{T(0)}{T_{op}}, \ y_1(0) = y_1^0, \ y_i(0) = 0, i = \overline{2,4}, \ \hat{\mu} = 0;
\tag{13}
$$

$$
\rho = 0, \ l = 0: \quad \dfrac{\partial y_i}{\partial \rho} = \dfrac{\partial y_i}{\partial l} = 0, \ \dfrac{\partial \Theta}{\partial \rho} = \dfrac{\partial \Theta}{\partial l} = 0;
$$

$$
\rho = 1: \quad \dfrac{\partial \Theta}{\partial \rho} = \dfrac{R_z \alpha}{\lambda^*} \left(\dfrac{T(0)}{T_{op}} - \Theta \right), \ \dfrac{\partial y_i}{\partial \rho} = 0, i = \overline{1,4};
\tag{14}
$$

$$
l = 1: \quad \dfrac{\partial \Theta}{\partial l} = \dfrac{L \alpha}{\lambda^*} \left(\dfrac{T(0)}{T_{op}} - \Theta \right), \ \dfrac{\partial y_i}{\partial l} = 0, i = \overline{1,4}.
$$

Here ρ is the dimensionless catalyst grain radius, $\rho \in [0,1]$ (independent spatial variable); l is the dimensionless length of the catalyst grain axis, $l \in [0,1]$ (independent spatial variable); τ is the dimensionless time, $\tau \in [0, +\infty)$ (independent time variable); $\Theta(\rho, \tau)$ is the dimensionless catalyst grain temperature; $y_i(\rho, \tau)$, $i = \overline{1,4}$, are the mole fractions of components in the gas phase of the reaction (the index 1 corresponds to oxygen, 2 to carbon monoxide, 3 to carbon dioxide, and 4 to water); $\hat{\mu}(\rho, \tau)$ is the dimensionless velocity of the Stefan flow; $q_c(\rho, \tau)$ is the mass fraction of coke on the catalyst grain; $z_1(\rho, \tau)$ and $z_2(\rho, \tau)$ are the mass fractions of hydrogen and oxygen in the coke deposit; $\theta_1(\rho, \tau)$ and $\theta_2(\rho, \tau)$ are the fractions of hydrogen-carbon and oxygen-carbon complexes on the coke granule surface; $\hat{S}(\rho, \tau)$ is the dimensionless area of coke granules; $\omega_j(\rho, \tau)$, $j = \overline{1,5}$, are the dimensionless rates of quasihomogeneous reactions taken from the kinetic scheme; $\omega_j(\rho, \tau)$, $j = \overline{6,7}$, are the rates of heterogeneous reactions taken from the kinetic scheme (g/mole); D^* is the effective diffusion coefficient (m²/sec); τ_k is the contact time (sec); R_z is the catalyst grain radius (m); L is the catalyst grain length (m); ε is the catalyst grain porosity; ν_{ij}, $i = \overline{1,4}$, are the stoichiometric coefficients from the reaction scheme; c_0 is the gas molar density (mole/m³); $T_{op} = 520°$ is the temperature at which the reaction rate constants are experimentally determined (K); c is the volumetric heat capacity of the catalyst (J/(m³ · K)); Q_j, $j = \overline{1,5}$, are the thermal effects of chemical reactions (J/mole); γ is the catalyst bulk density (g/m³); and M_C is the coke molecular weight (g/mole).

It should be noted that there is a decrease in the volume of the accumulated coke over time. This fact is taken into account in model (12) as a decrease of the reaction surface area $\hat{S}(\rho, \tau) = \left(\dfrac{q_c(\rho, \tau)}{q_c(\rho, 0)} \right)^{\frac{2}{3}}$, while the catalyst grain size remains constant.

The dimensionless model leads to a simplification of the computational domain: the integration domain is now the square $[0, 1] \times [0, 1]$.

3 The Numerical Algorithm

We solved the diffusion and heat transfer equations in system (12) by the integro-interpolation method. Using a three-stage implicit Runge Kutta method of the fifth order of accuracy, namely, Radau IIA [6], we separately solved the kinetic equations (splitting by physical processes).

Let us write the differential analogue of system (12):

$$\Theta_{i,j}^{n+1} = \Theta_{i,j}^n + \frac{\Delta t\, \lambda^*}{D^* \varphi i h_r^2} \left((i + 0.5) \left(\Theta_{i+1,j}^n - \Theta_{i,j}^n \right) - (i - 0.5) \left(\Theta_{i,j}^n - \Theta_{i-1,j}^n \right) \right) +$$

$$+ \frac{\Delta t\, \lambda^* \tau_k}{c^* L^2} \frac{\Theta_{i,j+1}^n - 2\Theta_{i,j}^n + \Theta_{i,j-1}^n}{h_z^2} + \left(\frac{\hat{S} c_0}{T_{op} c^*} \sum_{o=1}^{5} Q_o \omega_o \right)_{i,j}^n,$$

$$y_{i,j}^{n+1} = y_{i,j}^{n\,*} + \frac{\Delta t}{\varepsilon_k \varphi i h_r^2} \left((i + 0.5) \left(y_{i+1,j}^n - y_{i,j}^n \right) - (i - 0.5) \left(y_{i,j}^n - y_{i-1,j}^n \right) \right) -$$

$$- \frac{\Delta t}{\varepsilon_k \varphi i h_r^2} \left((i + 0.5) \left(\hat{\mu}_{i+1,j}^n y_{i+1,j}^n - \hat{\mu}_{i,j}^n y_{i,j}^n \right) - (i - 0.5) \left(\hat{\mu}_{i,j}^n y_{i,j}^n - \hat{\mu}_{i-1,j}^n y_{i-1,j}^n \right) \right) +$$

$$+ \frac{\Delta t\, R_z^2}{\varepsilon_k \varphi L h_z^2} \left((j + 0.5) \left(y_{i,j+1}^n - y_{i,j}^n \right) - (j - 0.5) \left(y_{i,j}^n - y_{i,j-1}^n \right) \right) -$$

$$- \frac{\Delta t}{\varepsilon_k \varphi i h_z^2} \left((j + 0.5) \left(\hat{\mu}_{i,j+1}^n y_{i,j+1}^n - \hat{\mu}_{i,j}^n y_{i,j}^n \right) - (j - 0.5) \left(\hat{\mu}_{i,j}^n y_{i,j}^n - \hat{\mu}_{i,j-1}^n y_{i,j-1}^n \right) \right) +$$

$$+ \left(\frac{\hat{S}}{\varepsilon_k} \sum_{o=1}^{5} \nu_o \omega_o \right)_{i,j}^n,$$

$$\hat{\mu}_{i,j}^n = \frac{1}{h_r + h_z} \left(h_r \hat{\mu}_{i,j-1}^n - \frac{h_z}{i-1} \hat{\mu}_{i-1,j}^n + h_r \hat{\mu}_{i-1,j}^n + \right.$$

$$\left. + h_z h_r \left(\varphi \hat{S} \sum_{o=1}^{5} \nu_o \omega_o \right)^n_{i-1,j-1} \right),$$

where $y_{i,j}^{n\,*}$ are the preliminary mole fractions of the components obtained by solving system (2)–(3).

The resulting difference scheme formed the basis of the software written in C++. A theoretical study of stability and convergence is impossible due to the complexity of the right side of system (12), so the study was carried out for different numbers of computational cells. The conclusion about its stability and convergence was made according to the correct operation of the numerical algorithm for grids of sizes $10^2 \times 10^2$, $2 \cdot 10^2 \times 2 \cdot 10^2$, and $4 \cdot 10^2 \times 4 \cdot 10^2$.

4   The Parallel Solution Algorithm

Currently, many tools speed up and simplify the work of complex computing systems. A special place is occupied by parallel technologies, which allow performing fast computations by distributing computational threads among processors.

In this article, calculations are carried out using the MPI standard. The choice of this technology is determined by several factors.

Previously, the authors developed a parallel algorithm using the Open MP technology for numerical simulation of the oxidative regeneration process of spherical grains taking into account the simple geometry of the domain [13]. It is worth noting that the solution of kinetic problems in the general body of the program leads to considerable step refinement, which entails significant time costs for calculations. In the present study, we use splitting by physical processes to solve separately the equations of chemical kinetics. However, it makes the use of the OpenMP standard inefficient.

Interprocessor exchange is necessary only at the boundaries of the partitioning regions since the transition to cylindrical coordinates and the nondimensionalization of the problem reduce the computational domain to the square $[0, 1] \times [0, 1]$. At the same time, an increase in the number of components in the chemical reactions does not lead to a critical increase in calculation time since solution of their equations will be distributed among the processors.

In addition, the study of the numerical algorithm stability in the formulation of refining grids requires a significant number of computational experiments. The MPI standard makes it possible to implement the computations for a large number of spatial cells.

The computational domain is divided into parts according to the number of processors used to organize the parallel computations.

The values of the variables corresponding to the concentrations and the temperature are calculated using the given initial and boundary conditions in each region. For the algorithm implementation, the temperature of the catalyst grain

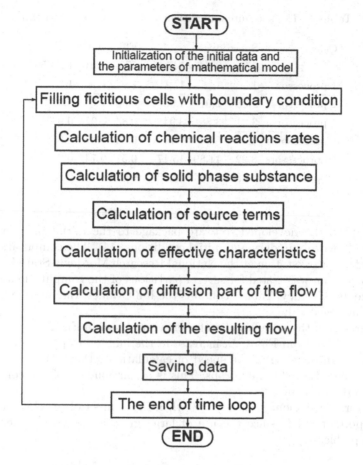

Fig. 1. The scheme of computation on a node

and the concentrations of the mixture components are defined as integral averages in the grid cells.

Parameters for calculating the reaction rates and effective thermophysical characteristics are stored on each processor, which can significantly reduce the amount of data involved in the interprocessor exchange. It is enough to carry out the exchange between adjacent processors in terms of boundary conditions.

Paired blocking functions MPI_Send() and MPI_Recv() are used in the code to send and receive data since there only occurs exchange between two processors in the parallel algorithm.

Figure 1 shows the flowchart describing the operation of one computing node on the example of computation of the dimensionless temperature $\Theta(\tau, \rho, l)$, the concentrations $y_i(\tau, \rho, l)$, and the Stefan flow velocity $\hat{\mu}(\tau, \rho, l)$.

Table 1. The speedup and efficiency of the parallel algorithm

Cells	Speedup			Efficiency		
	576	9216	147 456	576	9216	147 456
1 processor	1	1	1	1	1	1
2 processors	1.96	2.01	1.98	0.98	1	0.99
4 processors	3.31	3.88	3.94	0.83	0.97	0.98
8 processors	4.35	6.94	7.74	0.54	0.87	0.97
16 processors	8.22	11.89	15.17	0.51	0.74	0.95
32 processors	11.84	17.94	28.06	0.37	0.56	0.88

We applied the developed software package to the initial boundary value problem (12) with boundary and initial conditions (14). The computations were performed on a workstation at the National Research Mordovia State University.

The algorithm was tested for several partitions of the computational domain to analyze its efficiency. Table 1 contains the limit values; the intermediate ones are some averaged values.

The graphs of the speedup and efficiency are given in Fig. 2.

As we can see from Fig. 2, an increase in the number of processors leads, as expected, to an increase in the speed of calculations. However, if the number of cells is large, the efficiency drops. This is a consequence of the considerable amount of data transfer.

However, the efficiency reaches 88% when the number of cells increases. This is an important result since the use of large grids is necessary when solving practical problems.

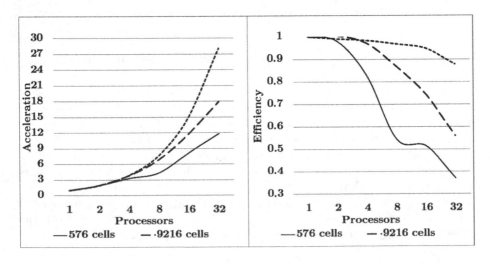

Fig. 2. The speedup and efficiency for different numbers of cells

5   The Computation Results

We applied the developed parallel algorithm to the numerical simulation of the process of oxidative regeneration in a cylindrical catalyst grain.

The values of the technological parameters were taken from [2,5]:

$$\rho_C = 1.8 t/m^3, \ \gamma_k = 0.7 \ t/m^3, \ \varepsilon_k = 0.5, \ \tau_k = 4.8 \ sec, \ c_0 = 15 \ mole/m^3,$$
$$R_C^0 = 10^{-8} \ m, \ T_{op} = 793 \ K, \ M_C = 12 \ g/mole, \ \theta_1^0 = 0.12, \ \theta_2^0 = 0,$$
$$y_1^0 = 0.05, \ \alpha = 11.5 \ W/(m \cdot s), \ \beta = 0.0115 \ m/sec.$$

The rate constants at a temperature of 720 K and the activation energies for stages (1) are given in [2] and [4].

The effective coefficients of heat capacity and thermal conductivity were calculated based on data given in [18–20]. The dependence of thermal conductivity and heat capacity for aluminum oxide and coke was approximated by parabolas.

The calculations were carried out under the assumption that the initial temperature of the catalyst grain corresponds to normal conditions (0°C), and the grain boundary is heated continuously by gas at a temperature of 520°C.

The catalyst chosen for the computational experiment is based on aluminum oxide. The grains have a cylindrical radius of 2 mm and a length of 4 mm. The size of the computational grid is 100 × 100 cells.

The concentrations of oxygen O_2, carbon monoxide CO, carbon dioxide CO_2, and water vapor H_2O are shown in Figs. 3, 4, 5 and 6.

Fig. 3. O_2 concentration

Fig. 4. CO concentration

Fig. 5. CO_2 concentration

Fig. 6. H_2O concentration

Figure 7 depicts the key indicator of the oxidative regeneration process: the decrease in coke's mass fraction in the catalyst grain. Figure 8 shows the temperature field pattern corresponding to the case when 40% of the coke's initial mass fraction is burnt off.

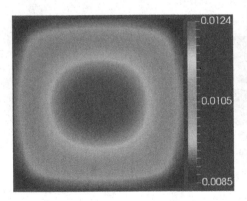
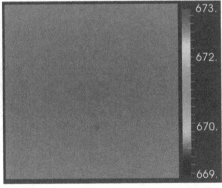

Fig. 7. Mass fraction of coke   **Fig. 8.** Grain temperature

It follows from the graphs in Figs. 3, 4, 5, 6 and 7 that the process is most active at the boundary zone, which agrees with the temperature distribution in the grain (Fig. 8).

The low oxygen concentration in the grain's center corresponds to a high concentration of other substances in the gas phase, in complete agreement with the law of conservation of mass. The coke burns out most quickly at the grain boundary, which is associated with the heat transfer in this zone and the supply of oxygen through the grain boundary.

6   Conclusions

In this article, we developed a numerical algorithm for the study of a model of a cylindrical grain during oxidative regeneration. The numerical algorithm was implemented in C++ using MPI technology. We analyzed the efficiency of the algorithm and compared it with a sequential version of the problem solution. Also, we gave the patterns of distribution over the catalyst grain for substances involved in the chemical reaction, provided the dynamics of the coke mass fraction, and analyzed the temperature field distribution over the catalyst grain while burning coke residua off.

By calculating the effective coefficients of thermophysical characteristics, we modified the model of the cylindrical grain during oxidative regeneration. Afterward, the resulting nonlinear system of parabolic equations underwent nondimensionalization. The resulting model is characterized by a high degree of stiffness. An approach based on splitting into physical processes was chosen for developing an efficient algorithm to solve the problem. The equations of diffusion and heat transfer were solved by the integro-interpolation method, while the kinetic equations were solved using a three-stage implicit Runge–Kutta method of the fifth order. This approach makes it possible to solve such problems in a reasonable time and conduct a large number of multiparameter numerical experiments.

The parallel algorithm showed its efficiency in the simulation of oxidative regeneration under different technological parameters. In the future, the model considered in this paper will be used, as part of the catalyst-bed model, in the study of the oxidative regeneration process. Also, we intend to extend the developed algorithm to a new model.

Acknowledgments. This research was partially funded by the Boreskov Institute of Catalysis (project AAAA-A21-121011390010-7) and the Institute of Petrochemistry and Catalysis of the Russian Academy of Sciences (theme № FMRS-2022-0078).

References

1. Kutepov, B.I.: Kinetics of formation and interconversion of coke oxidation products on modern cracking catalysts. Ufa, USSR (1980)
2. Masagutov, R.M., Morozov, B.F., Kutepov, B.I.: Regeneration of catalysts in oil processing and petrochemistry. USSR, Moscow (1987)
3. Ostrovskii, N.M.: Kinetics of catalysts deactivation. Nauka, Moscow (2001)
4. Gubaydullin, I.M.: Mathematical modelling of dynamic modes of oxidative regeneration of catalysts in motionless layer. Ufa, Russia (1996)
5. Gubaydullin, I.M., Yazovtseva, O.S.: Investigation of the averaged model of coked catalyst oxidative regeneration. Comput. Res. Model. **13**(1), 149–161 (2021). https://doi.org/10.20537/2076-7633-2021-13-1-149-161
6. Hairer, E., Wanner, G.: Solving Ordinary Differential Equations. Stiff and Differential-Algebraic Problems. 2nd edn. Springer Series in Computational Mathematics, vol. 14. Springer, Heidelberg (1996)

7. Shestov, A., Popov, A., Lee, S.-C., Kuksa, P., Glickson, J.: Fast parallel algorithm for large fractal kinetic models with diffusion (2018). https://doi.org/10.1101/275248
8. Tikhonova, M. V., Gubaydullin, I. M.: Computer processing of chemical experiments in solving inverse kinetic problems based on parallel computing. In: Vestnik OmGU, vol. 64, no. 2 (2012)
9. Adamov, D.P., Fazliev, A.Z., Mikhailov, S.A.: Software for modeling chemical kinetics by parallel programming methods for a computer cluster. In: Atmospheric and Ocean Optics (1999)
10. Gubaydullin, I.M., Zhalnin, R.V., Peskova E.E., et al. : Construction of parallel algorithms of high order of accuracy for modeling the dynamics of reacting flows. In: Parallel Computing Technologies (PaVT'2017): Short Articles and Descriptions of Posters XI International Conference, pp. 288–296. Kazan, Russia (2017)
11. Gubaydullin, I.M., Peskova, E.E., Yazovtseva, O.S., Zagoruiko, A.N.: Numerical simulation of oxidative regeneration of a spherical catalyst grain. Matem. Mod. **34**, 48–66 (2022). https://doi.org/10.20948/mm-2022-11-04
12. Gubaydullin, I.M., Peskova, E.E., Yazovtseva, O.S., Zagoruiko, A.N.: Numerical simulation of oxidative regeneration of a spherical catalyst grain. Math. Models Comput. Simul. **15**, 485–495 (2023). https://doi.org/10.1134/S2070048223030079
13. Yazovtseva, O., Grishaeva, O., Gubaydullin, I., Peskova, E.: Construction of a parallel algorithm for the numerical modeling of coke sediments burning from the spherical catalyst grain. In: Sokolinsky, L., Zymbler, M. (eds.) Parallel Computational Technologies. PCT 2022. Communications in Computer and Information Science, vol. 1618, pp. 248–260 (2022). https://doi.org/10.1007/978-3-031-11623-0_17
14. Pavlov, K.F., Romankov, P.G., Noskov, A.A.: Examples and tasks for the course of processes and apparatuses of chemical technology. USSR, Leningrad (1987)
15. Sampath, B.D.S., Ramachandran, P.A., Hughes, R.: Modelling of non-catalytic gas-solid reactions-I. Transient analysis of the particle-pellet model. Chem. Eng. Sci. **30**, 125–134 (1975)
16. Welty, J.R., Wicks, C.E., Wilson, R.E.: Fundamentals of Momentum, Heat, and Mass Transfer (1969)
17. Muhlenkov, I.P., Dobkina, E.I., Derjuzhkina, V.I., et al.: Tehnologiya katalizatorov. Leningrad, USSR (1989)
18. Sheludyak, E.Y., Kashporov, L.Y., Malinin, L.A., Tsalkov, V.N.: Thermophysical properties of combustible system components. Moscow (1992)
19. Chirkin, V.S.: Thermophysical Properties of Materials for Nuclear Engineering. USSR, Moscow (1968)
20. Kazantsev, E.I.: Industrial Furnaces: Reference Guide for Calculation and Design. USSR, Moscow (1975)

Research of the Influence of the Thermal State of an Air-Intake Model on In-Flight Icing Conditions

Anton O. Mikryukov$^{(\boxtimes)}$, Vladimir Ya. Modorskii⑩,
Stanislav L. Kalyulin$^{(\boxtimes)}$⑩, and Danila S. Maksimov

Perm National Research Polytechnic University, Perm, Russian Federation
anto-mikryuko@yandex.ru, ksl@pstu.ru

Abstract. We consider the impact of icing on in-flight conditions in the case of a structure with a heating element mounted to the aircraft skin, taking as an example an engine air-intake model (AIM). The prediction of the thermal state of the AIM allows choosing the optimal geometric and temperature parameters of the heating element. This reduces the risk of ice entering the engine flow path. With the help of the Ansys FENSAP-ICE simulation software, we researched the conjugate heat transfer between the structure and an external moist flow. Also, we conducted relevant numerical experiments using the High-performance Computational Complex at Perm National Research Polytechnic University. We present in this paper the main results relating to the influence of the heating temperature on the shape and thickness of icing in the AIM for temperatures in the range $1.0T_{st}$ to $1.05T_{st}$ (T_{st} is the flow stagnation temperature near the structure surface). Additionally, we give a comparative assessment of the icing problem scalability on AMD Barcelona-3 and Intel Xeon E5-2680 processors.

Keywords: Air intake model · Icing condition · Numerical simulation · High-performance computation · FENSAP ICE

1 Introduction

Aircraft icing has been a major challenge throughout the history of the aviation industry (mainly since the 1980s). Icing has a significant impact on the safety of aircraft operating under a wide range of meteorological conditions [1]. Icing may exert an extremely adverse effect on the structural elements of aircraft engines (AE), which manifests in various ways [1,2]:

1. Buildup of ice (due to the presence of small and large supercooled droplets in the air) on elements of the engine intake system, with its subsequent detachment (under the action of aerodynamic forces and vibration) and damage to the engine parts located further along the path of the ejected mass of ice.

© The Author(s), under exclusive license to Springer Nature Switzerland AG 2023
L. Sokolinsky and M. Zymbler (Eds.): PCT 2023, CCIS 1868, pp. 351–363, 2023.
https://doi.org/10.1007/978-3-031-38864-4_25

2. Deterioration of the operation efficiency due to ice buildups on the fan blades, the directing vane, low- and high-pressure compressors, and others. All this makes it difficult for the engine to compress the air and leads to a noticeable decrease in thrust and power.
3. Buildup of ice on optical sensors, which reduces the engine control efficiency and ultimately leads to loss of power or operation instability.
4. Buildup of ice on the fan blades, which can cause unstable flow, detachment by rotation, and "fluttering".
5. Cyclic loading and reduction of rotor resources due to uneven ice growth.

Several types of deicing systems (DIS) (anti-icing, electrothermal, mechanical, and their combinations; Fig. 1) have been developed and applied to minimize the negative effects of this phenomenon [3,4].

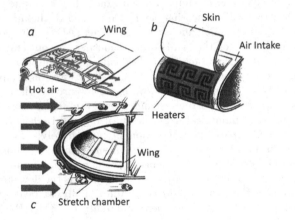

Fig. 1. Types of DISs [4]: (a) anti-icing; (b) electro-thermal; (c) mechanical

Electrothermal DISs are the most widely used in the modern aircraft industry because of their efficiency. They also offer the possibility of being mounted to the aircraft skin, made of metal and composite materials, and varying operating modes.

The need for studying the effect of icing on the air intake at the stage of designing and upgrading AEs is determined by statistical data: more than 40% of flight accidents and crashes occur due to icing of wings, fairings, and air intakes of engines [1,3,5]. The prediction of the thermal state of an air-intake model (AIM) allows choosing the optimal geometric and temperature parameters of the heating element mode and minimizing the negative consequences of ice entering the engine flow path.

Most works by foreign [5–9] and Russian research teams [1–3,10–21] consider icing processes from the standpoint of the occurrence of the phenomenon, experimentally and numerically applied to the aerodynamic profile of the wing.

In this paper, we consider the geometry of an axisymmetric small-sized air intake subjected to the negative influence of icing, namely, ice grows from the side of the AE flow path. The geometric layout is a modified version of an air intake based on a combination of airfoils NACA 5318 and NACA 4310. Such research requires interdisciplinary approaches to account for the thermal balance between the structure and the external moist flow. At the same time, finding the solution to the problems of this class is resource-intensive and requires the appropriate competence when using supercomputer technologies and parallelization.

In this research, we study how the thermal state of the AIM of an aircraft engine (with a heating element mounted to the skin) affects in-flight icing conditions, using various methods and approaches for the numerical simulation of conjugate heat transfer. Also, we consider the scalability of the icing problem on different processor architectures.

2   Materials and Methods

2.1   The Computational Domain

The initial geometry (without the elements of the flow path) of a small-sized axisymmetric engine is shown in Fig. 2 a. We pass from this initial geometry to the computational geometry (the AIM) shown in Fig. 2 b. The transition from the initial to the computational geometry is possible thanks to the fact that the considered design is axisymmetric, which, in the context of the processes under research, allows studying only a characteristic element, namely, an airfoil based on a combination of NACA 5318 and NACA 4310 airfoils.

The AIM consists of a leading edge, an inner panel (from the side of the flow path), an outer panel, and a rear fairing. The toe is a multi-layer structure consisting of a metal skin and an electrical insulator, inside which there is a heating element (HE).

We determine the dimensions of the computational domain based on the characteristic values of the computational geometry. To exclude the influence of the boundaries of the computational domain on the moist flow, we assume that the boundaries are moved away from the research object by five calibers in the direction of the flow and by four calibers in the direction perpendicular to the flow (by caliber, we mean the length L of the airfoil chord). Thus, the computational domain is a parallelepiped with dimensions $11L \times 8L \times 0.5L$. The computational domain with the representation of the regions for the subsequent adjustment of the boundary conditions is shown in Fig. 3.

2.2   Parameters and Methods

The influence of the thermal state of the AIM on in-flight icing conditions was studied in a three-dimensional unsteady formulation of the conjugate heat transfer between the AIM structure and the moist flow. In the research, we employed the Ansys FENSAP-ICE software complex, which allows studying the effect of

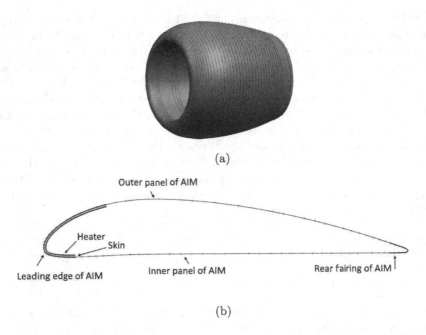

(a)

Outer panel of AIM

Heater
Skin

Leading edge of AIM   Inner panel of AIM   Rear fairing of AIM

(b)

Fig. 2. General view of the air intake engine geometry: (a) initial geometry; (b) computational geometry

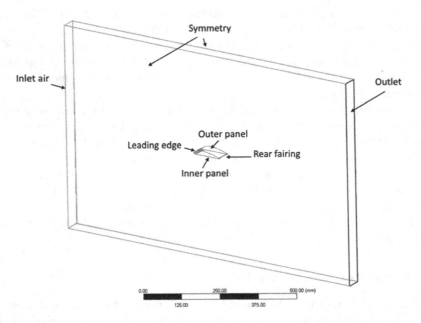

Symmetry

Inlet air   Outlet

Outer panel
Leading edge
Rear fairing
Inner panel

0.00   250.00   500.00 (mm)
      125.00   375.00

Fig. 3. Computational domain for the flow around the AIM construct by the moist flow

icing on structures through numerical simulations of processes and the operation of deicing systems in the context of the conjugate heat transfer approach [15–18]. Within the framework of this approach, the heat flows are conjugated at each time step from the solution of the heat balance equations, that is, from the thermal state of the structure (solutions to the heat conduction problem) and all the solutions of gas-dynamics and fluid problems for a moist airflow [8, 9, 18].

Our team of authors has vast experience in modeling icing in FENSAP-ICE [13–21], which we contributed to model the thermal anti-icing system. It should be noted that icing simulation is also possible using other engineering analysis complexes, including some designed in Russia, such as FlowVision, IceVision, and LOGOS Aero-Hydro. We plan to use these software tools in future research.

The following parameters were employed in the numerical simulations of the buildup of ice on the AIM:

- flight altitude: 1000 m;
- flight velocity: 30 m/s;
- ambient temperature: $-10°$C;
- humidity: 86%;
- liquid water content: 0.4 g/m^3;
- water droplet diameter: 36.6 μm;
- droplet size and water suspension distribution: Langmuir D distribution;
- icing duration: 5 min.

We studied the influence of the thermal state on the icing process under conditions of constant heating with a thermal power that maintains, on average, the temperature of the outer surface of the leading edge of the AIM within the range $1.0T_{ad}$ to $1.05T_{ad}$ (T_{ad} is the flow stagnation temperature near the structure surface).

The choice of flight conditions is determined by the fact that a given combination of temperature, pressure (determined by the flight altitude), and flight velocity (provided that there is no active deicing system) imply a high risk of icing on the side of the bottom panel of the structure or a similar shape during the whole period that these conditions are present. In the numerical simulation, we assume that the droplet size and the water suspension in the moist flow are distributed according to Langmuir D distribution (Fig. 4).

This distribution was chosen because, under real-life meteorological conditions, the airflow can contain drops in a wide range of sizes (from 5 to 75 μm and even larger [22]) when entering the icing zone. The Langmuir D distribution used for a given median droplet size makes it possible to take this factor into account.

2.3 Mesh Convergence Estimation

Three-dimensional mesh models were constructed with the help of the Ansys ICEM CFD finite element mesh generator using the *O-grid* block topology approach for the computational domain of the moist flow and geometry of the AIM

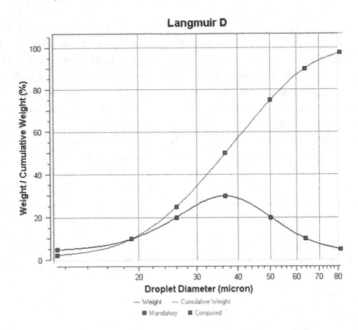

Fig. 4. Langmuir D distribution of droplet size and water suspension

leading edge structure. At the same time, the number of partitions along the mating surface in the region of the leading edge is identical for the mesh model of the flow and that of the structure.

To eliminate the influence of the "quality" of the constructed mesh models on the obtained results, we assessed the mesh convergence by varying the linear dimensions of the finite elements (the number of partitions of the generatrix of the AIM surface) until the "independence" of the results was established during the simulation of a steady gas dynamic flow around the AIM under in-flight conditions. The convergence factor for mesh models is defined as the average temperature value over the surface of the leading edge and the airfoil (i.e., the combination of the leading edge, the inner panel, the outer panel, and the rear fairing). The mesh convergence results are shown in Fig. 5.

From the analysis of the mesh convergence results, we concluded that 1.72 million elements are required as a minimum to obtain correct results in the subsequent modeling. Further increasing the number of elements does not significantly affect the results obtained. The corresponding mesh model (near the AIM surfaces), employed in further numerical simulations, is shown in Fig. 6.

Based on the number of partitions of the AIM surface, we developed a mesh model of the leading edge, which was required for further modeling of the conjugate heat transfer. While having an identical set of surface partitions for the structure, the total number of elements was 310 thousand.

Thus, for the subsequent modeling, we used mesh models with a total of 2.03 million elements.

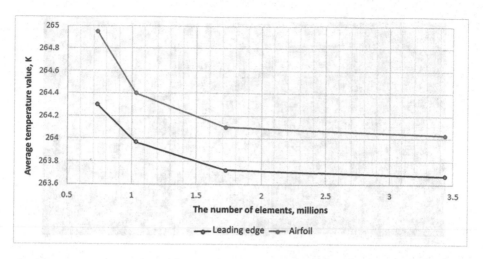

Fig. 5. Mesh convergence graphs: the temperature averaged over the leading edge surface (black curve) and over the airfoil surface (red curve) of the AIM versus the number of elements (Color figure online)

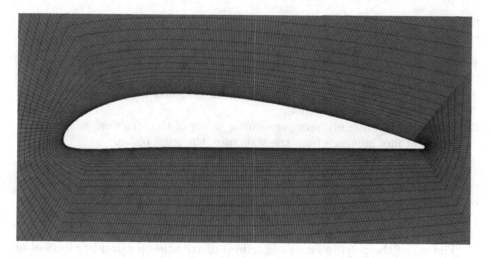

Fig. 6. A mesh model of the AIM external flow for research on the thermal state influence (ICEM CFD)

3   Results and Discussion

3.1   Speedup and Scalability

The research of interdisciplinary processes is resource-intensive and time-consuming because of the mathematical complexity of such tasks. Icing processes (either without conjugate heat transfer or with the conjugate exchange between

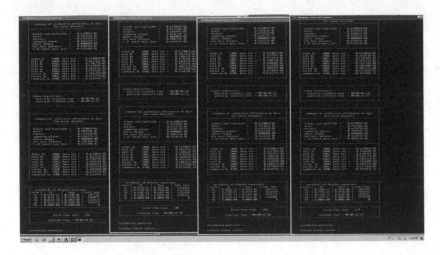

Fig. 7. An example of parallelization of a simulation task for modeling the liquid stage with the polydisperse droplet distribution

the external flow and the structure) are implemented within the framework of existing approaches and numerical methods in several phases:

1. Simulation of the distribution of gas-dynamics fields in the external flow: the gas-dynamics phase.
2. Simulation of the distribution of the water field and that of droplets in the external flow: the liquid phase.
3. Simulation of unsteady processes during icing of the structure without and with heat flux influence from the structure: the icing phase.

Each phase has implementation features that affect the overall acceleration of computations. The liquid phase has the most significant impact on the simulation of in-flight icing under the considered flight conditions since the solution using the Langmuir D droplet distribution for the water field is a weighted set of independent computations for each characteristic size (Fig. 4).

The use of the polydisperse Langmuir D distribution for droplets instead of a monodisperse one increases the computational cost by a factor of at least 7. An example of parallelization of a simulation task for modeling the liquid stage with the polydisperse droplet distribution is shown in Fig. 7. It should be noted that the architecture of the processors on which the parallelization takes place has a significant impact on the speed of the computations (Fig. 7).

To assess the scalability of the liquid phase solution, the following steps are performed:

- Estimation of the processor architecture influence on the parallelization of the liquid phase problem.
- Comparative analysis of the efficiency of parallelization of the liquid phase problem.

For the numerical experiments, we used the Ansys 2020 R2 licensed software on various architectures with different numbers of cores. The software was run on the high-performance computing cluster (HPC) of Perm National Research Polytechnic University (PNRPU) [14], whose main characteristics are as follows:

- 95 computing nodes;
- 128 four-core processors AMD Barcelona-3 (a total of 512 cores);
- 62 eight-core Intel Xeon E5-2680 processors (a total of 480 cores);
- peak performance: 24.096 TFLOPS;
- performance measured by the LINPACK benchmark: 78%;
- storage system capacity: 27 TB;
- RAM: 5888 GB (32 GB/node for nodes with AMD Barcelona-3, and 128 GB/node for nodes with Intel Xeon E5-2680);
- 12 NVIDIA Tesla M2090 GPUs (a total of 512 cores and 6 GB).

In the first stage, we made a comparative assessment of the required time for solving the problem of the liquid phase depending on the number of computational cores. Figure 8 contains the assessment results for the two processor architectures used on the PNRPU HPC, namely, Intel Xeon E5-2680 and AMD Barcelona-3, on test runs of the considered problem.

From the analysis of the required time versus the number of cores used, we drew the following conclusions. In the case of AMD Barcelona-3, the greatest time reduction was achieved (by a factor greater than 1.9) when the number of cores increased from 16 to 32. A similar picture was observed in the case of the Intel Xeon E5-2680. If we compare the computation times for AMD Barcelona-3 and Intel Xeon E5-2680, we see that the time required by the latter is less by a factor greater than 1.8.

We found that the optimal number of cores for parallelizing the task in Ansys FENSAP-ICE is 32, regardless of the processor architecture used. By further increasing the number of cores used, a decrease in speedup is observed due to overheads in network data exchange between nodes.

Thus, the subsequent numerical simulations of the AIM thermal state under in-flight icing conditions were carried out on 32 eight-core Intel Xeon E5-2680 processors.

3.2   Results for Heater Regimes

Based on numerical simulation results, we drew the following conclusions. We obtained the distributions of gas-dynamics fields, liquid water content and droplet velocities in the flow, and the thickness of the ice buildup on the AIM surfaces. The results for the ice shape and thickness on the AIM surfaces at the final time step T under various heating conditions are given in Fig. 9.

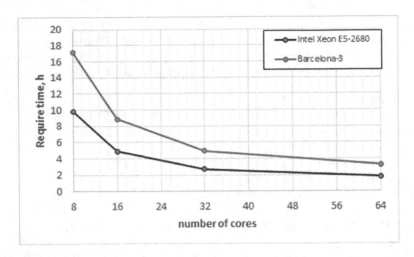

Fig. 8. Results of the problem parallelization for different numbers of cores using Intel Xeon E5-2680 and AMD Barcelona-3 architectures

From the analysis of the obtained shapes and thicknesses of the ice buildup on the structure of the AIM under various temperature conditions, we drew the following conclusions: We made the following conclusions based on the research results of the thermal state influence on the AIM in-flight icing conditions:

1. The ice shape that most distorts the external AIM aerodynamic profile grows over the entire structure surface under a constant power heat flux equivalent to $1.00T_{ad}$. In this case, the maximum thickness of ice buildups (relative to other temperature regimes of constant heating) reaches the value $h_{\max}$.
2. The thermal state with constant heating of the AIM leading edge from $1.00T_{ad}$ to $1.05T_{ad}$ under in-flight icing conditions does not ensure the absence of ice on the side of the engine flow path. As heating increases up to $1.02T_{ad}$, the ice thickness grows up to $h_{\max}$ on the surface from the side of the flow path; the ice buildup can become critical for the unit's performance as a result of subsequent detachment (under the influence of aerodynamic forces) and can cause damages to the engine parts located further along the path of the ejected ice mass. Nevertheless, an increase in temperature up to $1.05T_{ad}$ is sufficient to avoid ice buildups from the side of the inner panel, which significantly reduces the risk of ice entering the engine flow path.

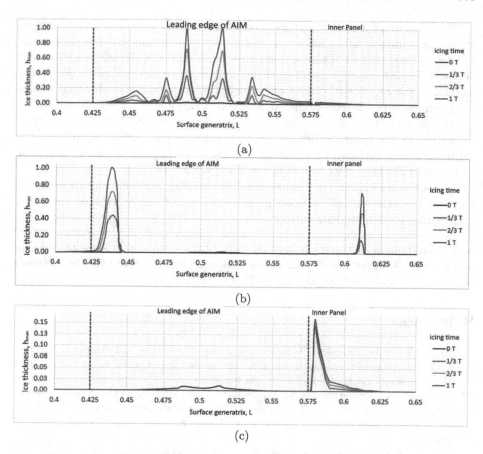

Fig. 9. The shape and thickness of the ice buildup on the AIM surface under constant heating of the leading edge and power heat flux equivalent to (a) $1.00T_{ad}$; (b) $1.02T_{ad}$; (c) $1.05T_{ad}$

4   Conclusions

We considered the air-intake model of an aircraft engine (with a heating element mounted to the skin) under in-flight icing conditions. For this, we used various methods and approaches for the numerical simulation of conjugate heat transfer (Ansys 2020 R2, FENSAP-ICE).

We conducted numerical experiments using the HPC resources of PNRPU to determine the thermal state influence of the air-intake model on in-flight icing conditions. The flight parameters considered in the simulations were: altitude: 1000 m m, flight velocity: 30 m/s, ambient temperature: $-10°$C, humidity: 86%, liquid water content: 0.4 g/m^3, the polydisperse spectrum of Langmuir D distribution of droplet size, average median diameter: 36.6 μm, and icing duration: 5 min.

We compared the estimated time required for the most time-consuming stages of the simulation of processes of conjugate heat transfer under icing conditions. We determined that 32 is the optimal number of cores for parallelizing the task in Ansys FENSAP-ICE, regardless of the processor architecture used. By further increasing the number of cores used, a decrease in speedup is observed due to overheads in network data exchange between nodes.

According to the results of numerical experiments of the AIM thermal state, the ice shape that most distorts the external aerodynamic profile occurs over the entire structure surface at a constant heating of $1.0T_{ad}$. At the same time, the maximum thickness of ice buildups reaches the value $h_{\max}$.

Moreover, an increase in temperature up to $1.05T_{ad}$ is sufficient to avoid ice buildups from the side of the inner panel, which significantly reduces the risk of ice entering the engine flow path.

Acknowledgments. The study was supported by the Russian Science Foundation (grant № 22-19-20118) and the Ministry of Education and Science of the Perm Region (agreement № c-26/1203, dated June 30, 2022).

References

1. Tsypenko, V.G., Shevkov, V.I.: Ensuring the flight safety of transport aircraft taking into account new certification requirements for icing conditions. Civil Aviat. High Technol. **22**(3), 45–46 (2019). (in Russian)
2. Gurevich, O.S., Smetanin, S.A., Trifonov, M.E.: Evaluation of the deterioration of the characteristics of gas turbine engines during crystalline icing and the possibility of its compensation by control methods. Aviat. Engines **3**(4), 17–24 (2019). (in Russian)
3. Milyaev, K.E., Semenov, S.V., Balakirev, A.A.: Ways of fight against frosting in the aviation engine methods of countering with icing in the aircraft engine. PNRPU Aerosp. Eng. Bull. **59**, 5–18 (2019). https://doi.org/10.15593/2224-9982/2019.59.01
4. Popov, S.N.: Aeroflot from A to Z. Book on demand, p. 183 (2012). (in Russian)
5. Cao, Y., Tan, W., Wu, Z.: Aircraft icing: an ongoing threat to aviation safety. Aerosp. Sci. Technol. **75**, 353–385 (2018). https://doi.org/10.1016/j.ast.2017.12.028
6. Yong, S.M.: Fiber-reinforced plastic material with de-icing capability for radome application **284**(2), art. no. 128943 (2021). https://doi.org/10.1016/j.matlet.2020.128943
7. Shen, X., Wang, H., Lin, G., Bu, X., Wen, D.: Unsteady simulation of aircraft electro-thermal deicing process with temperature-based method. Aerosp. Eng. **234**, 388–400 (2020). https://doi.org/10.1177/0954410019866066
8. Raj, L.P., Myong, R.S.: Computational analysis of an electro-thermal ice protection system in atmospheric icing conditions. J. Comput. Fluids Eng. **21**(1), 1–9 (2016). https://doi.org/10.6112/kscfe.2016.21.1.001
9. Reid, T. Baruzzi, G., Aliaga, C., Aube, M., Habashi, W.: FENSAP-ICE: application of unsteady CHT to de-cing simulations on a wing with inter-cycle ice formation. Am. Inst. Aeronaut. Astronaut. 1–11 (2010). https://doi.org/10.2514/6.2010-7835

10. Kashevarov, A.V., Stasenko, A.L.: Modeling of ice accretion on the airfoil surface in an air flow containing ice particles. J. Appl. Mech. Tech. Phys. **59**(4), 645–652 (2018). https://doi.org/10.1134/S0021894418040107
11. Alekseenko, S.V., Prikhodko, A.A.: Numerical simulation of icing of a cylinder and an airfoil: model review and computational results. TsAGI Sci. J. **44**(6), 761–805 (2013). https://doi.org/10.1615/TsAGISciJ.2014011016
12. Grinats, E.S., Miller, A.B., Potapov, Y.F., Stasenko, A.L.: Experimental and theoretical studies of the processes of icing of nanomodified superhydrophobic and ordinary surfaces. Bull. Moscow State Reg. Univ. Ser. Phys. Math. **3**, 84–92 (2013). (In Russian)
13. Kalyulin, S.L., Modorskii, V.Y., Cherepanov, I.E.: Numerical modeling of the influence of the gas-hydrodynamic flow parameters on streamlined surface icing. In: Fomin, V. (ed.) ICMAR 2018, AIP Conference Proceedings, vol. 2027, art. no. 030180 (2018). https://doi.org/10.1063/1.5065274
14. Modorskii, V.Y., Shevelev, N.A.: Research of aerohydrodynamic and aeroelastic processes on PNRPU HPC system. In: Fomin, V. (ed.) ICMAR 2016, AIP Conference Proceedings, vol. 1770, art. no. 020001 (2016). https://doi.org/10.1063/1.4963924
15. Kozlova, A.V., Modorskii, V.Y., Ponik, A.N.: Modeling of cooling processes in the variable section channel of a gas conduit. Rus. Aeronaut. **53**(4), 401–407 (2010). https://doi.org/10.3103/s1068799810040057
16. Kalyulin, S.L., Modorskii, V.Y., Paduchev, A.P.: Numerical design of the rectifying lattices in a small-sized wind tunnel. In: Fomin, V. (ed.) ICMAR 2016, AIP Conference Proceedings, vol. 1770, art. no. 030110 (2016). https://doi.org/10.1063/1.4964052
17. Kalyulin, S.L., Modorskii, V.Y., Petrov, V.Y., Masich, G.F.: Computational and experimental modeling of icing processes by means of PNRPU high-performance computational complex. J. Phys. Conf. Ser. **965**, art. no. 012081 (2018). https://doi.org/10.1088/1742-6596/1096/1/012081
18. Kalyulin, S.L., Modorskii, V.Y., Maksimov, D.S.: Physical modeling of the influence of the gas-hydrodynamic flow parameters on the streamlined surface icing with vibrations. In: Fomin, V. (ed.) ICMAR 2018, AIP Conference Proceedings, vol. 2027, art. no. 040090 (2018). https://doi.org/10.1063/1.5065364
19. Seregina, M.A., Babushkina, A.V., Modorsky, V.Y., Maksimov, D.S.: Numerical simulation of processes of interaction of a gas wave and a deformed barrier in a model channel aircraft engine. PNRPU Aerosp. Eng. Bull. **69**, 92–99 (2022). https://doi.org/10.15593/2224-9982/2022.69.10
20. Modorsky, V.Y., et al.: Influence of some parameters of the experimental anti-icing complex "filter" on the efficiency of protection of power plants from snow. PNRPU Aerosp. Eng. Bull. **69**, 100–109 (2022). https://doi.org/10.15593/2224-9982/2022.69.10
21. Maksimov, D.S., et al.: Developing cyber infrastructure and a model climatic wind tunnel based on the PNRPU high-performance computational complex. Commun. Comput. Inf. Sci. **2163**, 336–350 (2020). https://doi.org/10.1007/978-3-030-55326-5_24
22. Zhbanov, V.A., Kashevarov, A.V., Miller, A.B., Potanov, Y.F.: Study of icing under various conditions. Proc. MAI **105**, 1–17 (2019). (in Russian)

Author Index

© The Editor(s) (if applicable) and The Author(s), under exclusive license
to Springer Nature Switzerland AG 2023
L. Sokolinsky and M. Zymbler (Eds.): PCT 2023, CCIS 1868, pp. 365–366, 2023.
https://doi.org/10.1007/978-3-031-38864-4

Printed in the United States
by Baker & Taylor Publisher Services

Printed in the United States
by Baker & Taylor Publisher Services